Race, Money, and the American Welfare State

Race, Money, and the American Welfare State

MICHAEL K. BROWN

Cornell University Press

ITHACA AND LONDON

First published 1999 by Cornell University Press
First printing, Cornell Paperbacks, 1999

Printed in the United States of America

LIBRARY OF CONGRESS CATALOGING-IN-PUBLICATION DATA

Brown, Michael K.
    Race, money, and the American welfare state / Michael K. Brown.
        p.   cm.
    Includes index.
    ISBN 0-8014-3510-2 (cloth : alk. paper). — ISBN 0-8014-8510-X
(pbk. : alk. paper)
    1. United States—Social policy.   2. United States—Politics and
government—1933–1945.   3. United States—Politics and
government—1945–1989.   4. Social classes—United States.   5. United
States—Race relations.   I. Title.
HN57.B659   1999
361.6'1'0973—dc21   98-31999

Cornell University Press strives to use environmentally responsible suppliers and materials to the fullest extent possible in the publishing of its books. Such materials include vegetable-based, low-VOC inks and acid-free papers that are recycled, totally chlorine-free, or partly composed of nonwood fibers.

Cloth printing   10   9   8   7   6   5   4   3   2   1

Paperback printing   10   9   8   7   6   5   4   3   2   1

For
Eric and Walter

Contents

Figures

Tables

Preface

The inspiration for this book came to me in 1969 on a hot, smoggy March day in south central Los Angeles. I was working as a policy analyst for the city manager in Compton, California, helping plan its Model Cities program. Richard Nixon had just taken office, the Vietnam War did not appear to be ending, and the racial conflagration of the sixties loomed large. I had just been to the Watts office of the Concentrated Employment Project, a Lyndon Johnson program, where I had witnessed the futile efforts of administrators trying to stretch inadequate resources to remedy the poverty and unemployment in one of America's poorest ghettos. The lack of resources meant that public agencies and individuals spent as much time fighting for money as they did trying to help the poor.

Today it is commonly assumed that Lyndon Johnson threw unlimited amounts of money at poverty, with devastating results. The Great Society not only failed to remedy the problem of poverty, but created new problems. In a 1982 address to black Republicans, Ronald Reagan suggested that blacks would have been better off if the Great Society had never occurred. "The big taxers and big spenders in the Congress had started a binge [that] threatened the character of our people." Programs intended to help the poor had led to "a new kind of bondage for millions of American citizens."[1] Reagan's indictment of the Great Society has been turned into a justification for abandoning the poverty programs of the 1960s and leaving the residents of inner-city ghettos to fend for themselves.

In this book, I enter the debate over the Great Society from an angle that takes into account both the New Deal and the aftermath of the 1960s. The debate over the Great Society has stagnated. People either see current trends

---

1. "Reagan Says Blacks Were Hurt by Works of the Great Society," *New York Times,* September 16, 1982, sec. 1, p. 1.

in poverty, divorce, or crime as the legacy of Johnson's handiwork, or they bemoan multiculturalism, which they trace to the black nationalism of the 1960s. Whereas conservatives think that the Great Society accounts for continued high levels of poverty, many liberals and progressives think that a preoccupation with racism and racial equality has sabotaged any broad-based political movement for economic justice. Only color-blind policies, these liberals argue, will permit the revival of an effective political coalition dedicated to social reform and the alleviation of inner-city poverty. Both these views of the legacies of the 1960s reflect atavistic judgments of race and social class. In equating public social policies with black poverty and indolence, Ronald Reagan repeats a typical white view of African Americans that dates from slavery. The view took a new form in the 1930s with the inception of a national welfare state. Many progressives, on the other hand, merely embroider on the historical tale of how incipient alliances between black and white workers were undermined by racial conflict in the early years of the twentieth century. Then the culprits were businessmen who used black strikebreakers to forestall unionization and white workers who refused to integrate their unions. Today, it is blacks and their white allies who are thought to fan the flames of racial discord, insisting on race-specific remedies to economic problems. I take issue with both these arguments. They both seem to mischaracterize the relationship between race and social class since the 1930s.

One could write separate books about race or class in the U.S. welfare state—I often wondered if I was actually writing two books—but I am convinced that one cannot understand either the contemporary debate over the Great Society or the history of federal social policy without integrating them. In this book I explore how both race and social class bear on the political development of the American welfare state. In considering the role of social class, I focus on conflict over taxes and spending for federal social policies. I advance a fiscal theory of the welfare state, arguing that the builders of welfare states must deal with the rival claims of entrepreneurs and taxpayers in fashioning social polices. In considering the role of race, I examine the implications of racial discrimination in labor and housing markets, particularly regarding the relationship of whites and blacks to the welfare state.

Had we created a more capacious and comprehensive public welfare state, I argue, there would have been more racial equality within the welfare state, and racial hostilities would be less likely to serve as a channel for conflict over social policy. That we did not create such a state has to do with the class imperatives that influenced decision makers. Put another way, it was not the Vietnam War that strangled the Great Society's War on Poverty, but a more deeply rooted conflict over taxes and spending. One must see the Great Society from the vantage point of the New Deal to understand this.

My insistence on integrating these two arguments reflects my sympathy with the many African American intellectuals and political leaders who have understood the necessity of a political agenda based on both economic justice and racial justice. There is a profound irony at the heart of America's debate over race and social justice. Although many conservatives and progressives alike insist that race is only kept alive by racial interest groups pursuing race-specific agendas, African Americans have been the one group that has consistently demanded policies that would benefit all citizens. It was African Americans who kept the promise of a social democratic welfare state alive into the 1960s after white workers had abandoned it, just as they kept alive aspirations for universal citizenship during the struggle to end slavery after white propertyless men got the vote. Yet, unlike many white liberals, they have always understood that universalism without racial equality is a sham. I am indebted to those black writers and leaders who have shown that race and class could be neither conflated nor separated.

This book is also about the choices we have made and failed to make. The political leaders I examine in this book all had alternatives to the course of action they chose; they could have decided differently than they did. My concern with this problem is long standing. In an earlier book, I explored the choices that police officers make on the street, arguing that their decisions can be understood only in light of the moral dilemmas and organizational pressures they confront. The point was not to excuse them or to say that they could not act otherwise, but to understand "why some alternatives are consistently preferred over others" in order to reach a judgment about contemporary police work.[2] Both the builders of the welfare state and their opponents faced constraints on their power and influence; but they still had choices, and we are remiss if we fail to understand their choices and to act on that knowledge.

I am indebted to the University of California, Santa Cruz, Division of the Academic Senate and the Office of the Dean of Social Sciences for financial assistance during my research. Some of these funds supported the work of a group of able and resourceful research assistants. This book is immeasurably

---

2. Michael K. Brown, *Working the Street: Police Discretion and the Dilemmas of Reform* (New York, 1988), p. xiii.

better because of the work of Ricky Bluethenthal, Jesse Donahue, Tracy Kaplan, Burton Reist, and Todd Shuman. My many trips to presidential libraries were aided by grants from the Lyndon Baines Johnson Foundation, the Harry S. Truman Library Institute, the Franklin and Eleanor Roosevelt Institute, and the National Endowment for the Humanities Travel to Collections program.

Numerous colleagues and friends have my gratitude for their invaluable help in correcting my errors, straightening out my logic, and helping to clarify my thoughts. Amy Bridges, Eileen Boris, Michael Dawson, Robin Einhorn, Michael Goldfield, Nelson Lichtenstein, Sonya A. Michel, Ann Orloff, Adolph Reed, Jr., Wendy Sarvasy, Walter J. Szczepanek, and Margaret Weir all provided lively, insightful criticisms. My thinking on the Great Society also benefited from an earlier collaboration with Steven P. Erie. Bill Domhoff scrutinized the manuscript with care, rescuing me from errors while bolstering my confidence. Ron King and Frances Fox Piven gave me the kind of detailed, invigorating criticisms that only true friends and colleagues can. They helped me to make this a better book. Wendy Mink has been a source of inspiration, encouragement, and timely assistance. She also manages, somehow, to talk me out of a sizable chunk of my avocado crop every summer. Woody Sanders, always a fund of good advice and a master at finding obscure sources, has to take some of the blame for the result. Woody first dragged me over to the National Archives and told me I should take a look at the Budget Bureau records. David Wellman provided the illuminating criticisms of a dear friend; he was also there at some of the darkest moments along the way.

My research depended on the invaluable assistance of many librarians. My thanks to the many archivists and research librarians who guided me though the presidential libraries and the National Archives. Nor would I have been able to do the detailed historical research I did without the assistance of the able staff of Interlibrary Loan and Government and Public Affairs of UCSC's McHenry Library. I thank them all for finding hard-to-get books and esoteric government reports and suppressing knowledge of my many library fines.

My thanks to Peter Agree of Cornell University Press for his assistance, Grey Osterud, for her editorial hand, Cheryl Van de Veer, for catching numerous errors in the manuscript, and Pat Sanders, for repeatedly coming to my rescue. Vivian Brown has my gratitude for her support and for putting up with me during all the years I was writing this book.

An earlier version of Chapter 4 appeared as my article "Bargaining for

Social Rights," in *Political Science Quarterly* 112, no. 4 (1997–98): 645–74, and is reprinted here by permission.

This book is dedicated to my son Eric, who will have to grapple with the choices we have left his generation; and to Walter J. Szczepanek, who was there at the beginning and never lost faith.

MICHAEL K. BROWN

Santa Cruz, California

Note on Sources

This book is founded largely on research material drawn from a variety of archives. These collections include the five presidential administrations that are the subject of this study; the papers of the AFL-CIO, National Association for the Advancement of Colored People, and the National Urban League; and the Bureau of the Budget (which was renamed the Office of Management and Budget in 1971) and the Social Security Board. The abbreviations for the libraries and the manuscript collections I have consulted are listed below.

Library of Congress, Manuscript Division	LC
Papers of the National Association for the Advancement of Colored People	NAACP
Papers of the National Urban League	NUL
National Archives	NA
Records of the Budget Bureau	RG 51
Records of the Social Security Board	RG 47
Records of the Works Progress Administration	RG 69
Franklin D. Roosevelt Library	FDRL
President, Official File, 1933–45	OF
President's Personal File, 1933–45	PPF
President's Secretary's File, 1933–45	PSF
Harry S. Truman Library	HSTL
President, Official File, 1945–53	OF
John Fizgerald Kennedy Library	JFKL
President's Office Files	POF
Lyndon Baines Johnson Library	LBJL
White House Central Files	WHCF
Nixon Presidential Materials Staff, National Archives	NPMS
White House Special Files	WHSF
George Meany Memorial Archives	GMMA

Abbreviations Used in the Text

ADC	Aid to Dependent Children
AFDC	Aid to Families with Dependent Children
AFL	American Federation of Labor
AFL-CIO	American Federation of Labor and Congress of Industrial Organizations
AMA	American Medical Association
BAC	Business Advisory Council
BOB	Bureau of the Budget
CBC	Congressional Black Caucus
CDBG	Community Develoment Block Grant
CEA	Council of Economic Advisers
CES	Committee on Economic Security
CETA	Comprehensive Employment and Training Act
CIO	Congress of Industrial Organizations
COPE	Committee on Political Education
CORE	Congress of Racial Equality
ESEA	Elementary and Secondary Education Act of 1965
FAP	Family Assistance Plan
FERA	Federal Emergency Relief Administration
HEW	Department of Health, Education, and Welfare
MDTA	Manpower Development and Training Act of 1962
NAACP	National Association for the Advancement of Colored People
NLRB	National Labor Relations Board
NNC	National Negro Congress
NRPB	National Resources Planning Board
NUL	National Urban League
NWLB	National War Labor Board
OAA	Old Age Assistance
OASI	Old Age and Survivors' Insurance
OEO	Office of Economic Opportunity

OJT	On-the-Job Training
OMB	Office of Management and Budget (formerly the Bureau of the Budget)
PMC	Postwar Manpower Conference
PWA	Public Works Administration
RFC	Reconstruction Finance Corporation
SSB	Social Security Board
SSI	Supplemental Security Income
UAW	United Autoworkers
UMW	United Mineworkers
USES	United States Employment Service
USW	United Steelworkers
WPA	Works Progress Administration

Race, Money, and the American Welfare State

Introduction: Race and Money in the American Welfare State

[The American War on Poverty failed because it was] presented as a pro-Negro enterprise; it [was] not seen as a universalist problem of inequality, social injustice, exclusion. . . . How to include poor people, and especially poor coloured people, in our societies, and at the same time to channel proportionately more resources in their favour without inducing shame or stigma, remains one of the great challenges for social policy in Britain and the USA.

— RICHARD M. TITMUSS

The state lives as an economic parasite. It can withdraw from the private economy only as much as is consistent with the continued existence of . . . individual interest in every particular socio-psychological situation. In other words, the tax state must not demand from the people so much that they lose financial interest in production or at any rate cease to use their best energies for it.

— JOSEPH SCHUMPETER

In the four decades between the economic depression of the 1930s and the political malaise of the 1970s, the governments of industrialized societies used broadly inclusive social policies and full-employment economies to balance capitalist development with a measure of security and social justice. Private wages were supplemented with a social wage, the fear of an impoverished old age was banished, and the absence of adequate health care and housing was remedied for many people. The situation in the United States was no exception. Despite its reputation as a welfare state laggard, America made progress in extending social protection to its citizens, especially senior citizens and the poor. For the elderly, policymakers created a system of public social insurance based on social security pensions and Medicare that rivals the generosity of European welfare states and has eliminated extreme poverty among senior citizens. Means-tested cash payments and in-kind transfers (food and medical care) raised a substantial number of the rest of the poor above the poverty line.

Yet America's struggle for social rights remains unfinished. The failures of U.S. social policy have left a fragmented welfare state distinctive for its low public expenditures; its heavy reliance on means-tested policies, tax expenditures, and private health insurance; and its historically weak commitment to full employment. As Americans, we celebrate individual effort and opportunity, but we have created a system of social protection in which some individuals are thrown overboard or given a leaky life raft while others have been advantaged by government largess. It is notable that by 1980, the end point of the developmental phase of the American welfare state, approximately 35.1 million Americans were without any form of health insurance and that 40 percent of poor households received no cash transfers whatsoever.[1] By comparison few middle- or upper-income households were uncovered by private health insurance and pensions or failed to benefit from tax expenditures. Forty-six percent of all fringe benefits, for example, were received by people in the top 20 percent of the income distribution, and most of the value of tax deductions for mortgage interest and medical expenses goes to families in the upper one-third.[2]

For no group do these failures leave a more troubling and paradoxical legacy than for African Americans. Blacks were never extended the same social rights as white Americans; and, more so than whites, they are likely to have been thrown out of the life raft. Social Security may be the most comprehensive and generous social program in the United States, but blacks receive lower benefits, on average, than whites. And because the earnings of the median black household are lower than those of the median white household, black familes lose a higher percentage of their income to regressive social security payroll taxes. Black women, Jill Quadagno astutely observes, are less likely to qualify for the more generous spousal benefits yet end up, because of their greater involvement in the labor force, subsidizing white housewives.[3] Nor have many African Americans benefited from federal housing subsidies and mortgage loan guarantees, so they are, consequently, less

1. Sheldon Danziger, "Budget Cuts as Welfare Reform," *American Economic Review* 73 (1983): 66. Matters have only gotten worse since 1980. As of 1992 about 44 percent of poor households did not receive a means-tested transfer payment, according to *Statistical Abstract of the United States, 1997* (Washington, D.C., 1997), p. 376, table 583. The number of people without health insurance has risen to 41 million.

2. Daniel H. Weinberg, "The Distributional Implications of Tax Expenditures and Comprehensive Income Taxation," *National Tax Journal* 40 (1987): 245.

3. Gayle B. Thompson, "Blacks and Social Security Benefits: Trends, 1960–73," *Social Security Bulletin* 38 (1975): 30–39; Jill Quadagno, *The Color of Welfare: How Racism Undermined the War on Poverty* (New York, 1994), pp. 161–62.

able to take advantage of lucrative tax expenditures like the mortgage interest deduction.[4]

Yet today African Americans are blamed for the failures of the American welfare state. Conservative politicians commonly lament the "grim harvest of the Great Society" and pronounce its policies the cause of inner-city devastation by producing the "breakdown of the family structure."[5] Black poverty has become the fulcrum of a conservative assault on federal social policies, and blacks bear a disproportionate share of any reductions in services or transfers. Many, perhaps most, whites believe blacks are the authors, defenders, and prime beneficiaries of wasteful, feckless social policies that do more harm than good. Blacks, they think, are lazy, do not try hard enough to overcome economic liabilities, and are overly "dependent" on welfare. Such harsh, negative images have merely replaced the virulently negative prejudices of forty years ago, and, as Paul M. Sniderman and Thomas Piazza argue, these images foment opposition to more social spending among a wide swath of Americans that "goes beyond the ranks of bigots."[6] Proposals for new social policies bear the burden of demonstrating they are not simply "give-aways" in the name of racial equality.

America failed to create a welfare state that would treat blacks and whites alike. The problems of race, on the one hand, and the failure to create broadly inclusive social policies for all Americans, on the other, have become entwined. That fact would not have surprised Richard Titmuss, the doyen of British social policy. Like most European social democrats, he believed that redressing injustices, or "diswelfares"—compensating losers in the ongoing process of economic growth—could only take place through an infrastructure of universal social policies that would permit those in need to be helped without stigmatizing them. Universalism, social policies in which people are included without reference to their social or economic status, appeals to the values of equality and fairness yet has the added virtue of embracing disparate income and social strata and gives all citizens a stake in the welfare state. It avoids the penury and stigmatization of relief or means-tested assistance.

4. Melvin L. Oliver and Thomas M. Shapiro, *Black Wealth/White Wealth* (New York, 1995), pp. 39–40, 44.

5. William P. Barr speaking on "This Week with David Brinkley," April 26, 1992, quoted in Daniel Patrick Moynihan, "How the Great Society 'Destroyed the American Family,'" *Public Interest* (Summer 1992): 53. Barr, at that time, was attorney general for President George Bush.

6. Paul M. Sniderman and Thomas Piazza, *The Scar of Race* (Cambridge, Mass., 1993), p. 97. Also see Donald R. Kinder and Lynn M. Sanders, *Divided by Color: Racial Politics and Democratic Ideals* (Chicago, 1996), pp. 121–22.

Without universalistic, comprehensive social insurance or public transfers, Titmuss presciently argued, the political foundations of the welfare state would erode as the victims of "economic progress" were vilified.

Titmuss blamed the failure to build on the universal social insurance policies of the New Deal and create a welfare state that would benefit all working- and middle-class citizens on Lyndon Johnson, namely his misguided attempt to remedy the injustice of racism with policies designed to benefit mainly African Americans. William Julius Wilson, among others, has revived Titmuss's critique, charging Great Society liberals with creating a racially bifurcated pattern of social provision in big cities and adopting group-specific policies that singled out race as the decisive barrier to economic advancement. In doing so, these liberals alienated the white working-class core of the Democratic party coalition. Lyndon Johnson's Great Society, unlike the New Deal, was "modeled on the English poor laws," and wrecked whatever chance there had been for a genuine assault on economic and racial inequality.[7]

If Titmuss asks the right questions, however, his answers are misleading. Race has been implicated in the construction of the American welfare state from the New Deal on.[8] Federal social policies took shape and were implemented in a society where one region was governed by an extreme form of racial apartheid and the rest of the country was governed by pervasive labor-market and residential discrimination. It is vital to understand the difference racism in both the North and South has made for the political development of the American welfare state. Furthermore, universalism was not exchanged in the 1960s for group-specific policies, as Titmuss and Wilson assume. Lyndon Johnson and his advisers rejected policies that would have benefited most citizens, such as family allowances, for reasons that had less to do with the moral or political attraction of race-specific benefits than with their own ability and willingness to finance comprehensive social policies.

My approach to Titmuss's question emphasizes race and money. I explain why the political development of the American welfare state produced an uneven pattern of social provision, one sharply differentiated by race and social class. Compared to European welfare states, the United States combines comprehensive, universalistic social policies for the elderly with an assortment of means-tested transfers, social services, and private benefits for

7. William J. Wilson, *The Truly Disadvantaged* (Chicago, 1987), p. 119.
8. Jill Quadagno makes a similar point in *The Color of Welfare*, though my perspective on this problem is quite different.

the nonelderly. We may call this pattern of social provision truncated universalism. In a society characterized by pervasive racial discrimination in labor and housing markets, this outcome has led to a racially stratified welfare state: blacks have been disproportionately excluded from mainstream programs and have received lower benefits than whites. In addition, they have been made to depend on putative racially neutral means-tested programs, such as Aid to Families with Dependent Children (AFDC), that have become racially stigmatized. As a consequence, the relationship of African Americans to the welfare state mirrors the racial stratification of American society. This outcome would have been less likely had a more comprehensive welfare state emerged in America.

Beginning in the 1930s, race and money have been mutually entwined in the history of the American welfare state, serving as a fetter on its political development. The foundations were laid with the Social Security Act of 1935, which created contributory social insurance and decentralized public assistance programs with limits on federal contributions. To cope with unemployment, Franklin Delano Roosevelt created a temporary, underfunded work relief program. African Americans were excluded from old-age and unemployment insurance through statutory occupational exclusions, but they accounted for disproportionate numbers of those on means-tested work and general relief throughout the depression years. Federal social policy was racially stigmatized as a result. After World War II, New Dealers failed to go beyond the 1935 policy decisions and create a "cradle to grave" welfare state that might have diminished these racial distinctions. But new policies, including the G.I. Bill, and a labor union–instigated expansion of private health and pension policies contributed to the well-being of a growing middle class and fueled postwar prosperity. Even though the war accelerated the movement of African Americans into industrial employment, blacks failed to benefit from these new and rapidly growing programs because of discrimination in labor and housing markets. Public housing and Aid to Dependent Children became programs almost entirely for migrating black sharecroppers, and acquired a racial identification that was politically exploited by northern conservatives and white southerners opposed to the civil rights movement. On the eve of the civil rights movement, a racial fault line was embedded in the American welfare state.

Johnson's Great Society failed to undo the racially stratified social policies inherited from Roosevelt. Johnson responded to African American protest by building a redistributive welfare state. This policy revolution was predicated on a strategy of fiscal conservatism, which necessitated targeting social programs on the ghetto. In the midst of the political mobilization of blacks and the ensuing white backlash, such policy choices reinforced racial divisions within the welfare state. The Nixon administration partially reversed the redistributive thrust of the Great Society by limiting the growth of some social programs and replacing others with block grants. This policy shifted distribution of limited resources to middle-class constituencies and left the inner-city poor high and dry. Conservatives, then, could ascribe the failures of the Great Society to race and exploit these failures politically.

My account of these events is anchored by Joseph Schumpeter's theory of the "tax state" and Gunnar Myrdal's theory of how racial discrimination is reproduced in the welfare state. Schumpeter regarded all states as economic parasites that expand at the expense of the rival claims of entrepreneurs and citizens. One implication of this conflict is that the welfare state, as Daniel Patrick Moynihan has quipped, "is always short of money"—though some states more so than others. Welfare states tax and spend, and it is the capacity to tax and spend that determines what kind of welfare state emerges: universal social insurance conceived in the solidarity of all citizens or fragmented policies that divide citizens by social class, race and gender. The success of Scandinavian social democracy arguably lay in the ability of Swedish policymakers to combine high tax rates with universalistic transfers while promoting economic growth. The failures of the American welfare state, on the other hand, might be understood in light of a preference for tax cuts and a reluctance to spend.

Money—conflict over taxing and spending—is a neglected topic in the study of social policy and rarely considered as a factor shaping policy decisions. There are two reasons why it is important. First, questions of taxing and spending influence, and often determine, social policy choices. Since policymakers must worry as much about who will feel the tax bite as who will benefit from a new social policy, they are motivated to finance the welfare state with taxes that will minimize taxpayer resistance. They must also set tax burdens and levels of deficit spending in relation to concerns about inflation, unemployment, and investor confidence. Those political leaders seeking to build welfare states face conflicting demands for economic stabilization and growth (capital accumulation), on the one hand, and for creation of social rights and economic security, on the other. They cannot evade this conflict and will seek to negotiate it by choosing policies that maintain investor confidence and thus the conditions for economic prosperity while permitting the future expansion of social benefits. Second, money matters to the formation and durability of political coalitions championing or opposing the welfare state. Investors and wealthy taxpayers may oppose all but the most minimal levels of social protection; working citizens and poor people may be willing to spend much more. But whether taxpayers favor a social policy very often depends on whether they benefit. Means-tested policies are the classic example; backlash against welfare is assumed to be a "rational political activity for the majority of citizens."[9]

Questions of fiscal capacity—the ability of policymakers to raise revenues necessary to finance new policies and to spend—lie at the center of the political development of the American welfare state. Fiscal capacity was crucial to the design of both the 1935 Social Security Act and the Great Society programs. Roosevelt and Johnson presided over these two bursts of policy innovation with large liberal congressional majorities that momentarily opened the sluice gates of Madisonian democracy. Both presidents were dedicated to creating permanent institutions of social provision, yet both combined liberal social policy innovations with fiscal conservatism that undercut their policy revolutions. (In Johnson's case, all the important decisions were taken before he escalated the Vietnam War.) Why, when they had all the political leverage one can ever hope for in the normally fragmented American political system, did both Roosevelt and Johnson act this way? The answer lies in money; neither FDR nor LBJ could escape tailoring his social policies to the need to extract financial resources from unwilling investors and taxpayers.

Both of these episodes of welfare state–building were followed by a period of conservative control and reaction. In each period money played a crucial role in explaining the opposition to federal social policies and the changes in political coalitions. Liberal efforts to build on these policy revolutions and erect more universalistic and comprehensive policies were opposed by resurgent conservatives, Republicans with the support of New Deal apostates: white southerners during the 1940s and 1950s, and white union members and blue-collar workers during and after the Great Society. Conservatives, led first by Senator Robert Taft and later by President Richard M. Nixon, lacked the power or will to roll back liberal policies and adopted a strategy of containing liberal state-building. In both periods, there was some policy innovation because key conservatives (namely, southern Democrats and the Nixon administration) had monetary and electoral incentives to expand social policies selectively.

The fiscal restraint of Roosevelt and Johnson, the relative success of their

9. Walter Korpi, "Social Policy and Distributional Conflict in the Capitalist Democracies: A Preliminary Comparative Framework," *West European Politics* 3 (1980): 304–7.

conservative opponents, and the desire of whites to maintain their racial privileges produced a racially stratified welfare state in the United States. Racial stratification began as an inadvertent consequence of Roosevelt's fiscally circumscribed welfare state and the virulent labor-market discrimination of the depression; once in place, it became entwined with conflict over taxes and spending, structuring political battles and policy decisions. White southerners and white workers alike had no interest in supporting social policies that would erode their racial privileges or that were seen as benefiting African Americans; conservative opponents of the welfare state have since the 1940s exploited these facts.

To sum up, race and money explain why liberal policy innovations at defining moments were sacrificed on the altar of fiscal conservatism, the failures of the Democratic party coalition, and the political and economic consequences of the divergent fates of black and white, female and male, workers since the 1930s. Below, I elaborate on the theoretical arguments that underpin my historical analysis.

Myrdal's Rule: Reproducing the Color Line in the Welfare State

The problem of race and the welfare state is typically understood as one of racially motivated exclusion. This approach focuses on how whites have used their power over African Americans to enforce racial hierarchies by denying them entry into the welfare state or preventing them from receiving all the benefits they are legally entitled to. Southern fears that their system of racial apartheid could be altered by universal coverage of social insurance led to the statutory exclusion of agricultural and domestic workers from the Social Security Act, a step that effectively excluded almost three-quarters of black workers. State and local officials administered decentralized public assistance programs in a racially discriminatory manner; they denied eligible African Americans needed benefits or gave them lower benefits than eligible whites.[10] Nor were federal officials necessarily any better. Federal housing administrators used their power to construct white enclaves in the suburbs and to deny black families access to federally guaranteed mortgages

10. Jill Quadagno, *The Transformation of Old Age Security* (Chicago, 1988), pp. 115–16, 132–37; Lee J. Alston and Joseph P. Ferrie, "Labor Costs, Paternalism, and Loyalty in Southern Agriculture: A Constraint on the Growth of the Welfare State," *Journal of Economic History* 45 (1985): 95–117; Robert Lieberman, "Race and the Organization of Welfare Policy," in *Classifying by Race,* ed. Paul Peterson (Princeton, N.J., 1995), pp. 156–87.

until the 1970s.[11] In all of these cases federal social policy was racialized by exclusion, which, Melvin L. Oliver and Thomas M. Shapiro argue, limited the ability of African Americans to "acquire land, build community, and generate wealth" and which failed to relieve the obvious needs of an extremely poor people.[12]

Racist exclusion must be a central aspect of any analysis of race and the welfare state. Yet to assume that exclusion is the sole problem confronting African-American families risks oversimplifying the problem. Blacks have never been entirely excluded from social policies, even prior to the New Deal. Black Civil War veterans, for example, were eligible for veterans' pensions and received them for many decades after the war. One must account for patterns of inclusion as well as exclusion. Theda Skocpol suggests that black Civil War veterans were the beneficiaries of a cross-class coalition fostered by the party competition of the late nineteenth century.[13] Yet historically racial discrimination has been far more important. It has not only denied African Americans access to the welfare state; it has also determined how they are included and whether pejorative stereotypes are attached to social policies. An important question is whether social policies reproduce the racial hierarchies of American society within the welfare state. To see why this could occur requires considering how welfare states may become instruments of social stratification rather than social equality.

T. H. Marshall observed that if welfare states can abate distinctions of social class, they may also create "class privilege." Marshall's insight was that there is inevitably a tension between collective social provision and the fates of individual beneficiaries. He was concerned with the possibility that universal access to education in England would alter patterns of stratification because access to prestigious schools was limited. He went on to argue, however, that status differences conveyed by social policies retain legitimacy so long as "they do not cut too deep, but occur within a population united in a single civilization."[14]

What happens, though, when the status differences acquired by virtue of social policy occur in a racially stratified society? The role of the welfare state in generating or reproducing patterns of social stratification, Gosta

11. Kenneth T. Jackson, *Crabgrass Frontier* (New York, 1985), pp. 190–218.

12. Oliver and Shapiro, *Black Wealth/White Wealth*, p. 37.

13. Theda Skocpol, "African Americans in U.S. Social Policy," in Peterson, *Classifying by Race*, pp. 136–38.

14. T. H. Marshall, "Citizenship and Social Class," in *Class, Citizenship, and Social Development*, ed. S. M. Lipset (Chicago, 1964), pp. 93–94, 110, 115–16, 127.

Esping-Andersen has demonstrated, depends on the distributive effects of social policies—that is, it depends partly on the kind of social policies a society chooses.[15] Whether social policies override or reinforce differences of social class, race, or gender, depends first on coverage. Universal social insurance or noncontributory grants that cover substantially all of a population may diminish class differences; means-tested policies that single out citizens by income thresholds accentuate them. Although universalism denotes comprehensive coverage, there are few truly "universalistic" policies. Most contain implicit exclusions. Family allowances, often taken as the main example of a universal, noncontributory grant, exclude both single persons and childless couples. In general, though, broadly inclusive policies do reduce class or racial differences by promoting cross-class or biracial coalitions. This is the reason builders of European welfare states embedded means-tested policies within universalistic transfers.[16]

Social policies also affect income inequality. For example, flat-rate, non-contributory pensions ignore income differentials in the distribution of benefits, which is why unions and left-wing political parties preferred them for a long time. Most social policies are redistributive in the sense that they affect relative income distributions, though to different degrees. Means-tested policies are explicitly redistributive, using general revenues to augment the current income of the poor. Contributory old-age insurance may temper wage-related benefits by replacing a higher proportion of the wages of low-income retirees than those of high-income retirees. Opportunity policies, such as education or employment training given to the poor, redistribute budgetary resources but affect potential future income only. A society that combines noncontributory old-age pensions with wage-related contributory social insurance builds an equalitarian welfare state that will do more to offset differences in income than a society that relies on means-tested transfers, private pensions, or health benefits.[17] Means-tested policies are usually thought to be more efficient in getting money to poor families, but they stigmatize recipients. Universal social policies, on the other hand, may not be redistributive. America's surrogate housing allowance, the mortgage interest deduction, nominally covers all citizens, but since it rewards only home owners and excludes renters (and thus most low-income households), it contains an implicit *reverse* means-test. Universalism sometimes punishes the poor.

15. Gøsta Esping-Andersen, *The Three Worlds of Welfare Capitalism* (Princeton, N.J., 1990).

16. For a discussion of the advantages of this strategy in the United States, see Theda Skocpol, *Social Policy in the United States* (Princeton, N.J., 1995), pp. 250–74.

17. Esping-Andersen, *Three Worlds of Welfare Capitalism*, pp. 51–54, 69–77, 83–87.

The racial stratification of the American welfare state is defined by a long-term overlap between racial and programmatic boundaries, particularly among the nonelderly. This overlap is based on the relative exclusion of minority and female-headed families from the salient, non-means-tested, and private forms of social protection, the disproportionately low benefits these families do receive when included, and on their disproportionate inclusion in means-tested programs. Even though the programmatic overlap is relative rather than absolute (as it nearly is in the case of public housing), it is sufficiently large to matter.

The racial distinctions embedded in federal social policy are quite startling and have changed little in the sixty-year history of the American welfare state. As of 1986, white households received 90.5 percent of all non-means-tested transfers and 63.4 percent of means-tested payments, while black households receive only 8.2 percent of non-means-tested payments but 32.3 percent of means-tested payments. These differences are especially pronounced for black women who head families by themselves: just 3 percent receive a non-means-tested benefit.[18] The proportion of African American families on relief (means-tested policies) was only marginally higher in the late 1930s than the mid-1980s. And black families remain relatively excluded from many middle-class social programs. Data on the coverage and access of blacks to unemployment compensation, for example, indicate that blacks make up about 10 percent of all those receiving it, but most of the black unemployed must turn elsewhere or do without. (By 1980, only 30 percent of the black unemployed received unemployment compensation benefits.) They are also less likely to be covered by private health insurance (in 1980, 54 percent of blacks had such insurance compared to 78 percent of whites).[19]

Race is not the only basis for status differences within the welfare state.

18. United States Bureau of Census, Current Population Reports, ser. P-60, no. 164-RD-1, *Measuring the Effect of Benefits and Taxes on Income and Poverty: 1986* (Washington, D.C., 1988), p. 10; Diana Pearce, "Welfare is Not For Women: Why the War on Poverty Cannot Conquer the Feminization of Poverty," in *Women, the State, and Welfare*, ed. Linda Gordon (Madison, Wisc., 1990), p. 271. Obviously far more whites receive means-tested transfers than blacks, but that is not the point. The question is whether specific groups are more likely to be the beneficiary of one type of policy rather than another and what conclusions are drawn from this fact. The figures quoted in the text are the most recent data available that measures receipt of means-tested and non-means-tested payments by race. I doubt that it has changed much in the last ten years.

19. Robert B. Hill, *Economic Policies and Black Progress: Myths and Realities* (Washington, D.C., 1981), pp. 51–52; U.S. Bureau of the Census, Current Population Reports, P-70-83-4, *Economic Characteristics of Households in the United States: Fourth Quarter, 1983* (Washington, D.C., 1985), p. 5, table E.

Gender inequalities may also be reproduced by social policies. Women have been denied access to core social insurance policies in much the same way as African Americans and other minorities. Women have been affected by occupational exclusions, and they remain less likely to receive unemployment compensation than men. When they have been included under social security through survivor's benefits, the policy merely reinforced the patriarchal system. There is, moreover, an obvious overlap between race and gender: AFDC, perhaps the program that became most identified with racial stereotypes, did so on the basis of images that stigmatized women. Yet if all women suffer from the logic of patriarchal social policies and all experience labor-market discrimination, they do not all fare similarly in the welfare state, and there are sharp differences between the access of white women to non-means-tested social policies and that of African American women or Latinas.[20]

How did federal social policy become racially stratified? It is commonly assumed that the racial stratification of federal social policy dates from the Great Society. Jill Quadagno, among others, argues that the exclusion of African Americans from the Social Security Act and other New Deal legislation left a tangled, bitter legacy that reinforced racial inequalities. Social and political changes ignited by the New Deal set the stage for the unraveling of Jim Crow in the South and the second great wave of migration from southern sharecroppers' shacks to the tenements of northern ghettos. Lyndon Johnson responded to this migration and the civil rights movement by trying "to reorient the nation's social policy agenda so that it could eradicate, rather than reinforce, racial inequality."[21] The architects of the Great Society designed a variety of new social policies calculated to assimilate

20. Although a detailed analysis of gender and social policy is beyond the scope of this book, a consideration of where gender and race intersect and where they conflict is not. This intersection is explored in Chapters 2, 5, and 10. On gender and social policy see Carole Pateman, "The Patriarchal Welfare State," in *Democracy and the Welfare State,* ed. Amy Gutmann (Princeton, N.J., 1988), pp. 231–60; Diana M. Pearce, "Toil and Trouble: Women Workers and Unemployment Compensation," *Signs* 10 (Spring 1985): 456–57; and Ann Shola Orloff, "Gender and the Social Rights of Citizenship," *American Sociological Review* 58 (1993): 303–28. For studies that explicitly consider race and gender, see Gwendolyn Mink, *The Wages of Motherhood* (Ithaca, N.Y., 1995); Linda Gordon, "Black and White Visions of Welfare," *Journal of American History* 78 (1991): 559–90.

21. Quadagno, *Color of Welfare,* p. 10. This framework is fairly common; see Skocpol, *Social Policy in the United States,* pp. 218–21, and Skocpol, "African Americans in U.S. Social Policy," pp. 145–46.

African American migrants into the economy: the War on Poverty, Model Cities, and employment training, among others. These policies are commonly explained either as intentional efforts to address black political discontent with patronage and welfare or, alternatively, as policies for all poor people, regardless of race, that were overwhelmed and politicized by the rise of the black power movement and the demand for community control.[22]

There are two problems with this view. First, it cannot explain the union of race and social policy prior to the Great Society. Second, the Great Society held out a historic opportunity to break the pattern of racial stratification inherited from the New Deal, but instead it merely reproduced that stratification.

Why did policymakers fail to transform the racialized social policies they inherited? The argument that Democrats set out to create racially bifurcated social policies in big cities is unsatisfactory. Very few of the social policies of the 1960s were "race-specific" as that term is commonly understood; although the term typically refers to affirmative action policies, it cannot be stretched to cover many of the Great Society programs. Food stamps, Medicaid, education, and employment-training programs were all putatively "race-neutral" (though in some cases employment training programs were targeted to urban ghettos). The identification of the Great Society as of sole or exclusive benefit to African Americans derives from the public perception of the intended beneficiaries of the War on Poverty and the rise in the welfare rolls. Yet many Great Society programs—ranging from those ostensibly created for the poor, such as the Elementary and Secondary Education Act of 1965, to more universalistic ones—were of benefit to white middle-class families. Ironically, the explosive growth of the welfare rolls during the 1960s was of principal benefit to white women. The African American struggle for equality is obviously central to understanding what happened in the 1960s, but by itself it is insufficient. One must also consider the consequences of

22. For the first interpretation see Frances Fox Piven and Richard A. Cloward, *Regulating the Poor: The Functions of Public Welfare* (New York, 1971); for the second, see: Paul Peterson and J. David Greenstone, "Racial Change and Citizen Participation: The Mobilization of Low-Income Communities through Community Action," in *A Decade of Federal Antipoverty Programs,* ed. Robert Haveman (New York, 1977), pp. 241–78; Theodore Lowi, *The End of Liberalism,* 2d ed. (New York, 1979), chap. 8; Michael K. Brown and Steven P. Erie, "Blacks and the Legacy of the Great Society: The Economic and Political Impact of Federal Social Policy," *Public Policy* 29 (1981): 299–330; Margaret Weir, *Politics and Jobs: The Boundaries of Employment Policy in the United States* (Princeton, N.J., 1991), chap. 3, esp. pp. 87–89; Ira Katznelson, *City Trenches: Urban Politics and the Patterning of Class in the United States* (New York, 1981).

Lyndon Johnson's decision to build a redistributive welfare state rather than support more comprehensive social policies for citizens other than the elderly.

My approach to the question of how and why federal social policy became racially stratified begins with an observation Gunnar Myrdal made about the effects of New Deal relief policy:

> White people by means of the severe job restrictions they have imposed upon the Negro—and by denying him sufficient public health facilities— have forced him to accept public relief as one of his "major occupations." Therefore, if the Negro, in a sense, has become *"demoralized,"* it is rather because *white people have given him a smaller share of the steady and worthwhile jobs than of public assistance benefits.*[23]

In other words, labor-market discrimination is reproduced in the welfare state independent of the actions of administrators. Under pressure of job competition, whites seek to apportion a greater share of jobs among themselves, relegating African Americans and other subordinate racial groups to charity or the public system of social provision, normally relief. Myrdal's observation can apply to discrimination in any market, including housing or education.

Myrdal actually had the answer only half right; racial discrimination also limits access to non-means-tested policies and leads to differential benefits. Wage-related contributory social insurance forges a tight link between work and eligibility. The designers of the American system of social security were concerned to discourage "malingerers," understood as workers who move in and out of the labor force willingly or unwillingly. The legitimacy of the system, they believed, depended on its connection to work. Social security establishes a formal equality among recipients, but it is not "color-blind." Reliance on contributory, earnings-related policies magnifies patterns of both racial and gender discrimination. Job discrimination undermines the eligibility of black and female workers for unemployment benefits; wage discrimination appears in the way that social security benefits for blacks lag behind those of whites sixty years after the system was created.

National policy decisions have produced a welfare state that has combined comparatively slack labor markets with social insurance tightly circumscribed by work requirements and policies that sharply distinguish affluent citizens from those less fortunate. When implemented in a society with

---

23. Gunnar Myrdal, *An American Dilemma* (New York, 1944), p. 301.

pervasive racial discrimination, these policies have reproduced the color line within the welfare state (though obviously some African American families may be better off economically). The color line represents the entrenched system of racial inequality, and it is defined by the concepts of hierarchy and collectivism. "Hierarchy," writes Marguerite Ross Barnet, "specifically means the existence of a principle (racism) that ranks groups consistently and pervasively, *and is enforceable through social control.* Collectivism means that each individual member of a group is treated according to some principle that defines the whole."[24] Because of the persistence of racially stratified social policies since the 1930s, blacks are regarded as inferior to whites and denied their individuality.

The color line is made and remade historically. Race is not an independent, autonomous force in history but rather an element of the economic and political terrain contested by social classes and racial groups. Racial privileges and identity form as a relationship between dominant and subordinate groups, much like social classes, out of struggles over racial advantages. Dominant racial groups display a sense of entitlement and make prior claims to social status and economic advantages; they seek to maintain these entitlements and their sense of themselves as superior.[25] An analysis of how the color line is remade historically entails understanding how the practice of racism at an individual level is related to societal forces that either implicitly or explicitly affect behavior. "One must seek explanations for the reproduction of racist belief and behavior," Thomas Holt asserts, "not in individual pathologies but in social formations at specific historical moments that shape and make both self and other knowable."[26] I insist that one cannot account for the origins and persistence of racial stratification in the welfare state with a framework that considers only racial discrimination by politicians and administrators. Stratification must be understood in light of the racial order that took shape with the industrialization of the north and the migration of African American sharecroppers and workers, that is, as a consequence of the relationship of black and white workers.

24. Marguerite Ross Barnet, "A Theoretical Perspective on American Racial Public Policy," in *Public Policy for the Black Community,* ed. Marguerite Ross Barnet and James A. Hefner (New York, 1976), p. 20.

25. George Fredrickson, "Reflections on the Comparative History and Sociology of Racism," *American Studies in Southern Africa: Symposium Proceedings,* vol. 2 (1992), p. 6. Also see "Colonialism and Racism," in Fredrickson, *The Arrogance of Race* (Middletown, Conn., 1988), pp. 216–35.

26. Thomas C. Holt, "Marking: Race, Race-making, and the Writing of History," *American Historical Review* 100 (1995): 9–10.

African American workers entered the industrial order as a racially subordinate group. Migrating black workers were either denied membership in unions by white workers intent on protecting jobs or denied work altogether. Even before the depression, African American workers had higher unemployment rates than white workers. When blacks did find employment, they were relegated to the worst and lowest-paying jobs. White workers appropriated the skilled jobs for themselves and stoutly resisted the efforts of black workers to acquire experience or job skills. They regarded black workers as incapable of working with machines or in supervisory and managerial positions.[27] White workers, according to Robin D. G. Kelley, achieved both economic security and a sense of superiority from this. "Black workers," he writes, "had to perform 'nigger work.' Without the existence of 'nigger work' and 'nigger labor,' to white workers whiteness would be meaningless."[28] As a consequence, one avenue into industrial employment for black workers was as strikebreakers, a situation adroitly exploited by employers, widening the racial divide among workers.[29]

The point is that the American welfare state took shape in a racialized industrial order governed by Myrdal's rule. This has two implications. First, blacks fare less well in the welfare state relative to whites and are economically shortchanged. To the extent that work regulates access to the core social insurance policies or private fringe benefits, the victims of racial discrimination are denied access or, when included, denied equal benefits. Second, the derogatory social meaning inscribed on the work that African Americans do is reproduced in the welfare state. Work and the ideology of the work ethic reside at the core of the American welfare state. The legitimacy of a social policy and the status of its recipients may be said to turn on their relationship to work. Social security is an *earned* right; welfare is charity. The meaning of citizenship in America, as Judith Shklar has taught us, is deeply entwined with slavery and work. One mark of citizenship in America, she argues, is earning a living, a status that was historically defined

27. Warren Whatley and Gavin Wright, "Race, Human Capital, and Labour Markets in American History," in *Labour Market Evolution,* ed. George Grantham and Mary Mackinnon (London, 1994), pp. 270–91; William A. Sundstrom, "The Color Line: Racial Norms and Discrimination in Urban Labor Markets, 1910–1950," *Journal of Economic History* 54 (1994): 382–95.

28. Robin D. G. Kelly, *Race Rebels: Culture, Politics, and the Black Working Class* (New York, 1996), pp. 30–31. For a contemporary view see W. E. B. Du Bois, "Of Work and Wealth," in *Darkwater* (New York, 1920), pp. 81–104.

29. Warren Whatley, "African-American Strikebreaking from the Civil War to the New Deal," *Social Science History* 17 (1993): 525–58.

in relation to its racial opposite, slavery. Poor whites lived in fear they would be reduced to slavelike status under a wage labor system. To be a citizen was to be free, which meant to be an independent worker. The strength of the ideology of work in America derives from "the memory of slavery, rendered ever potent by racism, [and] still arouses predictable fears among white workers and haunts blacks."[30] Historically what has distinguished the "deserving" from the "undeserving" poor is work, and the idea of work has depended on its relationship to race, both in terms of labor-market discrimination—blacks' exclusion from decent jobs—and as the source of the ideology of the American work ethic. By denying work to African Americans and giving them relief instead, social policies are marked by the history of slavery and race and signify the hierarchy of white over black.

Race and Class in the Development of the American Welfare State

The reproduction of racial hierarchies within the welfare state depends on whether social policies reinforce or override labor-market and residential discrimination. Willard Townsend, a prominent African American trade unionist in the 1940s, summed up the implications when he observed, "you can't have unencumbered and prosperous white workers and unemployed black workers—for, if you let that happen, the white worker will have to carry the black worker on his back through relief or the dole."[31] Had the United States adopted, for example, noncontributory, universal transfers, a racially stratified welfare state would have been less likely to have emerged. This would not have granted African Americans civil or political rights; but it would have removed, or at least minimized, one source of conflict over social policy. Similarly, had LBJ made different choices, the contemporary discussion of poverty likely would have been much different. Such counterfactual speculations raise the question of what explains the political development of the variegated pattern of social provision in the United States.

My answer focuses on the strategic choices of policymakers (chiefly, presidents from Roosevelt to Nixon) and the self-interested actions of the main advocates and opponents of a federally controlled welfare state. These

30. Judith N. Shklar, *American Citizenship: The Quest for Inclusion* (Cambridge, Mass., 1991), pp. 85–86.

31. Willard Townsend, "Full Employment and the Negro Worker," in *A Documentary History of the Negro People in the United States,* ed. Herbert Aptheker, vol. 4 (New York, 1974), p. 520.

choices, I argue, were governed largely, but not entirely, by money and race. Understanding the role of money requires that we reverse our usual assumptions about the relationship between money and social policy and treat it as a cause rather than a result of policy decisions. Political leaders, especially when contemplating marked departures from the status quo, make decisions about taxes and budgets *prior* to choosing social policies, and those choices determine policy agendas. Put another way, major social policy decisions are framed by questions of fiscal capacity, the ability of policymakers to finance new ventures by imposing new taxes, raising existing taxes, or running budgetary deficits. The implications of alternative tax and budget policies for investors and taxpayers act as a filter for policy choices, ruling in some policies and ruling out others. Similarly, the social policy preferences of different social classes depend on assessments of who will pay for the welfare state and who will benefit. In the United States, though, class preferences are always complicated by the defense of white privileges.

The problem facing policymakers intent on building a welfare state is that governments are invariably dependent on investors to undertake and sustain economic activity and taxpayers to part with their hard-earned cash. Both Roosevelt and Johnson confronted demands to create new social rights and social policies while simultaneously igniting and sustaining economic growth. For both of these politicians economic growth was a preeminent concern. FDR had to find a way to bring the economy out of the depression but he also recognized that economic growth was integral to the development and well-being of a welfare state. Growth generates tax revenues to finance expensive social policies; it lubricates policy innovation by ameliorating distributive conflict; and, without it, anti-poverty programs are jeopardized. Demands for new social rights and policies actually increase the dependence of policymakers on investors and taxpayers. Policymakers like Roosevelt and Johnson, who were intent on building a national welfare state, thus faced a perverse dilemma: the success of their policy agenda required that they strengthen, not weaken, the economic machine.

Social theorists since Joseph Schumpeter have maintained that states face a structural conflict that cannot be evaded between demands for social rights and capital accumulation.[32] The "market is a prison," it is said, such that any attempt to change the distribution of income through taxes or to use

32. See, for example, James O'Conner, *The Fiscal Crisis of the State* (New York, 1973); Claus Offe, *The Contradictions of the Welfare State* (Cambridge, Mass., 1984); Milton Fisk, *The State and Justice: An Essay in Political Theory* (New York, 1989).

governmental resources for a social wage or otherwise bid up the price of labor inevitably leads to "deadweight losses," the withdrawal of needed resources from productive use whether by investors or taxpayers.[33] But just how real is this constraint? Can we assume that it would have mattered to Roosevelt and Johnson? There is certainly reason to doubt that the market is a prison; not every attempt to pass prolabor social policies has led to retaliation by investors, and not every tax annihilates private economic activity. There is not much empirical evidence on this question, but one important piece of research establishes that policymakers have choices: it is theoretically possible to evade the trade-off between social rights and capital accumulation by choosing consumption rather than income taxes. The Swedes have done just this, building the Cadillac of welfare states by "taxing capital lightly."[34] The Swedish case indicates that we should not assume that business confidence does not matter to policymakers, even though the strong version of the structural dependence theory may be untrue. In my analysis, I reformulate the theory to explain under what conditions policymakers will assume they are constrained by their dependence on investors and taxpayers and respond accordingly.

Policymakers fear a capital strike, but this fear waxes or wanes depending on political circumstances. Fred Block believes that business confidence is a powerful constraint on political leaders during periods of economic growth but its influence declines during economic depressions when low economic activity and popular discontent strengthens their hand and weakens business.[35] Actually, the relationship is just the opposite. Political leaders are more concerned about investment during periods of slack or sluggish economic growth. The need for political leaders to assuage the anxieties of resistant, unruly investors rises with the demand for a bustling, growing economy, and it is at a premium when the demand for economic growth coincides with a critical moment of policy innovation. This was precisely the sort of situation that FDR faced during 1934–35 when he was trying to

33. Charles Lindblom, *Politics and Markets: The World's Political-Economic Systems* (New York, 1977), pp. 172, 175.

34. Adam Przeworksi and Michael Wallerstein, "Structural Dependence of the State on Capital," *American Political Science Review* 82 (1988): 11–30; Seven Steinmo, "Social Democracy vs. Socialism: Goal Adaptation in Social Democratic Sweden," *Politics and Society* 16 (1988): 403–46.

35. Fred Block, "The Ruling Class Does Not Rule: Notes on the Marxist Theory of the State," in *The Political Economy,* ed. Thomas Ferguson and Joel Rogers (New York, 1984), p. 43.

jump-start the economy at the same time he was maneuvering to design and pass the Social Security Act and related legislation.

Investors do not bolt at the first sign of a tax increase. What matters most is their expectation of what governments will do. John Maynard Keynes argued that decisions by investors to purchase capital assets rather than hoard money was fraught with uncertainty, and governed by the "facts of the existing situation." He assumed that anticipation of large but uncertain changes in business conditions would weaken investor confidence. Keynes, who had ample opportunity to examine the psychology of investors first-hand, observed that "economic prosperity is excessively dependent on a political and social atmosphere which is congenial to the average business man."[36] The confidence of investors is particularly affected by the election of left-wing governments and by the capacity of such governments to act. Conservative governments do not inspire a lack of business confidence. When a left-wing government appears likely to act on its agenda, businessmen and investors are attentive to the implications of tax, spending, and labor policies for profits and labor discipline. Different businesses may have different economic interests, and there may be conflict between sectors of the economy, but as Michael Kalecki argued businesses also have an aggregate, or class, interest in issues of taxing and spending. There is some evidence that business confidence is affected by elections.[37]

Under these circumstances, left-wing governments with ambitious agendas are highly sensitive to expectations of investors and taxpayers. Adam Przeworksi, who is otherwise skeptical of the structural dependence theory, suggests "the state may be structurally dependent in the dynamic sense that, given the cost of anticipations, left-wing governments may best promote the interests of their constituencies by assuring capitalists that they would not pursue such policies."[38] These governments seek to reassure investors that they will not give away the store while paying for their social policies. As a consequence, we should expect left-wing political leaders to frame their policy agendas by choosing policies that minimize the concerns of investors regarding budget deficits, monetary inflation, the size and incidence of tax

36. John Maynard Keynes, *The General Theory of Employment, Interest, and Money* (New York, 1964), pp. 148, 162.

37. Michael Kalecki, "Political Aspects of Full Employment," in *Capitalism: Business Cycles and Full Employment,* ed. Jerzy Osiatynski, vol. 1 (Oxford, 1990), pp. 347–56; Christopher Heye, "Labor Market Tightness and Business Confidence: An International Comparison," *Politics and Society* 21 (1993): 185.

38. Adam Przeworksi, *The State and the Economy under Capitalism* (New York, 1990), p. 95.

increases, and the growth of the public sector relative to the private (which in the United States is usually understood to mean the size of the federal government in relation to the GDP). Both Roosevelt and Johnson kept one eye on the confidence of investors while crafting policies that would be supported by constituents. Both presidents negotiated the dilemma between capital accumulation and social rights by choosing tax and budget policies that minimized immediate conflict and permitted some future expansion of their programs as the economy grew.[39]

Political leaders must also pay attention to taxpayers. Tax resistance is pervasive and not (as is sometimes thought) especially unique to the United States, but the degree to which it strikes fear in the minds of political leaders varies. Tax resistance may become salient during periods of declining wages and incomes, which explains much of the hostility toward taxes today, and even more so during the tax revolt of the 1930s.[40] Rapidly rising tax burdens can also stiffen voter resistance to new taxes. This mattered during the 1940s when the war required income tax increases.

Money is not the only explanation for the choices of policymakers of course. An alternative approach centers on political institutions. Proponents of the polity-centered approach, as it is called, argue that the configuration of governmental institutions, party structure, and electoral rules condition the actions of politicians and social groups. In explaining the kind of social policies chosen by a nation, we should consider the historical formation of particular states and the way in which these institutional structures in turn determine the policy agenda, the problems attended to, and the goals and capacities of policymakers and social groups. This approach deemphasizes underlying social and economic factors. States are "sites of autonomous action" in which officials "do not just respond to socioeconomic transformations [but] pursue policies that reinforce the interests (and use the capacities) of the organizations within which their careers are embedded." Politicians pursue their own vision of the future with due regard to institutional constraints. The political identity of social groups and classes, moreover, is shaped by political institutions. For example, the early enfranchisement of white men in the United States diminished their sense of themselves as a class-conscious political force. Finally, policy legacies—the residue of past

---

39. For a similar approach to the analysis of business confidence with regard to tax policy, see Ronald F. King, *Money, Time, and Politics: Investment Tax Subsidies and American Democracy* (New Haven, Conn., 1993), pp. 75–77.

40. Michael J. Boskin, "Some Neglected Economic Factors behind Recent Tax and Spending Limitation Movements," *National Tax Journal* (supplement) 32 (1979): 38–40.

decisions and debates—influence the views, interests, and actions of future political leaders. Policies can determine politics.[41]

According to the polity-centered approach, different political institutions and party systems lead to different kinds of welfare states. Strong states—in which centralized power is neither culturally nor politically suspect; an independent civil service nurtures policy proposals; and the party system is organized around programmatic agendas—will produce a much different kind of welfare state than a fragmented and decentralized political system—in which the assertion of centralized political power is problematic; the party system is based on patronage; and policy ideas are generated by an assortment of reformers, party bosses, and interest groups. It is to the American configuration of political institutions that one must look for an explanation of the fragmented pattern of social provision created by the 1935 Social Security Act and the subsequent inability of policymakers to establish broad, universalistic social policies.

American political institutions have constrained the development of the welfare state in two ways. In the American federal system, weak political parties based on patronage and tied to local constituencies through single-member districts have led to a policymaking process that gives undue influence to those local constituencies and that facilitates legislative log rolling. This institutional structure promotes the adoption of policies that disperse social benefits geographically and obstructs the creation of nationally administered social policies. Additionally, the separation of powers and the anti-majoritarian effects of the Madisonian system frustrate the formation of cross-class political coalitions, which are deemed to have been essential to the construction of universalistic European welfare states. A farm-labor coalition failed to emerge in the late 1930s, for example, because the centrifugal features of the American political system frustrated Roosevelt's attempt to impose party governance. Similarly, the effort by Bayard Rustin and A. Philip Randolph to create a biracial political coalition in the 1960s foundered on the shoals of a decentralized political system. Together these factors and the two-tiered welfare state—the institutional separation between social insurance and welfare—molded the Great Society.[42]

41. Theda Skocpol, *Protecting Soldiers and Mothers: The Political Origins of Social Policy in the United States* (Cambridge, Mass., 1992), pp. 41–42, 47–50, 57–59; Skocpol, *Social Policy in the United States*, p. 40.

42. Margaret Weir, Ann Shola Orloff, and Theda Skocpol, ed., *The Politics of Social Policy in the United State* (Princeton, N.J., 1988), pp. 24–25, epilogue; Weir, *Politics and Jobs*, pp. 95–97; Michael Katz, *In the Shadow of the Poorhouse* (New York, 1986), chap. 9.

This argument obviously speaks to the realities of the American political system and the effects of decentralized political institutions on decision making. But the polity-centered approach begs the question of state autonomy and evades questions of fiscal capacity. Builders of welfare states can never act autonomously so long as they must extract needed resources from hostile investors and reluctant taxpayers. Money shapes the initiatives and decisions of policymakers every bit as much as political arrangements, if not more so. Political leaders, and especially presidents intent on building new institutions of social provision, cannot ignore the structural realities of capitalism. A choice between universalistic social policies and means-tested ones depends on the ability of politicians to finance comprehensive policies. A narrow focus on political institutions obscures this stubborn fact. This is the reason the polity-centered approach has difficulty explaining why, for example, first Johnson and then Nixon choose to reinvent the two-tiered welfare state.[43]

Questions of fiscal capacity may be mediated by political institutions. Consider the problem of federalism. It is usually argued that the fragmented, decentralized American welfare state stems from local resistance to the imposition of national standards and a desire to maintain local institutions. Yet liberal political leaders have been willing to decentralize control of social policies when the question of who would bear the tax burden was at issue. If most state politicians have sought historically to shift costs to the federal government, national politicians, beginning with FDR, have been reluctant to assume the full costs of the welfare state. Federalism thus mediates the question of tax burdens precisely because it provides an opportunity to shift responsibility for raising taxes. Ironically, the very policy that facilitates racial discrimination in the distribution of benefits—decentralized administration of public assistance—came about because FDR was seeking to minimize investor and taxpayer resistance to his policies.

Although this book focuses mostly on presidential decisions, it would be a mistake to assume that Congress has been continually dominated by the president. Yet much of the liberal policy agenda from the 1930s on was hatched in the executive branch, and at the two crucial moments of social policy innovation (the 1930s and the 1960s), presidential power was decisive in setting the agenda and shaping the outcome.

43. Prior to the 1960s, means-tested spending as a proportion of GNP remained stagnant, while middle-class payments to individuals (social insurance and other federal payments) were growing relative to means-tested transfers. Johnson and Nixon reversed this trend, and after 1965 the rate of growth of means-tested payments outstripped middle-class payments. (Author's calculation.)

Business confidence, I argue, provides a singularly important element in the explanation of FDR's and LBJ's policy agendas and decisions. It explains the paradox of two consummate politicians, who governed with over-whelming congressional majorities, choosing to combine liberal social poli-cies with fiscal conservatism. Conversely, business confidence did not really matter in the 1940s and 1970s, periods of conservative control in which presidents had less influence. My point is not that business confidence has been decisive throughout the entire fifty-year period of the development of the welfare state, but rather that it became important only with the election of left-wing governments that had the capacity to act. Business confidence was not an invariant constraint, but it did shape the policy agendas and choices of Roosevelt and Johnson.

Liberal and conservative political coalitions were divided over whether the welfare state should be based on universalistic social policies and be nationally administered. Some theorists commonly assume that there is a working-class agenda for the welfare state which is invariant across time and between countries, one that differs from the agenda of bourgeois parties. Historically, working-class political parties and labor unions have loathed poor laws and means-tested policies and stood for comprehensive, univer-salistic social policies and full-employment economies. The achievement of such policies, Gøsta Esping-Andersen argues, depends on the ability of la-bor parties to take power and implement their agenda.[44] The strength of working-class political parties does appear to explain variations in the generosity and comprehensiveness of social policies as well as the absence of means-tested policies. But, as Peter Baldwin has shown, the universalism of European welfare states cannot be attributed entirely to the mobilization of the working class; workers' parties often opposed extending coverage of pensions to citizens outside the safety net because workers were already cov-ered and reluctant to pay for anyone else. Universalism depended on middle-class support, which appeared when the middle class believed that exclusion from social policies was no longer acceptable. There is no invariant class agenda; class interest, Baldwin argues, is mediated by patterns of inclusion and exclusion in the welfare state that structure incentives for middle-class, as well as working-class, citizens.[45]

Baldwin clearly has a point. Yet class interest is not entirely encompassed

---

44. Esping-Andersen, *Three Worlds of Welfare Capitalism*, chap. 5.
45. Peter Baldwin, *The Politics of Social Solidarity* (New York, 1990), pp. 47–54, 143–46, 152–57, 201–3, 288–99.

by inclusion or exclusion from social programs; different social classes have a fiscal stake in whether the welfare state is expansive and generous or limited and punitive. Middle-class citizens, particularly conservative opponents of the welfare state, have a stake in tax rates and aggregate levels of spending. At the same time, working-class and poor citizens can be expected to think they would benefit from robust and expensive forms of social provision, and indeed they typically vote this way. Historically, conservatives and affluent middle-class opponents of the welfare state have sought to limit its long-run growth and to lower both spending and tax levels. The Republican party has preferred locally controlled means-tested transfers, private forms of social protection, fiscally constrained grants-in-aid (such as block grants), and tax cuts often calculated to "starve the beast" and reduce the capacity to spend.

Democrats and their labor allies have opposed this agenda, but the interests of the Democratic party coalition have proved to be far less unified than those of Republicans. The three constituent elements of the Democratic party coalition between the 1930s and the 1970s—union members, white southerners, and African Americans—have had disparate interests in the welfare state. Only African Americans have consistently expressed unqualified support for a comprehensive welfare state. Indeed, blacks are the one group whose policy aims and political program have invariably transcended narrow economic self-interest.[46] Both southerners and union members have had more ambivalent stakes in the welfare state and both have withheld their support for more comprehensive public social policies at crucial moments. The reason for these divergent stands is that in the United States class interest—the fiscal stake in social provision—competes with race in defining the interests of blacks, southern Democrats, and union members. In both the North and the South, whites have had a stake in preserving their racial privileges and maintaining a rigid color line socially, economically, and politically.

Southern Democrats figure in most accounts as the chief opponents of the American welfare state. Their opposition to progressive social policies is usually attributed to their desire to maintain southern apartheid at all costs. But some of the fiercest southern racists were also loyal New Dealers, for whom tax and spend was a byword. Southerners were not unabashed

---

46. On the origins of these beliefs see Michael C. Dawson, "A Black Counterpublic? Economic Earthquakes, Racial Agenda(s), and Black Politics," in *The Black Public Sphere,* ed. The Black Public Sphere Collective (Chicago, 1995), pp. 199–227.

opponents of a welfare state; rather they opposed a large universalistic, national welfare state. If the federal government was a potential threat to southern apartheid, it was also a source of needed revenues. Racial animosities could be tempered by the lure of federal dollars so long as social policies were confined to means-tested, locally controlled programs. These interests set southern Democrats apart from both their fellow Democrats in the North and from Republicans. They wanted a smaller and less comprehensive welfare state than northern Democrats but a more expensive one than Republicans. Southern Democrats were mostly interested in building a limited but racially segregated welfare state in their own region.

Although the labor movement failed to capitalize on its political leverage after the surge in mobilization during the 1930s, unions were central to the enactment of broad social policies in the postwar era. American unions may not have lived up to the ideals of European social democracy, but the AFL-CIO was important to the success of many national legislative battles.[47] Yet if labor leaders acted on behalf of broader social policies, individual unions and workers proved to be fickle supporters of a comprehensive welfare systems and turned their backs on the idea during the Great Society. Union rejection of the social-democratic creed of AFL-CIO chieftains was motivated by their economic and racial interests. After World War II, unions took the lead in constructing private welfare systems through collective bargaining; thereafter they had scant interest in new social policies. This economic interest was reinforced by the stake white workers had in maintaining their control of labor markets and racially segregated neighborhoods.[48]

For blacks, compelling economic (i.e., class) interests in a comprehensive welfare state are reinforced by racial interests. African Americans have historically pursued both an economic and a civil-rights agenda.[49] If these agendas were sometimes seen to be in competition prior to the New Deal, they were understood to be related afterwards when it became clear that full-

47. J. David Greenstone, *Labor in American Politics* (New York, 1969).

48. CIO as well as AFL unions followed this course, even though they actively recruited blacks after 1936. See Robert J. Norrell, "Caste in Steel: Jim Crow Careers in Birmingham, Alabama," *Journal of American History* 73 (1986): 669–94. The picture is by no means one of unrelieved working-class racism; there were unions that actively worked to build a biracial labor movement. See Michael Goldfield, "Race and the CIO: The Possibilities for Racial Egalitarianism during the 1930s and the 1940s," *International Labor and Working-Class History* 44 (1993): 1–32.

49. See Earl Lewis, *In Their Own Interests* (Berkeley, 1991); Dona C. Hamilton and Charles V. Hamilton, *The Dual Agenda: Race and Social Welfare Policies of Civil Rights Organizations* (New York, 1997).

employment and inclusive social policies were necessary (in addition to civil rights) to transcend racial divisions. Martin Luther King Jr. eloquently reaffirmed this in one of his last speeches when he suggested that the black struggle for civil rights and economic equality was fundamentally a struggle for all citizens. Black nationalists may have had bitter disagreements with integrationists over political ends and strategy; but they have rarely dissented from the enduring consensus among African Americans for a robust and comprehensive welfare state. To understand why African Americans have behaved more like European social democrats than the American labor movement has, one must consider the racial stakes of various social policies.

The argument that whites will coercively substitute relief for jobs is based on the assumption that blacks and whites compete in the labor market, but the intensity of this competition depends, quite obviously, on the existence of a labor surplus or shortage and on the availability of legal remedies to labor market discrimination. Civil rights remedies appeared rather late in the history of the American welfare state and thus did not affect the development of these patterns of social provision though they might have modified them. Historically more important, particularly from the point of view of African Americans, have been full-employment policies. Black trade unionists and civil rights leaders believed that the New Deal agenda for full employment and universal social insurance, combined with wartime economic advances, would mean an end to the color line in labor markets.

As African Americans have well understood since the 1930s, conflict over social policies in the United States has never been simply about economic interests. Even though public transfers have raised the standard of living for many African Americans, the racial stratification of social policy that emerged with the New Deal reinforced racist beliefs and contributed to white antipathy against federal social policy. An irony was thus embedded in the political development of the American welfare state: the victims of efforts to maintain racially discriminatory labor and housing markets are systematically blamed for their plight. Blacks came to be seen as both authors and defenders of social policies that whites regarded as invidious and detrimental, opening the way for conservative opponents of the welfare state to use this belief in their political wars.

My account of this story covers federal social policy from Roosevelt through Reagan. Although my analytic framework distinguishes between two periods of policy innovation and two periods of conservative control and reaction, I have proceeded chronologically. Episodic accounts of political conflict over social policies alternate with analyses of these policies' distributive and political implications for blacks and whites. Franklin Roosevelt and Lyndon Johnson become central figures in my examination of the formulation of liberal policy agendas. Southern Democrats and Richard Nixon assume pivotal roles in my study of the conservative rejection of liberal demands and the use of selected social policies to funnel northern money to the South and build a new electoral coalition. Chapter 4 is devoted to understanding why the labor movement made private social policies a key demand in collective bargaining. This is an important story in its own right, but also has enormous implications for the union response to the Great Society. Chapters 2, 5, 8, and 10 consider what happened as federal social policies were implemented in a society pervaded by racism. I pay particular attention to the debate within the African American community over the relationship between race and class and to the racial structuring of social policy. Whites figure in these chapters as both the instigators and beneficiaries of a welfare state marked by racial distinctions. The concluding chapter considers the implications of this study for the present debate over the future of the American welfare state.

PART ONE

THE ANTINOMIES OF RACE AND CLASS IN THE NEW DEAL

CHAPTER ONE

The Policy Settlement of 1935

The businessmen of this country are deeply apprehensive of the future. This is because they see in some of the things the Administration has done, but even more in things various of its spokesmen have said, trends and tendencies which, if developed further, will bring serious trouble if not disaster.

— MARC A. ROSE

[The Economic Security Act] is, on the whole, reasonably economical, so that we may hope to carry this structure financially without making too great inroads upon the private purses of individuals contributing.

— FRANCES PERKINS

Franklin Delano Roosevelt announced his plans to establish a permanent system of economic security in his 1935 State of the Union address. Declaring that the "federal government must and shall quit this business of relief," FDR proposed replacing the Federal Emergency Relief Administration (FERA) with universal entitlements to work-related social insurance for the elderly and the unemployed; state-run categorical public assistance, or means-tested income transfers for "unemployables" (the elderly, single mothers, and the blind); and a temporary, federally subsidized work-relief program for "employables" (individuals out of work because of the depression). These decisions, the culmination of an executive-branch planning effort dominated by the Committee on Economic Security (CES), laid the foundation for a national welfare state.

As important and far-reaching as these innovations were, the New Dealers failed to resolve the question of the federal government's permanent responsibility for minimizing unemployment and gave up substantial national control over social policy. The work relief program failed to become the basis for a right to work, as many of Roosevelt's advisers hoped it would, and never served more than 30 percent of the unemployed. Control over old-age insurance was given to the federal government but states retained authority over unemployment insurance and categorical public assistance. All these policies were financed by regressive payroll and sales taxes. Although payroll taxes attracted most of the criticism from reformers, the main New Deal contribution to regressive taxation was the general sales tax. Only five states had adopted general sales taxes when Roosevelt took office; by the end of 1937, twenty-eight states had imposed a sales tax. Most of these new sales taxes were a consequence of the 1935 policy settlement.[1]

For all its sweep, Roosevelt's policy revolution was predicated on fiscal conservatism. When Secretary of Labor Frances Perkins announced submission of the CES's report to Congress, she said that "no *federal* financial aid was contemplated in either the unemployment insurance plans or the permanent program for old age pensions."[2] Perkins went out of her way to reiterate the program's fiscal conservatism in her congressional testimony, stressing the administration's intention to minimize tax burdens. Just how frugal the administration was is apparent from FDR's fiscal year 1936 budget. It not only explicitly rejected a general tax increase, but made no mention of any permanent spending for public assistance or other programs contemplated in the administration's economic security plan. The fiscal structure of the policy settlement of 1935 appeared to minimize the federal role: poor relief was given back to the states and federal assistance was expressly limited; work relief was financed by temporary borrowing and "self-liquidating" projects that would pay themselves off; and social insurance was taken out of the normal appropriations process and placed on a "self-sustaining" basis.

Paradoxically, Roosevelt joined fiscal conservatism to liberal policy reform just as he strengthened his leverage in Congress. His large partisan majorities in the House of Representatives and the Senate were augmented by gains in the 1934 elections that increased Democratic party strength in the House to 322 seats and gave them better than a two-thirds majority in the Senate. Many of the new members of Congress were well to the left of the New Deal or were third-party candidates committed to far-reaching reforms. They joined a House of Representatives in which over half the members had served less than two terms and most were committed New Dealers ready to do the president's bidding. The policy settlement of 1935 took shape and was

1. W. Brooke Graves and David H. Kurtzman, "New State Taxes," *State Government* 9 (1936): 156–57; Neil H. Jacoby, *Retail Sales Taxation* (New York, 1938), pp. 72–74.
2. "Roosevelt Limits Social Aid Grants," *New York Times,* January 12, 1935. (Emphasis added.)

passed during an on-going critical realignment of the electorate, a moment when the localistic and incremental character of congressional policymaking was superseded and the constitutional barriers to policy innovation were easily surmountable.[3] Roosevelt could act with the knowledge that his decisions would be ratified in Congress. Yet for some people, both within and outside the administration, the question was not whether to act; it was how to cope with "money radicalism" and the wild-eyed spenders of the new Congress. Indeed, the generally conservative press interpreted Roosevelt's announcement of his economic security plans as a shift to the right and a rejection of the so-called radical ideas then surfacing in Congress and the country.[4]

What accounts for FDR's preference for fiscally circumscribed policies and regressive taxation despite his apparent political leverage in Congress? It is often assumed that FDR crafted his policies to avoid opposition from southern legislators or that the planning effort was dominated by reformers with strong ties to corporate leaders. Actually, what mattered most to FDR was money. He and his closest aides made a set of choices about public spending and taxes that independently shaped the design of the 1935 Social Security Act and work relief program.

FDR Maneuvers between Recovery and Reform

Roosevelt settled on a decentralized welfare state, a temporary means-tested work relief program, and contributory social insurance to avoid large tax increases and minimize permanent federal deficits. These decisions were his solution to the quandary faced by all would-be builders of a welfare state: the necessity of balancing conflicting demands from the right and left, of extending social protection while trying to stimulate economic growth and sustain capital accumulation. FDR was trying to launch his welfare state at the same time he was trying to jump-start the economy. In an open letter, John Maynard Keynes bluntly warned FDR of the dilemma he faced in trying to bring about both recovery and reform. "For the first [recovery]," Keynes wrote, "speed and quick results are essential. The second [reform] may be

3. William E. Leutchenburg, *Franklin Roosevelt and the New Deal* (New York, 1963), pp. 116–17; David W. Brady, *Critical Elections and Congressional Policy Making* (Stanford, Calif., 1988), pp. 103–4, 107.

4. *Business Week,* November 17, 1934, p. 5, December 8, 1934, p. 36; Mark Leff, *The Symbolic Uses of Reform* (New York, 1984), pp. 120–21; *New York Times,* January 2, 1935, sec. 4, January 5, 1935, sec. 1.

urgent too; but . . . even wise and necessary reform may, in some respects, impede and complicate recovery. For it will upset the confidence of the business world and weaken its existing motives before you have had time to put other motives in their place."[5]

By the time he created the Committee on Economic Security in June 1934 and charged it with fashioning a comprehensive social welfare policy, FDR faced conflicting demands for reform and recovery. The voice of reform emerged from discontented people among the unemployed, the elderly, farmers, dissident third-party movements, and middle-class professionals, many of whom found themselves radicalized by the depression. The unemployed objected to the seeming withdrawal of aid when FDR decided to dismantle the Civil Works Administration, a massive public employment effort that had abandoned means tests and, at its peak, successfully employed over four million men and women. Francis E. Townsend, a retired physician, organized the elderly to petition for a universal $200 annual pension "on the condition that they spend the money as they get it." Earnest Lundeen of the Minnesota Farm-Labor party introduced a radical unemployment bill in Congress in February 1934 that would have set benefits equal to local wages and been administered by local committees of workers. Social workers moved left and called for large-scale income-maintenance policies financed with progressive income taxes.[6] All of these groups criticized FDR for not taking bolder steps; they attacked the social security bill for its regressive taxation scheme and lack of national standards for unemployment insurance. One left-wing critic acidly commented that Roosevelt's "view that local authorities can finance the care of the unemployables and of the able-bodied not absorbed by public works can only be described as fantastic."[7]

Popular, left-wing pressure is thought to have been vital in galvanizing the administration to act and opening the way to passage of the Social Security Act. What is less well understood is that popular protest was not the only, or even the most, influential voice Roosevelt heard in 1934. Many businessmen had soured on the administration by then and believed that "recovery is imperiled by reform." Although Roosevelt had periodically come

---

5. *New York Times,* December 31, 1933, sec. 1.

6. Frances Fox Piven and Richard Cloward, *Poor People's Movements* (New York, 1979), pp. 66–67; Alan Brinkley, *Voices of Protest: Huey Long, Father Coughlin, and the Great Depression* (New York, 1982), p. 223; Linda Gordon, *Pitied but Not Entitled: Single Mothers and the History of Welfare* (New York, 1994), pp. 210–11, 226–29, 234–41.

7. Mark Leff, "Taxing the Forgotten Man," *Journal of American History* 70 (1983): 364–65; Wayne McMillen, "Still Forgotten," *New Republic,* February 6, 1935, pp. 353–54.

under attack for his handling of labor conflict, the issue that mobilized business opinion was legislation he had introduced to regulate the securities markets. Richard Whitney, president of the New York Stock Exchange, believed that if the securities bill was enacted, it would stifle capital investment. His program for recovery was simple: "Provide adequate incentives for private enterprise! Grant management the maximum of freedom! Restore confidence to Capital!"[8]

Many business executives agreed with Whitney, although few criticized the administration openly, as he did. Business leaders were deeply apprehensive about Roosevelt's intentions. Private investment remained flat as banks were reluctant to make business loans. One businessman rather tartly summarized the business view when he said that FDR should be "more thrifty; less shifty." Another business executive told Louis Howe, who monitored business opinion for FDR, that a private survey had discovered that businessmen thought recovery was progressing but believed future economic growth was being hindered by uncertainties over future actions. "There is a strong feeling that experimentation has gone far enough and that it is time to consolidate the gains already made and smooth out the inconsistencies in New Deal policies." Businessmen in the northeast believed the depression had led to "an increased dependency brought about by lavish government relief" and "the growth of class feeling." All this added up to an erosion of business confidence. Telling FDR that only business investment would get the country out of the depression, a New York life insurance executive wrote, "what the big business of this country needs today is a guarantee from you that you will not interfere in any way with them."[9]

Aside from labor policy and the securities legislation, what concerned the men who owned and ran the American economy were issues of taxes and work relief. Rexford Tugwell, a member of Roosevelt's brain trust, noted in his diary that the broad attack on FDR, "had a loose financial orientation." Many businessmen fully expected FDR to propose a large tax increase on the order of $500 million by the end of the year. The editors of *Business*

8. Linda Keller Brown, "Challenge and Response: The American Business Community and the New Deal, 1932–1934" (Ph.D. diss., University of Pennsylvania, 1972), pp. 254, 262–63; Herman E. Kross, *Executive Opinion* (New York, 1970), pp. 179–80.

9. Robert Skidelsky, *John Maynard Keynes: The Economist as Savior, 1920–1937* (London, 1992), p. 504; John Cary to Louis Howe, May 31, 1934; A. A. Dougherty to Franklin D. Roosevelt, August 11, 1934, OF 172, FDRL. Judging from the evidence in Roosevelt's office files, the administration appears to have tracked business opinion quite carefully.

Week thought the administration's intentions were worrisome because opening up tax questions "might more sharply formulate the issue between human rights and property rights with repercussions upon the 1936 elections that would not help business." Henry Harriman, president of the Chamber of Commerce, linked taxes and work relief in an August meeting with FERA officials. He told them that the cost of relief must be reduced and taxes could not be raised. In short, many businessmen believed that continued deficit spending and social reform would inevitably lead to massive increases in tax rates.[10]

These fears were articulated in the context of a massive taxpayer revolt that spread as the depression deepened. The property tax revolt, ignited by rate hikes to pay for relief, was inspired and led by realtors, farmers, and other property owners. By the early 1930s, state and local officials faced angry taxpayers, a confrontation described by one reporter as "the nearest thing to a political revolution in the country. . . . For the first time in a generation taxpayers are wrought up to the point of willingness to give up public services."[11] The National Association of Real Estate Boards and individual taxpayer leagues sought both to reduce the tax burden for specific groups of taxpayers and to limit the growth of government expenditures. Proposals for new taxes to replace the property tax were often accompanied by demands to consider tax limitations or deductions first. Local taxpayer leagues, which formed the organizational basis of resistance, appeared in many northern cities in the early years of the depression. William B. Munro wrote in 1933 that "the loudest protests today are not being directed . . . against the proposal to tax this or that, but against the idea of levying any new taxes at all."[12]

Both state-mandated tax limitations and locally inspired exemptions

10. Rexford Tugwell diaries, September 1934, p. 28, FDRL; *Business Week,* September 8, 1934, p. 5; "Memorandum of the Principal Points in the Policy Presented by Mr. Harriman," August 16, 1934, Harry Hopkins Papers, box 19, folder "Memoranda of Jacob Baker," FDRL. Also see Douglas A. Hays, "Business Confidence and Business Activity: A Case Study of the Recession of 1937," *Michigan Business Studies* 5 (1951): 116–17, 120.

11. David Beito, *Taxpayers in Revolt: Tax Resistance during the Great Depression* (Chapel Hill, N.C., 1989), p. 8.

12. William B. Munro, "Taxation Nears a Crisis," *Current History* 37 (1933): 661; William O. Suiter, "State Limits on Local Property Taxes," in *The Municipal Yearbook 1936,* ed. Clarence E. Ridley and Orin F. Nolting (Chicago, 1936), pp. 332–33; Beito, *Taxpayers in Revolt,* pp. 15–18; Jo Ann E. Argersinger, *Toward a New Deal in Baltimore* (Chapel Hill, N.C., 1988), pp. 28–29, 52–53.

spread throughout the 1930s. Fourteen states passed property tax limitation laws during 1933–34, and in seven states the limits took the form of constitutional amendments. Overall tax rate limits were popular, and some states pioneered "blanket" limits that were multi-jurisdictional. Other states imposed spending limits; the California legislature required local governments to limit spending increases to 5 percent of total expenditures. Another strategy deployed by states in response to tax protest was to pass constitutional exemptions that removed property from the tax rolls or exempted specific groups, often veterans. Over one hundred tax limitation bills were introduced in state legislatures in 1935, and, as Simeon E. Leland aptly put it, "the crop of exemptions thrives each year, in spite of drought or rain."[13] While the origins of the tax revolt of the 1930s antedated the coming of the New Deal and focused on state and local governments, tax protest was a continuing feature of the politics of the 1930s.

If businessmen believed that reform imperiled recovery, Roosevelt's problem was just the opposite: recovery potentially imperiled reform. He had to reassure intransigent businessmen of the administration's fiscal prudence and avoid arousing the fears of an electorate agitated by tax protest while, at the same time, responding to the vocal pressure to accommodate those Americans cut down by the depression. The key to recovery was investment, but by the fall of 1934, FDR's economic policies left him with few ways to get it, other than by sweet-talking businessmen. Roosevelt and his brain trust initially gravitated to industrial policies—the National Industrial Recovery Act and the Agricultural Adjustment Act—that tried to promote investment by stabilizing competition and propping up prices. To this, Roosevelt added a policy of temporary deficit spending and, importantly, federal credit policy. In his 1934 budget message, FDR and his advisers—Rexford Tugwell, Adolph Berle, and Jesse Jones of the Reconstruction Finance Corporation (RFC)—indicated that they believed federal intervention in credit markets would bring economic recovery.[14] Acting on this premise, various New Deal agencies, including the RFC, made loans and investments in banking, real estate, farm land, farm commodities, railroads, and manufacturing. By the summer of 1934 New Deal agencies had constructed a flourishing market

13. Simeon E. Leland, "Municipal Revenues," in *Municipal Yearbook 1936*, pp. 32–33; Suiter, "State Limits on Local Property Taxes," pp. 328–38; Mabel Walker, "The States Search for Money," *National Municipal Review* 23 (1934): 367–68.

14. Michael A. Bernstein, *The Great Depression: Delayed Recovery and Economic Change in America, 1929–1939* (New York, 1987), pp. 188–89; Louis H. Kimmel, *Federal Budget and Fiscal Policy, 1789–1958* (Washington, D.C., 1959), p. 180.

in consumer loans and the RFC was poised to provide the commercial credit that was thought necessary for recovery.[15]

FDR's reliance upon credit policy as the central means to stimulate investment and, thus, recovery made the success of the administration's economic strategy entirely dependent on business cooperation. Jesse Jones and others in the RFC assumed that business complaints of a lack of demand for commercial loans were exaggerated, and with direct RFC loans and an accommodating business environment recovery would be forthcoming. This policy was just the opposite of the kind of government intervention John Maynard Keynes believed necessary to induce investment. As he observed in a letter to an American friend, "one fears your President is depending far too much on psychological as distinct from real factors . . . such as open-market operations and public works [which] are being tackled much too timidly."[16] Deference to the insecurities of businessmen became the order of the day and guided Roosevelt's spending and tax policies. Both he and his treasury secretary, Henry Morgenthau Jr., believed their budget policies would affect the willingness of businessmen to invest. "The possibility that business reactions against the policy of spending and deficits would depress investment and so retard recovery was a consideration always present in administration thinking," Herbert Stein concluded. Roosevelt's "desire to strengthen confidence was a force tending to hold expenditures down."[17]

Roosevelt is often depicted as being a rather sincere fiscal conservative, but his decisions were guided more by his preoccupation with business confidence than by any ideological conviction in favor of fiscal conservatism. In 1932 he did run on a pledge to balance the budget and made numerous public statements disparaging deficit spending, so clearly one cannot ignore his fiscal conservatism. Nonetheless, conservative ideology was less important to his policy decisions than business confidence. Although Roosevelt ran very large deficits, exceeding 5 percent of GNP in 1934–36, he endeavored to assuage the anxieties of investors by emphasizing that the deficits were temporary. Enacting permanent social programs required tax increases, however. If FDR were truly a big-government fiscal conservative (as Harry Truman was) he could have reconciled a national welfare state with a balanced budget by choosing suitable tax policies. But businessmen

15. James Olson, *Saving Capitalism: The Reconstruction Finance Corporation and the New Deal, 1933–40* (Princeton, N.J., 1988), chap. 5.

16. Keynes to M. C. Rorty, Keynes Papers, L/33, cited in Skidelsky, *John Maynard Keynes*, p. 491.

17. Herbert Stein, *The Fiscal Revolution in America* (Chicago, 1969), pp. 68, 89.

were always less concerned about temporary spending than about the substantial tax increases they assumed would be necessary to finance old-age pensions, unemployment compensation, work relief, and other welfare policies.[18]

There is abundant evidence of Roosevelt's concern with business confidence and his efforts to allay the fears of investors. Once the Securities Exchange Bill was enacted, he quickly appointed Joseph P. Kennedy as chair of the Securities and Exchange Commission, believing that Kennedy would help "break the 'strike of capital'" that was impeding economic recovery. During the fall of 1934, FDR made solicitous overtures to businessmen, reassuring them about the NRA and taxes and pointedly rejecting the advice of Harry Hopkins, administrator of the Federal Emergency Relief Administration (FERA), who urged him to shift the New Deal in a more left-wing, interventionist direction. Roosevelt went out of his way to insist that the administration would not raise taxes and that spending would be contained. Thus, he cast the mold that would shape his reform policies.[19]

Money and Social Reform

Money dictated the outlines of the 1935 policy settlement, and it accounts for the decisions that left much of the new welfare state subject to the control of state governments, for the rejection of noncontributory pensions for contributory social insurance, and for the decision to use an underfunded, temporary work relief program to cope with unemployment. Money was far more influential than other commonly discussed factors. Theda Skocpol believes that the policy decisions of 1935 can be understood only in light of "decentralized federalism, the legacies of the patronage-oriented forms of democratic politics that prevailed in the nineteenth-century United States, the weakness and fragmentation of the new realms of public administration built from the late nineteenth century onward, and public policy-making processes centered in legislative logrolling rather than in programmatic

18. Stein, *Fiscal Revolution in America*, p. 74.

19. Thomas K. McGraw, *Prophets of Regulation* (Cambridge, Mass., 1984), pp. 183–84, 186; Searle F. Charles, *Minister of Relief: Harry Hopkins and the Depression* (Syracuse, 1963), pp. 95–97; Stein, *Fiscal Revolution in America*, pp. 62–63; Theron F. Schlabach, *Edwin Witte: Cautious Reformer* (Madison, Wisc., 1969), p. 104. It is not clear whether the New Deal actually had adverse effects on business confidence; the evidence is contradictory. My point is that Roosevelt and his advisers acted as if business confidence did matter and crafted their policies accordingly. For a discussion of the problem of business confidence and the New Deal, see Bernstein, *Great Depression*, pp. 193–98.

political parties or executive planning agencies."[20] In this interpretation, the crucial decisions were made by the reformers who dominated the CES. These reformers feared the reckless spending habits of patronage political parties and frequently expressed their concern that adoption of noncontributory old age pensions advocated by the Townsend movement would lead to national bankruptcy. They preferred contributory social insurance on the grounds that it would actually limit spending. Lack of national control reflected the federal structure of the American state: the ability of southern legislators to veto key provisions such as national standards for public assistance, and the constraints imposed on decision makers by existing state old-age and mothers' pensions.[21] There is no compelling evidence that reformers were motivated by a fear of "patronage democracy"; if anything their actions are more consistent with Carolyn Weaver's claim that they were dedicated to expansion rather than fiscal restraint.[22] Nor can Roosevelt's choice, over opposition from southern Democrats, to decentralize the welfare state and enjoin states to assume part of the burden of public assistance be attributed to the structural realities of federalism.

Another explanation of the Social Security Act stresses the influence of reform-minded business elites in successfully advocating contributory social insurance modeled on the welfare capitalism of the 1920s. Although these studies are informative about the views and maneuvering of businessmen and business reformers, they are less successful in explaining why the administration would accept business-inspired plans rather than any of the alternatives.[23]

Both approaches, in fact, tend to minimize presidential will and obscure the political calculations that Roosevelt and others made. It is Roosevelt's choices that must be explained. Even though Congress made its presence felt by voting to remove national standards for categorical public assistance and to exclude specific occupations from coverage (agricultural workers, domes-

20. Theda Skocpol, *Social Policy in the United States* (Princeton, N.J., 1995), p. 138.

21. Theda Skocpol and John Ikenberry, "The Political Formation of the American Welfare State in Historical and Comparative Perspective," *Comparative Social Research* 6 (1983): 129–30; Theda Skocpol and Edwin Amenta, "Did Capitalists Shape Social Security?" *American Sociological Review* 50 (1985): 574.

22. Carolyn Weaver, *The Crisis in Social Security* (Durham, N.C., 1982), pp. 7–8, 95, 103–6.

23. See Jill Quadagno, *Transformation of Old Age Security* (Chicago, 1988), chap. 5; G. William Domhoff, *State Autonomy or Class Dominance?* (New York, 1996), chap. 5. It is worth noting that both Quadagno and Domhoff, like Skocpol, stress the importance of the South to this outcome.

tics, governmental workers, and employees in nonprofit organizations), the Social Security Act is not a case where Congress subverted the president's intentions. FDR made all the crucial decisions, even in the case of national standards. He may have consulted with members of Congress occasionally during the planning, but he retained tight control over the CES and the small group developing the work relief program. He backed away from proposing a centralized welfare state that integrated relief with social insurance or linked non-means-tested entitlements to general revenues, a plan that was advocated by Harry Hopkins and Rexford Tugwell and was preferred by many reformers. "Harry and I argued . . . with [the president] for nearly two hours the other day," Tugwell wrote in his diary, "and I doubt whether we made very much impression."[24] Once the legislative package was introduced in Congress, FDR took strenuous measures to ensure passage of his policies intact. The president was described by reporters as tightening "administration lines" in order to "prevent blocs amending seriously either the work or security bills; plans were laid to keep 'pork' out of the first and to prevent the latter from being over liberalized."[25]

All of Roosevelt's decisions were calculated to manage the conflicting imperatives of recovery and reform. Federal subsidies for locally controlled general relief were abandoned in order to shift more of the burden to state and local governments; unemployment insurance and work relief were trimmed to meet the objections of businessmen concerned about taxes; payroll taxes and a reserve for old-age insurance were embraced in deference to investors.

Uncooperative Federalism

The New Deal ushered in "cooperative" federalism—shared fiscal responsibility for the poor and the unemployed—not centralized authority and control. Most New Deal social policies either provided states with statutory independence regarding eligibility, benefits, and other requirements or were administered in a way that was implicitly deferential to local authorities. This outcome was neither inevitable nor a consequence of the structural realities of federalism. Quite the opposite: Roosevelt chose to build a decentralized welfare state. For the president and his chief advisers, the governing reality

24. Tugwell diaries, December 28, 1934; Joseph P. Lash, *Dealers and Dreamers* (New York, 1988), pp. 244–45.
25. *New York Times,* January 19, 1935.

was that of coercing uncooperative state legislatures to assume some fiscal responsibility for relief and social welfare. Federalism mattered only insofar as it provided FDR with a way to minimize federal tax burdens. Many in Congress, notably southerners, bitterly resisted. Cooperative federalism had to be imposed with a velvet fist.

Initially, New Deal relief policy was highly centralized, extending federal dominion over the states. The Emergency Relief Law of 1933 gave the FERA administrator, Harry Hopkins, the power to assume control of state relief efforts if necessary and to monitor state actions closely and intrusively. These powers were supplemented by discretionary funds that could be used to cajole or otherwise persuade state and local officials to improve relief operations.[26] Hopkins did not hesitate to use his powers, and relations between the FERA and state governments were often frayed and hostile. Aside from conflict over who would pay for relief, there was discontent over FERA demands that states conform to national policies and standards. There were limits to Hopkins's power over states—for example, he and Aubrey Williams, his chief deputy, had to tailor their relief policies to accommodate the demands of southern plantation owners for cheap farm labor by curtailing relief payments to agricultural laborers and sharecroppers—but overall, the relief effort was radically centralized.[27]

The Federal Emergency Relief Administration was potentially the foundation for a centralized welfare state. Yet Roosevelt and Hopkins abandoned it for work relief and a federal subsidy to state-run programs for the elderly and widowed mothers. They did so largely for fiscal reasons, to stem the threat to the federal budget of rising financial obligations for relief during 1934. By the summer, the administration faced an impending relief crisis. Federal relief rolls expanded rapidly from October 1933 to December 1934, rising from 3.4 million to 5.2 million cases; at the same time, the administration was embroiled in protracted disputes with state governments over who would pay the costs of relief, a fight obviously exacerbated by the tax revolt. Fifteen states, nine of them in the South, failed to pass laws funding emergency relief in 1933, and in 1934 state legislatures became noticeably more reluctant to fund relief. State governments also successfully shifted the burden for the so-called unemployables—the elderly, single mothers, children, and the chronically ill—to federally assisted relief, an action which

26. William Brock, *Welfare, Democracy, and the New Deal* (New York, 1988), pp. 168–69, 173–74, 182ff., 201.

27. Paul Mertz, *New Deal Policy and Southern Rural Poverty* (Baton Rouge, La., 1978), pp. 48–49 n. 10.

especially vexed Hopkins. FERA officials estimated that unemployables made up 20 to 40 percent of the caseload.[28]

FDR portrayed his decision to dismantle the FERA's national cash relief policy and replace it with state-run public assistance and a work relief program as a federal government divestment of a historically state and local responsibility that had been assumed temporarily during the depression. It was actually a calculated strategy to reduce the pressure on federal relief rolls and shift more of the burden for permanent, direct (cash) relief to state and local governments. Hopkins had been preoccupied with state and local reluctance to fund relief for a long time, telling Lewis Douglas, FDR's budget director, "when I came . . . the Federal Government was paying over 70% [of relief costs] and this seemed to me to be an unfair proportion so we thought we would try to get the States to put up part of the money."[29] State assumption of an increasing proportion of the costs of relief was central to the administration's plans for economic security and a path to reform calculated to minimize the dangers to recovery. The immediate benefits were obvious. A national work relief program was seen as an expedient way to assist individuals regarded as capable of work until their "absorption in a rising tide of private employment." Williams told Hopkins, "with the forcing back upon the states of the unemployables, it would be possible to shear off approximately 15% of the total present load."[30]

Although permanent federal responsibility for part of the costs of state old age assistance and mothers' pensions was regarded by many at the time (and even today) as "revolutionary," it is stretching matters to construe the three categorical public assistance titles of the Social Security Act (Old Age Assistance, Aid to Dependent Children, Aid to the Blind) as a form of fiscal relief for state and local government. Neither Hopkins nor Roosevelt understood the policy that way. Congress initially required that state and local governments contribute one-third of emergency relief money in 1933–34, but it applied this requirement only to half the $500 million appropriation and left the FERA substantial discretion in spending the remainder. The state

28. Arthur E. Burns, "Federal Emergency Relief Administration," *Municipal Yearbook* 4 (1937): 389; "Testimony of Mr. Harry L. Hopkins before Bureau of Budget," January 22, 1934, pp. 26–27, Hopkins Papers, box 80; "Security Employment—A Part of a Program of National Economic Security," November 21, 1934, p. 3, Hopkins Papers, box 48; Edward A. Williams, *Federal Aid for Relief* (New York, 1939), p. 91; Josephine Brown, *Public Relief, 1929–1933* (New York, 1940), pp. 162–63.

29. "Testimony of Hopkins before Bureau of Budget," January 22, 1934, p. 2.

30. Williams to Hopkins, October 20, 1934, Hopkins Papers, box 49, folder "Memoranda of Jacob Baker."

contribution was effectively rescinded by Hopkins in late 1933, reducing the state and local share of the costs of relief. The Social Security Act, on the other hand, actually increased the state share of public assistance costs on average. Under the FERA regime, the federal government financed 70 percent of the cost of relief (excluding work relief); the federal share declined to about 40 percent under the Social Security Act.[31]

The policy settlement not only ended any subsidy for general or local relief; it statutorily limited the federal share of relief. The CES recommended replacing the "discretionary and equalization" grant-in-aid, which had been the source of Hopkins' power, with a policy that combined a ceiling on federal contributions to old age assistance and mothers' pensions with national benefit standards. The ceiling on federal contributions, it was thought, would prevent escalating federal payments to the states. FDR made his intentions, as well as his reasons, quite clear at a press conference, when he said he would not consider raising the maximum federal contribution for public assistance (which was then set at fifteen dollars). The states could raise the money, he pointed out, and the limit was necessary "to keep the federal budget in balance."[32]

Members of Congress were hardly oblivious to the possible effects of the Roosevelt-Hopkins strategy for state spending and taxation. The issue in the congressional debate over national standards was taxes, the question of who would bear financial responsibility for what. By replacing the FERA with a grant-in-aid system subject to national standards, the administration shifted part of the burden to the states while both retaining federal leverage and diminishing somewhat the actual power of federal administrators. The CES recommended giving the administrator of the public assistance titles discretionary authority over the standards because of the worry that Congress would set them too low at the insistence of southerners. If the administration thought they could ease legislators' fears by abandoning the FERA model, they were mistaken. The ceiling on federal contributions meant that any raise in benefit standards would raise state financial obligations. Edwin Witte, the executive director of CES, admitted this when he told members of the Ways and Means Committee that the federal administrator might require a state to contribute more than the fifteen dollar federal maximum to

31. Williams, *Federal Aid for Relief,* p. 218. (Calculations by author.) Obviously, the states were better off than they were before the New Deal. But by 1934 that mattered less than the question of how much the states would have to pay.

32. Richard E. McEvoy, "State-Federal Public Assistance, 1935–1946" (Ph.D. diss., University of Maryland, 1980), p. 59.

guarantee "reasonable subsistence."[33]

All of the rather vague language defining national standards was removed by the Senate after Harry Byrd of Virginia and other southerners attacked the provisions. The southerners were clearly provoked by their experience with the FERA. Federal relief payments and jobs raised the standard of living for all of the rural poor. One southern plantation owner objected "to the practice of providing Negro clients such 'luxuries' as the tomato juice given to prevent rickets."[34] Experience with the FERA had also made many non-southerners wary of federal control; John McCormack of Massachusetts feared that discretionary national standards would permit the federal government to "dominate and control private charitable activities." States' experiences with the FERA's centralization of social welfare policy and the fears of southern planters that high relief payments would undermine their power over agricultural workers may have facilitated resistance to national standards, but it was money that made the difference. Control over eligibility and benefit standards was tantamount to control over state and local spending for social welfare and the tax bite needed to finance it. Howard W. Smith, a congressman from Virginia, strongly stated his opposition to a law that would give a federal administrator "the right to say that we have to double our taxation in order to go along." Byrd made similar although exaggerated claims in the Senate. Witte and other New Dealers, in contrast, played down the effects on state and local taxes.[35]

The most unusual aspect of the congressional debate over the public assistance titles was the southern campaign to shift the entire fiscal burden to the federal government. Most southern legislators were more ambivalent about the federal role than was Byrd. Southern fears of centralization and an expanding federal government were always tempered when the question of money came up. The state of Virginia, for instance, was quite willing to care for the poor so long as the federal government paid the bill. Byrd's political machine ruthlessly opposed state appropriations to meet FERA demands for a state contribution.[36] The South had a lot to lose with the pub-

33. Brown, *Public Relief, 1929–1939*, p. 308; McEvoy, "State-Federal Public Assistance," pp. 62–63.

34. Mertz, *New Deal Policy*, p. 51.

35. U.S. Congress, House, Committee on Ways and Means, *Economic Security Act, Hearings on H.R. 4120*, 74th Cong., 1st sess., 1935, pp. 286–87, 974–75; U.S. Congress, Senate, Committee on Finance, *Economic Security Act, Hearings on S. 1130*, 74th Cong., 1st sess., 1935, pp. 245–47; George Tindall, *The Emergence of the New South* (Baton Rouge, La., 1965), pp. 477–80.

lic assistance provisions of the Economic Security Act. Under the FERA regime, the federal government paid an average of 94 percent of all costs of relief in the eleven former Confederate states, compared to a national average of 70 percent. While Harry Byrd led the charge to eviscerate national standards in the Senate, the Texas delegation in the House, led by Tom Connally, tried to eliminate the state contribution altogether, either permanently or for a specified period, and Representative William Colmer of Mississippi demanded a permanent ban on state contributions. Many southerners argued that the federal government should pay for unemployment and old-age relief just as it had paid for Union pensions after the Civil War. The congressional debate revealed that many members of the House thought federal payments were too low and the matching requirements too onerous. Frances Perkins reported to FDR in late February, "there is . . . a movement now to grant aid to the States for old age pensions at more than 50–50 rate, the federal government to pay 3/4 or 9/10 of the money if the president finds that the State is too poverty stricken to provide adequate pensions."[37]

This congressional maneuvering casts doubt on assertions that the institutional structure of federalism, and especially southern resistance, stood in the way of a more centralized welfare state. It is by now an axiom in studies of the Social Security Act that the decentralization of public assistance was mainly due to southern fears that national benefit standards would undermine Jim Crow by precluding segregated or differential benefits. Southerners were certainly concerned about this possibility, yet they were far less worried in 1934–35 than they would be in the 1940s.[38] If southerners recognized the dangers of federal relief policy, they were also well aware of the advantages. The sharecropping system in the South was breaking down, and plantation owners turned to federal relief as a replacement for "furnishing." As Pete Daniels has pointed out, New Deal work and relief policies enabled

36. Mertz, *New Deal Policy,* p. 51.

37. McEvoy, "State-Federal Public Assistance," pp. 70–72, 78, 192; Perkins to Franklin D. Roosevelt, February 25, 1935, OF 121A, FDRL.

38. Robert Lieberman argues that southerners were mainly motivated by their desire to uphold the racial hierarchy of the South and cites, as evidence, a statement by Howard W. Smith. Smith was undoubtedly concerned to protect Jim Crow, but he, like Byrd, objected to the tax increases required by national benefit standards. The problem with Lieberman's argument is that it assumes that FDR had little choice but to acquiesce to southern demands, when in fact he had considerable leverage that he chose not to use. See Lieberman, "Race and the Organization of Welfare Policy," in *Classifying by Race,* ed. Paul Peterson (Princeton, N.J., 1995), pp. 180–81. Cf. Gareth Davies and Martha Derthick, "Race and Social Welfare Policy: The Social Security Act of 1935," *Political Science Quarterly* 112 (1997): 217–35.

planters "to dump onto the government the paternalistic remnants of the tenure system, [and] so long as federal relief policy did not disperse the seasonal work force or drive wages too high," they accepted it.[39] The decisive point, in any event, is that FDR could have obtained a policy with greater federal control had he been willing to compromise on the funding. He got his way when the House rejected several amendments by Arkansas and Mississippi representatives to place the full burden for Old Age Assistance on the federal government.

Coerced federalism provided federal assistance to state and local governments while at the same time provoking tax increases. All this exacerbated the property-tax revolt that was sweeping the country, fueling state property-tax limitations while nourishing the proliferation of general sales taxes. Neither FERA nor Works Progress Administration (WPA) officials hesitated to pressure state and local politicians to raise taxes to meet demands for state contributions. Caught between irate property owners, declining revenues, and Roosevelt and Hopkins's insistence on state contributions to relief and federal programs, state legislators turned to general sales taxes, which were easily imposed and could not be evaded. These taxes were quite regressive. Most states adopted narrowly based taxes that excluded many items consumed by the wealthy and typically applied only to tangible personal property. Only a few states exempted food. The resulting sales tax rates were about 60 percent higher for low-income groups than for high-income groups.[40]

Roosevelt got what he wanted, a reduced federal role, but at the cost of diminished federal control over public-assistance spending and regressive sales taxes. The irony of all this was nowhere more apparent than when William Green, president of the American Federation of Labor (AFL), plaintively told the Senate Appropriations Committee during hearings on the work relief bill, "we have reached the point where now the recipient of our relief, in spending the dole supplied him by the Government, must pay out of that his sales tax for the food he buys, and the shoes he wears, and the fuel he consumes."[41]

39. Pete Daniel, *Breaking the Land* (Urbana, 1985), pp. 72, 78, 88; Mertz, *New Deal Policy*, pp. 48, 56.

40. Jacoby, *Retail Sales Taxation*, pp. 78–79, 173, 182, 190–92; Burns, "Federal Emergency Relief Administration," p. 400.

41. U.S. Congress, Senate, *Emergency Relief Appropriations: Hearings on House Joint Resolution 117*, 74th Cong., 1st sess., 1935, Supplemental Hearings, p. 29; Thomas M. Renahghan, "Distributional Effects of Federal Tax Policy, 1929–1939," *Explorations in Economic History* 21 (1984): 59, 61.

Permanent and Temporary Policies for "Employables"

Passage of unemployment insurance did not settle the question of what the federal government ought to do about unemployment, nor was that the intent. Unemployment compensation was regarded by Hopkins, Tugwell, and even FDR as a side-show to the main action, the work relief program. It was never regarded by New Dealers as anything more than an ameliorative, short-term policy intended to compensate for temporary and limited unemployment, which today is called frictional unemployment. Extended unemployment was another matter. Hopkins was convinced early that any permanent solution to unemployment had to go beyond social insurance. He and Tugwell argued to FDR "against reliance on unemployment insurance and for a guarantee of jobs on public works," and they convinced FDR to change the CES report and insert a strong claim for a right to work "so that it minimized the part of unemployment pensions in a national security scheme and threw the emphasis upon a works program as the real effort toward security."[42]

The New Deal's public commitment to a right to work was vitiated by the failure to create a permanent public employment policy and FDR's willingness to tailor his final decisions about both unemployment compensation and work relief to business demands. Even though the two programs were developed more or less separately, the tension between the objectives of reform and recovery and the concern with business confidence mattered. FDR regularly solicited the views of Wall Street financier Russell Leffingwell and other businessmen about his financial options for relief. And the technical board of the CES advised that "the final scope of the [unemployment compensation] program, as well as the rate at which it can be adopted, must be formulated in light of business and fiscal conditions."[43]

The unemployment compensation title of the Social Security Act was later regarded by many New Dealers as their most egregious blunder. They ended up with a policy that gave state governments control over benefits and eligibility and generated incentives for businesses to keep benefits and payroll taxes low, since these were paid entirely by employers. The administration is usually understood to have rejected a national plan based on a federal subsidy to states in favor of a tax-offset plan that would remove the main

42. Tugwell diaries, September 1934, p. 87, December 31, 1934, p. 172; "Testimony of Hopkins before Bureau of Budget," January 22, 1934, pp. 13, 25, 28.

43. Henry Morgenthau Jr., diaries, "Memorandum of Conference at the White House," October 16, 1934, p. 96, FDRL; "Preliminary Recommendations of the Technical Board to the Committee on Economic Security," September 1934, p. 1, Hopkins Papers, box 48.

obstacle to states enacting their own plans. The tax-offset plan was really an enabling law that would neutralize interstate competition by requiring employers to pay a 3 percent payroll tax into a national trust fund, 90 percent of which would be refunded if the employer paid into a state run program; hence federal taxes were offset by creation of a state-run program. There were sharp differences of opinion within the administration over the two plans. However, the real choice confronting New Dealers and Congress in 1934–35 was not between a tax-offset plan and a federal subsidy, but whether or not to establish national standards.

Paul Kellogg, a prominent social reformer, put his finger on the problem in his testimony before the Senate Finance Committee. So long as there were no national standards, he told them, the law would fail to "scotch the snake of interstate competition." Once the states created unemployment compensation programs, the tax-offset lever limiting competition "goes limp and becomes a hose, piping the Federal tax money back into the States without any provisions that will safeguard the unemployed themselves."[44] Witte admitted to the same committee that national standards were entirely compatible with a tax-offset plan and the differences between the subsidy and tax-offset plans were exaggerated. The arguments waged in the CES over these policy alternatives acquired intensity only because what was really at stake was the content of the standards: pooled versus individual reserves, merit rating, eligibility criteria, and benefit levels.

Roosevelt's decision in favor of the tax-offset plan is usually interpreted as a reflection of the centrifugal power of federalism and a defeat for the corporate reformers who favored a national plan.[45] FDR had sound political reasons for adopting the permissive tax-offset plan. It avoided the necessity of taking sides in a bitter dispute between two groups of reformers while providing an escape hatch from a negative Supreme Court decision. The CES assumed that state plans would be preserved if the national law was rescinded.[46] But Roosevelt's preference for the tax-offset plan was also

44. Senate, *Economic Security Act,* 74th Cong., 1st sess., 1935, p. 239. Kellogg made the same point to FDR; Kellogg to Howe, February 12, 1935, OF 1086, FDRL.

45. Skocpol, *Social Policy in the United States,* pp. 158–59; Skocpol and Amenta, "Did Capitalists Shape Social Security?" p. 572.

46. The administration's fears were not unfounded. There is ample evidence that Justice Brandeis was opposed to any national plan and some evidence that the administration took this into account. See *Roosevelt and Frankfurter: Their Correspondence, 1928–1945,* annotated by Max Freedman (Boston, 1967), p. 224; Arthur Altmeyer, *The Formative Years of Social Security* (Madison, Wisc., 1968), pp. 14–15, 19; Tugwell diaries, December 31, 1934, p. 172.

predicated on his opposition to raising federal taxes. Businessmen in fact cared more about taxes and national standards than anything else. Marion B. Folsom of Kodak Company, for example, told the Ways and Means Committee that he did not feel strongly about state versus national control but was adamant about the need for individual, rather than pooled, reserves and merit rating. These views were echoed by other businessmen.[47]

On the crucial issue of national standards, FDR resolved most of the serious questions in favor of businessmen. Kellogg urged the president to raise the payroll tax from 3 percent to 4 or 5 percent so that higher benefits could be provided for longer periods of time. Lewis Howe tartly informed Kellogg that FDR refused, saying "of course, we would all like to see better standards, but it is a matter of finance and we cannot eat the whole cake in one meal."[48] Roosevelt did the same with respect to merit rating and knowingly reintroduced the snake of interstate competition into the unemployment scheme. Merit rating allowed tax rates to vary depending on the experience of the employers in preventing unemployment. The Ways and Means Committee eliminated merit rating from the bill precisely because they thought it would foster interstate competition. The Senate put it back in because Roosevelt, responding to pressure from Folsom and other businessmen, insisted.[49] In the end, businessmen obtained the unemployment insurance policy they wanted from Roosevelt: low taxes, merit rating, and private reserves.

In deciding in favor of the tax-offset plan, Roosevelt and Perkins took the path of least resistance; they could do this precisely because the work program was understood to be a backstop to the perceived inadequacies of unemployment compensation. Hopkins and his two alter egos, Aubrey Williams and Corrington Gill, started out with the intention of creating a program much like the short-lived Civil Works Administration. Accordingly, their initial public employment proposals either rejected means tests or suggested they be as "light" as possible; sought benefits equivalent to those of

47. House, *Economic Security Act,* 74th Cong., 1st sess., 1935, pp. 773, 991; Senate, *Economic Security Act,* 74th Cong., 1st sess., 1935, pp. 915–17.

48. Howe to Kellogg, February 7, 1935, OF 1086, FDRL.

49. William T. Haber, Columbia University Oral History Project, pt. 5, "New Deal," pp. 58–59; Sanford M. Jacoby, "Employers and the Welfare State: The Role of Marion B. Folsom," *Journal of American History* 80 (1993): 540–41. Jacoby blames the deletion of merit rating and private reserves on Republicans seeking to "gum up the works." This may be true, but it does not account for Democrats like Jere Cooper of Tennessee who were seeking to minimize interstate competition.

unemployment insurance; and recommended that ongoing planning for public employment be institutionalized. They were clearly thinking in terms of a long-term, permanent program that would put most of the unemployed to work—early cost estimates assumed a program that would employ six million workers. Yet the plan actually produced was a pale imitation of these ideas, a limited program tailored to conservative objections about cost and scope.

The business press and lobbyists waged an unrelenting assault on the administration's rumored work relief policies. The price tag on Hopkins's plan was potentially very high. Winthrop W. Aldrich of the Chase National Bank, who was a member of the Rockefeller family, argued in a widely distributed pamphlet that work relief would cost three times as much as "home relief."[50] Cost was not the only issue here; many businessmen feared, like Aldrich, that the planned work relief program would compete with the private sector, raise wages, and increase the deficit. They were not entirely wrong. Several major business groups announced their opposition to a permanent relief effort, and one businessman advised FDR to "separate the emergency jobs from the long-range objectives," which is exactly what he did.[51]

Direct relief costs much less than work relief and posed an obvious dilemma for Roosevelt. A costly work relief program that appeared to herald an expanded and permanent federal role in the economy was not calculated to bolster business confidence. The way out of this dilemma was through so-called self-liquidating public works projects, a scheme ostensibly designed to recover project costs over time, much as a loan was repaid. In fact, the administration contemplated funding work relief projects with loans to state and local governments. For these reasons, work relief was to be preferred to direct relief. One of Hopkins's aides, Jacob Baker, explained the rationale as follows:

> The cost of present relief—National, State and Local funds—is two billion dollars a year. None of the money is paid back and not nearly enough is produced by its use. If a reasonable sum is added to it, and arrangements made to get as much back as possible, we shall have a program that will create new national wealth and will finally return much of its cost to the

50. "The Financing of Unemployment Relief," p. 16, Hopkins Papers, box 50.

51. Letter to Franklin D. Roosevelt from the president of the American Institute of Food Distribution, Inc., August 14, 1934, OF 172, FDRL; *Business Week*, September 15, 1934, p. 9; Joanna C. Colcord and Russell H. Kurtz, "The Business of Federal Relief," *Survey* 71 (1935): 23–24.

National Treasury. If five billion dollars is spent on a security work program and three-quarters of it is paid back, the Treasury saves almost a billion dollars.[52]

Roosevelt was noticeably enthusiastic about such self-liquidating projects, telling Hopkins to bring the idea up at meetings of the planning group. A work relief program based on self-liquidating projects, he discovered, was a real bargain. At the October 10, 1934, meeting of the planning committee, three alternative plans were considered: the status quo or cash relief; cash relief plus a small public works program; and a work relief program for six million employables. Direct cash relief cost an estimated $2.4 billion, none of which was repayable, according to an analysis submitted by Hopkins and Harold Ickes, secretary of interior. Adding $1 billion in public works spending, of which $400 million might be recoverable, brought the cost to $2.8 billion. But a relief plan that shifted the burden of unemployables to state and local governments and relied upon a $6 billion work relief program would cost the Treasury just $850 million, a rather substantial savings. How was it possible to spend twice as much for work relief yet reduce federal outlays? Hopkins and Ickes assumed the federal government would save $1.5 billion by shifting the unemployables to state and local governments, which left the estimated cost of public assistance for the federal government at $350 million. Work relief would cost only $500 million in direct outlays; the rest of the expenditure would be paid back or somehow recovered.[53]

Roosevelt's enthusiasm for self-liquidating projects had limits. When the Treasury Department's chief legal adviser asked why such projects could not be expanded until all the unemployed were at work, the president replied that "this would bring up the old question of balancing the budget."[54] Estimates of total cost and the proportion of projects that might be self-liquidating were scaled down over the course of the planning process, but the idea remained integral to the administration's plans. Tugwell wrote in his diary that "the only questions the President had in his mind were (1) whether sufficient works could be got underway so that relief might be got rid of in from six to eight months and (2) what proportion of them could be self-

52. "A National Program of Economic Security," November 13, 1934, p. 5, Hopkins Papers, box 48.

53. Franklin D. Roosevelt to Hopkins, November 8, 1934, OF 444, FDRL; Morgenthau diaries, pp. 88–92, box 2; also see notes on meetings of October 1 and 16, Morgenthau diaries, pp. 84–86, 96–102, box 2; Hopkins and Ickes to FDR, October 6 and 16, 1934, Hopkins Papers, box 49.

54. Morgenthau diaries, p. 89, box 2.

liquidating so that the financial scheme we had in mind could be used."[55] Although the administration believed that self-liquidating projects were a way to hold down costs, the idea was mainly attractive as a device to disguise the cost of work relief.

Cost depended on more than assumptions about self-liquidating projects. It also depended on the number of people employed, and the administration repeatedly scaled back the scope of the work relief program. Hopkins's dream of providing employment for most unemployed workers disappeared by late November as a consequence of fiscal pressures. The problem, as Williams ruefully announced to Hopkins, was that the creation of a serious work relief program would dramatically increase the number of men and women applying for relief. Williams assumed that "loan-liquidating" projects served as one limit; he added two others, means-tests and the security wage. "By these two means, the one requiring that people shall show that they face destitution, hunger, and eviction prior to receiving employment, and second, that the wage shall be less than what they can earn in private industry," Williams's report said, "it is believed that the number who are to be given aid could be definitely limited and controlled."[56] This provision would reduce the number of jobs to four million rather than the six million actually needed. Congress approved the president's request for a $4.8 billion relief appropriation, substantially below the $8 or $9 billion that many people assumed the administration intended to spend.

The program was also temporary. Why did the administration decide not to seek a permanent program, especially since officials were at pains to stress the role of work relief as the main defense against prolonged unemployment? One answer is that Roosevelt and others did not think they would need a work relief policy for more than three years at most. They thought that the government could divest itself of responsibility for the unemployed rather quickly. None of the FERA officials deluded themselves, however, and Hopkins and Williams had long thought that a permanent program was needed. The real reason for this decision was financial. Opposition to a permanent program came from Roosevelt's financial advisers, notably Morgenthau and the director of the Bureau of the Budget, whose arguments prevailed. These men preferred a temporary program that would end when the economy picked up.[57]

55. Tugwell diaries, November 28, 1934, p. 125.
56. Williams to Hopkins, November 30, 1934, p. 4, Hopkins Papers, box 49.
57. Morgenthau diaries, pp. 84, 91, box 2; Arthur MacMahon, John D. Millett, and Gladys Ogden, *The Administration of Federal Work Relief* (Chicago, 1941), p. 27.

Roosevelt's decisions left the New Deal's commitment to a right to employment uncertain, subject to the prevailing political and economic winds and to his preoccupation with business confidence. Workers experienced both feast and famine as surges in WPA employment alternated with purges. Work relief employment rose rapidly to over 3 million workers by February 1936 and then commenced a long march downward, reaching a depression-era low of 1.4 million workers by September 1937, a decline of 50 percent. The downward march was interrupted only by a slight jump just before the 1936 election but resumed afterwards; WPA employment dropped by almost 1 million workers between the election and its nadir ten months later. The WPA caseload then rose rapidly with the onset of the 1937–38 recession and FDR's decision to start spending again. After the 1938 election, however, the caseload turned around again. The ratio of WPA employment to estimated unemployment steadily declined from 34 percent in 1936 to just 26 percent during 1939.[58]

The main reason for limited coverage and the changing fortunes of unemployed workers was a lack of money. Democratic senator Claude Pepper of Florida in 1939 ruefully described the decision making process regarding relief bills: "We did not decide how many needed work; we decided how much money we could make available for work."[59] Work relief expenditures were always insufficient because Roosevelt persisted in manipulating his budget policies in deference to businessmen or to curry favor with congressional conservatives. His spending policies were only marginally constrained by congressional resistance, however. Congress never refused to grant FDR whatever funds he requested for relief, and even during the fractious debate over relief spending in the summer of 1937 efforts to limit or target spending were easily defeated. Roosevelt may have requested what he thought Congress would provide, but it was "unconstrained bargaining" between Hopkins, Morgenthau, and the Bureau of the Budget that determined the request. In this struggle Roosevelt's own fiscal and political preferences mattered greatly, and he opted to hold the line on spending.[60]

In the wake of his 1935 legislative triumphs, Roosevelt remained convinced that a balanced budget was necessary for recovery; he also thought he was vulnerable on the issue of spending in his reelection campaign. He

58. *Security, Work, and Relief Policies,* Report of the Committee on Long-Range Work and Relief Policies to the National Resources Planning Board (Washington, D.C., 1942), p. 236, table 51.

59. MacMahon et al., *The Administration of Federal Work Relief,* p. 185.

60. Ibid., p. 174.

fudged relief costs in his January 1936 budget message, telling Congress it would suffice to rely on funds carried over from the current fiscal year 1936 budget, pending a continued rise in the level of employment. Only later that spring did Roosevelt request additional money for the WPA for the new fiscal year. FDR's balanced budget strategy ended when he and Hopkins realized they would have to drastically slash WPA rolls before the election. To avoid this, Hopkins went on a spending binge in October. By December, after the elections, Roosevelt and Hopkins concluded that they would need a supplemental appropriation of $790 million, which FDR requested and Congress dutifully provided.

The president turned around in January 1937 and unveiled yet another balanced budget, this one calculated to reassure investors that the administration was on the right track. Trumpeting rising employment, FDR said it was now possible "to reduce for the fiscal year 1938 many expenditures of the Federal Government which the general depression made necessary."[61] Again he avoided submitting a request for relief funds, though he acknowledged that another $1.5 billion would be needed. That request, plainly insufficient to sustain WPA employment at current levels, was smuggled into a separate message that once again proclaimed Roosevelt's intent to balance the budget within the coming fiscal year. While Roosevelt did encounter some congressional resistance to relief spending in 1937, he tempered his request mainly to build support for his court packing and reorganization plans in Congress, notably among Republican progressives.

There was more than a grain of truth to the charge of Roosevelt's critics that the administration was abandoning many otherwise needy people and reinstitutionalizing poor relief. Yet the administration remained implacably opposed to a permanent work relief policy until after the "Roosevelt recession" of 1937–38. Harry Hopkins told Congress in 1936 that he opposed the creation of a permanent program "until a time when we can envisage the extent of the problem as a permanent problem far better than we can today."[62] Nor was Roosevelt interested. He publicly opposed a permanent program and called attention to his favorite alternative to spending for unemployment: reducing the supply of labor. Was it not possible "and right," he asked in a speech, "to limit the active working ages at both

---

61. *The Budget of the United States Government, Fiscal Year 1938* (Washington, D.C., 1937), p. v.

62. Quoted in Josephine Brown, "Present Relief Situation in the United States," *Proceedings of the National Conference of Social Work,* 63d Annual Meeting (Chicago, 1936), p. 425.

ends?" Pension off the elderly, send the young to school, and ask employers to shorten the work week—all were among Roosevelt's favorite nostrums for unemployment.[63]

The Origins of the "Annuity Fiction"

The decision to propose wage-related social insurance for both the elderly and the unemployed that was financed by regressive taxes is the third pivotal choice made in 1934. All of the proposed alternatives were noncontributory policies and relied heavily on general revenues. Tugwell's opposition to the tax-offset plan and payroll taxes rested squarely on the issue of tax equity. He backed the federal subsidy plan for unemployment insurance because he would rather stand "on the ground of the more equitable incidence of Federal taxation than on any other"; he argued to Roosevelt that payroll taxes were like sales taxes and pointed out that FDR himself was against sales taxes.[64]

Contributory social insurance had two related virtues in the minds of New Dealers, both of which spoke to the program's fiscal conservatism and depicted it as an alternative to profligate spending and runaway deficits. The contributory scheme was widely understood to be an antidote to "dependency," which meant that workers would save for their retirement or for a spell of unemployment and what they saved would be roughly commensurate with what they earned. It entailed no giveaways, no redistribution of income. According to its most determined advocates, contributory social insurance would reward effort while penalizing sloth. Arthur Altmeyer, who became chair of the Social Security Board in 1936, explained: "The social insurance approach proceeds upon the assumption that it is desirable to retain so far as possible the advantages of a truly competitive society. . . . [It] stimulates individual initiative and thrift because it gears benefits directly to the wage-earning history so that the steady, long-time worker receives more benefits than the unsteady, short-time worker."[65]

---

63. "The Period of Social Planning Is Only at Its Beginning—Address to the Young Democratic Club," Baltimore, Md., April 13, 1936, *The Public Papers and Addresses of Franklin Delano Roosevelt*, vol. 5 (New York, 1938), pp. 162–63. See also Richard Jensen, "The Causes and Cures of Unemployment in the Great Depression," *Journal of Interdisciplinary History* 19 (1989): 571–75.

64. Tugwell diaries, December 17, 1934, p. 161; Leff, "Taxing the Forgotten Man," pp. 364–65. I am indebted to Leff's provocative analysis.

65. Altmeyer to Wilcox, December 2, 1936, RG 47, Chair's Files, box 60, NA.

Second, as Frances Perkins suggested in her press conference, the federal government's role in providing old-age and unemployment insurance would be minimal; social insurance contributions were not thought of as taxes and the program would not entail public expenditures. The federal government, it was assumed, was only involved financially when it committed general revenues. Payroll taxes were rationalized as a cost of production that would be passed on to consumers and reflected in the price of goods and services, thereby precluding the necessity of subsidizing the elderly or the unemployed through general taxation. In this sense, a contributory policy was thought to be self-supporting, much like a private annuity, and it was argued that, over time as workers built up a social security nest egg, the obligation of both federal and state governments for the elderly would diminish. J. Douglas Brown, one of the two authors of the old-age insurance plan, recalled years later that "we argued strenuously that a contributory old age insurance system would lift the burden from both the federal government and the state governments in increasing degree."[66] These assumptions also applied to unemployment insurance, since benefits were tightly linked to the solvency of reserves and stringent wage-related eligibility criteria, which excluded those with a weak attachment to the labor market (in the political lexicon of the times, "the undesired relief element"). The dreaded dole only surfaced when the government attempted to cope with unemployment through deficit spending. These arguments were made, of course, in a context in which taxes, government spending, and the very idea of deficits had become politicized and were believed by many businessmen to threaten economic recovery.[67]

The social insurance proposals, then, were portrayed as fiscally conservative, prudent measures that would not entail a tax increase or large government expenditures either immediately or in the future. These assumptions and arguments amounted to the invention of an annuity fiction, which paralleled the assumption of self-liquidating work relief projects financed by loans. Just as self-liquidating projects were a mark of fiscal prudence, so too contributory old-age pensions were assumed to restrain costs compared to the noncontributory pensions advocated by the Townsend movement. Brown said, "Barbara Armstrong and I fought for . . . a constructive device

66. Altmeyer to Wilcox, December 12, 1936, RG 47, Central Files, box 60, NA; J. Douglas Brown, Columbia University Oral History Project, pt. 3, "Social Security," p. 113.

67. Harry Malisoff, "The Emergence of Unemployment Compensation III," *Political Science Quarterly* 54 (1939): 580–81.

that would keep old-age assistance from getting bigger and bigger and bigger."[68] Both ideas spoke to business hostility to federal spending and deficits.

The attraction of the contributory model to Roosevelt and others did not stem, as some have suggested, from an inordinate fear of patronage democracy and runaway spending. Indeed, all the evidence demonstrates that the authors of this legislation had expansionist aims. The New Dealers themselves did not believe in the fiction of a self-supporting program. Frances Perkins openly admitted to the Senate Finance Committee that the old-age "annuity" proposed by the Committee on Economic Security was really an intergenerational transfer. J. Douglas Brown pointed out to the Ways and Means Committee that it was unnecessary to require the old-age insurance program to accumulate a surplus or reserve because the "taxing power of the federal government was your true reserve." In fact, most of the reformers involved in creating the program assumed that at some point general revenue financing would be necessary, whether a federal subsidy for old-age pensions in the future (estimated to be needed by 1965) or for a federally financed work relief program in case of a severe economic downturn.[69]

Most New Dealers from Roosevelt on down were more interested in creating a governmental commitment to care for the elderly and the unemployed than in fending off the spending binges of patronage democracy. In a now-famous statement made six years after the inception of the policy, FDR insisted that the discussion of contributory social insurance in 1935 turned on the questions of how to establish a moral right to benefits and how to prevent conservatives from undoing the policy. How far Roosevelt was actually motivated by such a calculation is unclear, as Mark Leff cogently observes, but there is ample evidence that among those who fashioned and subsequently defended the policies, such as Edwin Witte, J. Douglas Brown, and Arthur Altmeyer, there was a passionate concern with the creation of a social right, a politically secure claim to a benefit. Contributory financing appealed to them because they realized that a program financed by a *dedicated* tax would be outside the normal appropriations process—that is, politically insulated and autonomous. This autonomy was far more important to the social insurance reformers than their litany of fiscal prudence and fear of expensive schemes. An important piece of evidence for this

68. Brown, Oral History Project, pp. 12, 17.
69. Ibid., p. 17; Senate, *Economic Security Act,* 74th Cong., 1st sess., 1935, p. 109; House, *Economic Security Act,* 74th Cong., 1st sess., 1935, pp. 245–46.

argument comes from the debate within the Advisory Committee to CES between those who preferred the tax-offset unemployment proposal to a federal subsidy. One of the main reasons that the seven members who voted against the federal subsidy preferred the tax-offset plan was their belief that contributory social insurance would avoid the congressional appropriations process entailed by any federal subsidy plan.[70]

Yet the preference for contributory taxes reflected another, more immediate concern: taxes and the implications of any tax increase for the administration's political support, for its ties to business, and for the prospects of economic recovery. Roosevelt insured that a distinction between general revenues and contributions would be the foundation of national policy in June 1934, when he indicated his preference for a contributory program and his aversion to a general tax increase, a statement that worried Edwin Witte. But Roosevelt's preference for a contributory plan was taken as a guideline for planning by the CES. Witte's fears that Roosevelt's aversion to general taxation would guide policy proved correct when Roosevelt demanded just prior to submitting the proposals to Congress that the financing plan for old-age insurance be changed by adding a reserve, the so-called Morgenthau Amendment, so the program would be fully "self-sustaining."[71]

Roosevelt faced insurmountable difficulties in financing new social policies while asserting that deficit spending was only temporary and calming the apprehensions of business leaders. This situation led to his willingness to cater to business demands for a 3 percent rather than 5 percent payroll tax for unemployment insurance, to reject (insofar as possible) funding by general revenues, and to rely on self-liquidating work relief projects. A payroll tax was the least onerous of the revenue options that he could have proposed, and it was insufficient for many businessmen if it did not include employee contributions. Gerard Swope and Marion Folsom continued to criticize the unemployment proposal in the spring of 1935 because of the absence of employee contributions. But as Howard S. Cullman, chairman of the New York Conference for Unemployment Insurance Legislation and an old friend of Roosevelt, noted in a letter to the president, "we have repeatedly pointed out

70. "Report of the Advisory Committee to the Committee on Economic Security, Presenting Its Recommendations Relating to Unemployment Compensation," December 1934, p. 3, RG 47, CES Files, box 5, NA.

71. Samuel Rosenman, ed., *The Public Papers and Addresses of Franklin D. Roosevelt*, 3:291; Edwin Witte, "Basic Questions of Policy on Which Early Decisions Are Deemed Very Necessary," August 11, 1934, RG 47, CES Files, box 1, NA; Leff, "Taxing the Forgotten Man," pp. 368–71.

[to businessmen] that because of the limited amount of time of benefits, workers will bear a large part of the cost of unemployment in any event. As consumers, workers, whether employed or unemployed, will ultimately carry the cost of unemployment insurance which will be passed on to the public." Businessmen saw through the fiction that social security contributions were not taxes, but their reaction to Roosevelt's budget message in early January was generally one of mild approval or relief. They recognized a conservative policy when they saw it.[72]

Fiscal Imperatives and the New Deal Welfare State

As an example of budget legerdemain, Roosevelt's 1935 budget message is unequaled. The pledge not to raise taxes referred only to general revenues, not payroll taxes, and the old-age insurance reserve was calculated to mask the deficit. Self-liquidating work relief projects, a congressional committee was told, did not really mean that the projects would generate income in order to finance the cost, but rather that they were "indirectly" self-liquidating. In this sense, health projects that reduced sickness or even unemployment were self-liquidating.[73] Yet the budget message and the policy settlement it reflected represented Roosevelt's attempt to carve out a new and limited role for social policy that did not conflict with his economic policies and the support he needed to sustain them.

All of the core decisions of the 1935 policy settlement were motivated by the fiscal realities confronting the administration. Concern about business confidence and deference to disgruntled taxpayers, rather than fear of patronage democracy or the institutional realities of American electoral democracy, were most important to the outcome. The policy settlement was crafted to reassure investors and avoid large tax increases, rather than prevent unlimited spending. FDR had far more leverage over southern legislators than is usually assumed, and it would be a mistake to conclude that he simply acquiesced to southern demands. The administration could have had national benefit standards for the public assistance titles had it been willing to pay for them. It also could have had national standards that would have made

72. Howard S. Cullman to Franklin D. Roosevelt, April 16, 1935, OF 121A, FDRL; Leff, "Taxing the Forgotten Man," pp. 377–78. Colin Gordon shows that many businessmen had more specific reasons to favor the policy as well; see his *New Deals: Business, Labor, and Politics in America, 1920–1935* (New York, 1995), chap 7.

73. U.S. Congress, House, *Emergency Relief Appropriations: Hearings on House Joint Resolution 117*, 74th Cong., 1st sess., 1935, p. 10.

unemployment compensation less favorable to employers, but chose otherwise.

To be sure, some institutional factors did matter, especially the realistic fear that the Supreme Court would overturn a national unemployment compensation scheme. Some of what FDR did was deceptive—"smoke and mirrors" if you like—and some decisions, such as social security, contained the seeds of long-term expansion, while others, such as work relief, did not. But the question of investor confidence is always confronted in the short run, and there is evidence that, on the crucial matter of provision for all this legislation, FDR framed his policies with a clear understanding of their implications for investors and taxpayers. FDR faced an erosion of investor confidence, which he took into account while planning a permanent security program. Business confidence does not explain every decision taken during the winter of 1934–35, but it explains a lot.

Despite its inherent conservatism, the policy settlement of 1935 contained the seeds of a far more expansive welfare state than anyone envisioned at the time: it institutionalized at least limited social rights for workers and established a basis for future growth. Yet it was not a New Deal for African Americans. Charles Houston characterized the Social Security bill as a "sieve with holes just big enough for the majority of Negroes to fall through."[74] He estimated that three-fifths of black workers were not covered by the act because Congress excluded agricultural laborers and domestic workers. Houston and other African American political leaders also worried about any social policy that left the states in control. Walter White of the NAACP warned Eleanor Roosevelt that "if the Federal Government continues to make lump grants to the States and leaves expenditures to the States it should not abandon all responsibility to see that Federal funds are not used to grind a section of its citizenry further into the dust."[75] Because of the occupational exclusions and state control of public assistance, African Americans were denied the same social rights as white Americans, though the effects of these decisions would only become fully apparent after World War II. During the depression, African Americans acquired a foothold in the welfare state, but they did so as the recipients of relief, not as workers entitled to social rights. Relief was banished in name only as the New Deal—hobbled by the assumptions and mistakes of 1934–35—failed at its most elementary and

74. U.S. Congress, Senate, *Economic Security Act,* 74th Cong., 1st sess., 1935, p. 641.

75. White to Eleanor Roosevelt, November 13, 1934, folder "'Interracial' FERA," cited in Allen F. Kifer, "The Negro Under the New Deal" (Ph.D. diss., University of Wisconsin, 1961), p. 234.

important task, that of providing security to all citizens through public or private employment. By the end of the depression, the idea of "dependence" had been indelibly tied to race. This connection, rather than occupational exclusions or discrimination by local administrators, was the crucial racial legacy of Roosevelt's policy settlement.

CHAPTER TWO

The Origins of a Racially
Stratified Welfare State

There is the danger of making the Negro, as a race, a chronic dependent
and . . . of developing racial friction through creating resentment on the
part of the majority public against the presence of so many Negroes on
the relief rolls.

—Forrester B. Washington

The traditional racial stereotypes—which have been inherited from the
master-slave tradition and which have been employed by the ruling class
of large landholders in the South and industrialists in the North to give effective expression to their determination to keep the Negro in a servile
condition and as a profitable labor supply—remain, and are indeed often
heightened by the New Deal.

—Ralph J. Bunche

The New Deal appealed to the common fears of the destitute and near-
destitute and to the collective aspirations and hopes of the "ill-housed,
ill-clad, and ill-nourished." New Dealers equated a common plight with the
common good. Roosevelt's jeremiads at economic royalists, Harry Hopkins's
ruminations about "idle men, money, and machines," and Aubrey Williams's
assertion of the right to work as "simply economic realism . . . the quickest
and cheapest way to attain full economic recovery" articulated claims to
work-related social rights. These universalistic claims to economic security
were based on social class and were so understood. Workers believed that
by "voting Democratic and supporting the New Deal . . . they were affirming rather than denying their class status."[1] Class identity overwhelmed
ethnic and racial status.

Yet the political appeal of New Deal universalism concealed a racial bifurcation at the core of the emerging welfare state. The unification of race

1. U.S. Congress, Senate, *Unemployment and Relief Hearings,* 75th Cong., 2d sess.,
p. 1351; *New York Times,* July 2, 1938, sec. 1, p. 2. Lisabeth Cohen, *Making a New Deal*
(New York, 1991), pp. 287–89.

and class in the New Deal electoral coalition and in the efforts of black political elites to build a biracial alliance was contradicted by the antinomy between a party coalition forged in the crucible of social class and an emerging welfare state that reconstituted the color line. Rather than incorporating African Americans into the New Deal as working-class citizens entitled to security and merging their problems in the predicament of all low-income citizens, New Deal social policy erected a new structure of dependence.

Race did not figure in the construction of the New Deal welfare state, as white liberals suppressed or ignored questions of racial inequality. Racial liberals of the 1930s—principally Harold Ickes of the Public Works Administration and Will Alexander, one of the architects of the New Deal's rural rehabilitation policies—believed racial hostilities would evaporate with the incorporation of blacks into the new political order. New Deal reforms responded to the needs and aspirations of all working-class citizens, Ickes believed. The "Negro problem," he wrote, "merges into and becomes inseparable from the greater problem of American citizens generally, who are at or below the line in decency and comfort from those who are not." Both Ickes and Alexander, like FDR, avoided confronting southern apartheid and the more obvious forms of segregation in the North. The reason was not just the political risks to New Deal policies entailed by any engagement with racism. These men shared an ineluctable faith that New Deal reforms would alter the economic status of African Americans, thereby removing the single most important source of racial prejudice. White hostility would diminish as black income and education rose.[2]

Gunnar Myrdal's theory of the vicious circle—an apt metaphor for the New Deal's racial liberalism—explains why New Dealers thought social reform would diminish white racism. Racial prejudice, he argued, was propelled by a cumulative cycle of causation in which white racism led to the degradation of African Americans, and then in turn confirmed to whites their superiority and justified their racial privileges. "White prejudice and Negro standards thus mutually 'cause' each other," as Myrdal put it.[3]

New Deal economic aid was presumed to mitigate racism insofar as it raised the standard of living of African Americans, yet the New Deal had precisely the opposite effect, inverting Myrdal's vicious circle. New Deal

2. John Kirby, *Black Americans in the Roosevelt Era: Liberalism and Race* (Knoxville, 1980), pp. 32–35, 46, 52–54, 60–61; Harold Ickes, "To Have Jobs," *Negro Digest* (1946): 73, quoted in Kirby, p. 32.

3. Gunnar Myrdal, *An American Dilemma* (New York, 1944), p. 75.

social policy did raise the living standards of African Americans, but Ralph Bunche concluded it reproduced a historical narrative about African Americans' inferiority to whites. This racial narrative focused on the disproportionate number of African American families on the dole. Forrester B. Washington, director of Negro Affairs for the FERA until he resigned in 1934, found this alarming. He recognized the importance of relief to the survival of black families; Washington thought many blacks, particularly in the South, were better off on relief since "in some communities the minimum budget for food and necessities exceeds their previous highest wages." But Washington also believed that long-term "dependence" on relief was as horrid a fate as the exploitation and discrimination that African Americans faced everyday. Washington was convinced that dependence on relief would only reinforce white animosities toward blacks.[4]

The inversion of Myrdal's vicious circle resulted from the virulent labor-market discrimination of the 1930s (which displaced blacks from the labor market to relief rolls) and from the combined effects of New Deal budget and labor policies. In the fiscal logic of the New Deal's work- and social-insurance policies and in whites' appropriation of jobs lay the origins of a racially stratified welfare state.

Job Discrimination and the Logic of New Deal Social Policy

Blacks entered into the new political order as part of a class coalition rather than as an exploited racial group. Roosevelt's was the first federal administration since Lincoln's to actively minister to the needs of black Americans. FDR did refuse to back congressional efforts to pass an antilynching law, and there was pervasive discrimination in the administration of relief and other programs; nonetheless, the New Deal provided limited but important economic assistance to African Americans and opened the door to the civil rights movement. In addition to federal relief payments, blacks benefited from Public Works Administration job quotas, public housing assistance, and especially the programs of the National Youth Administration. African American representation in New Deal agencies by the mid-1930s may have been more symbolic than influential, but it gave members of Roosevelt's Black Cabinet, as his African American appointees were called, a foothold to

---

4. Forrester B. Washington, "The Negro and Relief," *Proceedings of the National Conference of Social Work, 1934* (Chicago, 1934), p. 184.

agitate for changes in federal policies that would minimize racial discrimination and mitigate its effects.[5]

The class logic of the New Deal appealed strongly to many African Americans. Two of the most prominent and influential black New Dealers, Mary McLeod Bethune and Robert Weaver, firmly believed in the liberating possibilities of New Deal reform for blacks and remained in federal agencies until the end of the war. Black voters responded both to the logic of class and to Roosevelt personally and, rather than hold him responsible for the failure to pass an antilynching law, they swelled the Democratic party rolls in northern cities.[6] But nowhere was the growing salience of class consciousness more apparent than among black elites in the main African American political organizations—National Urban League (NUL), National Association for the Advancement of Colored People (NAACP), and National Negro Congress (NNC)—who came to believe that only through a class-based alliance of black and white workers could economic deprivation be overcome. Many black organizations broadened the base of their alliances with whites by including union leaders on their governing boards and openly advocated downplaying an explicitly racial agenda.

The NNC, a national umbrella organization formed at the insistence of John L. Davis and Ralph Bunche, traveled farthest along the road to class consciousness. Organizers of the NNC believed that black poverty was largely due to economic causes: African Americans were first members of the working class, and any solution to their poverty could only be alleviated by finding common ground with white workers. Of all black political organizations, the NNC was the most closely allied with the labor movement, particularly CIO unions, and had close ties to members of the Communist party as well.[7] The conservative NAACP was pulled into class-based politics during the 1930s by militant young blacks such as Abram Harris, who sought to modify longstanding NAACP civil rights policies by adding economic goals.

---

5. Nancy J. Weiss, *Farewell to the Party of Lincoln* (Princeton, N.J., 1983); Harvard Sitkoff, *A New Deal for Blacks* (New York, 1978).

6. Kirby, *Black Americans in the Roosevelt Era,* pp. 110–31; Weiss, *Farewell to the Party of Lincoln,* pp. 209–35.

7. Charles R. Lawrence, "Negro Organizations in Crisis" (Ph.D. diss., Columbia University, 1953), chap. 5; John Baxter Streater Jr., "The National Negro Congress, 1936–1947" (Ph.D. diss., University of Cincinnati, 1981), pp. 60–61, 97–98, 104–5, 109, 152; see also Cicero Alvin Hughes, "Toward a Black United Front: The National Negro Congress Movement" (Ph.D. diss., Ohio University, 1982), chaps. 2–4.

"Instead of continuing to oppose racial discrimination on the job and in pay and various manifestations of anti-Negro feelings among white workers," Harris argued in a searching reexamination of NAACP policies, "the Association would attempt to get Negroes to view their special grievances as a natural part of the larger issues of American labor as a whole. It would attempt to get white workers and black to view their lot as embracing a common cause rather than antithetical interests."[8] Similarly, T. Arnold Hill and Lester Granger of the NUL struggled tirelessly to put the Urban League on the side of the working class, a marked turnabout for a middle-class organization woefully dependent on the money of capitalists. Hill and Granger formed Workers' Councils to persuade black workers of the advantages of joining unions in addition to lobbying New Deal agencies. In response to one critic of the Urban League, Granger wrote, "We are urging upon Negro workers that they cast aside the old interracial method and approach and join hands with white fellow workers. Please do not construe the Councils as any purely Negro reform movement."[9]

The fight against racism was never abandoned, and one should not exaggerate the strength or depth of class consciousness among African Americans. The call for an alliance of black and white workers was accompanied by demands from men like Ralph Bunche to exclude whites from black organizations and by strenuous efforts to counter racism in the administration of New Deal programs and in unions. Nor were all black elites captivated by racial liberalism or the vision of a unified working class. Walter White of the NAACP never truly abandoned the traditional agenda of the organization despite acceptance of much of the Harris report; T. Arnold Hill and Lester Granger's plan to align the NUL with the CIO and convince black workers to join unions was undermined by lack of funding and the opposition of local Urban League chapters that were dominated by close ties with local economic elites and, hence, primarily responsive to black middle-class interests. W. E. B. Du Bois was openly skeptical that class could ever override race. "Today it is white labor that keeps Negroes out of decent low-cost

---

8. "Future Plan and Program of the NAACP" (Harris Report), in *Black Protest Thought in the Twentieth Century*, ed. August Meier, Elliot Rudwick, and Francis L. Broderick (New York, 1971), p. 180.

9. Workers' Council Correspondence files, National Urban League, cited in Lawrence, "Negro Organizations in Crisis," p. 263; Dona Cooper Hamilton, "The National Urban League during the Depression, 1930–1939" (Ph.D. diss., Columbia University, 1982), chap. 4.

housing," he argued, "that confines the protection of the best unions to 'white' men, that often will not sit in the same hall with black folk who already have joined the labor movement."[10]

Even though many blacks recognized that there were limits to the class logic of the New Deal, they put their faith, for a time, in a class-based strategy for political change. Yet their efforts were undermined by endemic racial exploitation and the logic of New Deal social policy. New Deal labor law rendered a key source of hostility between black and white workers obsolete but, at the same time, left African Americans more vulnerable to the racist inclinations of white workers. Prior to the New Deal, racial conflict between black and white workers was defined by the struggle to unionize northern industries. A cycle of violence and hatred ensued when white workers denied union membership and jobs to blacks, who responded by acting as strikebreakers. The Wagner Act removed this source of racial hostility by outlawing the use of strikebreakers. This prevented industrialists from exploiting white racism against the unions. But Congress failed to add an antidiscrimination provision, as black political leaders had requested. Roy Wilkins of the NAACP commented that the act "rigidly enforces and legalizes the closed shop . . . [and] plainly empowers organized labor to exclude from employment in any industry those who do not belong to a union."[11] This provision increased the incentives for black political leaders to promote a biracial class coalition. But it left black men and women with little protection from white workers who believed that their racial privileges were more important than class solidarity.

White workers cast African Americans as the villains during the depression and used their power to forcibly displace blacks from work and make them accept lower-paying jobs. Horace Cayton and George Mitchell vividly portrayed the racist violence endemic to depression-era labor markets in their study of black railroad firemen:

> The causes of the murderous campaign against the Negro road service men [in which twenty-one were killed, wounded, or shot at] may be traced to the accentuated unemployment among railroad employees. . . . The change in the character of firemen's work, the generally embittered racial feeling of the Deep South, the peculiar operation of the rules of seniority under

10. "A Negro Nation within the Nation," in *W. E. B. Du Bois: A Reader,* ed. David Levering Lewis (New York, 1995), p. 566; see also Du Bois, "Social Planning for the Negro, Past and Present," *Journal of Negro Education* 5 (1936): 120–25.

11. Herbert Hill, *Black Labor and the American Legal System* (Madison, Wisc., 1985), p. 105.

the ban against Negro promotions, the willingness of the companies concerned to permit replacement of murdered Negroes with whites, the lax enforcement of law, and the conspiracy of white road service men combined with the unemployment situation to make possible the inauguration of a reign of terror.[12]

The experience of black firemen, absent the violence, was typical of black workers during the depression. White workers organized to force black workers from scarce jobs and limit employment in recovery programs to white workers, actions which local public officials often explicitly condoned. Skilled white workers displaced black workers. The National Urban League told Roosevelt in a 1937 memorandum, "the area of so-called 'Negro jobs' had been steadily invaded by disemployed whites during the past decade, and this invasion, increased tremendously during the past five years, has practically eliminated any type of work 'reserved' for Negro workers." Many of these black workers as were displaced because white workers "appropriated 'Negro jobs'" they had previously scorned. Job displacement was especially severe for black women in the North, who lost their jobs in domestic or personal service to whites.[13]

Evidence of discrimination and job displacement over the decade is substantial. One study estimated that the wage rates of black workers as compared to whites declined by 3.6 percent for every 1 percent increase in the unemployment rate.[14] Blacks experienced very high unemployment rates compared to whites throughout the depression, rates that remained high while white rates declined. Unemployment peaked in 1933 when 25 percent of the labor force was out of work and declined to 14.6 percent in 1940. During the depths of the depression, black unemployment rates in northern cities were almost twice the white rate, approaching 50 percent in some places. As the depression lengthened, the ratio of black to white unemployment increased because the white unemployment rate sharply declined while

12. Horace R. Cayton and George S. Mitchell, *Black Workers and the New Unions* (Chapel Hill, N.C., 1939), pp. 439–45.

13. National Urban League, "The Negro Working Population and National Recovery," a special memorandum submitted to Franklin Delano Roosevelt, January 4, 1937, p. 3, NUL Papers, ser. 1, box 1, LC; Arthur M. Ross, "Race, Cultural Groups, Social Differentiation," *Social Forces* 18 (1940): 551; William A. Sundstrom, "Last Hired, First Fired? Unemployment and Urban Black Workers during the Great Depression," *Journal of Economic History* 52 (1992): 415–29; Forrester B. Washington, "The Negro and Relief," p. 183; Hamilton, "The National Urban League," pp. 83–91.

14. Orley Ashenfelter, "Changes in Labor Market Discrimination over Time," *Journal of Human Resources* 4 (1970): 406–8.

the black rate remained high. Overall the ratio increased from 1.49 to 1.66, but in some northern cities the change was more dramatic. In Cincinnati, for example, the ratio rose from 1.9 to 4.5 between 1933 and 1937. By 1940 the combined work relief and unemployment rates for urban black workers was 2.3 times that of whites. There were also sharp declines in the black labor force participation rate while the white labor force participation rate actually increased.[15]

When combined with the logic of New Deal social policy, white appropriation of black jobs extended the color line into the welfare state. Relief, not social rights, was at the core of Roosevelt's social policies. Rather than consolidating an inclusive welfare state based on accepted social rights, the New Deal left fragmented but austere relief and public assistance programs as the only source of support for many people. One of the ironies of the New Deal is that it extended relief while condemning it. New Dealers remained virulently antirelief throughout the 1930s, ruthlessly insisting relief was debilitating and corrupting. The "dole" was unacceptable policy, Roosevelt remarked in late 1935. "Most Americans," he went on to say, "want to give something for what they get. That something, in this case honest work, is the saving barrier between them and moral disintegration."[16] Harry Hopkins reiterated this theme when he pointed to the pervasive poverty and enduring unemployment of the late 1930s and called for a larger, permanent security program. "The federal government," he told Congress, "should never return to a direct-relief program. It is degrading to the individual; it destroys morale and respect. . . . We should do away with direct relief for the unemployed in the United States."[17]

Yet, paradoxically, New Deal social policy deepened the dependence of many people on relief. The assumptions underlying contributory social insurance, notably the wage-related eligibility requirements, were discordant with the realities of depression-era labor markets. FDR's fiscal conservatism and heed for business confidence, both during and after the 1935 policy settlement, eroded any commitment to a right to work. In its place, means-

15. E. Franklin Frazier, "Some Effects of the Depression on the Negro in Northern Cities," *Science and Society* 2 (1938): 490; Myrdal, *American Dilemma*, pp. 298–99, 302–3; Lawrence, "Negro Organizations in Crisis," p. 195; Sundstrom, "Last Hired, First Fired?" pp. 419–20.

16. Quoted in Robert H. Bremner, "The New Deal and Social Welfare," *Fifty Years Later: The New Deal Evaluated*, ed. Harvard Sitkoff (Philadelphia, 1985), p. 75.

17. U.S. Congress, Senate, *Unemployment and Relief Hearings*, 75th Cong., 2d sess., pp. 1341, 1348.

tested relief flourished, vitiating any clear distinction between WPA and the dole. Most of the outlays for social spending in the 1930s were dedicated to means-tested transfers; public assistance and relief expenditures accounted for 79 percent of all social outlays in 1936, declining to 64 percent by 1940.

One of the reasons for this, as I have already indicated, was that the Social Security Act was universal in name only. After Congress excluded domestic and agricultural workers, public employees, and workers in nonprofit, voluntary organizations, just 53 percent of all gainful workers (about 26 million people) were covered. Less than half of all gainful workers were covered by unemployment compensation.[18] Restrictive wage-related eligibility criteria further reduced the number of workers entitled to New Deal social rights: Congress imposed a national earnings requirement for old-age insurance; all states passed employment requirements (typically, one year) for unemployment compensation by 1940; and all but two states had minimum earnings requirements. Social insurance was designed to reward stable, long-term employment while penalizing intermittent employment, regardless of the reason for it. But in the middle of a prolonged, severe depression, wage-related eligibility criteria doubled the injury to unemployed workers by rendering them ineligible for social insurance. For most wage earners the right to unemployment benefits regardless of need was a meaningless abstraction.

Molly Dewson, a member of the Social Security Board, bluntly informed James Roosevelt: "Unemployment Compensation will have little effect on the relief load this winter."[19] Dewson was not exaggerating. An average of 17 percent of all covered workers in the United States in 1940 were excluded from unemployment compensation, although there were wide variations between states. Mandated exclusions affected nearly half of the labor force, but altogether two-thirds of the national labor force was not entitled to unemployment benefits in the late 1930s under any circumstances. Moreover, only twenty-three states were paying benefits by January 1938, the peak of the Roosevelt recession, and in many cases workers were entitled to receive benefits for only a few weeks because of insufficient employment. Unemployment benefits were so low during the depression that many eligible

18. The more restrictive coverage of unemployment compensation was due to the exclusion of firms employing fewer than eight workers (William Haber and J. J. Joseph, "An Appraisal of the Federal-State System of Unemployment Compensation: The Need for a Federal Plan," *Social Service Review* 15 [1941]: 212–16).

19. Molly Dewson to James Roosevelt, December 13, 1937, OF 1710, box 1, FDRL.

workers—30 percent in Detroit, according to one study—were forced to turn to general (local) relief to survive.[20]

An inadequate unemployment insurance policy might not have mattered so much if the administration had made good on its proclaimed commitment to a right to work. For Harry Hopkins, Aubrey Williams, and many other New Dealers, the right to work for the nonelderly was a corollary to an earned right to a pension and the defining premise of New Deal social policy. Yet Roosevelt's budget policies mocked the "right to work" rhetoric of Williams and others. At no time did the federal work relief program provide employment for more than 30 percent of the unemployed, nor did it assist all the individuals certified as eligible. In some states the WPA was less successful than the FERA in finding work for the employables.[21]

Roosevelt's and Morgenthau's preoccupation with balanced budgets and business confidence required that the administration carry out periodic purges of the rolls. FDR's fiscal 1938 budgetary decisions necessitated a forced reduction of 600,000 men and women from the relief rolls. WPA planners anticipated reducing the rolls to 1.5 million by October 1937 and sustaining that until the end of the year. This purge cut deeply, denying help to the most desperate as well as the merely unfortunate. The policy implementation statement noted:

> The prevailing instructions that no person who is in need of relief shall be separated from the WPA are canceled. No attempt will be made to establish categorical priorities of persons for removal from the WPA, i.e., single persons, persons eligible for security benefits, persons over the arbitrary age limit etc., and no attempt will be made to determine *relative* need among certified persons making removals.[22]

Relief spending rose with the 1937–38 recession, but FDR tightened up again in late 1938 and turned down Hopkins's plea to release money held in

20. National Resources Planning Board, *Security, Work, and Relief Policies* (Washington, D.C., 1942), pp. 110, 207–13; Haber and Joseph, "Appraisal of Federal-State Unemployment Compensation," pp. 212–14; Daniel Creamer and Arthur C. Wellman, "Adequacy of Unemployment Benefits in the Detroit Area during the 1938 Recession," *Social Security Bulletin* 3 (1940): 8, table 5.

21. William R. Brock, *Welfare, Democracy, and the New Deal* (New York, 1988), pp. 284–85.

22. "Memorandum Covering Policies to Govern the Operation of the Works Progress Administration Program during the Remainder of the Fiscal Year 1937, and through the Fiscal Year 1938," p. 1, Hopkins Papers, box 54, folder "FY 1937–1938," FDRL.

reserve. "It is absolutely definite," he remonstrated to Hopkins, "that I told Mr. Williams about the middle of October that no emergency could be declared and that he would have to get on without such a declaration. In other words, the money must last until March first. That is that." Once again quotas for WPA employment were imposed, and even though FDR backed off from some of the more draconian cuts, this only meant they would be imposed by state relief agencies subject to a fixed budget.[23]

Work relief was predicated on destroying the dole, or at least relegating it to the sidelines. Yet the administration's decision to replace the FERA with an inadequately funded work relief program necessitated the use of means-tested policies and led to an expansion of unsubsidized general, or locally controlled, relief. Originally, Roosevelt and Hopkins decided to impose a means test for the WPA in order to control the growth of the relief rolls. The 1935 executive order establishing the WPA required that 90 percent of recipients be drawn from the relief rolls (later this was raised to 95 percent). This decision may have pleased businessmen and many local officials, including the U.S. Conference of Mayors, who always denounced any loosening of eligibility requirements, but it provoked severe criticism from labor unions, social workers, and of course the unemployed themselves. Hopkins and Williams defended means tests as a way of stretching limited resources; even people opposed to means tests in principle accepted them in practice. And most of the public believed that the most needy should be assisted first. Yet these justifications were mingled with the antirelief rhetoric of the late 1930s, whether uttered by New Dealers or their opponents, eroding any distinction between ennobling qualities of work relief and the dole.

Congress imposed the first legal requirement that WPA beneficiaries must be certified as needy in 1939. Until this time, WPA administrators zigged and zagged between emphasizing employment and acknowledging they were administering a relief policy. Caught on the prongs of a hybrid program, Hopkins and others tried to run a "work program in which the less said about relief and standards of need the better," a compromise that could be sustained only so long as Congress did not consciously seek to shape the policy. But by this time the careful distinctions of 1935 between employable and unemployable and between the dole and work relief were blurred beyond

23. Franklin D. Roosevelt to Hopkins, November 18, 1938, M. H. McIntyre to Hopkins, November 22, 1938, and Franklin D. Roosevelt to Hopkins, April 28, 1938, box 9, OF 444c, FDRL; Harry Hopkins, Memo to the File, December 1938, Hopkins Papers, box 55, folder "Memos RE: WPA Funds."

recognition.[24] Their dilemma was mostly self-inflicted, of course. Most New Dealers were hard-pressed to do away entirely with some kinds of needs test, since it was the only plausible way to ration the limited resources Roosevelt was willing to commit to work relief. The WPA developed a standard of "relative need," which required distinguishing between the more and less needy in order to ensure that the most needy received aid, but as a result, many otherwise impoverished people were relegated to the vicissitudes of local poor-law administrators.

General relief became the catch basin for employables removed from WPA rolls or for those who could not qualify for one of the three public assistance programs. Expenditures for general relief rose sharply in 1935–36, averaged 15 percent of total outlays for relief between 1935 and 1940, and exceeded spending for Old Age Assistance until 1940. Caseloads for general relief remained very high after 1935 and are negatively correlated with the WPA caseload, rising sharply during the two purges of the WPA rolls during 1937 and 1939 (see figure 1).[25] Even though general relief was the only source of public support for many people, it was all but nonexistent in the South and uncertain elsewhere. As state and local expenditures for relief costs escalated, so did political conflict. States sought to reduce relief costs by reimposing stringent pre–New Deal eligibility requirements. Residence requirements, for example, were tightened as the number of states requiring three years of residence to attain eligibility increased from 12 to 16. So-called employables were either denied assistance or were purged when relief funds were insufficient.[26]

The inadequacies of New Deal social policies and Roosevelt's demand for state financial contributions provoked conservative opposition to relief. State legislatures in both Illinois and Ohio, for example, refused to appropriate adequate funds for general relief, forcing city officials in Chicago and Cleveland to implement draconian cuts in caseloads and benefits.[27] Relief

24. Don D. Lescohier, "The Hybrid WPA," *Survey Midmonthly* 75 (1939): 167–69; Donald Howard, *The WPA and Federal Relief Policy* (New York, 1943), pp. 351–53, 361–63, 370–71, 381–83, 406; William W. Bremer, "Along the 'American Way': The New Deal's Work Relief Programs for the Unemployed," *Journal of American History* 62 (1975): 643–44, 646; Bremner, "The New Deal and Social Welfare," p. 75.

25. Arthur E. Burns and Edward A. Williams, *Federal Work, Security, and Relief Programs* (Washington, D.C., 1941), pp. 116–17.

26. Howard, *The WPA*, pp. 59–60. In the South a person was considered employable if he or she could walk to the relief office and apply.

27. *Security, Work, and Relief*, pp. 150–51; David J. Maurer, "Relief Problems and Politics in Ohio," in *The New Deal: The State and Local Levels,* ed. John Braeman, Robert H. Bremner, and David Brody (Columbus, Ohio, 1975), pp. 96–97.

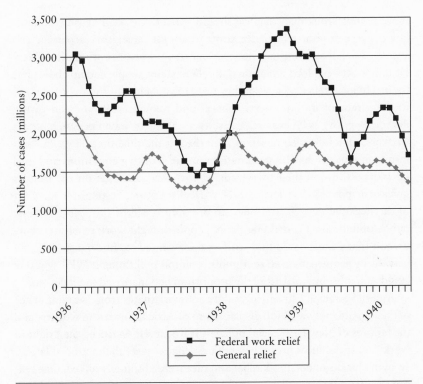

Figure 1. Relief caseloads by month, 1936–1940. *Source: Security, Work, and Relief Policies* (Washington, D.C., 1942), app. 9, pp. 557–58.

policy became captive to the tax revolt with discernible electoral consequences in some states. In Baltimore, where politicians and business interests were especially tenacious in their efforts to limit access to relief rolls, the Taxpayers League organized against the incumbent mayor when he proposed a tax increase to deal with unemployment and rising relief costs. While the mayor escaped defeat on a platform pledged to efficiency and reduced spending, the opposition to both relief and tax increases spread throughout the state. About one-third of the governors in states that passed sales taxes (which were used to fund relief) went down to defeat at the next election, though the proportion was higher in competitive northern states than in the one-party South.[28]

To many people none of this seemed necessary. Senator Robert La Follette posed the obvious question when he said, "there was never anything

28. Jo Ann Argersinger, *Toward a New Deal in Baltimore* (Chapel Hill, N.C., 1988), pp. 46–48, 52–53; Susan Hansen, *The Politics of Taxation* (New York, 1983), pp. 165–66.

more preposterous than that we should expand the old English common-law concept of poor relief in an effort to meet a cataclysmic economic crisis."[29] What Roosevelt had done, ironically, was to restore the pre–New Deal link between local taxation and relief. Many people had no choice but to turn to local relief agencies if they were to get help, but this exposed them to the wrath of irate property owners and taxpayers. By the end of the decade even the WPA was regarded as a haven for incompetent, shiftless workers. One informed observer remarked at the time that the WPA "has meant so much in hardship, humiliation, bad working conditions and jobs [to workers] not in their own trade, that they want to get off the rolls as quickly as possible."[30] The anti–New Deal press was responsible for a lot of the negative images, and one can discount much of this. Nevertheless, public opinion data reveal that many people thought work relief was charity and that people could find work if they wanted to. In August 1937, 55 percent of people surveyed in a public opinion poll thought WPA workers could find jobs; by April 1939 the proportion had increased to 69 percent.[31]

America's racially stratified welfare state originates from the confluence of the racially motivated job displacement of African American workers and the failures of New Deal social policies. If Roosevelt sacrificed the "right to work" on the altar of his budget policies, blacks were the sacrificial lambs. As many blacks understood, relief and race were absolutely linked. One reason the National Urban League publicly embraced an alliance between black and white workers and adopted a policy of seeking jobs rather than relief for blacks was their fear that relief would become racially stigmatized.[32]

Race and the Dole

New Dealers assumed their reforms would submerge the problems of race in economic concerns common to all citizens and, thereby, remove it from the national debate over the New Deal. Yet the plight of African Americans in the middle of the depression was a matter of considerable discussion. "One

29. Quoted in Howard, *The WPA*, p. 355.
30. Quoted in Richard J. Jensen, "The Causes and Cures of Unemployment in the Great Depression," *Journal of Interdisciplinary History* 19 (1989): 578; Barbara Blumberg, *The New Deal and the Unemployed* (Lewisberg, Penn., 1979), pp. 223, 225, 283.
31. Hadley Cantril, ed., *Public Opinion, 1935–1946* (Princeton, N.J., 1951), p. 895, tables 17, 18, p. 896, table 35.
32. Hamilton, "The National Urban League," p. 326.

of the major topics for private conversations at luncheon clubs throughout the country," wrote Edward Lewis, secretary of the Baltimore Urban League, is "why is there such a disproportionate number of Negroes on relief?" Lewis was not exaggerating. Senator Millard Tydings, no friend of the New Deal to be sure, had posed this question before a congressional committee. The FERA was sufficiently concerned to launch a series of studies in mid-1935. And Newton D. Baker, a trustee of the Carnegie Foundation, planted the seed for Gunnar Myrdal's famous study when he told a meeting of the trustees that the foundation should investigate the "Negro problem" in northern cities. Baker, a native of Cleveland who had a life-long obsession with the dangers of ethnic conflict, was appalled by the number of African Americans on relief and the high level of black unemployment. Baker proposed a study because he was worried about the danger of race riots in housing projects and about rising urban black poverty; he was fearful of "the consequences of a generation of young people growing up without work or a work ethic."[33]

Richard Sterner later said that during the depression "more Negroes obtained their main livelihood from relief . . . than from any single productive occupation except agriculture and domestic and personal service."[34] By the spring of 1935 when the FERA relief rolls peaked, 22 percent of all black families received relief compared to 13 percent of white families. The gap was substantially higher in urban areas (where over one-third of black families were on relief compared to one-eighth of white families) and in northern cities than in the rural South. (See table 1a.) Fifty-four percent of black families in northeastern cities were on relief, compared to 14 percent of white families. The relief rates in midwestern cities were comparable to those on the eastern seaboard; in southern cities the relief rates were lower, although the rate for black families exceeded that for whites: 26 percent compared to 11 percent. Only in the rural South did white relief rates exceed those of blacks, and then only slightly.

The heavy concentration of blacks on federal relief persisted into the early years of the war. Black workers were more likely to be on work relief than whites by the late 1930s; indeed, after 1938 the proportion of blacks on

33. Edward Lewis, "The Negro on Relief," *Journal of Negro Education* 5 (1936): 73; Walter A. Jackson, *Gunnar Myrdal and America's Conscience* (Chapel Hill, N.C., 1990), p. 22.

34. Richard Sterner, *The Negro's Share: A Study of Income, Consumption, and Housing* (New York, 1943), p. 214.

Table 1a. Relief rates for families by race and region, 1933–1940 (percentage of families on relief)

	Cash relief, 1933		Cash relief, 1935		Work relief, 1940	
	White	*Black*	*White*	*Black*	*White*	*Nonwhite*
Urban U.S.	10.0%	30.9%	13.5%	36.4%	3.5%	8.2%
Urban Northeast	9.5	35.8	14.2	53.7	3.1	9.1
Urban North Central	10.9	42.1	13.5	51.3	4.0	14.3
Urban South	10.0	25.6	11.4	25.5	3.3	6.0
Rural South	12.3	10.8	12.3	7.3	5.2	2.6

Table 1b. Blacks on general relief by city as a percentage of caseload and population, 1937

	New York	Chicago	Detroit	Philadelphia	Baltimore	St. Louis
Caseload	21.7%	25.0%	31.8%	44.2%	47.1%	40.0%
Population	6.4	8.3	9.3	13.0	19.4	13.4

Sources: (Table 1a) Federal Emergency Relief Administration, *Unemployment Relief Census, October 1933* (Washington, D.C., 1934), table 5; Philip M. Hauser, *Workers on Relief in the United States in March 1935,* vol. 1, *A Census of Usual Occupations* (Washington, D.C., 1938), tables 19, 20, 21 (data on the number of families are drawn from the 1930 census); *United States Census, 1940 Population: Families, Employment Status, Regions, Cities, 1,000,000 or More* (Washington, D.C., 1942), tables 5, 13, 15. *(Table 1b) Security, Work, and Relief Policies,* p. 117.

WPA rolls actually *increased.* The total number of workers on the WPA rolls declined substantially by 1940, but the work relief rates for urban black families remained three to three-and-one-half times those of urban white families in northern industrial states (table 1). Among urban workers throughout the country, black workers made up 17.2 percent of work relief rolls in 1940, down slightly from 18.7 percent in 1935. But the proportion of black workers on the work relief rolls increased in the North Central region and declined sharply in the South. In large northern cities (see figure 2), the proportion of black workers on work relief increased by an average of 3.3 percentage points between 1935 and 1940, with large increases in Detroit (13.4 percent) and Chicago (10.6 percent) and smaller increases in New York (4.4 percent), Indianapolis (4.5 percent), and Baltimore (5.2 percent). In southern cities, by contrast (see figure 3), the proportion of blacks on work relief declined by almost 10 percent on average, apparently because whites in the South were less likely to be forced off the WPA rolls than blacks. Nonetheless, the proportion of blacks on work relief in southern cities remained very high (38 percent) compared to northern cities (31 percent). Overall, in 1940 black workers made up about one-third of the workers on

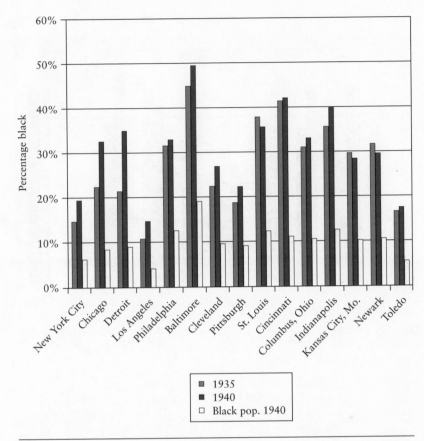

Figure 2.   Black workers on federal relief in northern cities, 1935–1940. Includes all cities over 250,000 people in which at least 5 percent is African American. *Sources:* Philip Hauser, *Workers on Relief in the United States in March 1935*, vol. 2, tables 1, 2; *United States Census, 1940, Population*, vol. 3, *The Labor Force* (Washington, D.C., 1943), tables 41–47.

work relief in the nation's largest cities, which was greatly in excess of the proportion of blacks in the total population of these cities.[35]

35. Sterner, *Negro's Share*, p. 241. The 1940 census apparently underestimated the number of workers on WPA rolls because of enumerator error; there was a significant discrepancy between the census count and WPA payrolls. There is no way to estimate what difference, if any, this would make in the figures (*U.S. Census, 1940, Population*, vol. 3, *The Labor Force*, pt. 1, p. 3). But the census data is consistent with other studies of the number of black workers on WPA rolls in the early 1940s. Sterner, for example, reports a similar trend based on WPA data (*Negro's Share*, pp. 239–44).

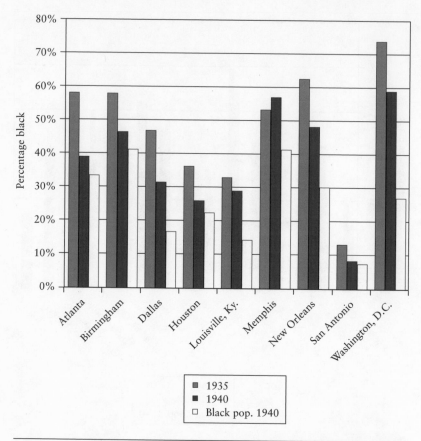

Figure 3. Black workers on federal relief in southern cities, 1935–1940. Includes all cities over 250,000 people in which at least 5 percent is African American. *Sources:* Philip Hauser, *Workers on Relief in the United States in March 1935*, vol. 2, tables 1, 2; *United States Census, 1940, Population*, vol. 3, *The Labor Force* (Washington, D.C., 1943), tables 41–47.

Federal statistics on the WPA rolls understate the number of black workers and families on relief in the late 1930s because they do not include data on general relief. The proportion of blacks on general relief remained high in northern states and cities, and it was usually higher than that of blacks on the WPA, according to African American newspapers of the period. The proportion of blacks on the general relief caseload ranged from about one-fifth in New York City to two-fifths or more in St. Louis, Baltimore, and Philadelphia. (See table 1b.) Some studies indicate that black workers and their families relied on general relief, "the dole," as much or more than on the WPA. In Cleveland the total relief rate (combining WPA and general relief) for families in census tracts with a more than two-thirds African American presence was an astounding 92 percent in 1935. This declined to 45 percent by 1937. The relief rate for all families in Cleveland declined from 35 to 17 percent in the same two-year period. A 1938 New Jersey study of the relief rolls in 15 cities revealed that almost half of black families relied upon some form of relief for their livelihood, and there were more black families receiving general relief than there were on the WPA (26 percent versus 22 percent). A similar pattern is apparent in New York City, where blacks comprised 22 percent of the general relief rolls but only 8 percent of WPA slots. In Pennsylvania blacks made up 24 percent of so-called employables receiving general relief, but only 5 percent of the total number of employables in the population and only 11 percent of those on the WPA rolls.[36] And in Chicago, a survey reported by the *Houston Defender* revealed that 92,000 blacks were on direct relief and 55,000 on the WPA. Upon learning how many St. Louis blacks were on relief, an Urban League official commented that "the submerged status of the racial group in the working class is alarming," an observation that easily applied to all these cities.[37]

Compared to whites, more African Americans were on relief, were on the rolls for a longer period of time, and were more likely to receive general relief than work relief. Lewis noted that in "off-the-record" discussions whites resorted to the staples of racist discourse to explain these facts, describing blacks as "lazy, irresponsible, indolent." The truth, as Myrdal pointed out at the time, is that whites were coercively substituting relief for jobs. New Deal social policies did little to mitigate the effects of private labor-market discrimination. Because of the wage-related eligibility provisions, unemployed black workers had less access to unemployment compensation than

36. Howard Whipple Green, "Nine Years of Relief in Cleveland, 1928–1937" (Cleveland Health Council, June 1937), tables 3, 6; and Green, "Two Hundred Millions for Relief in Cleveland" (Cleveland Health Council, 1938), table 13 (my calculations); *Report of the New Jersey State Temporary Commission on the Condition of the Urban Colored Population* (Trenton, N.J., 1939), p. 16; Cheryl Lynn Greenberg, *Or Does It Explode? Black Harlem in the Great Depression* (New York, 1991), p. 158; Commonwealth of Pennsylvania, *Employability of Pennsylvania's General Assistance Case Load, April 1941* (Department of Public Assistance, June 1941), p. 13; *Characteristics of the Population: United States Summary—Divisions and States,* 16th Census of the United States, vol. 1 (Washington, D.C., 1943), tables 37, 40.

37. Weekly Press Summaries for the week ending January 29, 1938, *St. Louis Star-Times,* p. 7; *Houston Defender,* July 1, 1939, RG 69.70/71, WPA, Division of Information, Negro Press Digest and related clippings, box 4, 1936–1940, NA.

did white workers. Data on unemployment compensation are not available, but it is reasonable to assume that exclusion rates for old-age insurance were similar to those for unemployment insurance. By the end of the decade, 42 percent of the black workers who were employed in covered industries and who paid payroll taxes for old-age insurance were uninsured; only 20 percent of comparable white workers were uninsured. Black women were the most severely affected group: 55 percent of black women were uninsured, compared to 40 percent of black men, 30 percent of white women, and 17 percent of white men. Black women were also disproportionately affected by the statutory exclusion of domestic workers from social insurance since 90 percent worked as domestics.[38]

Other New Deal policies were instrumental in forcing blacks onto the relief rolls. New Deal agricultural policies pushed many black farmers and sharecroppers off the land; many then migrated to cities, swelling the relief rolls. Employers responded to the wage policies of the National Recovery Administration by imposing color bans. In fact, efforts by the National Urban League and other black organizations to equalize wages between white and black workers led to threats by employers to replace black workers with white workers.[39] The most important New Deal policies implicated in the new color line, however, were the work and labor policies. Black workers faced the same competition with white workers for work relief that they encountered in the private labor market. Alfred Edgar Smith, an African American aide to Hopkins who submitted monthly reports on the experience of African Americans under the New Deal, wrote that "Negro workers apparently have not been and are not being assigned to work relief in their direct relief proportion, and view with alarm the prospect of being left on state supported direct relief rolls."[40] Very often blacks were either excluded or displaced from work and labor programs, usually because of an alliance between local labor unions and the officials running public works programs. But the competition for public jobs was made worse by Roosevelt's budget decisions, which limited the number of available jobs.

African American workers fared less well with early New Deal agencies,

38. Wayne F. Caskey to Jacob Perlman, September 27, 1940, RG 47, Social Security Board Files, box 41, no. 050.01, NA.

39. Hamilton, "National Urban League," pp. 114, 116; Michael S. Holmes, "The Blue Eagle as 'Jim Crow' Bird," *Journal of Negro History* 57 (1972): 278; Raymond Wolters, *Negroes and the Great Depression: The Problem of Economic Recovery* (Westport, Conn., 1970), chap. 6.

40. "Negro Clients on Federal Unemployment Relief," December 31, 1935, p. 3, FERA, General Subject Series, box 31, no. 060, NA.

when the aggregate unemployment rate was higher and hence white efforts at displacement were fiercer, than they did with the WPA. The Civilian Conservation Corps, an extreme example of discriminatory implementation of a New Deal policy, imposed a quota on black participation, since many blacks were on relief and would have qualified. In other cases, skilled black workers were excluded from Public Works Administration (PWA) projects because of the pressure of local craft unions and the refusal of employment agencies to refer blacks. Although it served blacks better, the WPA was not immune to such pressures. African Americans were often denied work relief on the grounds that they did not need work because their standard of living was lower than that of whites and they could presumably survive on general relief. Sometimes their applications were deliberately processed more slowly than those of white workers, which meant that the limited slots were given out to whites first. In New York City, WPA subcontractors refused to hire blacks, and an NAACP survey discovered only forty-one black men employed on twelve construction projects. A St. Louis NUL official reported that "even a sidewalk project set up in St. Louis employing about 100 men does not include a single Negro because Negroes are not permitted into the union and it is now a union job. On the other hand, there are many white men who have never touched cement in any way but through politics were signed on the project from the union."[41]

WPA policies often facilitated exclusionary practices. Harry Hopkins issued a policy directive in early 1936 requiring contractors to hire workers through union representatives and giving union members priority for work relief. The National Urban League protested, telling Hopkins and other WPA officials that "the average business agent would recommend first all the white men in the union who are on relief rolls, and would then seek by any possible means to avoid referring Negro union members, if there were any." WPA officials first tried to deny that the policy would lend itself to discrimination; then they admitted that the policy might have unfortunate effects but said "it was issued in response to pressure brought upon the department from AFL unions."[42] Only after Lester Granger threatened both retaliation at the polls and legal action did Hopkins issue a nondiscrimination policy. But this policy was toothless. Local unions remained in control of job allocation, to the detriment of black workers.

41. Hamilton, "The National Urban League," pp. 104–5, 142–44; Greenberg, *Or Does It Explode?* pp. 156–57.

42. National Urban League, Bulletin no. 11, The Negro Workers' Councils, June 11, 1936, pp. 5–6, NUL Papers, ser. 1, box 9, LC.

Table 2. Duration of work relief by race and city, 1937

	Under 6 months	6–12 months	13–24 months	Over 25 months
Total urban workers				
White	77.8%	71.7%	65.7%	65.3%
Nonwhite	22.2	28.3	34.3	34.5
Atlanta				
White	72.6	65.5	49.1	61.9
Black	27.4	34.6	50.9	38.1
Baltimore				
White	57.8	52.1	67.7	51.6
Black	42.1	47.9	32.3	48.4
St. Louis				
White	71.0	68.8	55.8	47.5
Black	29.0	31.2	44.2	52.5
San Francisco				
White	97.6	76.1	83.8	85.3
Nonwhite	2.4	23.9	16.2	14.7

Source: "Works Progress Administration Separation Study, 1937," Urban Areas, RG 69, Division of Research, box 45A, NA.

Not only were blacks forced onto the relief rolls in greater numbers, they were less likely to get off. More precisely, they shifted from relief to private jobs at a much slower rate than white workers. In the mid-1930s the turnover rates for blacks were much lower than for whites, and when blacks were removed from the WPA rolls they were less likely than whites to be reemployed. In fact, during one of the work relief purges, black political organizations urged administrators "not to drop Negroes from WPA rolls as fast as whites, since the rate of absorption of Negroes in private industry is much slower."[43] Data from a WPA separation study examining the effects of the 1937 purge in urban and rural locales showed that whites were more likely than blacks to be on the rolls six months or less, and less likely than blacks to stay on a year or more, especially in industrial cities. In St. Louis, for example, white workers made up 71 percent of those on the rolls six months or less, but only 56 percent of those on for thirteen to twenty-four months and 48 percent of those on for two years or longer. Blacks, on the other hand, accounted for just 29 percent of those on the rolls for less than six months, but 53 percent of those on for over two years (table 2). This difference is apparent in three other urban areas the WPA studied—Atlanta, Baltimore, and San Francisco— although the pattern is not quite as sharp as that in St. Louis.

43. Sterner, *Negro's Share*, p. 229; quoted in Alfred Edgar Smith, Report of July 1937, p. 3, RG 69, WPA Central Files, box 92, NA.

By the late 1930s many black workers and their families were caught in a relief cycle. This explains why the proportion of blacks on relief rolls increased. The general pattern is quite clear: as blacks were laid off or displaced from private sector jobs they were cycled onto cash relief and then off cash relief to work relief only as white workers departed for private sector jobs. There is evidence that blacks were less likely to move from cash to work relief than were whites. After the creation of the WPA, two-thirds of white workers on the cash-relief rolls in New York City moved onto the WPA rolls, compared to just one-third of black workers. Evidence from the New Jersey study of urban blacks confirms the prevalence of this pattern. In six cities, including Newark and Jersey City, black families made up almost one-third of the general relief rolls (31.5 percent) but less than one-fifth (19 percent) of the cases transferred to the WPA rolls during 1938. White workers, by comparison, were more likely to move into private sector jobs when they left local relief rolls than blacks. In Wayne County, Michigan (Detroit), 48 percent of blacks suspended from local relief rolls took WPA jobs; only 35 percent of suspended white workers did so, for whites were more likely to find work in the private sector.[44] White workers purged from the WPA rolls were more likely to end up in private employment and purged blacks more likely to end up on general relief or with no income. In St. Louis, for example, blacks were twice as likely as whites to end up on general relief after being "separated" from the WPA. This was also true in San Francisco, though it was Mexican Americans and Asian Americans who were put through the relief-wringer there (table 3).

The experience of blacks and whites in St. Louis and San Francisco was typical of northern cities but not of the South, where the pattern of discrimination was quite different. In Atlanta it was whites, not blacks, who stayed on the WPA rolls. The anomalous pattern in Atlanta reflected the southern relief officials' habit of excluding blacks from WPA in favor of whites and forcing them into subsistence-wage jobs instead. They used WPA jobs as a tool to regulate agricultural and other low-wage labor markets and made no bones about it. Mississippi administrators reported to Alfred Edgar Smith that "all WPA clients who can pick cotton have been made available for this type of private employment with the assurance that as it constitutes

---

44. Greenberg, *Or Does It Explode?* p. 158; *New Jersey State Commission*, pp. 16–17, 85–86; Irene E. Murphy, "Social Effects of Prolonged Unemployment on Negro Family Life," *Michigan State Conference on Employment Problems of the Negro* (Detroit, October 8, 1940), p. 38, RG 183, Lawrence A. Oxley Files, box 1398, NA.

Table 3.   Source of income of purged WPA workers by race, sex, and city, 1937

	White workers			Black workers		
	Total	Male	Female	Total	Male	Female
Total urban workers						
Private work	56.9%	61.0%	43.5%	62.3%	67.8%	54.7%
Relief	19.9	17.3	28.2	12.3	14.8	8.3
Other source	10.0	7.0	19.9	14.6	9.9	21.7
No income	13.2	14.7	8.4	10.7	7.5	15.3
Atlanta						
Private work	59.5	77.3	36.7	73.9	88.3	68.2
Relief	9.7	4.1	16.8	0	0	0
Other source	28.6	17.6	42.6	23.6	11.7	28.3
No income	2.3	1.1	3.9	2.5	0	3.5
Baltimore						
Private work	76.3	80.3	32.9	79.2	84.7	41.6
Relief	6.9	5.3	23.7	1.0	1.0	0
Other source	8.5	10.6	19.7	14.6	9.1	51.7
No income	8.3	6.9	23.7	5.4	5.2	6.8
St. Louis						
Private work	72.0	72.2	71.1	43.5	44.2	42.6
Relief	12.3	12.4	12.0	26.4	33.3	18.4
Other source	9.1	9.0	9.4	8.8	9.3	8.2
No income	6.6	6.4	7.6	21.4	13.3	30.8
San Francisco						
Private work	39.3	38.8	44.6	27.4	29.1	22.4
Relief	32.3	29.1	44.4	43.8	39.8	55.3
Other source	3.2	1.0	1.8	7.1	9.2	1.2
No income	25.2	31.7	9.2	21.7	21.9	21.2

Source: "Works Progress Administration, Separation Study, 1937," Urban Areas, RG 69, Division of Research, box 45A, NA.

employment of a temporary nature their status with the WPA will not in any way be altered." And if people, mainly African Americans, objected, the report noted that "insofar as this WPA is concerned, no force of any nature has even been indicated, but persons refusing normal private employment which they are capable of performing are not looked upon with favor for WPA employment." African Americans were outraged by such exploitation, and the black press was full of stories of how white cotton farmers got WPA jobs and blacks were immediately "shifted to the sugar cane field to harvest the crop." After the WPA purges, Smith regarded this exploitation as one of the most serious problems confronting black workers, noting in his July 1937 report to Hopkins that, "Negro farm workers complain of being forced to accept jobs on farms at starvation wages, with impossible working conditions."[45]

The relief cycle left black workers with few alternatives: they were forced onto relief, and their only alternative to cash relief was work relief. In fact, as the data make clear, they could bounce like a ping-pong ball between the two, depending on whether it was Harry Hopkins or local relief officials doing the purging. Life was especially difficult for black women, many of whom were worse off on general relief or public assistance after 1935 than they had been under the FERA.[46] But the consequences of Roosevelt and Hopkins's decision to dismantle federal relief and reinstitutionalize poor relief in 1935 was not just the abandonment of the poor. The failure of New Deal employment policies—the purges of WPA workers and the creeping stigmatization of recipients—consigned African Americans to local poor relief, racially marking Roosevelt's rhetoric about the dole.

African Americans' response to these developments was vigorous and varied. They focused their struggle on access to jobs. T. Arnold Hill of the Urban League pointed out in a speech to the National Conference of Social Work, "in the United States we still have unprotected marginal labor, and the Negro is it. The very fact that the number of Negroes on relief is from two to five times their percentage in the population is proof of the fact that every effort should be made to get them WPA employment and private jobs."[47] The Urban League was one of the few mainstream political organizations publicly and vigorously to demand a permanent public employment program. Dona Hamilton, who takes a somewhat revisionist view of the Urban League's efforts during the depression, argues that the NUL favored a centralized and universalistic welfare state and was far more pro–New Deal and prolabor than most blacks were during the 1930s. But the Urban League rarely operated alone and was often overshadowed by local organizations.

Grassroots protests by African Americans erupted in cities across the North after 1935. Among the most important were the "Don't-Buy-Where-You-Can't-Work" campaigns, which picketed stores that refused to hire black workers. These campaigns were conceived as a tangible way to acquire jobs at a time when antidiscrimination laws were unheard of. Yet in

---

45. Smith, Report for September 1937, pp. 6–7, Report for July 1937, p. 7, RG 69, WPA Central Files, box 92; *Pittsburgh Courier,* November 19, 1938, p. 1, RG 69.70/71, WPA, Negro Press Digest, box 4, 1936–1940, NA.

46. Howard, *The WPA,* pp. 291–93; Sterner, *Negro's Share,* pp. 245–46.

47. "Social Significance to Minority Groups of Recent Labor Developments," May 27, 1937, p. 7, NUL Papers, ser. 4, box 5, LC.

some cities the protest was organized not by black merchants but black workers. By 1940 the principal grassroots organization in Cleveland, the Future Outlook League, had evolved from an organization dedicated to consumer protests to one representing the interests of black workers.[48] The NUL, along with the NAACP and the NNC, tended to press their claims by lobbying New Deal administrators or local officials, yet all of these organizations became more militant with the spread of grassroots protests. For example, the NUL, limited in what it could do by its dependence on white philanthropists, found itself precariously balancing the tension between the demands of a downtrodden black clientele and its white benefactors. Led by its feisty president, A. L. Foster, who said that "the League should never take a vacillating position in matters affecting Negroes" even if it affected the group's financial support, the Chicago chapter of the NUL functioned somewhat like a protest organization over the decade. Other chapters, however, were far less militant.[49]

As important as it was, rising black militancy did not involve large numbers of people and was insufficient to alter the unfolding relationship between African Americans and the New Deal welfare state. Even though the number of blacks on relief declined between 1935 and 1940 and the total number of blacks on relief was small—most African Americans still lived in the rural South where relief was mostly nonexistent—the rising proportion was regarded with concern and contributed to a perception that there was a link between blacks and "dependency." One indication of this perception is the appearance of fretful reports on African American migration toward the end of the decade. The New Jersey Commission investigating the plight of African American workers noted that much of the public believed that blacks were migrating to the North for the "sole purpose of getting on public relief," something they were at pains to disprove, and commented that "the Negro population has consistently been treated as a dependent group to which relief of a sort must be given." A report by Alfred Edgar Smith to Hopkins in the spring of 1938 mentioned various disturbing findings: apprehension in Chicago over a steady increase in the city's black population; efforts underway in Washington, D.C., to discourage southern migrants from settling in the District; and comments in a congressional debate on a relief appropriations bill that referred to black migration as "a

48. Greenberg, *Or Does It Explode?* chap. 5; Kimberley L. Phillips, "Heaven Bound: Black Migration, Community, and Activism in Cleveland, 1915–1945" (Ph.D. diss., Yale University, 1992), pp. 239–42, 282, 293–95.

49. Christopher Robert Reed, "A Study of Black Politics and Protest in Depression-Decade Chicago: 1930–1939" (Ph.D. diss., Kent State University, 1982), pp. 270–71.

disturbing factor in the relief situation to be reckoned with in the future." Even prominent blacks, both conservatives and New Dealers, voiced their concern. Arthur Howe, president of the Hampton Institute (Virginia), said in a speech that "the living standards of 15,000,000 Race members in the United States will have to be raised or they might become a permanent relief problem."[50] Given the widespread racist stereotypes about black workers, the increasing proportion of blacks on both WPA and general relief rolls undoubtedly contributed to the erosion of public support after 1938 for expanding WPA and relief expenditures, despite continuing high levels of unemployment.[51]

Blacks understood the precarious nature of work relief, preferring permanent jobs. When ten thousand people, most of them black, stormed a government agency to apply for a minuscule number of jobs, the *Afro-American* editorialized: "Everywhere men and women are showing increased dissatisfaction with work relief. They are chafing at the prospect of having to continue this kind of thing. What they want, as the Washington incident demonstrates, are steady jobs upon which they can count and plan, and not the spirit-breaking uncertainty of work relief."[52] But blacks also believed that enactment of tighter eligibility standards for relief and the reduction of relief funds in the late 1930s by state and local governments was motivated by hostility toward blacks themselves. They were concerned when the Chicago city council voted to appropriate $3 million from the general fund to pay the wages for work relief while refusing to rescind a 15 percent cut in general relief and were angered by eligibility restrictions imposed by the Illinois state legislature. "The belief that most of the migrants into Illinois were Race persons," a columnist for the *Chicago Defender* wrote, "had something to do with the legislature's decision to lengthen the residence requirement for relief as a bar to migration. Probably the fact that large numbers of Race persons are on WPA had something to do with the decision of Congress to reduce the appropriation. In any event the appropriations have been reduced and the Race must suffer."[53]

50. *New Jersey State Commission*, p. 18; *Second Report of the New Jersey Temporary Commission on the Condition of the Urban Colored Population* (Trenton, N.J., June 1940), section on relief; Smith, Report of May 1938, p. 4, RG 69, WPA Central Files, box 92, NA; *Chicago Defender*, September 14, 1939, RG 69.70/71, WPA, Negro Press Digest, box 4, 1936–1940, NA.

51. Brock, *Welfare, Democracy, and the New Deal*, p. 334.

52. *Afro-American*, October 22, 1938, RG 69.70/71, WPA, Negro Press Digest, box 4, 1936–1940, NA.

53. *Chicago Defender*, October 15, 1938, August 5, 1939, RG 69.70/71, WPA, Negro Press Digest, box 4, 1936–1940, NA.

What would become a familiar drama pitted a rural-dominated conservative legislature against urban jurisdictions. In Maryland, rural opponents made a fateful connection when, in the context of the relief politics of the late 1930s, they objected not just to city profligacy but to "the presence of 'large numbers of Negroes' who, after having sampled the pleasures of 'relief allotments, refused to work any more.'"[54] How widespread these views were is difficult to tell, but state politicians were not the only ones who voiced such sentiments. Prominent Republicans searching for ways to peel off voters from Roosevelt's coalition or repeal New Deal policies made the connection between relief and race a matter of public discussion. Robert Taft, a conservative Republican Senator from Ohio, publicly commented that it is "virtually essential" that the Negro race escape from the "demoralizing help" of the WPA.[55] Other Republicans peddled this line during the late 1930s for the electoral benefits. Already by the end of the 1930s, conservative and anti–New Deal politicians were engaged in linking race, taxes, and welfare in the voters' minds.

The Legitimate and the Illegitimate: Black Women and New Deal Social Policy

The racial bifurcation of New Deal social policy intersected with gender to entrench permanently the color line in the American welfare state. Gender inequality was imported into the welfare state with the wholesale adoption of mothers' pensions as one of the three public assistance titles to the Social Security Act and the addition of survivor's benefits to Old Age Insurance in 1939. Women's inclusion hinged on their status as mothers, not as workers. Aid to Dependent Children (ADC) presumed the dependence of single mothers on a male wage earner and entitled the children of single (typically widowed) but "unemployable" mothers to assistance. The 1939 amendments to the Social Security Act made married women eligible for old-age and survivor's benefits and drew an implicit distinction between widows and other single mothers. Subsequently, access to the welfare state depended on family structure and was structurally differentiated by race and gender. Exclusion of much of the black labor force from social insurance meant that African American widows would fare less well than white widows. And by

54. Argersinger, *New Deal in Baltimore*, p. 53.
55. *Atlanta World*, June 24, 1939, RG 69/70.71, WPA, Negro Press Digest, 1936–1940, box 4, NA.

distinguishing between widows and divorced, separated, or unmarried mothers, the black family (and thus the behavior of black women) inadvertently became an object of public scrutiny.

Congress adopted mother's pensions intact at the insistence of maternalist reformers who objected to Hopkins's effort to create a federal subsidy for general relief by making all needy families with children under sixteen eligible. Hopkins's proposal would have ended the isolation of single mothers as a category of social policy. Katherine Lenroot, Grace Abbott, and maternalist reformers opposed the broader definition because they thought that any provision for federally subsidized general assistance would undermine the carefully built standards of mothers' pensions. They also wanted to make sure that single mothers would not be forced into the labor market at the expense of their domestic duties to their children. The upshot was that single mothers were statutorily labeled as unemployable and poor two-parent families were excluded from public assistance altogether.[56]

Survivor's benefits radically transformed social security from protecting individual workers to "a closely interlocking system of protection for both the aged and for dependent survivors of all ages," or for the social protection of families.[57] The Social Security Advisory Council justified dependents' allowances for mothers and children as a necessary replacement for ADC. They drew a comparison with the relationship between Old Age Insurance and Old Age Assistance saying "the arguments for substituting benefits as a matter of right in the case of children are even more convincing than in the case of aged persons."[58] The Social Security Board had reported that in 43 percent of families receiving ADC the father was deceased, so the family would be eligible for survivor's benefits. Whatever the official rationale, the 1939 amendments put adequate social protection for nuclear, two-parent families at the core of the policy, and thus drew an arbitrary distinction between married and unmarried women, legitimate and illegitimate families. The incentives written into the act reinforced the notion that women's place was in the home, not in the work force. Working women were at a singular disadvantage: they were precluded from attaining eligibility by

56. Josephine Brown, *Public Relief, 1929–1939* (New York, 1940), pp. 310–11; Gwendolyn Mink, *The Wages of Motherhood* (Ithaca, N.Y., 1995), pp. 130–32. See also Linda Gordon, *Pitied but Not Entitled* (New York, 1994), chap. 9.

57. J. Douglas Brown, *An American Philosophy of Social Security* (Princeton, N.J., 1972), p. 132.

58. *Final Report of the Advisory Council on Social Security, 1937–38* (Washington, D.C., 1938), pp. 17–18.

occupational exclusions, and they paid what amounted to a marriage tax since single wage earners would subsidize families. Wives' benefits were superior to the benefits that could be actually obtained by most working women, whose survivors and dependents remained uncovered by the 1939 amendments.[59]

The 1939 amendments also drew a fine distinction between the offspring of legitimate and illegitimate relationships, thereby importing a distinction based on marital status into the heart of the act. Neither divorced nor deserted women with dependent children were entitled to survivors' benefits; all children below the age of eighteen were eligible provided they had not been adopted and were dependent upon the beneficiary. The complicated provisions of the law were primarily intended for widows (the language of the Advisory Council Report and the law refer directly to widows) and surviving dependents, not the progeny of illicit or quasi-illicit relationships. Illegitimate children were specifically excluded. The law required that dependent beneficiaries demonstrate a legal relationship to the deceased but covered worker, which meant, Congress explicitly stipulated, that the relationship be recognized as legal under state intestacy or inheritance laws. Children born out of wedlock or in common-law marriages were typically excluded from inheritances, though state provisions varied widely. Most states at the time required fathers to support illegitimate children, but, ironically, under the provisions of the 1939 amendments "benefits must be denied in many instances to surviving children who have been in fact supported by a father even though he has contributed to a system designed to protect fatherless children."[60] Family organization thus became an arbiter of one's relationship to the welfare state.

Aside from ritualistic pronouncements that survivors' benefits would reduce ADC caseloads, little thought was given to the relationship between the two. The congressional hearings were devoid of any concern with this question. Insofar as mothers' pensions was a social policy for "gilt-edged"

---

59. See also Alice Kessler-Harris, "Designing Women and Old Fools: The Construction of the Social Security Amendments of 1939," in *U.S. History as Women's History*, ed. Linda K. Kerber, Alice Kessler-Harris, and Kathryn Kish Sklar (Chapel Hill, N.C., 1995), pp. 87–106.

60. Oscar C. Pogge, "Family Relationships and Old-Age and Survivor's Insurance," *Social Security Bulletin* (1945): 8; Michael Fooner, "Some Child Welfare Problems in Social Insurance," *Social Service Review* 16 (1942): 652–53. Fooner says that there is no record in either congressional hearings or debates of the intestacy provision, and thus it is unclear why the law was written this way.

widows, it was now replaced by survivors' benefits, leaving ADC for all other single mothers and thus altering the character and goals of that policy. Moreover, reeling under the fiscal pressures of the depression, state governments acted to change the composition of beneficiaries. Massachusetts, for example, broadened the definition of eligible mothers in order to shift women and children to federally subsidized ADC and relieve fiscal pressure on unsubsidized general relief. As a consequence, the proportion of widows receiving ADC declined from 71 percent in 1935 to 47 percent in 1942; unmarried mothers made up an increasing proportion of the ADC caseload, rising from 2 percent of the beneficiaries in 1936 to 7 percent in 1939.[61]

Together the 1939 amendments and state policies forged distinctions between widows and other mothers, between legitimate and illegitimate recipients of public aid. Mothers of so-called illegitimate children were entitled to aid but the children of two-parent but needy families were not. In the context of the social insurance exclusions and widening means tests of the late 1930s, this inevitably led to racial distinctions in social policy. Mothers' pensions had historically aided white women and children, a pattern that began to shift during the depression despite racially motivated exclusion. Although ADC remained a program used primarily by white women at the end of the depression, the process of occupational displacement and the exclusion from social insurance operated to increase the proportion of black families receiving public aid, except in the South. Black families accounted for 3 percent of the mothers' pensions caseload in 1931, increasing to between 14 and 17 percent by 1937–40.[62]

The growing concentration of African Americans on work relief, general relief, and ADC was accompanied by rising concern over the implications of prolonged unemployment for the structure of black families. Long before the Moynihan Report made illegitimacy and black female-headed families central to the debate over welfare, New Dealers, social workers, and black elites were already using similar language. E. Franklin Frazier reported that anywhere from 10 to 30 percent of black families in the North were headed by women, and that, in comparison to their white counterparts, a larger proportion of black women on relief were "unattached women." Frazier

61. Martha Derthick, *The Influence of Federal Grants* (Cambridge, Mass., 1970), pp. 61–63; Elizabeth Alling and Agnes Leisy, "Aid to Dependent Children in a Postwar Year," *Public Assistance Report,* no. 7, Social Security Administration (Washington, D.C., 1950), p. 8.

62. Winifred Bell, *Aid to Dependent Children* (New York, 1965), p. 9; Myrdal, *American Dilemma,* p. 359.

thought that the depression undoubtedly eroded the foundations of the black family under pressure from unemployment and migration, though reliable evidence on this question is hard to come by. The FERA apparently believed that black poverty, unlike white poverty, was a problem of "female dependency often involving children."[63] The St. Louis Urban League worried about the "increasing number of Negro women who are finding their way into domestic service as a way of taking up the slack resulting from the scarcity of jobs for men; that this development portends a bad future for Negro family life and the welfare of its children, no one can deny." The Urban League's strong stand in favor of a permanent public employment program was undertaken in light of such fears.[64] In a comment all too redolent of contemporary discourse, a Detroit social worker said "Negro women are frequently left as the economic heads of families when their husbands can neither contribute prestige nor security and drift away from the family scene."[65]

The Legacies of New Deal Social Policy

The very New Deal policies that Ickes, Hopkins, and others assumed would diminish racial prejudice actually embedded the color line in the nascent welfare state and reproduced the racism of Myrdal's vicious circle. This outcome reflects an antinomy between the logic of New Deal social policy—which was predicated on business confidence and the fiscal assumptions underlying employment policies—and labor markets riddled by racial discrimination. In the absence of either a faster recovery and a larger job creation program, or a more concerted effort to allocate jobs on the basis of racial quotas, blacks would be relegated to general relief and work relief. Outside of Harold Ickes's job quotas in the PWA, which were not altogether successful, none of the New Dealers were prepared to make race an issue, as concerned as they were over racial discrimination.

The New Deal put blacks and whites on a different footing in the new welfare state, and in this context, all too many whites equated relief with black indolence. Although many African American families were saved from

63. Frazier, "Some Effects of the Depression," p. 494.

64. Nancy J. Weiss, *The National Urban League, 1910–1940* (New York, 1974), p. 253; Hamilton, "The National Urban League," p. 326.

65. Murphy, "Social Effects of Prolonged Unemployment," pp. 33–34. Murphy's prescient report reads as if it were written yesterday.

extreme deprivation and degradation, by the end of the decade, Newton Baker's fears about the effects of relief had become an object of political comment. An aide to Thomas Dewey voiced a widely held view when he told a black newspaper that "the New Deal segregated the Negro out of America's productive life and provided for him a separate relief economy which was without a future."[66]

African Americans were ambivalent about the implications of the new political order. The *Kansas City Call* sounded an optimistic note at the end of the decade. In a hopeful editorial defending work relief, it argued:

> "The United States has from the moment it gave the freed Negro employment, called him lazy and paid him less than white workers on the claim that only by keeping him 'broke' could he be made to work. Today it pays the WPAs a wage above what that Negro was given for his full time and best endeavor. The same public which accepts the WPA's indifference and accounts for it on the ground that no better is to be expected for so little money, cannot help acquitting the underpaid Negro worker of being lazy."[67]

Other African Americans were far less sanguine and warned of the dangers of joblessness and relief in a society that had historically taken independent work as an alternative to slavery.

The failures of racial liberalism aside, African Americans abandoned neither their desire for an alliance with white workers nor New Deal universalism. This was the outcome of an African American debate over race, class, and the New Deal in which Ralph Bunche and W. E. B. Du Bois occupied opposite poles. Bunche remained a staunch proponent of a biracial working-class coalition, characterizing "Don't-Buy-Where-You-Can't-Work" protests as "narrowly racial" and an impediment to any alliance with white workers.[68] Du Bois's critique was aimed at what he regarded as the myopic, even naive, beliefs of prominent black radicals like Ralph Bunche or Abram Harris, who deluded themselves about the possibilities for a biracial working-class coalition. "White labor has to hate scabs," Du Bois argued, "but it hates black scabs not because they are scabs but because they are black."

66. *California Eagle,* May 25, 1940, RG 69/70.71, WPA, Negro Press Digest, 1936–1940, box 4, NA.

67. *Kansas City Call,* September 10, 1938.

68. Ralph Bunche, "Negroes in the Depression" in *Black Protest Thought,* pp. 122–31.

Although he advocated self-organization for economic security, even if it had to be done on a segregated basis, Du Bois was less a separatist than an advocate of what would later be called black power.[69]

By the end of the decade, however, the fury of this debate had dissipated, and the most important outcome was the insertion of social class and economic issues into a political program that hitherto had been dominated by middle-class demands for civil rights. William Hastie of the NAACP had publicly endorsed a broad economic agenda and enjoined local chapters to combine agitation for the black disadvantaged with agitation for the white disadvantaged.[70] Du Bois's call for blacks to come forth and demand their share coexisted comfortably with Bunche's insistence that black workers join unions. Among middle-class organizations such as the NUL and grassroots organizations such as Cleveland's Future Outlook League, race and class were combined in fruitful ways.

African Americans at the end of the depression believed that racial equality and New Deal universalism could be combined, and they had an interest in both. Without civil and political rights, blacks would be relegated to a nether world; but any solution to racial inequality would fail without broad, comprehensive social policies. Overcoming the antinomy between race and class would necessitate undoing the racial stratification of New Deal social policy, and whether or not that would happen would be decided by the furious struggle over the future of the American welfare state waged in the 1940s.

69. W. E. B. Du Bois, "A Negro Nation within the Nation," p. 566, and *Dusk of Dawn* (New York, 1968), pp. 203, 205–8. Du Bois's ideal black politician was Chicago Alderman William L. Dawson, whom he approvingly quoted as saying, "I am not playing Party politics but race politics."

70. William H. Hastie, "A Look at the NAACP," in *Black Protest Thought,* p. 219.

PART II

THE EMERGENCE OF
TRUNCATED UNIVERSALISM

CHAPTER THREE

Stacking the Deck: The Truncation of Universalism, 1939–1950

The Negro voter will support a political party which by words and deeds shows its determination to work for full citizenship status for thirteen million American Negroes and to better the lot of all disadvantaged people in this country. . . . The party or candidate who refuses to support a progressive public program for full post war employment or opposes an enlarged and unsegregated program of government-financed housing, or seeks to destroy organized labor is as much the enemy of the Negro as is he who would prevent the Negro from voting.

— A DECLARATION BY NEGRO VOTERS

The best reason to reduce taxes is to reduce . . . inflated ideas of the proper scope of bureaucratic authority.

— SENATOR ROBERT A. TAFT

Harry Truman's aborted Fair Deal, a turning point in the development of the American welfare state, embodied an agenda for a comprehensive, universalistic welfare state. The plan for this state was first approved by Roosevelt at the outset of the war and included national health and disability insurance, revisions to social security, nationalization of unemployment compensation, public housing legislation, federal aid to education, and changes in the minimum wage. Most of these legislative proposals were defeated; all that survived were increased benefits and coverage for Old Age and Survivor's Insurance (OASI), public housing, and the minimum wage. Congress left unemployment compensation under control of the states, substituted a new categorical public assistance title for disability insurance, and used temporary policies, tantamount to a new WPA, for deserving groups of men—veterans, rail workers, seamen—to avert unemployment after the war. The outcome was a pattern of social provision I call *truncated universalism,* a welfare state that mingled the equalitarian promise of universal social insurance with a fragmented assortment of public policies (veterans and housing programs) and private social policies (health and pension benefits) subject to collective bargaining.

This chapter examines the origins and triumph of truncated universalism. It grew out of a three-cornered struggle between Republicans and the polarized Democratic party, in which southern Democrats served as both opponents and proponents of the welfare state. After the 1938 elections, liberal Democrats confronted a coalition composed of a resurgent and homogeneous Republican party, which was hostile to the New Deal, and southern Democrats. Democratic losses to Republicans in the Northeast and Midwest made the party more dependent on southern Democrats, who held 50 percent of Democratic seats (a margin they maintained until 1964). FDR lost the flexibility he had had in 1934–36, when southerners held only two-fifths of Democratic seats and he could depend on the support of Progressive Republicans.[1] That the conservative coalition put a hammerlock on the postwar agenda of New Deal liberals is well known; that it offered an alternative is less well understood or appreciated.

Southern Democrats were the arbiters. They were not unalterably opposed to the idea of a welfare state, but neither did they simply go along with the wartime New Deal agenda. Southerners had a different view of acceptable social policy than northern Democrats.[2] They were also at loggerheads with those Republicans opposed to spending or adding to the New Deal. The marriage of Republicans and southern Democrats was neither simply a tactical alliance that drew like-minded politicians from different parties together nor a consequence of the lack of programmatic parties and the historical weakness of the U.S. state.[3] It was a class coalition uniting regional business elites with small-town and rural economic interests in the North and South against a national welfare state. It was a fragile coalition, frequently ruptured

1. Milton Plesur, "The Republican Congressional Comeback of 1938," *Review of Politics* 24 (1962): 543–44; David Brady, *Critical Elections and Congressional Policy Making* (Stanford, 1988), pp. 96–97, 102; David Mayhew, *Party Loyalty among Congressmen* (Cambridge, 1966), pp. 165–67.

2. Ira Katznelson, Kim Geiger, and Daniel Kryder ("Limiting Liberalism: The Southern Veto in Congress," *Political Science Quarterly* 108 [1993]: 283–306) argue that the main differences between the northern and southern wings of the Democratic party centered on labor and racial issues, not social policy, although I think they overstate southern agreement with liberal social policies during and after the war.

3. Theda Skocpol and Edwin Amenta, "Redefining the New Deal: World War II and the Development of Social Provision in the United States," in *The Politics of Social Policy in the United States*, ed. Margaret Weir, Ann Orloff, and Theda Skocpol (Princeton, N.J., 1988), pp. 81–123.

when the class agenda for a limited welfare state conflicted with competing demands for spending by regional (southern) and interest-group blocs.

This three-cornered partisan struggle was mediated by conflict over money and race. Support or opposition to social policies often depended on how the question of racial equality or the conflict over tax and spending measures determined preferences for specific policies and decisions. Partisan conflict over the welfare state coincided with the birth of the modern civil rights movement. War unleashed racial conflict, fostering racial consciousness and raising the stakes of any policy change for southerners. African Americans, whether trade unionists or civil rights leaders, were among the most steadfast defenders of a national, universalistic welfare state. Both the black leaders who signed the "Declaration by Negro Voters" and black workers believed that the struggle for civil rights was also a struggle for economic and social rights.[4] Indeed, Roy Wilkins, Lester Granger, Clarence Mitchell, and many other African Americans regarded social rights as sufficiently important that they testified in Congress on behalf of bills for national health insurance and full employment even though none of the bills contained any antidiscrimination provisions.[5] But if northern Democrats wanted southern votes for social welfare legislation, they had to temporize on the question of southern apartheid. Republicans hostile to liberal social policies used nondiscrimination riders to drive away southern votes.

Money, however, complicated any calculations of racial interests for southerners, who were intent on using federal resources to industrialize the South. Conflict over taxes and spending also framed policy alternatives and dictated choices for Republicans and northern Democrats. For Republicans, tax cuts were the centerpiece of their agenda upon acquiring majority control of the 80th Congress in 1946, a position that often put them at odds with southerners. And Truman's Fair Deal agenda was molded in a fiscal context governed by inflation rather than unemployment and a concern for business confidence. Truman's social policy choices, thus, were shaped by the fiscal imperatives of the high-tax regime that was a legacy of the war, the emerging

4. The "Declaration by Negro Voters," issued before the 1944 elections, was signed by many of the most important black leaders of the time, including Thurgood Marshall, A. Philip Randolph, Mary McLeod Bethune, William H. Hastie, George L.-P. Weaver, Walter White, and Max Yergan.

5. Dona Cooper Hamilton and Charles V. Hamilton, "The Dual Agenda of African American Organizations since the New Deal: Social Welfare Policies and Civil Rights," *Political Science Quarterly* 107 (1992): 442–43; Earl Lewis, *In Their Own Interests* (Berkeley, 1991), pp. 174, 187.

budgetary commitments of the cold war, and his commitment to the agenda of the Third New Deal.

This chapter focuses on the roots of the 1940s political alignments and explores how money and race led to the demise of the Third New Deal and eventuated in the truncation of New Deal universalism.[6]

Race and Money in the Political Alignments of the 1940s

The political struggle over the Fair Deal, as the *Congressional Quarterly* reported in its summary of the debate over social security during the late 1940s, centered on "whether the basic Old Age and Survivor's Insurance system should be improved in order to fulfill its originally intended role, or whether it should be scrapped or reduced in favor of more emphasis on the charity approach."[7] This issue of whether to expand social insurance or replace it with means-tested policies was fundamental to the political debate regarding the welfare state and defined the alternative agendas of liberal Democrats and the conservative coalition.

The Third New Deal was obliquely announced by FDR in his 1942 budget message in a request to extend coverage of social security as a way of financing the war. It was the postwar agenda of a dynamic and centralizing executive. Its origins can be traced to the formal reassessment of New Deal social policy that followed the recession of 1937–38. The Roosevelt administration was intent on remedying the most egregious deficiencies of the 1935 policy settlement and erecting on the foundations of the 1935 Social Security Act a "cradle to grave" welfare state. It planned to extend coverage of old-age and unemployment insurance to excluded occupations, mainly agricultural and domestic workers; to establish national standards for unemployment compensation; and to augment categorical public assistance programs with the creation of a new general public assistance program, which amounted to federalizing general relief. To the original policy settlement the administration proposed adding three new social insurance programs—temporary disability, permanent disability, and national health insurance—and

6. My interpretation of the events of the 1940s differs from that of Ira Katznelson and Bruce Pietrykowski, "Rebuilding the American State: Evidence from the 1940s," *Studies in American Political Development* 5 (1991): 301–39. For my analysis of their argument, see "State Capacity and Political Choice: Interpreting the Failure of the Third New Deal," *Studies in American Political Development* 9 (1995): 187–212.

7. Congressional Quarterly, *Congress and the Nation, 1945–1964* (Washington, D.C., 1965), p. 1245.

a scheme for variable public assistance grants to increase the ability of poor (mostly southern) states to undertake welfare programs and liberalize eligibility and benefit standards.[8]

New Dealers anchored their proposals in a "new bill of economic rights" encompassing the right to work, fair play, economic security, freedom from want, and a broad conception of equality of opportunity. Spending was at the core of their agenda and the vehicle to ensure a fair distribution of the fruits of capitalism. The Third New Deal fused economic growth with equity. "We stand on the threshold of an economy of abundance," said the National Resources Planning Board (NRPB). "This generation has it within its power not only to produce in plenty but to distribute that plenty." This credo signified a metamorphosis of New Deal liberalism from a concern with structural reform of the economy to a commitment to economic growth. The role of the government was akin to that of a balance wheel: it undertook the planning necessary to stabilize the business cycle and maintain aggregate demand without altering the structure of the economy.[9]

The "growth with equity" credo reflected the fusion of left-Keynesian and social-work critiques of New Deal policies. Throughout the late 1930s, social workers hammered away at the failures of the WPA, the inadequacies of unemployment compensation, and the need for a more inclusive welfare state. Keynesian economists and New Dealers allied with labor lobbied for a regime of compensatory spending and mass consumption. The merger of these forces occurred when Mariner Eccles and Harry Hopkins convinced Roosevelt to abandon temporarily the administration's so-called balanced budget policy during the 1937–38 recession. Hopkins fought for a permanent work relief policy, while Eccles agitated for an alternative to the structural economic reforms of the early New Deal. With the onset of war, the Hopkins-Eccles critique was integrated into the postwar planning effort by the NRPB.[10]

The liberal agenda for social renewal was propelled forward by a mixture

8. National Resources Planning Board (NRPB), *Security, Work and Relief Policies* (Washington, D.C., 1942), chaps. 12–13; Social Security Board, "An Expanded Social Security Program," April 23, 1941, RG 51, ser. 39.27, box 43, NA.

9. NRPB, *National Resources Development: Report for 1943,* pt. 1, *Post-War Plan and Program* (Washington, D.C., 1943), pp. 3–4; Patrick G. Brady, "Toward Security: Postwar Economic and Social Planning in the Executive Office" (Ph.D. diss., Rutgers University, 1975), pp. 49–50, 90–91; Alan Brinkley, *The End of Reform: New Deal Liberalism in Recession and War* (New York, 1995).

10. Frederick Delano to FDR, August 25, 1939, app. D-1, OF 1092, NRPB, box 3, FDRL. Delano certainly reflected the views of Hopkins and others when he told Roosevelt, "the relief problem is no longer an emergency sickness—it is chronic. We need a long range policy."

of bureaucratic initiative and electoral pressure. Arthur Altmeyer, by then chair of the Social Security Board (SSB), embarked on an ambitious and calculated political strategy to add health and disability insurance to OASI and make universal coverage a reality. He advised Roosevelt that "it seems increasingly possible to provide cradle-to-grave insurance against unemployment, sickness, permanent disability, old age, and death, without any increase in the employers' payroll taxes beyond the automatic step-up schedule now contained in the Social Security Act, if there were equal three-way contributions by employers, employees, and the government."[11] This development occurred against a backdrop of furious agitation over the shortcomings of social insurance by the labor movement and the Townsend movement, which were clamoring for an alternative to social security. Both the Congress of Industrial Organizations (CIO) and Townsendites favored replacing social security with noncontributory, "flat" pensions. Unemployment insurance became an issue with the introduction of the McCormack Amendment during congressional debate on the 1939 Social Security amendments. Inspired by business demands for a reduction in unemployment taxes as reserves accumulated, the amendment would have lowered payroll taxes. Labor officials were apoplectic, screaming that "benefits would be permanently frozen at low levels."[12]

The Third New Deal, taken together, amounted to a proposal for a massive expansion in the infrastructure of social protection. It was, quipped one of the Keynesian economists in the Budget Bureau, a "painless way to achieve full employment, preserve private enterprise, and deter a shift to fascism or socialism."[13] Although some conservative Republicans and southern Democrats preferred to repeal the New Deal, and pursued this goal with uncommon zeal during the war, most were intent on containing and reshaping the liberal impulse for social reform. Their political strategy was analogous to that used by businessmen to thwart resurgent unions by responding with tough, legalistic action that did not interfere with organizing efforts but asserted managerial prerogatives and enforced discipline.[14] In

---

11. Altmeyer to Steven Early, March 30, 1940, p. 2, OF 1710, box 2, FDRL; Social Security Board, "Expanded Social Security Program," p. 2.

12. United States Senate, Committee on Finance, *Hearings on H.R. 6635*, 76th Cong., 1st sess., 1939, pp. 335, 343; Jerry Cates, *Insuring Inequality: Administrative Leadership in Social Security, 1935–1954* (Ann Arbor, Mich., 1983), pp. 54, 56–57.

13. Brady, "Toward Security," p. 198.

14. Howell Harris, *The Right to Manage: Industrial Relations Policies of American Business in the 1940s* (Madison, Wisc., 1982), p. 29.

acting to halt the New Deal, congressional conservatives disavowed the Third New Deal's dictum that public aid should be permanent, preferring temporary programs to deal with unemployment. And they concentrated on establishing a means-tested welfare state that subordinated social policy to the prerogatives of business and local political elites. Robert Taft, one of the foremost exponents of this alternative, said:

> [The free enterprise system] has certain definite faults. . . . While the average is high, the necessary inequality of the system leaves millions poor. . . . If the free enterprise system does not do its best to prevent hardship and poverty, it will find itself superseded by a less progressive system which does. . . . [Congress] must undertake to put a floor under essential things to give all a minimum standard of living, and all children an opportunity to get a start in life."[15]

Conservatives combined means-tested redistribution with privatization through federal underwriting of voluntary health and pension plans and private housing credit. Redistribution had a double meaning, signifying the potential benefits to the South, the poorest region in the nation, as well as to the poor. What Taft and others were proposing was a locally controlled, public means-tested grant-in-aid system that would be tilted toward the poorer states, which in the political lexicon of the late 1940s meant the South. It was publicly juxtaposed to voluntary, private systems of social support, such as private health insurance, for middle-class Americans.[16]

The conservative architects of this agenda sought to uncouple the link New Dealers had fashioned between social policy and macroeconomic policy. They did not reject deficit spending; they were quite willing to cut taxes even if it meant increasing the deficit. What they rejected was a regime of permanent spending, denying that there was any linkage between social welfare spending, consumption, and economic growth; instead, they embraced temporary remedies for unemployment. Conservatives were strongly opposed to using social policy to raise the standard of living throughout the country, a posture which would drive up local wage rates. They favored local control in order to subordinate federal social policy to the market. Closely linked to these aims was a desire to limit the long-run costs of social policy. This could be done, conservatives thought, by relying on

15. James T. Patterson, *Mr. Republican: A Biography of Robert A. Taft* (Boston, 1972), p. 319.

16. The most complete statement of this alternative was Lewis Merriam, *Relief and Social Security* (Washington, D.C., 1946), chaps. 17–22.

means-tested policies and fashioning private, voluntary alternatives to a public welfare state.

Race and money explains both the rise of a conservative opposition to the New Deal and the appearance of a conservative alternative. Together they reveal the two faces of southern politics. Race was injected into the partisan struggle over the welfare state when A. Philip Randolph threatened a march on Washington, D.C., over the denial of defense jobs to African Americans. Roosevelt responded by creating the Fair Employment Practices Commission (FEPC). Anger over racial discrimination in defense industries and wartime hypocrisy provoked conflict, demonstrations, and rioting at military bases and elsewhere as blacks abandoned their World War I stand. This stand had called for suppressing racial grievances for the duration of the war; most blacks believed that agitation for democracy at home was just as important as victory abroad.[17] As the war was ending, African Americans were poised to move forward with a broad civil rights agenda, armed with the knowledge that their votes mattered for Democratic presidential candidates. Both Roosevelt and Truman worried about the erosion of the black vote as southern hostility to civil rights rose, and in a 1944 campaign speech in Chicago, FDR—to the cheers of 200,000 African Americans—denounced the poll tax, proclaimed his opposition to racial barriers, and said he would fight for a permanent FEPC. Truman followed Roosevelt's wartime gestures with a decision to desegregate the army as well as with the appointment of a commission on civil rights, which he did after a group of whites assaulted and murdered a black serviceman in South Carolina. By 1948 it was clear to Truman and his advisers that his reelection required explicit appeals to black voters, even if it raised the ire of southern democrats.[18]

Southerners saw a direct and immediate threat to Jim Crow in these events. Their opposition to any national social policies became a foregone conclusion when the NRPB made racial justice part of the liberal social welfare agenda. The NRPB Report, *Security, Work, and Relief Policies*, concluded "it is . . . evident that the majority of Negroes are at a marked disadvantage in access to public aid" and repeatedly called attention to the racial prejudice of southern relief efforts and varied patterns of exclusion in the North.

17. Richard M. Dalifume, *Desegregation of the U.S. Armed Forces* (Columbia, S.C. 1969), p. 109.

18. St. Clair Drake and Horace Cayton, *Black Metropolis: A Study of Negro Life in a Northern City* (New York, 1945), p. 359; Charles Hamilton, *Adam Clayton Powell, Jr.: The Political Biography of an American Dilemma* (New York, 1991), pp. 168–69; Clark Clifford to President, November 19, 1947, pp. 12, 39–40, Clark Clifford Papers, box 2, HSTL.

It specifically recommended that racial discrimination in the distribution of public aid be prohibited and called for "equal access to elementary and high school education" for all children.[19] The Democratic party, not surprisingly, became more polarized over social welfare issues during the late 1940s; the gap between the percentage of northern Democrats and southern Democrats supporting the Democratic administrations of this period increased from 26.7 percent during 1939–46 (76th–79th Congresses) to 44.4 percent during 1947–52 (80th-82d Congresses). Southern Democrats supported the Truman administration's social welfare initiatives 46 percent of the time compared to 91 percent for northern Democrats.[20]

Yet, paradoxically, southern Democrats were often in the forefront of efforts to increase federal spending for social welfare. Many southerners remained committed spenders—even rabid racists like Theodore Bilbo, who by 1944 had declared war on the northern Democratic party. One of the most revealing congressional votes during the war occurred when Roosevelt, on Morgenthau's advice, tried to reduce funding for the WPA. This vote aligned Roosevelt with his arch foes, Walter George, "Cotton Ed" Smith, and Harry Byrd, all of whom voted to cut the WPA, and against southern liberals such as Allen Ellender, Claude Pepper, Hattie Caraway, and populists like Bilbo, who voted in favor of spending.[21] Many southerners resisted the siren call of fiscal conservatism and cared more about distributive politics than balanced budgets. After failing to secure full federal funding of public assistance in 1935, southern politicians agitated for redistributive or variable grants-in-aid that would link state income or fiscal capacity with proportionate federal assistance. Opposition to spending was never a reliable indicator of southern proclivities. Senator James Byrnes (a Democrat from South Carolina) waged a ferocious battle against WPA spending, but after 1938 when relief expenditures were increased and later when Congress adopted a policy of equalizing WPA wage rates, Byrnes and the rest of the South eagerly accepted federal dollars. As Donald Howard cynically

19. NRPB, *Security, Work and Relief,* pp. 160, 519, 548; Robert Garson, *The Democratic Party and the Politics of Sectionalism, 1941–1948* (Baton Rouge, La., 1974), pp. 21–23, 41–42, 48, 52–53.

20. Barbara Sinclair, *Congressional Realignment, 1925–1978* (Austin, Tex., 1982), pp. 55, 57. See also John Robert Moore, "The Conservative Coalition in the United States Senate, 1942–1945," *Journal of Southern History* (1967): 368–76.

21. Lawrence H. Curry Jr., "Southern Senators and Their Roll-Call Votes in Congress, 1941–1944" (Ph.D. diss., Duke University, 1971), p. 166. See also Katznelson, Geiger, and Kryder, "Limiting Liberalism," pp. 291–93.

observed, southern states were quite willing to reduce regional differences in wages so long as the federal government paid.[22] This devotion to spending meant a southern signature could be found on many proposals for new social policies during the 1940s.

Southern ambivalence toward the welfare state—opposition to a national welfare state, but support for federal spending—had less to do with the lure of patronage than with southern poverty. Beginning in the late 1930s, both Roosevelt and southern politicians independently schemed to use federal policies and funds to industrialize the South. New Dealers directed defense contracts to the South during the war. Their sensitivity to southern poverty was accompanied by rising pressure for federal investment in roads, harbors, airports, and agriculture, as well as in welfare spending. Harry Byrd's fiscal conservatism was not so much atypical of southern politicians as it was more relentlessly pursued. Yet not even Byrd was immune to the lure of federal dollars: many roads were built by the Byrd machine in Virginia with federal assistance. Indeed, almost one-third of all federal dollars spent under the federal highway program after 1940 were spent in the South. Federal dollars were sought by a nascent industrial elite fully committed to the industrialization of the South. It was an elite which had replaced an older leadership rooted in the South's agrarian past. What was distinctive about these "southern Whigs," as Bruce Schulman has called them, was their commitment to ending the South's economic and political isolation and their more moderate stance on the question of civil rights. They embraced federal assistance, knowing that it would spur economic development, but fought against the imposition of federal policies that would regulate business, advantage labor, or undo southern apartheid.[23]

These reflections cast the political alignments of the 1940s in a much different light than arguments which stress the role of political institutions. While it is true that the fragmentation of American political institutions frustrates broad coalitions rooted in divisions of class and reinforces the localism characteristic of American politics, an analysis of the conservative coalition in light of institutional structure is insufficient. It omits the class basis of opposition to the New Deal that was undeniably present. Moreover,

22. Donald Howard, *The WPA and Federal Relief Policy* (New York, 1941), pp. 162–63, 771; George Tindall, *The Emergence of the New South, 1913–1945* (Baton Rouge, La., 1967), pp. 483–84.

23. Bruce J. Schulman, *From Cotton Belt to Sunbelt: Federal Policy, Economic Development and the Transformation of the South, 1938–1980* (New York, 1991), pp. 116–17, 123–31.

an institutional analysis cannot explain the emergence of the conservative alternative to the Third New Deal. The conservative coalition aligned regional business elites. These were people who had common interest in preventing the ascendance of a national, federally controlled welfare state—mostly because of its implications for wage rates and the growth of the public sector—but who had divergent economic interests. Northern businessmen opposed federal spending while southern businessmen stood to benefit. Hence regional polarities within the party system competed with, and overlapped, class divisions, and this situation frequently led to conflict within the conservative coalition. These facts account both for opposition to the Third New Deal and for support of means-tested redistribution.

The stalling of the New Deal in the early 1940s resulted from the convergence of different kinds of opposition (class- and interest-group-based opposition, the latter most often regional) and its solidification into an alliance. Presidential initiatives for national social policies and the aggressive use of federal power to manage the economy not only challenged the power and prerogatives of a resurgent business class in the North and the economic and racial interests of white southerners. Southern members of Congress intent on protecting the building blocks of the southern New Deal—public works, welfare, veterans programs, and agriculture—opposed presidential control of the budget. Institutional and class divisions converged, or to put it another way, congressional fears of a centralizing presidency were buttressed and fueled by increasing class conflict over the shape of the welfare state.[24]

This pattern of conflict is apparent in the struggle over federal spending, the central domestic political conflict of the 1940s. Although debates over spending and deficits were always couched in the language of fiscal conservatism and the need for balanced budgets, they really centered on two conflicts. The first was an institutional conflict between a centralizing presidency and Congress, where the key issue was who controlled federal spending. Since any centralization of spending diminished congressional control and the alliance between congressional committees and federal agencies, it was opposed by an alliance of regional and nonregional interest groups. Such opposition was never against spending.[25]

The other axis of conflict turned on the implications of *increased* public spending for economic and social purposes. Most businessmen thought

24. Arthur Holmans puts it this way: "the institutional clash became merged with the straight-forward political clash when the anti-Roosevelt coalition gained control of the Congress" (Holmans, *United States Fiscal Policy, 1945–1959* [New York, 1961], p. 28).
25. Brady, "Toward Security," p. 10.

spending could not be contained; the lure of distributive politics and citizen demand would inevitably lead to a bloated public sector and permanently high levels of taxation. As Robert Collins observed, "the spending solution posed a clear challenge to some of the more entrenched verities of business ideology. . . . Nor was it clear that government involvement could or would be minimized so as to ensure continued business domination of economic decision-making." A full-employment policy based on deficit spending also threatened to bid up the price of labor and to diminish labor discipline. At a time when the relationship between business and labor was unstable, with each side seeking leverage, as was the case during the war, it is easy to see why the idea of deficit spending became so politicized.[26]

The conservative coalition was fully united when the issue involved an opposing class agenda. Yet conflict between southern Democrats and Republicans was never far below the surface, arising with tax policy and variable grants for public assistance. Republican party platforms throughout the 1940s supported means-tested policies and the redistribution of federal aid to the South, although the party made an exception of Old Age and Survivor's Insurance. Robert Taft's more active involvement in fashioning a conservative alternative to the Third New Deal reflected not just constituency pressures and a narrow election victory in 1944 but his presidential ambitions. Taft was not alone among Republicans, but the spending implications of means-tested redistribution were not acceptable to those Republicans ardently pursuing tax and expenditure cuts. Support for means-tested redistribution was always stronger among Senate Republicans than House Republicans, a reflection to some degree of the importance of union voters in statewide elections.

Roosevelt and northern Democrats were put in the position of luring southern support with fiscal gambits if they wanted new social policies. This consideration explains Roosevelt's change of mind on variable grants. After rejecting the idea when Congress considered it in 1939, he strongly endorsed it when he announced his social security proposals, publicly saying that low public assistance payments in the poorer states, mainly the South, were due to lack of fiscal capacity, not any reluctance to pay higher benefits. In a calculated appeal to the South, FDR said, "We will reverse the old idea 'To him that hath shall be given' and go to help the people that 'hath not.'" FDR's acceptance of variable grants reflected the change in Democratic attitudes

---

26. Robert Collins, *The Business Response to Keynes* (New York, 1981), pp. 10–11, 135.

toward the South. They not only saw the South as an economic basket case, but believed that southern support for the Third New Deal could be bought with federal assistance. The Social Security Board never passed up an opportunity to point out that the South would be a major beneficiary of any expansion of Social Security.[27]

Variable grants—or rather, finding ways to divert more public assistance money to the South—remained a prominent feature of the Democratic party agenda for the next twenty years. It was the price of victory in any knotty legislative battle. In a memorandum on the Knowland amendment to the 1950 Social Security Act, one of Truman's advisers explained the underlying quid pro quo that governed Democratic legislative strategy. Truman was opposed to an amendment which would allow states, if they so chose, to deny unemployment benefits to workers on strike and defy federal law, but he was faced with a conference report that contained the amendment and was unable to veto the bill. His only recourse was recommittal of the report. But to do so he had to buy off the South. His adviser stated that "if [the administration] seriously desired to get recommittal, the leadership would be adding the so-called Mills formula for increased public assistance funds (this means a $120 million kitty mostly for the Southern Senators). Since the Mills formula is not to be one of the arguments for recommittal, we should take for granted that the fight is not seriously intended."[28]

Accepting southern support for a welfare state or any spending policy meant northern acquiescence to racial apartheid in the South. The Social Security Board tended to downplay the matter of racial discrimination while importuning the South, yet rarely could discrimination be avoided. Republicans, not northern Democrats, eagerly introduced race into the political fray, wielding nondiscrimination amendments as a tool to sink social welfare legislation. Federal aid to education provides a stunning illustration of a casualty of Republican intransigence. Lister Hill, a southern liberal, and Elbert Thomas, a western Democrat, introduced a bill in 1943 authorizing $200 million in federal aid to schools that had strong southern support until a Re-

27. Schulman, *Cotton Belt to Sunbelt,* pp. 48, 50–52, 60–61; Ellen S. Woodward, "What Social Security Can Mean to the South," *Social Security Bulletin* (July 1945): 2–5. See also the reports of the Social Security Advisory Councils, especially its 1948 report on OASI.

28. Neustadt to Spingarn, August 5, 1950, Charles Murphy Papers, box 27, folder "Social Security," HSTL. Like Roosevelt, Truman consistently supported variable grants; see, for example, his Message to Congress, May 24, 1948, *Public Papers of the Presidents of the United States: Harry S. Truman, 1948* (Washington, D.C., 1949), pp. 274–75.

publican offered an amendment stipulating that the funds must be spent equally for white and black schools. Republicans were never averse to manipulating racial issues in order to get their way. When southern support for a tax cut failed to materialize in 1947, one angry Republican threatened to introduce an anti–poll tax bill "to get even with Southern Democrats who helped kill the income tax reduction bill."[29] Use of the "race card" gave opponents of the welfare state a formidable weapon that remained in their arsenal until passage of the Civil Rights Act of 1964 and put northern Democrats in a position of accepting, or at least not opposing, Jim Crow social policies.

The Conservative Undoing of FDR's Plans for the Third New Deal

Senator Robert Wagner, in a letter to an old friend during the war, described the emerging conservative strategy to derail liberal plans for a comprehensive welfare state, presciently forecasting the outcome:

> All our Congressmen are for security for the returning armed forces. So are we and the provisions of the bill will show it. Our Republican friends and some Southern democrats want to limit the expansion of social security to the returning armed forces and no one else. . . . [Senator Arthur] Vandenberg [Republican, Michigan] also wants to freeze . . . the [social security] tax at the present rate. . . . He expects it will help him with the large employer.[30]

The initial skirmishes over the postwar welfare state concerned two issues: whether to freeze scheduled increases in the social security tax and whether to federalize unemployment compensation and pass a full employment policy. Both issues were fundamental to enactment of the liberal agenda, and in both cases conservatives won the legislative battle.

The fight over the social security tax increases was a fight over whether to have an integrated system of national social insurance. Arthur Altmeyer planned to finance the addition of disability and health insurance to the social security system by tapping into reserves of the old-age and unemployment trust funds, which were rapidly accumulating in the wartime economy. Altmeyer and the other members of the Social Security Board remained wedded to a social security reserve during the 1940s precisely because of its

29. Holmans, *U.S. Fiscal Policy,* p. 78.
30. Robert Wagner to Maurine Mulliner, 1943, Wilbur Cohen Papers, box 1, FDRL.

advantages for expansion, even though Congress abandoned it for a pay-as-you-go system in 1939. By the time war broke out Altmeyer was worried that Congress would postpone a scheduled rise in the OASI tax rate in 1942 and state legislatures would cut unemployment taxes. Either action would have doomed his plans. At the same time FDR had decided that an increase in social security taxes would dampen war-induced inflation. Gerhard Colm, an influential Keynesian economist within the administration, thought it would be possible to raise taxes and increase benefits since "the increase in payroll taxes would presumably curtail mass luxury consumption of wage earners while the increase in social insurance benefits would presumably add to the consumption of life necessities of persons deprived of earning power," a sentiment echoed by Lauchin Currie, one of Roosevelt's key aides. The marriage between an expansion of social security and war finance was consummated when Henry Morgenthau Jr., gave the treasury's enthusiastic approval.[31]

Arthur Altmeyer's dream of an integrated social insurance program, enacted at one blow, died with the social security tax freezes of the 1940s. Between 1939 and 1950 Congress deferred scheduled tax increases on eight separate occasions, and with the exception of some minor amendments in 1946, Congress refused to raise benefits, and it deferred consideration of whether to extend coverage to those excluded from old-age insurance. The turning point for the administration came when the Senate accepted Vandenberg's amendment to the 1942 Revenue Act to freeze the social security tax. The conservative coalition was not decisive to this decision; southern opposition was relatively unimportant, as almost three-fifths of southern senators opposed the amendment and Democrats from states with strong Townsend organizations split evenly. On the other hand, 40 percent of northern Democrats voted in favor of Vandenberg's amendment (see table 4). By 1944, however, southern opposition to the tax freeze had evaporated and less than a third of southerners opposed it. If the conservative coalition had emerged by 1944 with two victories, it remains true nevertheless that northern Democratic support was tepid at best.

One reason for northern Democrats' strong support for the freeze was rising antitax sentiment. The administration's attempt to leverage expansion of social security with war finance backfired as members of both houses of

---

31. Colm to Jones, May 27, 1941, September 12, 1941, RG 51, ser. 39.27, box 43, NA; Currie to Roosevelt, October 7, 1941, p. 174, Morgenthau diaries, box 457, FDRL; Morgenthau diaries, September 17, 1941, p. 267, box 441, FDRL.

Table 4. Congressional votes against OASI tax freeze by party, 1942–1944

	Senate			House of Representatives	
	1942	*1944a*	*1944b*	*1944a*	*1944b*
Northern Democrats	62%	59%	60%	66%	54%
Southern Democrats	54	30	28	17	34
Republicans	7	9	5	4	18

Source: Congressional roll call votes.

Notes:

1942: Vandenberg amendment to 1942 Tax Act freezing OASI tax rate at 1 percent.

1944a: Vote to freeze OASI tax rate (HR 5564) at 1 percent through 1945.

1944b: Amendment to 1945 Revenue Act freezing OASI tax rate at 1 percent through 1946.

Congress, including prominent liberals, proposed reducing taxes. Emanuel Celler said in a speech on the House floor that payroll taxes should be cut by one-third and the reserves spent down through higher benefits.[32] Passage of income tax bills in 1940–41 to finance the war substantially raised taxes and broadened the income base. When added to the administration's social security proposals, the combined average rate for income and social security taxes was estimated to be 15 percent. One insider thought the administration faced a conflict between income taxes and social security taxes, suggesting that "every increase in the payroll taxes diminishes the amount available for general revenue purposes."[33] Antitax fever was even more relevant in 1944. Congress was reluctant to approve any tax increase in the face of an incipient middle-class tax rebellion caused by the broadening of the income tax base. This, more than anything else, explains why opposition to the tax freeze by northern Democrats in the House declined from 66 to 54 percent over 1944 (table 4).

If opposition to tax increases stimulated support for a freeze, however, it was not the only issue nor even the most important factor in the outcome. Opposition to the Third New Deal was more fundamental. Many members of Congress were convinced that a decision to raise social security taxes had little to do with Old Age Survivor's Insurance. Congressional opponents of the tax increase plausibly argued that the accumulating social security reserves were sufficient to sustain the program and there was no need for a

32. U.S. House of Representatives, *Congressional Record*, 77th Cong., 1st sess., 1941, 87, pt. 13:A4089.

33. Sullivan to Morgenthau, October 14, 1941, Morgenthau diaries, p. 330, box 450, FDRL.

tax increase.[34] But the fight over the size of the reserve was a smoke screen for the real issue: whether to go forward with an integrated welfare state based on social insurance. Just as Altmeyer understood the virtues of a large reserve for expansion, so conservatives feared it. Daniel Reed, a Republican congressman from New York, put the point baldly in the 1944 House debate over the tax freeze: "The money collected as a pay-roll tax for old age benefits should not be poured into the General Treasury to be spent for whatever fantastic scheme may be incubated within the inner circle of the boondoggling fraternity of the New Deal." Senator Walter George, a Georgian who expressed the fears of many southern Democrats that the reserve could be used to revive the New Deal, said "the social security tax . . . should be levied only for the purpose of maintaining the integrity of the reserve fund."[35]

In freezing the social security tax, the conservative coalition acted to forestall expansion of the welfare state and prevent any use of the war to create new national social policies. Similarly, they wrested control of the debate over postwar planning and full employment from the administration and defeated its plans to create a capacity for national economic planning. Few people in the administration or Congress dissented from the proposition that with the end of the war America would be visited with widespread unemployment, perhaps approaching the levels of the depression. With Roosevelt camped on the sidelines, congressional liberals proceeded to introduce several proposals, notably the Murray-Kilgore bill of 1944 and the Full Employment Act of 1945. Both bills sought to join social policy with economic management and lay the foundations of a broader welfare state. Congress proceeded to gut these bills and used the G.I. Bill to address the specter of postwar unemployment by returning national employment policy to the jerry-built arrangements erected in 1935. The G.I. Bill became the 1940s version of the WPA: it was temporary and politically expedient.

Liberals believed that reform of unemployment compensation was a first, but absolutely necessary, step toward the full-blown macroeconomic planning they envisioned. Without a nationalized unemployment compensation system, efforts to manage the economy would go awry. The 1944 Murray-Kilgore reconversion bill proposed to rectify the system's inadequacies with

34. Mark H. Leff, "Speculating in Social Security Futures: The Perils of Payroll Tax Financing, 1939–1950," in *Social Security: The First Half-Century*, ed. Gerald D. Nash, Noel H. Pugach, and Richard F. Tomasson (Albuquerque, 1988), pp. 246–48.

35. *Congressional Record*, 78th Cong., 2d sess., 1944, 90, pt. 7:8845, 9042, 9052.

national standards. It broadened coverage, raised the maximum benefit, and stipulated that benefits should be 75 percent of average wages and be paid for a minimum of twenty-six weeks. The Full Employment bill, which succeeded Murray-Kilgore, was designed to commit the federal government to make up any "investment deficit," or the shortfall between anticipated private investment and the total needed to reach full employment. The bill entailed a legal commitment to full employment and the creation of a planning mechanism to reach it.[36]

The conservative coalition turned back any and all attempts to federalize unemployment compensation, beginning with the Murray-Kilgore bill, and otherwise limited the capacity of the federal government to deal with unemployment. The Full Employment Act was stripped of its capacity to use spending as a tool of economic policy, though the bill that passed retained at least a symbolic commitment to full employment and created the Council on Economic Advisers (CEA) to provide Congress and the president with economic advice. Opponents of the Full Employment Act were determined to bury any notion of a regime of permanent spending by decoupling economic and social policy. The bill would have shifted substantial discretionary control over spending to the executive branch and threatened not just those who feared full employment and a larger welfare state but also those with a stake in federal spending. There is no reason to believe that conservatives were acting on the basis of a tried-and-true fiscal conservatism or fear of deficits, since no one in Congress advocated a balanced budget in 1945–46, and Republicans pressed their case for tax cuts in 1945 oblivious to implications for the deficit. Fiscal orthodoxy was at best politically expedient, as Barton Bernstein has observed: "Though Congressmen might rail against government spending when opposing particular programs or resisting expansion of the federal bureaucracy, and their assaults relied upon the rhetoric of fiscal orthodoxy, budget balancing was not central to their political faith."[37]

Congressional conservatives opposed changes in unemployment compensation for many of the same reasons they gutted the full-employment bill. Those signing the minority report for the Murray-Kilgore bill said they did "not believe that aid to the unemployed should be used as a method of sta-

36. Stephen A. Bailey, *Congress Makes a Law* (New York, 1950), pp. 47–50.
37. Barton Bernstein, "Charting a Course between Inflation and Depression," *Register of the Kentucky Historical Society* 66 (1968): 60–61. On the fate of the full-employment act, see Brady, "Toward Security," pp. 247–50, 271–72; Bailey, *Congress Makes a Law*, pp. 130–32, 148.

bilizing wages and pay. Its sole purpose should be to prevent want for the necessaries of life by those who, because of lack of places to work, cannot support themselves." One Republican opponent said on the Senate floor, "we must not, under color of helping the unemployed, establish a new idea or form of government." Equally important was opposition to the level of benefits, a matter of some concern to southerners. The proposed level of benefits exceeded those of the G.I. Bill, which had been controversial, and Vandenberg argued that the bill would raise state benefits by 100 to 130 percent.[38]

Employment legislation was an instance in which the interests of southern Democrats and northern Republicans converged, and the conservative coalition held sway in all the votes on it. In rejecting the employment bills, conservatives did not deny the need for a postwar policy on unemployment. What they were willing to do, particularly in the Senate, was to pass temporary, politically popular programs to deal with the impending threat of a postwar recession and unemployment. The G.I. Bill is the chief case. It was more than a just payment to soldiers for the sacrifices of war; it was understood to be part of an ensemble of policies that would help the country cope with reconversion. The administration intended to use veterans benefits as a way of advancing its postwar agenda. The report of FDR's Postwar Manpower Conference (PMC) advocated federalization of unemployment benefits, for example, on the grounds that it was necessary to ensure that veterans received assistance in addition to the proposed mustering-out pay and social security credit for time served in the military.[39] FDR lost control of the debate, however, when an omnibus bill written by the American Legion was substituted for separate administration bills.

The innovative feature of the 1944 act was the readjustment benefits that Congress substituted for a bonus payment or other cash transfer. Readjustment benefits offered veterans educational opportunities, access to separate unemployment benefits, and guaranteed home and business loans in addition to the usual veterans compensation, service-connected pensions, and medical benefits. They were distinctive for their generosity and separateness. Congress established a series of temporary entitlements with no offsets and placed them under the control of the Veterans Administration as the American Legion had demanded. The absence of an offset meant that veterans

38. *Congresssional Record*, 78th Cong., 2 sess., 1944, 90, pt. 5:6811–12, 6823. Vandenberg's figures are suspect.

39. David R. B. Ross, *Preparing for Ulysses: Politics and Veterans during World War II* (New York, 1969), pp. 61–62.

could take advantage of more than one program without losing any benefits. The main fight in Congress was not over whether veterans benefits should be integrated with other social policies, as FDR wanted, but over their generosity.

John Morton Blum argues that the G.I. Bill was an electorally shrewd maneuver on Roosevelt's part, as it presumably advanced social legislation at a time when no other legislation was possible and served as the opening gambit for the 1944 election.[40] Yet the G.I. Bill also united opponents of the Third New Deal, who used it to subvert the liberal agenda. The battle over veterans benefits brought together conservatives such as John Rankin, a southern Democrat, who said, "I do not want to make the World War veterans the common carriers for the enormous appropriations that I can see in the distance for all the social uplifting that we will have and all the social and physical rehabilitation that may be undertaken," with veterans organizations seeking to maintain the exclusive and separate treatment of veterans.[41] The fight over the G.I. Bill was characterized by David R. B. Ross as a conflict between universalism and particularism that pitted the administration against veterans organizations and set the pattern for postwar debate, as in fact it was in many ways. But it would be a mistake to construe the political maneuvering over veterans benefits as simply a triumph of interest group politics.

Veterans policies represented a conscious attempt by Congress to devise ad hoc, temporary remedies for reconversion as opposed to permanent extensions of social security or anything else. The PMC report gave this view some legitimacy; it saw the educational benefits as a labor-market strategy, arguing that extended educational benefits would divert returning veterans from searching for jobs and therefore tighten up postwar labor markets. This was exactly the sort of supply-side employment strategy implicit in many New Deal policies, such as the Civilian Conservation Corps, National Youth Administration, and Fair Labor Standards Act.[42] The initial version of the administration's educational bill incorporated these ideas. Veterans unemployment benefits, the "52/20" provisions, were seen as a way of shoring

40. John Morton Blum, *V Was for Victory* (New York, 1976), pp. 248–49.
41. Ross, *Preparing for Ulysses*, pp. 42, 43.
42. NRPB, *Demobilization and Readjustment* (Washington, D.C., 1943), pp. 42–43. Supply-side schemes to deal with unemployment abounded in the mid-1940s. The Labor Department drafted a plan in mid-1944 to pay younger workers education allowances in lieu of unemployment compensation "to eliminate them from the post-war labor market." Smith to President, August 31, 1944, Harold D. Smith Papers, box 4, FDRL.

up a weak unemployment compensation system. And veterans credit policies had obvious implications for economic growth.

Congress regularly liberalized veterans readjustment eligibility and benefits, and resolutely deployed it as a surrogate unemployment program throughout the postwar period. Between 1944 and 1958, Congress enacted three temporary unemployment programs for veterans; the last, the Ex-Servicemen's Unemployment Compensation program, was made permanent. Congress also created special unemployment programs for railroad workers and seamen who served in the Merchant Marine. In other words, Congress consciously sought to deal with unemployment by enacting temporary policies. New permanent policies, with the single exception of disability insurance in 1956, were invariably means-tested or created for specific beneficiaries.

Veterans benefits occupy the same place in the postwar economy as the WPA did in the middle of the depression. But by creating a vast source of educational opportunities, they perverted ideas about education and youth that flowered in the late 1930s. Instead of the inclusive policy of educational opportunity the NRPB articulated in *Security, Work, and Relief Policies,* the new policies produced a narrow entitlement for a select group of men. This was the entering wedge of truncated universalism.

Fiscal Politics and the Denouement of the Fair Deal

Once plans for an integrated national welfare state had been subverted, the main struggle over postwar social policy involved discrete legislative proposals for public housing, national health insurance, old-age insurance, public assistance, and aid to education, among others. Taft and the southern Democrats were unsuccessful in enacting most of their means-tested proposals, but much of the domestic legislation that was passed by the end of the Truman era was sharply redistributive to southern states. Truman's Fair Deal failed to obtain national health insurance, but succeeded in raising social security benefits and establishing OASI as the institutional core of the American welfare state. Crucial to this outcome was the postwar politics of taxing and spending. Both the successes and failures of the alternative agendas were linked to the different budgetary and tax preferences of Republicans, southern Democrats, and the Truman administration.

Republican advocacy of selected social policies competed with their affection for tax cuts, arguably the central objective of their postwar policy agenda. The minute the shooting stopped, Republicans and their business allies pressed for large tax cuts. Upon gaining control of Congress in 1947, the House Republican Steering Committee called for a 20 percent reduction in income taxes, a demand widely supported within the party. Republicans wanted to reduce the burden of the income tax, which as a consequence of wartime tax increases was much heavier, and they argued that tax cuts would stimulate business investment. Yet for many Republicans, tax cuts were a way to prevent a revival of the New Deal. Harold Knutson, the chair of the Ways and Means Committee, said during the heat of the election that tax cuts were necessary to "cut off much of the government's income by reducing taxes and compel the government to retrench, live within its income." Even Robert Taft shared this view.[43] Republican success, however, depended on the votes of southern Democrats, who were predictably divided on the issue, since Truman was dead set against any tax cuts and publicly said he would veto them.

Northern liberals pressed ahead with social insurance while crafting housing and aid to education policies to attract Southern support. Southerners played hard-to-get while collaborating with Republicans to fashion policies that funneled resources south of the Mason-Dixon line and maintained local control. Both sides wooed southern votes. The education aid bills of the 1940s are indicative of the legislative maneuvering. All of the bills contained "equalization" provisions based on a minimum federal subsidy for elementary and secondary education, ranging from forty dollars to sixty dollars per pupil. This money was allocated on the basis of a redistributive formula with no state match, which would have sharply tilted federal funding toward the South. In both of the Republican bills reported out of House and Senate committees in 1947, 54 percent of all authorized funds would have gone to the eleven southern states. Liberal Democrats typically countered by outbidding the Republicans. Taft and his allies never proposed more than $300 million in federal aid for education, but Senate liberals promoted bills that authorized up to $2 billion in aid. While it is true that northern liberals saw spending as necessary to cultivate an alliance with southern Democrats (a strategy which often failed), they sincerely believed that federal spending was necessary for economic growth and development. As a consequence, they were usually willing to support any spending policy.

The postwar political conflict over social policy and tax cuts was fought out in an economy dominated by inflation. The postwar inflationary pressures facing Truman were unexpected, and they were exacerbated by the 1945 tax

---

43. Holmans, *U.S. Fiscal Policy,* pp. 60–61.

cut and Truman's insistence on abandoning wage and price controls as soon as possible (although it is not clear that he could have sustained them for very long anyway). After some floundering, the administration turned to fiscal policy as the main instrument for controlling inflation and proposed a succession of deflationary budgets with high taxes and limited expenditures.[44] Until Truman unveiled the Fair Deal proposals in January 1949, there was a massive discrepancy between his rhetoric and his actual budget proposals. When Truman announced his tight fiscal policy in early 1947, the administration also called for a major expansion in social welfare. Yet the budget provided little money for anything: proposed outlays for new programs amounted to $484 million, only $88 million of which was for social policy, and most of that was earmarked for public assistance. The administration was "shadow boxing" with the Republican Congress, advocating liberal alternatives not because Truman and his advisers thought they would pass but to build an agenda for the 1948 election.

Truman's tight budget policies were less a reflection of his stated ideological preference for balanced budgets than of the severe fiscal and economic pressures confronting the administration. These fiscal policies in turn framed the Fair Deal agenda and determined the administration's legislative strategy. The administration confronted a three-pronged assault on the budget by 1948: tax cuts, the cold war, and veterans programs. Republican efforts to cut taxes was rewarded after three tries when Congress overrode Truman's veto to pass the 1948 tax bill.[45] Truman's ire over the tax cut is understandable; it came at a time when the spending implications of the cold war had finally become apparent. The fall of Czechoslovakia in March 1948 led to new demands for foreign aid and, most important, for defense spending (the joint chiefs of staff requested a $9 billion supplemental appropriation, though they had to settle for $3 billion). Spending estimates for the fiscal year 1949 budget (introduced in January 1948) were radically revised upward. Meanwhile, the growth of veterans spending, which averaged 20 percent of the federal budget during the late 1940s, added to the budgetary pressures facing Truman. When it came to veterans benefits, Congress cast

---

44. Craufurd D. Goodwin and R. Stanley Herren, "The Truman Administration: Problems and Policies Unfold," in *Exhortation and Controls*, ed. Craufurd D. Goodwin (Washington, D.C., 1975), pp. 33–34.

45. The tax cut was less a triumph of the conservative coalition than an election year gambit by Congress; support for the cut was drawn from both parties and all regions. This is further evidence that the lure of tax cuts or spending always trumped fear of deficits. Holmans, *U.S. Fiscal Policy*, pp. 93–97.

fiscal prudence aside. Veterans payments rose almost $700 million during the first half of 1948, almost entirely a result of veterans taking advantage of liberalized readjustment allowances. It is worth noting that other programs were growing as well; public assistance payments were increasing in real terms at an annual rate of 25 percent. Truman acknowledged his plight when he told a press conference that veterans, defense, and foreign aid consumed 60 percent of the federal budget, leaving less than a third, after interest payments, for everything else.[46]

These conflicting budgetary demands and inflationary pressures dictated the administration's legislative agenda. Truman linked his Fair Deal to a substantial tax increase, adopting what might be called an implicit policy strategy of "high-tax–high-spend." Inflation remained the ostensible economic constraint for the administration. Truman told Thurman Arnold, who had complained of cuts in the Federal Trade Commission's budget, "I have had to make up an exceedingly tight budget and shall expect to continue that tight budget in operation until we find the money to make a more liberal one." Yet he simultaneously ordered cabinet departments to develop legislation to implement his campaign commitments, thus putting the administration in a bind. The administration was faced with a choice of either balancing the budget and funding needed programs as revenues became available or acting to "do everything we can possibly do to speed the programs [to which the President is committed] up to the limits imposed by deficit financing and . . . expand those limits right now for planning purposes in terms of the maximum increased revenues we can hope to get by taxation." All of Truman's liberal advisers—Leon Keyserling, Clark Clifford, and Charles Murphy— argued for an antiinflation, social welfare strategy for the fiscal year 1950 budget, and Truman decided to expand the limits of the deficit.[47]

The Fair Deal budget called for $8.16 billion in new spending (including slated increases in social security benefits), of which two-thirds was for cold war expenses, in addition to $6 billion in new taxes. The administration requested $4 billion dollars of new corporation, estate, and gift taxes and pos-

46. *Public Papers of the Presidents: Harry S. Truman, 1947* (Washington, D.C., 1948), pp. 385, 386–87.

47. President to Arnold, November 26, 1948, OF 79, box 364, HSTL; Neustadt to Staats, November 22, 1948; Staats to Director (BOB), December 17, 1948; Director (BOB) to President, December 1948, Richard E. Neustadt Papers, box 10, folder "Addendum, Budget Policy," HSTL; William O. Wagnon, "The Politics of Economic Growth: The Truman Administration and the 1949 Recession" (Ph.D. diss., University of Missouri, 1970), pp. 45–46, 48, 51, 54–55.

sibly increased rates for the "upper and middle brackets"; the remaining $2 billion was payroll taxes, though Truman insisted they had nothing to do with the operation of the government since they were contributions to the social security trust fund and would not reduce the public debt.[48]

While the tax increases were consistent with the presumption that inflation remained the salient economic reality, the overall effect of the budget would have been expansionary and the taxes would not have had much effect on demand. Truman was entirely serious, even though he never submitted a tax message to Congress, and one cannot explain his fiscal policies simply as another manifestation of his ingrained fiscal conservatism.[49] Rather the scope and magnitude of the tax proposals point to an attempt to resolve the conflict between fiscal reality—the belief in the need for a tight budget policy and competing budgetary demands—and the administration's social policy agenda.

Truman's high-tax–high-spend policy of the late 1940s entailed an implicit commitment to state socialism. It was not a strategy of commercial Keynesianism. Many left-Keynesians in the government assumed that a balanced budget either would entail sacrificing full employment or would threaten the private sector, since a balanced budget and full employment could be had only with substantial *increases* in outlays and taxes. Deficit spending was regarded as the only politically realistic way to get full employment. Michael Kalecki, a Hungarian economist who anticipated much of Keynesian economics, advised Senator James Murray that redistribution and high taxation "will be extremely difficult because they will involve a drastic 'squeezing' of profit margins . . . or a very heavy taxation of profits."[50] Truman's fiscal policies may have defied the political wisdom of the left-Keynesians, and they may have been somewhat self-defeating since the administration's credit policies (particularly with regard to housing) diminished the anti-inflation effects of the fiscal policy; but this was not the point in 1949.

How did these conflicts between Truman, his Democratic allies, and their Republican opponents affect the outcome of their policy agendas? Succinctly stated, Republican preferences for tax reductions undercut Taft's

48. *Public Papers of the President: Harry S. Truman, 1949* (Washington, D.C., 1950), pp. 20, 29.

49. Holmans, *U.S. Fiscal Policy,* pp. 104, 107–8.

50. Kalecki to Murray, May 5, 1945, Gerhard Colm Papers, HSTL. Roosevelt and Truman, on the other hand, always operated on the assumption that deficits were politically risky.

ambitions for means-tested redistribution. Furthermore, northern and southern Democrats collaborated on new spending programs subject to tight budget constraints. The failure of health insurance and the triumph of social security legislation, by contrast, resulted from the failure of Truman's high-tax–high-spend policy.

The initial skirmish over means-tested redistribution was fought over variable grants for public assistance, perhaps the most important policy on the southern Democrats' agenda at the end of the war. They lost this particular fight, revealing the limited appeal for House Republicans of Taft's strategy for gaining southern Democratic alliances. But the southerners won the larger battle. Unlike the late 1930s, conflict over variable grants was never a matter of sectional politics. Variable grants represented a crucial instance of a "rare coalition of Southerners and left-wing Democrats."[51] The opposition came from House Republicans, who objected to higher social welfare spending, not to regional disparities. Spending was the chief issue in the 1946 fight over variable grants, when House Republicans were able to prevent the adoption of a variable grant proposal first in the House and then, after the Senate passed a similar proposal, in conference committee. Republican opponents charged that the legislation was a "raid on the Treasury," saying "the democratic majority is perfectly willing to increase benefits as long as Uncle Sam can be relied upon to bear a disproportionate, and unfair, share of the cost, knowing full well it would lead to a 3-for-1 rule, a 4-for-1 rule, and ultimately a 100 percent federalized system."[52] House Republicans buried the issue of variable grants until the late 1950s, even though they compromised on an amended formula that raised the federal share of public assistance costs and in the process provided more federal dollars to southern states. If support for means-tested redistribution within the Republican party was shallow, this was less because of regional disparities in funding than because of opposition to any significant expansion in funding for the welfare state.[53]

Federal aid formulas were revised nine more times before variable grants were approved in 1958, each time emerging from Congress with a southern

51. *New York Times,* July 31, 1946, sec. 1, p. 1.
52. *New York Times,* July 3, 1946, sec. 1, p. 25.
53. Of course, one might ask, given that the cost of public assistance goes up anyway, Is it not the case that the fight was really about regional benefits? There are two reasons to reject this view. First, the change was only temporary, though it was made permanent in 1948; and, second, the Republicans had to compromise—from their point of view what was bothersome were the long-term implications of spending.

tilt. Incremental adjustments of the public assistance formulas based on the 1946 compromise raised the average federal shares of OAA payments from 55.5 percent to 65 percent and of ADC payments from 56 to 67 percent. These formulas created powerful incentives for southern states to admit large numbers of people to the welfare rolls while maintaining low benefits. Unlike a variable grant, which relates state fiscal capacity to federal contributions, the public assistance formulas of the 1940s subsidized state payments on a sliding scale up to a maximum payment. Under the 1948 Old Age Assistance formula, for example, the federal government paid three-quarters of the first twenty dollars and one-half of the next thirty dollars up to a maximum of fifty dollars, or a total federal share of 60 percent. Southern states maintained low average payments, rarely exceeding the lower ceiling for calculating the federal share, but maintained large caseloads—a neat policy that guaranteed federal dollars would flow South while limiting local contributions and, thus, the tax burden, as well as ensuring that benefits would not drive up wages.

Despite the opposition of House Republicans, the alliance between northern and southern Democrats held, and they were able to siphon off a sufficient number of Republican votes to establish redistribution to the South as national policy. The Hospital Construction Act (Hill-Burton) and school lunch program are two examples of narrowly framed social legislation that incorporated formulas for redistributive funding. The southerners' most spectacular success came with public housing. The 1949 Housing Act grew out of an agreement between Taft, southern Democrats, and urban liberals, notably Robert Wagner, to tie an expansion of public housing to a new slum clearance program. Taft, who was instrumental in persuading other northern Republicans to join in supporting the housing legislation, saw it as a straightforward alternative to "the dangers that a general socialistic housing plan might bring about."[54] The southern thirst for federally supported public housing was driven by a severe shortage of housing for low-income families in the urban South, and it reflected a blend of southern populism and southern liberalism. Pushing the legislation were Allen Ellender (a product of the Huey Long machine in Louisiana who combined New Deal liberalism with racism), Wright Patman (who also depended upon a populist, low-income base of support), and southern liberals such as Claude Pepper, Lister Hill, Albert Gore, and Estes Kefauver, all of whom depended to some degree on labor support. With the exception of Pepper, these southerners usually voted

54. Patterson, *Mr. Republican,* p. 316.

Table 5. Federal social welfare grants in the South, 1962

Type of grant	Percentage of grants to South	Year established	Year fiscal capacity provision added	Proportion of funds redistributed
Hospital construction	37%	1946	1946	100%
Vocational Rehabilitation	34	1926	1954	100
School lunches	35	1946	1946	100
Child welfare services	31	1935	1958	10
Crippled children's services	35	1935	1935	41.2
Maternal and Child Health	33	1935	1935	37.3
Community health services	25	1961	1961	100
Mental health	24	1946	1946	30.3
Old Age Assistance	36	1935	1958	43.7
Aid to Blind	36	1935	1958	37.4
Aid to Disabled	38	1935	1958	35.7
Aid to Dependent Children	18	1935	1958	25.7
Impact Aid for Schools	26			
Vocational Education	30			

Source: Advisory Commission on Intergovernmental Relations, *The Role of Equalization in Federal Grants* (Washington, D.C., 1964), pp. 43, 179–84, 193–95.

Note: The South, here, refers to the eleven former confederate states.

against national social insurance, favoring some version of means-tested redistribution. Liberals saw public housing as a part of a policy for urban redevelopment. Both Truman and Taft preferred public housing to a means-tested rent subsidy that had been recommended by real estate interests because it was cheap and there were no immediate budgetary outlays.

The success of the southern strategy was clear by the end of the 1950s; federal grants-in-aid for social welfare were sharply redistributive to the South. About one-third of all social welfare spending by 1962 found its way south of the Mason-Dixon line, a region with just 24 percent of the nation's population. (See table 5.) The strategy of holding benefits down while admitting large numbers of people to the OAA and ADC rolls shifted most of the costs to the federal government. By 1955, 70 percent of OAA payments and 75 percent of ADC payments in the South were picked up by the federal government, compared to a national average of 56 percent. And once tax burdens are calculated, the southern advantage relative to other regions was quite large.[55] The South was favored even in discretionary federal programs. One-third of vocational rehabilitation and education funds flowed

55. "Policies in Major Grant Programs," U.S. Bureau of the Budget, draft report, pp. 17–19, RG 51, ser. 39.3, box 56, folder no. 329, NA. Author's calculations.

southward, and the region benefited substantially from public housing programs. The two states with the largest number of public housing projects in the late 1950s were Texas and Georgia, and by 1970 over half of all projects were in Chicago or New York City (12 percent apiece) or small southern towns (36 percent).[56]

Of the Third New Deal's agenda for universal social insurance, only old-age insurance was left standing. This outcome is less perplexing than it appears once the politics of taxing and spending are considered. What sealed the fate of national health insurance was the 1949 recession and the collapse of Truman's high-tax–high-spend policy. At the first hint of recession, fiscal conservatives in Congress launched a drive to cut federal expenditures, while arguing that a tax hike in a recession was unwise. This contradictory stance, taken by Walter George among others, reflected opposition to the Fair Deal proposals and thus was less a sign of balanced budget orthodoxy than an opportunistic attempt to slash domestic spending. Truman and his advisers were in a bind. They acknowledged the collapse of their high-tax–high-spend strategy by dropping the request for the $4 billion tax hike, and they had no alternative proposal. The temptation to increase veterans spending— the one spending policy Congress might have accepted—as an antirecession measure had a disadvantage. Truman's budget adviser warned that "it is a practical certainty that bad economic conditions would result in strengthened demands for enactment of increased or new benefits," which would limit the administration's ability to fund other social policies.[57] Although Truman reluctantly approved a modest increase in veterans spending, the administration faced excruciating conflicts among budgetary priorities and had no choice but to change their social policy agenda.

Health insurance was not one of the Truman administration's top policy priorities. The administration had little to do with the preparation of health proposals and informed congressional Democrats that social security was the priority. Charles Murphy, Truman's chief domestic policy adviser, told Wilbur

56. Robert M. Fisher, *Twenty Years of Public Housing: Economic Aspects of the Federal Program* (New York, 1959), p. 111; Henry J. Aaron, *Shelter and Subsidies: Who Benefits from Federal Housing Policies?* (Washington, D.C., 1972), pp. 120–21.

57. M.S. March, April 22, 1949, RG 51, ser. 39.3, NA; Frank Pace told Truman that extending "52–20" unemployment benefits for veterans would "indicate a willingness to provide special benefits beyond the terms of the Veterans Readjustment Act, which could open the door and prove embarrassing at a later date with respect to possible bonus or other special veterans' legislation." Director to President, July 8, 1949, OF 396, box 1076, HSTL.

Mills that the administration did not want the Ways and Means Committee to consider the health legislation until after hearings on social security were finished.[58] After pushing health insurance in 1948 and making it a central part of his legislative program, Truman made only half-hearted efforts on behalf of the proposal. National health insurance, like OASI, was publicly justified as contributing to the administration's anti-inflation policies. The scheduled tax increases would result in a $3 billion surfeit of taxes over benefit payments, Oscar Ewing told Congress in early February. After the recession vitiated the rationale for these taxes and the administration imposed budget ceilings for the fiscal year 1951 in order to limit the deficit, the administration's interest in health insurance evaporated. The administration's legislative clearance procedures stipulated that Truman endorse only those bills that clearly met its budgetary requirements; since the proposal Democrats introduced did not meet those requirements, the legislation went forward as a bill in which the president was "generally in accord" rather than as an administration bill.[59]

The interesting question about national health insurance is why the various alternatives to it were never considered rather than why it was defeated. By the summer of 1949, it was clear that the one Democratic policy that could not be enacted was national health insurance. Aside from Truman's demurral, numerous interest groups and public agencies were opposed, including the Veterans' Administration (which saw health insurance as a threat to its own medical programs) and various Catholic social organizations (who "feared that the extension of social insurance would result in an encroachment of taxation upon religious and charitable institutions").[60] The labor movement had publicly proclaimed its support, but by late 1949 most unions were well along the road to using collective bargaining to obtain health insurance. The administration's lackluster support for national health insurance after the collapse of its high-tax–high-spend strategy allowed conservatives to kill the legislation in committee.

But several alternatives were introduced. All of them linked private health insurance to a program of welfare medicine for the poor, and all but one

58. Murphy to President, February 14, 1949, and Charles S. Murphy, Memorandum for the Files, February 11, 1949, Murphy Papers, box 27, Social Security, folder no. 2.

59. Testimony by Oscar R. Ewing, Federal Security Administrator, before the Joint Committee on the Economic Report, February 14, 1949, Oscar R. Ewing Papers, box 34, HSTL; Monty Poen, *Harry S. Truman versus the Medical Lobby* (Columbia, Mo., 1979), pp. 156–57.

60. Poen, *Truman versus the Medical Lobby,* p. 162; "Broad Health Bill Doomed, Says Taft," *New York Times,* April 20, 1949. See also Daniel M. Fox, *Health Policies, Health Politics* (Princeton, N.J., 1986), pp. 156–57.

were means-tested, stipulated local control, and redistributed money to the South. The one non-means-tested proposal, the Flanders-Ives bill, would have created a national plan by providing federal subsidies to voluntary health insurance. These alternatives were strongly opposed by the labor movement and by many liberal democrats, but the opposition of the Truman administration brought their demise. Once the high-tax–high-spend strategy unraveled, the administration was reluctant to support new spending programs for anything.

The fate of social security was different precisely because all of the contending parties by 1949 had a fiscal stake in saving a contributory pension system. The failure to raise benefits and extend coverage contributed to the urgency the administration attached to the OASI proposals; but strong defense of a contributory system was also dictated by the short-run fiscal pressures facing the administration and the long-term implications of continued budgetary conflict. Truman's budget advisers believed contributory social insurance was endangered by alternative programs, notably OAA and veterans pensions. They were not imagining the threat. In late 1948, the administration tried to get a ceiling on public assistance expenditures and "to reestablish the insurance principle before it was too late to head off veterans pensions and other grabs from the Treasury."[61] A number of pending bills in Congress removed any ceiling on federal contributions to public assistance payments, thus reversing FDR's insistence on state effort. A bigger threat came from an archfoe of the Fair Deal, John Rankin, who had fought for the G.I. Bill as a way to sink the Third New Deal. He tried to sabotage Truman's 1949 social security proposals with a bill that gave all veterans of the two world wars a ninety-dollars-a-month pension. The measure attracted substantial support from Republicans, who were lukewarm about social security anyway, and was defeated by just one vote. Its passage would likely have killed the Social Security reforms, as Rankin intended. The Truman administration estimated it would cost an additional $5 to $6 billion annually and believed "it would be in direct competition with social security. . . . To permit veterans' pensions to be received unchecked would weaken the social security program."[62]

61. Hubbel to Labovitz, October 27, 1949, no. 831; Stark to Smithies, April 23, 1948, no. 821, RG 51, ser. 39.14a, NA.

62. Neustadt to Director (BOB), February 18, 1949, attached memo, p. 1, Neustadt Papers, box 10; "Rankin's Pension," *New Republic,* April 4, 1949, p. 7. It is worth noting that Congressional conservatives used the same strategy to sink any effort to revive national health insurance by widening veterans' health coverage to cover dependents. See Stephen J. Spingarn, Memo of August 24, 1950, Stephen J. Spingarn Papers, box 27, HSTL.

Direct evidence is hard to come by, but a close reading of Truman's public statements in 1948 and 1949 indicate that he wanted to reduce reliance on OAA and veterans' pensions and put social security beyond the budgetary battles with Congress. His 1949 budget message clearly enunciated the principle that OASI was an alternative to veterans' pensions. Perhaps more significant, Truman and his advisers decided in favor of creating a fiscally autonomous social security system. They discarded a key element of the Third New Deal, the belief that OASI should be partly funded out of general revenues so as to enhance its usefulness as a tool of macroeconomic management. The administration continued to make budgetary decisions and fiscal policy on the basis of the cash-consolidated budget, which took account of the effects of OASI outlays on the economy; at the same time, it had decided an autonomous social security system was preferable to the alternatives. Truman and his closest advisers publicly treated OASI as separate and apart from the rest of the government, maintaining that it was irrelevant to any deficit or surplus. In short, the administration had an urgent stake in insulating social security from fiscal conflict, warding off untoward alternatives, and firmly establishing it as the core of the American welfare state. Without OASI there would be little opportunity in the future to add disability or health insurance.

Both Republicans and southern Democrats had strong reasons to support a pay-as-you-go contributory insurance system by 1949. Some business organizations, notably the Chamber of Commerce, had concluded that in the long run contributory social insurance was cheaper, and a politically insulated contributory system would resolve conservative fears about the potential uses of the reserves. Southern support derived from the mounting fiscal pressures of OAA and their failure to enact a variable grant system. Congress's decision to freeze OASI benefits and taxes shifted much of the burden of caring for the elderly to the Old Age Assistance program. By 1949 more people were receiving means-tested OAA benefits than received OASI benefits, and the average old-age benefit was higher than social security payments in 1949 (OAA paid an average of forty-five dollars per month compared to twenty-six dollars for OASI). But because agricultural workers were excluded from coverage, there were very few retirees receiving social security in rural, mostly southern states, while OAA caseloads, if not benefit levels, were much higher than in the North.[63] The fierceness with which southern

63. Jill Quadagno, *The Transformation of Old Age Security* (Chicago, 1988), pp. 147–49; Edward Berkowitz, *America's Welfare State: From Roosevelt to Reagan* (Baltimore, 1991), pp. 56–57.

politicians pursued variable grants was partly due to this difference. Under these circumstances a limited contributory system that did not include all agricultural workers was preferable to the status quo.

The 1950 amendments to the Social Security Act fully institutionalized old-age insurance. Congress acted to "save" the program politically and eliminate any real threat from alternative policies. But if OASI was firmly established at the core of the American welfare state, henceforth it occupied a separate realm, subject to its own rules and dynamics.

The Racial Legacy of Truncated Universalism

With the defeat of the Fair Deal, the political conflicts unleashed by depression and war were provisionally settled. The liberal dream of an integrated welfare state was lost, cutting short the promise of the New Deal. This outcome resulted from two different but related patterns of political conflict during the decade. The Third New Deal succumbed to an alliance between those opposed to a comprehensive welfare state or higher taxes (businessmen and middle-class opponents) and those seeking to minimize presidential control of spending. This coalition managed to freeze social security and defeat postwar legislative proposals that would have nationalized unemployment compensation and created the fiscal capacity to maintain a robust, full-employment economy. Opponents perversely modeled their alternative for the postwar economy on Roosevelt's temporary, stopgap WPA, and they deployed veterans' benefits as an alternative to a national full-employment policy, the addition of health and disability insurance, and the continuation of OASI (though unsuccessfully in the last case). This alliance of Republicans and southern Democrats ruptured, however, over means-tested redistribution. In this phase of legislative conflict, the shifting alliances for and against various social policies depended closely on preferences for different tax and spending policies. These preferences explain Republican defections (largely in the House) from means-tested redistribution; the acceptance of public housing by all three parties over rent subsidies; Truman's lackluster support of national health insurance (including the failure to pursue any of the alternatives); and the convergence of support for contributory social insurance. These changes, when combined with the advent of collectively bargained social policies, remade the New Deal.

Northern Democrats paid a heavy price for their limited successes. Race was the arbiter between northern aspirations and southern intransigence. Catering to southern interests enabled northern Democrats to assemble legislative majorities, but in the process they sacrificed any presumption of racial equality, thus reviving the New Deal antinomy between the Democratic party coalition and the racially biased effects of its policies. All of the postwar aid-to-education bills mocked their justification, equalization of the opportunity for education, as all of them were premised on "separate but equal" education in the South. Aid to education went nowhere; but many of the social policies that were enacted reaffirmed *Plessy v. Ferguson*. The School Lunch Act of 1946 is indicative. When Adam Clayton Powell introduced an amendment to the act that would have barred discrimination (the first of many antidiscrimination riders he would introduce) northern liberals convinced him to reword the amendment to avoid mention of schools or separate school systems. This amendment passed in the House, only to be replaced in the Senate by a nondiscrimination provision that would have killed it. The legislation was "saved" when southern Democrats, with northern votes, changed the nondiscrimination amendment into one that provided school lunch funds even to states that maintained separate school systems as long as they distributed the money equally. "Separate but equal," after all, was the law of the land.

Southerners took full advantage of the capitulation of northern Democrats. Locally controlled public assistance and nutrition programs were administered in ways that maintained the subservience of African-American sharecroppers, while federal agricultural policies hastened the mechanization of farming and undermined sharecroppers' ability to earn a living.[64] Southerners also used federal grants to outfit Jim Crow with racially segregated social services. Most of the social programs of the era contained "nonintervention" provisions, which precluded federal supervision or control of the administration or operation of projects.[65] Grants for the construction of public facilities or publicly subsidized buildings were seized upon to extend the color line. Veterans Administration and Hill-Burton funds were used to build badly needed but segregated hospitals and other health facilities. The Hill-Burton Act of 1946 prohibited racial discrimination but stipulated that "separate but equal" would meet this requirement. All ninety of the hospi-

---

64. James C. Cobb, "'Somebody Done Nailed Us on the Cross': Federal Farm and Welfare Policy and the Civil Rights Movement in the Mississippi Delta," *Journal of American History* 77 (1990): 912–36.

65. United States Commission on Civil Rights, *Employment* (Washington, D.C., 1961), pp. 84–85. An exception was the Vocational Rehabilitation Program, in which, the commission concluded, blacks received benefits in proportion to their number in the population in both the North and South (see p. 203, n. 118).

tals constructed by 1960 were rigidly segregated. Southern cities were much more likely than nonsouthern cities to raze black neighborhoods, and redevelopment projects were often deployed as buffers between black and white residential areas.[66]

Southerners were not shy about all this, nor did they regard the use of federal money to reinforce racial segregation as discrimination. After noting there was little or no discrimination in a Louisiana veterans' hospital, VA officials in a letter to the NAACP observed "the ratio of plumbing fixtures to patients is low in the wards occupied by white veterans and colored veterans alike. This is receiving consideration with a view to corrective action." The NAACP fought back, and after a furious battle, prevented the construction of a segregated hospital on the site of Booker T. Washington's birthplace. But they were not always so successful, and most veterans' hospitals were rigidly segregated.[67]

The conflict between the racially discriminatory distribution of federal funds and the passage of social legislation intensified after Truman's Civil Rights Commission made an issue of it. Until then the NAACP had believed that passage of social policies that would benefit African Americans was more important than staving off discriminatory uses of federal funds. At its 1949 convention, however, the NAACP passed a resolution condemning the use of federal funds to strengthen southern apartheid. There was opposition to this position from some African American organizations, but from that point on the NAACP's chief congressional lobbyist, Clarence Mitchell, joined forces with Adam Clayton Powell to introduce nondiscrimination riders to social legislation. No longer would the Republicans be alone in this practice. Northern liberals were furious as Powell proceeded to introduce his amendments, provoking Roy Wilkins to write one critic, "it would seem that the friends of federal aid might well expend some of their persuasive powers on those who want to have their cake (segregation) and eat it too (federal aid)."[68] Liberal anger obviously did not dissuade Powell and Wilkins

66. Heywood T. Sanders, "The Politics of City Redevelopment: The Federal Urban Renewal Program and American Cities, 1949 to 1971" (Ph.D. diss., Harvard University, 1977), pp. 335, 337–44.

67. Griffith to Dedmon Jr., November 6, 1945; Frank T. Hines (V.A. administrator) to Leslie Perry, February 1, 1945, and Perry to Hines, February 7, 1945, NAACP Papers, group 2, ser. 1, box 642, Veterans Policies, LC.

68. Hamilton, *Adam Clayton Powell, Jr.*, pp. 172, 225–27, 231–32; Wilkins to Frederick F. Greenman, November 15, 1955, NAACP Papers, group 2, A-267, LC, quoted in Hamilton, p. 232.

or their allies. But it meant that until passage of the "universal Powell amendment," Title VI of the 1964 Civil Rights Act, social policy was hostage to the racist inclinations of southern Democrats.

Liberals got little out of their pact with Jim Crow. "Growth with equity" was a dead letter by the end of the Truman years. The fiscal regime left by the policy decisions of the 1940s was inflexible, though capable of moderating the effects of recession. What it did not create was the capacity to manage the economy through a coherent fiscal policy or launch new social policies. The capacity of Democratic administrations to stimulate and sustain economic growth through spending policies foundered on the inclinations of southerners. Although a majority of southern Democrats could be mobilized in favor of spending, their support was selective, depending on the type and level of spending. After 1950 the archetypal southern Democrat was Olin Teague of Texas, chair of the House Veterans Committee, not Theodore Bilbo or Harry Byrd. Teague hewed to a line that incorporated both fiscal conservatism, which endeared him to Republicans, and the spending impulses of Democrats. He consistently beat back schemes to liberalize veterans' benefits at the same time that he devised veterans' policies that would largely benefit rural constituencies such as his own. Teague was intent on keeping a lid on spending, and with his fellow southerners, voted down most northern schemes that would have raised wage rates or undermined southern apartheid.[69]

Northern Democrats thus found themselves politically hobbled after 1950 by their tortured relationship with southern Democrats and by widening racial conflict. Their weaknesses might have been overcome by the political capacity of a powerful labor movement. But labor's capacity to defend public social provision was eroded after unions linked their fate to collective bargaining for private social policies.

69. Alec P. Pearson Jr., "Olin E. Teague and the Veterans Administration" (Ph.D. diss., Texas A&M University, 1977), pp. 86–87, 102, 109, 162.

CHAPTER FOUR

Bargaining for Social Rights: Unions and the Reemergence of Welfare Capitalism

It appeared in the interest of sound governmental policy to encourage rather than confine or prohibit voluntary private plans aiding citizens by medical care, hospitalization, or other methods protecting their health and well-being and easing the blow of physical or economic misfortune and distress. These plans decrease the responsibility and burdens of the State. Legal restrictions, or prohibitions would, on the other hand, tend to increase the public burden and responsibility and the dependence of the wage earner upon the State.

—SENATOR JAMES MURRAY

I think the development of . . . health insurance through collective bargaining . . . took the heat out of the pressures for national health insurance, but also the pressure for national health insurance gave great stimulus to them.

—NELSON CRUIKSHANK

The political struggles of the 1940s culminated in a fragmented and truncated public welfare state that represented a victory neither for those seeking a more comprehensive welfare state nor those advocating public means-tested social policies. The resulting gaps in the American welfare state were filled through the growth of private social policies—pensions, health and disability insurance, even unemployment benefits. Most individuals receive private social benefits as employee benefits, financed by employer supplements to wages and salaries. Entitlement to these benefits is based on employment, not citizenship. Such policies are not absent from other welfare states, but the United States has made a virtue of what many countries consider an unwanted stepchild. Even when compared to the less capacious welfare states of Britain or Australia, much less the comprehensive continental European or Scandinavian welfare states, American reliance on private social protection is anomalous.[1]

1. The United States spends a higher fraction of GNP for private pensions (1.4 percent) than any other industrial society, and 57 percent of all U.S. health expenditures are

Private social benefits became a core element in the American welfare state during the late 1940s. It was in this period that the choice between public and private forms of social protection was made explicit, although the issue never became a matter of overt political conflict. The explosive growth of private pensions and private health and disability insurance after 1945 was tantamount to a revival of the private welfare capitalism that had flourished in the 1920s but expired with the depression. Pre–New Deal corporate managers had melded paternalism with efficiency and offered workers housing schemes, pensions and profit sharing arrangements, and health and recreation programs. Striped of its paternalistic veneer, the welfare capitalism of the 1920s was fundamentally anti-union, and it largely succeeded as an instrument of labor control, although workers were never entirely docile or loyal.[2] Yet when private welfare capitalism reemerged after World War II, it was not the product of a conservative plot to halt the Democratic party agenda of an expanded welfare state. In fact, the new welfare capitalism came with a union label.

American labor unions and their European counterparts emerged from the war explicitly committed to creating a universal, "cradle to grave" public welfare state. Despite their rivalry, both the American Federation of Labor (AFL) and the Congress of Industrial Organizations (CIO) supported the Third New Deal's blueprint for a comprehensive public welfare state.[3] Black workers willingly signed on and eschewed the appeal of racial consciousness during the war, much as they had in the 1930s. They believed that the union agenda for full employment and universal social insurance presented a chance to "establish a framework favorable to the continuing occupational advancement of the black worker; and to the removal of the white worker's fear of him as an economic rival."[4] But, despite its public agenda, the American labor movement was instrumental to the expansion of private social welfare by making fringe benefits (principally, paid vaca-

private, compared to an average of 20 percent in other welfare states. Gøsta Esping-Andersen, *The Three Worlds of Welfare Capitalism* (Princeton, N.J., 1990), pp. 71, 83.

2. Gerald Zahavi, "Negotiated Loyalty: Welfare Capitalism and the Shoe Workers of Endicott Johnson, 1920–1940," *Journal of American History* 71 (1983): 602–20; Stuart Brandes, *American Welfare Capitalism, 1880–1940* (Chicago, 1976); David Brody, *Workers in Industrial America* (New York, 1980), pp. 48–81.

3. Julie Meyer, "Trade Union Plans for Postwar Reconstruction in the United States," *Social Research* 11 (1944): 491–505.

4. Willard S. Townsend, "Full Employment and the Negro Worker," in *A Documentary History of the Negro People in the United States,* vol. 4, ed. Herbert Aptheker (New York, 1974), p. 524.

tions, health insurance, and pensions) objects of collective bargaining. Unions in other countries eventually incorporated private pensions, but not other social benefits, into collective bargaining. But nowhere was collective bargaining over private benefits taken up as early and with such aggressiveness as in the United States. Other national labor movements were implacably opposed to bargaining over pensions. The British Trades Unions Council, for example, steadfastly opposed such bargaining, finally accepting it only because of pressure from the government.[5]

Unions were actively aided in their campaign by northern Democrats, including Harry Truman and Senator James Murray from Montana, one of the few authentic social democrats to emerge from American soil. During the congressional debate on a provision of the Taft-Hartley Act to outlaw union contributions to health and welfare funds, Murray justified private social benefits to his fellow Democrats in terms that Robert Taft or the American Medical Association (AMA) could have accepted. The AMA, in fact, publicly applauded the union fight to make health insurance subject to collective bargaining. Nelson Cruikshank, the AFL's chief lobbyist on social welfare matters, believed that the AMA would not have been as successful in deflecting the movement for national health insurance if union demands at the bargaining table had not taken some of the steam out of it.[6]

The role of unions in reviving welfare capitalism governed the relationship of American unions and individual workers to the welfare state after the 1940s. Critics at the time argued that private social benefits "assure great inequality" because many workers will not be covered: unorganized workers, individuals with an intermittent attachment to the labor force, or employees of small firms. Eveline Burns, one of the architects of Roosevelt's plans to go beyond the social policies of the 1930s, presciently warned that union programs will "inevitably weaken the interest of those workers covered by welfare plans negotiated by unions in pressing for extensions and liberalizations of our public programs."[7] Grant McConnell, among others, has seen in these events an atavistic impulse toward voluntarism, the business

5. Jill Bernstein, "Employee Benefits in the Welfare State: Great Britain and the United States since World War II" (Ph.D. diss., Columbia University, 1980), pp. 344–46, 353–60, 389–91.

6. Nelson Cruikshank, Columbia University Oral History Collection, pt. 3, Labor, p. 9.

7. *New York Times*, December 2, 1949; Clark Kerr, "Social and Economic Implications of Private Pension Plans," *Commercial and Financial Chronicle*, December 1, 1949, p. 21.

unionism of the pre–New Deal era when many union leaders championed trade union autonomy and opposed public social insurance.[8] The ability of unions to act in the interests of all working people, union and nonunion alike, as well as to override the hostility between black and white workers, depends on their relationship to the welfare state. The significant questions about unionized welfare capitalism are whether unions took themselves out of the struggle for a comprehensive welfare state, and, if so, whether this removal contributed to labor's transformation from a broad social movement in the 1930s to a narrow interest group in the 1950s. These questions are better addressed after we analyze the paradox of union and liberal-Democrat support for private welfare capitalism.

Why did the labor movement chose to abandon its postwar agenda by pursuing private social protection at the bargaining table? Why did northern Democrats compromise their dream of a broad, inclusive welfare state by supporting the labor movement's change of priorities? At the time, it was commonly assumed that conservative opposition to a public welfare state was an "invitation to unions to . . . 'get [their] pensions from private industry.'"[9] Some labor leaders, Walter Reuther for example, went so far as to justify union actions as a shrewd political strategy calculated to induce business support for public social welfare policies by ratcheting up the cost of fringe benefits.[10] Unionized welfare capitalism was never just a question of whether to have public or private social policies, either for the labor movement or for its allies in the Democratic party. It would be foolish to discount entirely the effects of conservative opposition to the expansion of federal social policy. But this was always less relevant to unions than the question of their status and power with respect to that of managers. Ironically, private welfare capitalism's postwar reconstruction tacitly aligned the labor movement with purveyors of the new managerial ideology for private provision of social protection and with the AMA, while inspiring managerial opposition to collective bargaining of social policies.

Those postwar businessmen advocating privatization of social welfare

8. Grant McConnell, *Private Power and American Democracy* (New York, 1966), chap. 10; see also Nelson Lichtenstein, "From Corporatism to Collective Bargaining: Organized Labor and the Eclipse of Social Democracy in the Postwar Era," in *The Rise and Fall of the New Deal Order, 1930–1980,* ed. Steve Fraser and Gary Gerstle (Princeton, N.J., 1989), pp. 122–52.

9. "Pensions Reconsidered," *Nation,* November 19, 1949, p. 484.

10. Jill Quadagno, *The Transformation of Old Age Pensions* (Chicago, 1988), pp. 159–71.

were inclined to see private social benefits as a bulwark against "state socialism." They accepted the language of economic rights popularized by Roosevelt during the war but sought to establish these rights privately. "Businessmen and industrialists *must* concern themselves with economic rights," wrote Russell W. Davenport, a prominent figure in the creation and articulation of the postwar doctrine of social responsibility for corporate managers; they must take action so as to "transfer the private responsibility, and therefore the initiative, from government to private hands."[11] Davenport extolled efficiency rather than paternalism in tones that echoed the rationale for welfare capitalism in the 1920s, arguing that private social insurance was not just a prophylactic for a public welfare state but would allow executives "to produce a better product at lower cost."

Most corporate managers ignored Davenport's appeal and continued to believe that provision of employee benefits was a managerial prerogative. The older, anti-union rationale for corporate social benefits remained a vital feature of managerial ideology and strategic practice. Corporate managers proved noticeably reluctant to embrace a course of action manifestly in their interest and remained less than enthusiastic, even deeply opposed, to negotiating with unions over pensions and social insurance in 1949. One corporate lobbyist told Congress "it could not have been the valid intent of the Wagner Act to compel employers to bargain away their advantage and responsibility in relation to pension and retirement plans," since it was this "responsibility," he suggested, that constituted "the major remaining factor in establishing friendly relations and assuring permanence and loyalty" with employee personnel.[12] Businessmen may have disliked much of Truman's Fair Deal, but Davenport's alternative seemed just as pernicious. These businessmen lobbied furiously during Congressional hearings on the operation of the Taft-Hartley Act to outlaw collective bargaining over health and welfare funds, arguing strenuously against union involvement. Many businessmen saw collectively bargained social protection not as the last bastion between a free society and "state socialism" but as "privately imposed sales taxes for the benefit of a particular group."[13]

Unionized private welfare capitalism emerged from a bitter postwar

11. Russell W. Davenport, "The Greatest Opportunity on Earth," *Fortune* 40 (October 1949): 68.

12. United States Congress, Hearings, Joint Committee on Labor-Management Relations, 80th Cong., 2d sess., *Operation of the Labor-Management Relations Act, 1947*, pt. 1 (Washington, D.C., 1948), p. 565.

13. Ibid., p. 507.

struggle between opposing classes and, as such, was a matter of labor policy. It triumphed only because New Deal liberals from Truman on down were driven to support the unions at crucial moments in their push for collectively bargained social rights. Bargaining over fringe benefits bore directly on the security of union membership, a question that was reopened when the closed shop was outlawed by the Taft-Hartley Act. For labor leaders, fringes were a device to insure the loyalty of workers to unions; for businessmen they were a way to promote company loyalty and undermine unions.

Collective Bargaining and Social Rights

The revolution in collective bargaining was led by the three most powerful industrial unions of the era: the United Mine Workers (UMW), United Steel Workers (USW), and the United Auto Workers (UAW). These three unions represented over two million workers in 1945 and were led by three of the most influential and tenacious labor leaders of the time: John L. Lewis, Philip Murray (president of both the USW and the CIO), and Walter Reuther. By the end of the war, about 600,000 workers were covered by health and welfare funds through collective bargaining. The unions that had secured such benefits were drawn from both the AFL and CIO, but they were a diverse group and in no position to influence the direction of the postwar labor movement. Lewis, Reuther, and Murray were in such a position, however, and it is doubtful that unionized welfare capitalism would have had the impact it did were it not for the pivotal role of these union chieftains.

Initially, the emergence of a private alternative to public social welfare was an inadvertent consequence of wartime tax and labor policies. Changes in the internal revenue code and the decision of the National War Labor Board (NWLB) to permit fringe benefits in lieu of wage increases during the war furnished labor leaders and business executives with ample incentives to demand and give fringes. Although the labor movement did not inaugurate the shift toward private social protection, it was clearly responsible for its rapid growth and its legitimacy. Unions not only extracted pensions and health plans from corporate managers, they reworked the idea of social rights to include collectively bargained benefits. What labor demanded, Donna Allen points out in her suggestive study of vacation benefits, was "an employee benefit, social in nature, which the employer owed them by reason of his use of their services."[14]

14. Donna Allen, *Fringe Benefits: Wages or Social Obligation* (New York, 1964), p. 93.

Labor leaders initially chose to make collective bargaining of health and welfare benefits an issue in the fall of 1946. Walter Reuther spoke for many in the labor movement when he told the CIO convention that year, "there is no evidence to encourage the belief that we may look to Congress for relief. In the immediate future, security will be won for our people only to the extent that the union succeeds in obtaining such security through collective bargaining."[15] CIO delegates passed a resolution affirming the principle of "security through collective bargaining." William Green, president of the AFL, praised John L. Lewis's successful strike to gain a health and welfare fund for mine workers, telling the AFL convention in October 1946 that all AFL affiliates would be encouraged to negotiate health and welfare funds. David McDonald of the steelworkers sounded the charge at the CIO convention, proclaiming, "we of the Steelworkers Union, and I know of some of the other unions, intend to press these demands very vigorously in the coming collective bargaining conferences. . . . We contemplate that any plan which is negotiated shall be paid for exclusively by the employers."[16]

Private pensions and social insurance were contested terrain for the next three years, the major battles being fought in 1949. Philip Murray, president of the CIO, announced after the 1948 election that labor would stress social insurance, not wages, in the 1949 bargaining sessions; and Reuther wrote UAW locals in early 1949 saying the union was going to take "pension and social security plans out of the category of fringe demands and put them at the top of the agenda." Murray and Reuther, who were reported to be studying actuarial tables in order to frame their demands for health and welfare funds and pensions, were not alone: "Scores of AFL and independent unions will be in the field," the press announced, "to add their members to the total of 3.5 million unionized workers now covered by welfare programs."[17] The unions won important contracts containing health plans and other fringes that year. The flood gates were opened, and by 1954 three-quarters of union members, over 11 million workers, were covered by a health plan or pension through collective bargaining, up from one-eighth of union members in 1948 (table 6).

Both AFL and CIO unions avidly sought employer concessions on health

15. Quoted in Frank G. Dickinson, "The Trend toward Labor Health and Welfare Programs," *Journal of the American Medical Association* (1947): 1286.

16. *New York Times,* October 8, 1946, October 13, 1946; Congress of Industrial Organizations, *Report of the Proceedings of the 8th Constitutional Convention,* 1946, pp. 185–86, quoted in Bernstein, "Employee Benefits," pp. 408–10.

17. *New York Times,* April 2, 1949, p. 2; *Business Week,* January 22, 1949, pp. 19–20.

Table 6.   Private social benefits among all union members and by union federation, 1948–1954

	All union members	Members of AFL	Members of CIO	Independents
1948				
Total covered	11.7%	68.5%	31.5%	
1950				
Total covered	56.5	35.1	47.5	17.5%
HWF[a] and pensions	33.9	33.0	77.9	66.1
HWF only	18.7	· 50.8	20.6	31.1
Pensions only	3.9	16.2	1.4	2.8
1954				
Total covered	75.1	45.2	43.6	12.2
HWF and pensions	46.0	41.3	75.8	84.0
HWF only	27.8	55.3	23.6	16.0
Pensions only	1.3	3.4	0.6	

Sources: "Employee Benefit Plans under Collective Bargaining, Mid-1950," *Monthly Labor Review* 72 (February 1951), table 1, p. 156; "Health, Insurance, and Pension Plans in Union Contracts," *Monthly Labor Review* 78 (September 1955): table 1, p. 994.

Note: The data in the first column is based on the total number of union members in 1948, 1950, and 1954, respectively. The data in the last three columns is based on the number of union members covered by an employee benefit plan under collective bargaining.

[a]Health and welfare funds.

and pension benefits. Two-thirds of union members covered by a health and welfare fund and/or pension in 1947 were from AFL unions. After the CIO surge of 1949–50, there was little difference between the proportion of AFL or CIO workers protected. Where the AFL and CIO did differ was in their preferences for social protection: AFL unions were more inclined to bargain for health benefits than for pensions. By 1954, three-quarters of CIO workers were covered by plans combining health and pension benefits, compared to 41 percent of AFL workers; a majority of AFL workers, on the other hand, were covered by separate health and welfare benefits.

Differences between rival union federations are trivial compared to differences in coverage between union members and all other workers. Access to the private safety net was determined by whether a worker was in a union or an industry that was heavily unionized (see figure 4).[18] Overall, private employee benefits such as pensions, group health, and life insurance made up a large fraction of employee compensation by 1980. Private wage

18. Estimates of union density in figure 4 are based on H. M. Douty, "Collective Bargaining Coverage in Factory Employment, 1958," *Monthly Labor Review* 83 (1960): 345–49; and Richard B. Freeman and James L. Medoff, "New Estimates of Private Sector Unionism in the United States," *Industrial and Labor Relations Review* 32 (1979): 143–74.

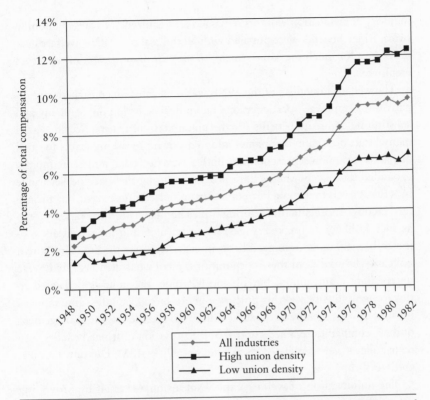

Figure 4. Private wage supplements by union density, 1948–1982. *Source: The National Income and Product Accounts of the United States: Statistical Tables, 1929–1982* (Washington, D.C., 1986), tables 6.4B, 6.13.

supplements accounted for about 2 percent of total employee compensation in 1948; by 1980 they were almost 10 percent of the total, and made up almost two-thirds of total wage supplements compared to just half in 1948. High-union-density industries paid out almost 3 percent of compensation for social insurance and pensions in 1948 compared to 1 percent in low-union-density industries. By 1980 the figure was 12.2 percent for high-union-density industries and 6.3 percent for low-union-density industries.

Unions stimulated spending on private social benefits, and the threat of unionization was a key force in the growth of fringes in large nonunion companies. Such companies remained a small but significant segment of the core economy even during the turbulent days when unions were ascendant. One study estimated that 5 percent of Fortune 500 companies were nonunion and found a much larger segment to be predominately nonunion since a majority of production workers remained unorganized.[19] In large nonunion firms, fringe benefits were pursued with all the zeal of a 1920s welfare capitalist and for much the same reason: to prevent unionization of the firm's employees.

The welfare capitalism of the 1920s was predicated on constructing alternatives for employee "participation" and influence within the company and substituting company benefits for the union version. During World War II many large, nonunion companies adopted private social programs to quell demands for union representation. Both Eastman-Kodak and Sears rapidly expanded their corporate welfare programs during the war and set fringe benefits at levels that could be obtained in unionized firms, according to Sanford Jacoby. Another manufacturing firm, Thompson Products (later known as TRW), diligently tracked wages, seniority rules, and other matters subject to bargaining in unionized firms in order to frame the company's own policies. The actions of these corporations, Jacoby has demonstrated, were unrepentantly anti-union, but obviously ironic: the policies dedicated to thwarting unions served this purpose only to introduce "the same reforms the unions were seeking at the same time."[20] Nevertheless, the management of these companies retained control of the provision of fringe benefits, and their policies were replicated elsewhere, notably by IBM, Dupont, Eli Lilly, and Northrup.

The unionization of welfare capitalism insinuated itself by provoking defensive maneuvers among anti-union employers and by incorporating nonpecuniary obligations into the wage bargain. The language of social rights, which was then being used to establish a public obligation for social welfare, was embedded in collective bargaining and spread to nonunion settings. The idea of a right to social benefits was interpreted by labor leaders as an obligation by management to provide for the health and security of workers and as an entitlement due workers. As one union official explained, "the vast army of organized workers, not content to wait for possible legislation, have pressed for the attainment of some of these benefits now as a complement to the weekly payroll check. Workers want these benefits as

19. Fred K. Foulkes, "Large Nonunionized Employers," in *U.S. Industrial Relations 1950–1980: A Critical Assessment,* ed. Jack Stieber, Robert B. McKersie, and D. Quinn Mills (Madison, Wisc., 1981), p. 133; Richard Freeman, "The Effect of Unionism on Fringe Benefits," *Industrial and Labor Relations Review* 34 (1981): 496, 499–502.

20. Sanford M. Jacoby, "Norms and Cycles: The Dynamics of Nonunion Industrial Relations in the United States, 1897–1985," UCLA, Institute of Industrial Relations, Working Paper Series 123 (Los Angeles, 1987), pp. 22–23.

part payment for their labor and not as a grant bearing the stigma of charity."[21]

Two ideas were important to unions: that the benefit be earned, a form of deferred compensation; and that the payment be a legitimate cost of doing business. Labor leaders often invoked analogies between labor and machines, arguing that providing for retirement or vacations was no different than replacing worn-out machinery. Like many labor leaders, Philip Murray saw the matter of collective bargaining and pensions as a moral issue:

> I would take an old steelworker who has reached the age of 65, and who has rendered years of yeoman service, and given of his sweat and his blood, and perhaps a limb to industry, and is about to get out, he is about to leave, he is done, he is tired, and he has no pension except a measly form of social security. . . . I . . . should stand beside that old man here in this room a piece of metal, a piece of ordinary metal, and our system provides replacement, our system provides monies of a very substantial nature for wear, tear, and depreciation of that piece of iron, that piece of metal. There you have the man, the old man, the human machine, the creature, the man, possessing, as he does, the dignity of a man, and a creature of God. He gets nothing. And the same corporation that gives to him nothing expends $146,000,000 in the year 1948 for the wear and tear and depreciation of the inanimate machine, the piece of metal.[22]

Labor leaders were angered that corporate managers received lucrative pensions while workers received little or nothing. Business leaders denounced these arguments, but public policy had already begun to shift toward labor. The War Labor Board took the initial step when it adopted the view that vacations were an earned right rather than a management prerogative. This principle was then imported into labor disputes, often by third-party arbitrators. Acceptance of an obligation for private social benefits thus spread, reinforcing the anti-union inclinations of many employers.[23]

It is doubtful that business ever fully accepted the labor ideology of welfare capitalism; but business did come to accept fringes as part of the wage contract and collective bargaining, notwithstanding the intransigence of the

21. Helen Baker and Dorothy Dahl, *Group Health Insurance Plans and Sickness Benefits in Collective Bargaining* (Princeton, N.J., 1945), p. 19.

22. Proceedings of the Executive Committee, October/November 1949, Congress of Industrial Organizations, pp. 34–35, GMMA. See also L. S. Buckmaster, "CIO Views on Pensions," *Commercial and Financial Chronicle* 170 (December 1, 1949): 20. Buckmaster was president of the United Rubber, Cork, Linoleum, and Plastic Workers, a CIO affiliate.

23. Allen, *Fringe Benefits*, pp. 136–40, 168.

National Association of Manufactures. Davenport's argument for private social welfare became an intrinsic part of corporate ideology, even if notions of economic rights were discarded, and it contributed to the diffusion of employee benefits. At the same time, unionized welfare capitalism was incrementally extended and undergirded by law. In 1952, the National Labor Relations Board (NLRB) ruled that it was illegal for either employers or unions to restrict fringe benefits to union members; and the Davis-Bacon Act was amended in 1964 to include fringe benefits in the definition of "prevailing wages," obligating contractors in federally financed construction projects to pay for pensions and health care, not just wages.[24]

The Wages of Insecurity

CIO and AFL unions made collective bargaining over social rights an issue because it was central to the viability of unions as institutions. The union shift in priorities was neither a reluctant turn to voluntarism in the face of an intransigent Congress and a more conservative political environment nor a strategy to erode business opposition to the welfare state. The unions' decision grew out of the conflicts endemic to an emerging system of collective bargaining in the late 1940s.

Alternative explanations are not very persuasive. CIO leaders justified their 1949 bargaining initiatives as a way to expand public welfare policies, but there is no evidence that this gambit ever worked or that it was anything more than a rationalization for the 1949 collective bargaining strategy. In congressional testimony, Walter Reuther said, "we fought for a noncontributory pension plan in industry because we knew that that was the key to getting action at the Federal Government level." Reuther claimed that the UAW tried to negotiate pension agreements that would reduce a company's contribution to a private pension plan as social security benefits were raised, so "the employer will have an incentive to go down to Washington and fight with us to get the Government to meet this problem."[25] Reuther succeeded in extracting such an agreement from Ford Motor Company, yet this may have been less a consequence of the UAW's bargaining strategy than employer intransigence. One report on the negotiations said that both the UAW and United Steel Workers were seeking a pension with no offset so that both

24. Isadore Katz and David Jaffe, "Illegal Pension and Welfare Funds," *Labor Law Journal* 4 (1953): 13–18; Stuart R. Wolk, "The Fringe-Benefit Amendment to the Davis-Bacon Act," *Labor Law Journal* 15 (1964): 673–77.

25. Quoted in Charles L. Dearing, *Industrial Pensions* (Washington, D.C., 1954), p. 47.

public and private pension benefits would rise together, but they lost at the bargaining table.

Nor was the failure to liberalize social security, improve unemployment benefits, and pass national health insurance the main reason why unions decided to add social rights to collective bargaining. It is true that labor leaders sought private remedies in the face of public failure, but CIO and AFL unions would have made bargaining over corporate welfare programs an issue regardless of the outcome of legislative struggles. CIO officials endorsed a two-track strategy in 1949 that combined public and private social policies, and they indicated they had no intention of relenting in their efforts to make employers ante up for pensions and social insurance.[26] Liberalization of OASI benefits would not have quenched labor's thirst for private pensions because they were viewed as a supplement to social security rather than an alternative. According to the UAW, "As improvements are made in federal Social Security, a larger portion of the Ford Company's 8.75 cents contribution will be used to retire past service credits. As increased federal benefits make it possible to pay off past service credits at a faster rate, the road will be cleared for the union through collective bargaining to win additional company-financed pensions and hospital and medical programs."[27] Labor elites were concerned about maintaining the standard of living for retiring workers, and social security (even if liberalized) was deemed insufficient. The UAW-GM pension agreement of 1950, in fact, abandoned the goal of a one hundred dollar per month minimum pension linked to OASI by allowing social security benefit increases to take effect with no reduction in management's contribution to private pensions.[28]

Moreover, the public failure hypothesis begs the question of labor's choice to launch a massive campaign to obtain private social protection after Truman's reelection, the one moment when the possibilities of enacting new social policies seemed brightest. Even if it were true that the 1949 pension agreements were sought to force action on social security legislation, this does not explain the drive for health benefits. There was, in fact, little debate over the implications of the labor strategy for Truman's health insurance bill. The choice of 1949 was not dictated by conservative opposition to the welfare state; it was made before the Truman administration introduced pension and health legislation and was based on a calculation

26. Bernstein, "Employee Benefits," p. 417.

27. *United Auto Worker,* October 1949, p. 4, quoted in *Pensions and Health and Welfare Plans in Collective Bargaining,* ed. Anne P. Cook (Los Angeles, 1950), p. 13.

28. A. H. Raskin, *New York Times,* December 27, 1949.

that wage increases were unattainable in a year in which the economy was widely perceived to be sliding into a recession. Health and pension benefits seemed more attainable.[29]

The union preference for fringes is more accurately understood in the context of postwar conflict between unions and corporate managers to control the development and shape of the system of modern collective bargaining. Organized labor emerged from the war as a formidable social force in American society. Unionized workers made up 30.4 percent of the nonfarm labor force in 1945, and the number of workers organized into unions increased by 6 million between 1939 and 1945 (union membership had grown by only 3 million from 1933 to 1939).[30] Unions obtained these membership gains with the aid of the NWLB by accepting a no-strike pledge and wage stabilization policies in exchange for government-guaranteed security of membership. When the war ended, unions had finally secured a position in the industrial order and strengthened their organizational capacity, but their power and prerogatives relative to business within the new system of industrial relations as well as the political leverage of the labor movement remained to be established.[31]

The difficult negotiations and frequent, bitter strikes that took place from 1945 to 1950 were never simply about wages and hours; the very terms of collective bargaining were at issue in this war. Labor and business meant quite different things by the term collective bargaining. Most businessmen at the time were either explicitly anti-union or dedicated to containment, a strategy that entailed a variety of measures: confining bargaining to as narrow a scope as possible ("wages, hours, and conditions of employment"); circumscribing the status of unions by refusing to consult labor leaders; going to the mat no matter what the cost; and attempting to communicate with workers directly. Corporate chieftains were visibly angered that unions publicly justified their wage and fringe benefit demands with appeals to human rights, purchasing power, or "the American standard of living."[32]

29. This was widely reported at the time; see *Business Week*, January 22, 1949, p. 19; *New York Times*, March 28, 1949.

30. Leo Troy and Neil Sheflin, *U.S. Union Sourcebook* (West Orange, N.J., 1985), pp. III-10–III-11.

31. Howell J. Harris, *The Right to Manage* (Madison, Wisc., 1982), pp. 43–60; Nelson Lichtenstein, *Labor's War at Home* (New York, 1982), pp. 73–81; Robert M. MacDonald, "Collective Bargaining in the Postwar Period," *Industrial and Labor Relations Review* 20 (1966–67): 554–58.

32. Harris, *Right to Manage*, p. 60.

GM management, Frederick Harbison and Robert Dubin point out, always construed "bargaining with the union" and "dealings with our employees" as distinct activities. Nor was GM unique. General Electric executives followed a labor strategy designed to break down communication and ties between workers and unions while cultivating a direct employer-employee tie. The point was to relegate unions to a confined and narrow niche in the industrial order.[33]

Labor elites took a much broader view of collective bargaining, though it would be incorrect to ascribe unanimity to the labor movement. Reuther thought that political ends could be obtained through collective bargaining. Just as the war ended, he demanded a 30 percent wage increase from General Motors with no price increase, thus putting the corporation's pricing policies on the bargaining table. Reuther's demands reflected what has since come to be called "social unionism," the idea that the labor movement embodied the aspirations of all people, consumers and unorganized workers as well as union members. Elements of this vision, central to the CIO at the time, could be found in Philip Murray's corporativist scheme for planning and in CIO agitation for the guaranteed annual wage. Reuther's bold initiative was perhaps quixotic in its assumption that collective bargaining was a suitable vehicle to gain political ends in an otherwise fragmented labor movement. His strategy failed when other CIO unions defected, accepting the wage increases they had gained from the strike and letting others worry about prices.

The broad-gauged CIO strategy of 1945–46 gave way to a more narrowly framed collective bargaining strategy by the fall of 1946 as Reuther and Murray—with William Green and the AFL following suit—embraced unionized welfare capitalism. For Murray and Reuther, arguably the two most influential CIO leaders, this amounted to abandoning any link between collective bargaining and political ends, even though they denied it at the time. Their decision was influenced by the wide assault on unions then being advanced by conservatives and by the failure to tie wage increases to price controls or to negotiate a guaranteed annual wage. But if such events pointed to the limits on union power, they did not dictate the sharp shift in the CIO agenda that actually took place. Nor did the preference for fringe benefits originate from rank and file demands. Most union members remained

33. Frederick H. Harbison and Robert Dubin, *Patterns of Union-Management Relations* (Chicago, 1947), pp. 46, 51; Ronald W. Schatz, *The Electrical Workers* (Urbana, Ill., 1983), p. 171; see also Jacoby, "Norms and Cycles," pp. 18–38.

indifferent if not hostile to the idea, preferring wage increases to private social benefits.[34] The demand for collective bargaining of social rights derived from the preoccupations and concerns of union elites, especially in the three most influential unions—miners, steelworkers, and autoworkers. Indeed, the shift in strategy was imposed from above; it was Lewis, Murray, and Reuther who changed course.

John L. Lewis's demand in 1945–46 for a company-funded union health and welfare fund was arguably the single most influential action taken by a union leader at the time; it was far more decisive for the future of the labor movement than Reuther's abortive collective bargaining strategy. The mine workers' success legitimized the pursuit of private social rights within the labor movement and put the onus upon other labor leaders to show they could do just as well. Yet Lewis's actions would have made little difference had the CIO not changed its mind and the steelworkers and autoworkers not succeeded in making fringes an object of negotiation. Both unions put fringes on the bargaining table for the 1947 round. The UAW wanted management to contribute 3 percent of payrolls to an insurance fund for health and sickness benefits (including maternity benefits) and survivor's benefits, and the steelworkers asked for a guaranteed annual wage and social insurance. It was the success of these two unions that opened the door to widespread bargaining over private social rights.[35]

For these three unions, the shift to unionized welfare capitalism was more a response to internal organizational dilemmas, aggravated by the ongoing struggle with management, than it was a political strategy to use collective bargaining to gain business support for public social welfare or a reaction to Reuther's aborted campaign to link profits and wages. Putting private social benefits on the bargaining table was often integral to the long-run viability and success of a union. This factor, more than any other, explains John L. Lewis's bold demand for a company-funded health and welfare fund in the spring of 1945. Lewis's behavior is often explained by the latent voluntarism in the soul of this AFL unionist; Raymond Munts describes him as a "Republican on vacation" during the New Deal.[36] Lewis, unlike many labor

34. Baker and Dahl, "Health Insurance and Collective Bargaining," p. 22; E. Robert Livernash, *Collective Bargaining in the Basic Steel Industry* (Washington, D.C., 1961), p. 86.

35. The UAW demands were formulated prior to the 1946 election. Martin Halpern, *UAW Politics in the Cold War Era* (Albany, N.Y., 1988), p. 188; *Business Week,* December 7, 1946; Livernash, *Collective Bargaining,* pp. 255–56; Harold M. Levinson, *Collective Bargaining in the Steel Industry* (Ann Arbor, Mich., 1962), p. 25.

36. Raymond Munts, *Bargaining for Health* (Madison, Wisc., 1967), p. 32.

leaders, had abandoned the New Deal to strike out on his own and his rhetoric was stridently voluntaristic by the time Harry Truman was reelected. But it is dubious whether one should attribute his actions to a simple bread and butter voluntarism, the idea that unions should go it alone. Lewis's so-called voluntarism was less important than the health of the union membership and the union's long-run bargaining strategy.

The UMW faced a somewhat unusual set of problems in the late 1940s. Mine workers were older and less healthy than workers in many other industries. The average age of UMW miners was forty-five by 1944; only 16 percent were below the age of thirty, and one-third of these had been classified as 4-F during the war. There were over eleven thousand miners over the age of sixty-five still working. Confronted with an older and less healthy work force in a dangerous, accident-prone industry, Lewis had ample incentive to make an issue of health and welfare benefits.[37] Pensions, Lewis argued, could only enhance the efficiency of the industry by retiring older workers and opening up opportunities for younger workers. More important for Lewis's strategy, though, was the union's decision to sacrifice jobs in order to mechanize the mines.

The UMW bargaining strategy was based on sustaining the long-run viability of the industry through increasing productivity and eliminating competition in the perennially chaotic coal industry. Besides improving the economic status of miners, the UMW sought to stabilize wage rates in cyclical downturns, which in its view was a function of excess capacity. The union also adopted a policy of equalizing wage differentials, both within mines and regionally. From the union's point of view, the long-run health of the union depended on the elimination of competition within the industry and its mechanization. Lewis described the strategy as raising "wages high enough to induce the employer to exchange jobs for machines and then take still more wages out of the machines."[38] The demand for health and welfare funds and company pensions was essential since it made possible the necessary reduction in the work force required by the union's bargaining strategy. A health and welfare fund and mechanization dovetailed in myriad ways: the fund provided the means to compensate displaced miners; and

37. Melvyn Dubofsky and Warren Van Tine, *John L. Lewis: A Biography* (New York, 1977), p. 459; Morton S. Baratz, *The Union and the Coal Industry* (New Haven, Conn., 1955), p. 114.

38. Lewis is quoted by Lloyd Ulman, "Forward," in Paul T. Hartman, *Collective Bargaining and Productivity* (Berkeley, 1969), p. ix; Baratz, *Union and the Coal Industry*, p. 51, 69.

since the fund was noncontributory and tied to productivity, it worked against high-cost mines (which the union wanted to push out of business) and made the income of the fund independent of the number of men employed. Employment in mining dropped dramatically after 1950, as did UMW membership, but those remaining in the union had little cause to complain. Besides a generous health and welfare fund, wages in the coal industry remained high; the ratio of wages in the coal industry to all manufacturing industries increased from 1.16 to 1.25.[39]

Mechanization was not the only reason that union elites demanded businesses negotiate private social rights. Many union leaders saw fringe benefits as a way to make gains when large wage increases were ruled out, typically during periods of either recession or inflation, or as a distributive good that union leaders could use to attract followers and consolidate power. But the main reason unions put private social protection on the bargaining table was union security. In an assessment of the Taft-Hartley Act, Clark Clifford, an adviser to President Truman, was told that unions "are numerically strong but organizationally insecure. . . . They are forced to fight with every weapon at their command what they consider threats to the development and maintenance of group solidarity among their members."[40] If unions were impervious to a complete rollback in the postwar period, they had by no means escaped challenges to their security and power. Union security was always an issue for labor leaders given the deeply rooted and distinctive hostility of American businessmen to their very existence. What typifies American businessmen, argues Sanford Jacoby, is their unremitting antagonism to unions, a hostility that hardly abated after depression and war, and their considerable ability (compared to their European counterparts) to act on it. Legal guarantees of security were regarded as insufficient by most union leaders. As one UMW official said at the time, "It is not the union shop which stabilizes union membership in the captive mines, but other informal devices for membership control."[41]

Union security remained a concern of union leaders in the late 1940s, and at the root of their fears was Taft-Hartley. Paul M. Herzog, chair of the NLRB,

39. Baratz, *Union and the Coal Industry,* p. 116; William H. Miernyk, "Coal," in *Collective Bargaining: Contemporary American Experience,* ed. Gerald G. Somers (Madison, Wisc., 1979), pp. I-11, I-24, I-44–I-47.

40. E. Wright Bakke to Clark Clifford, June 14, 1947, Clark Clifford Papers, box 8, folder "HR 3020," no. 2, HSTL.

41. Jacoby, "Norms and Cycles," pp. 3–4, 9–12, 32–33; Robert C. Spencer, "Bargaining with the Government: A Case Study in the Politics of Collective Bargaining in the Basic Steel Industry" (Ph.D. diss., University of Chicago, 1955), p. 91. "Captive mines" refers to coal mines owned by steel companies.

did not accept the union view that Taft-Hartley was a "slave labor" law, but he did regard it as a significant shift in federal policy, noting that Title I "taken as a whole will inevitably have the effect of weakening government protection of employee rights and discouraging collective bargaining."[42] The bill stacked the deck against union power, enlarging opportunities for businesses to resist unions or crush weak unions, and diluting union power in the workplace. The union security provisions of the law were especially threatening. The Taft-Hartley Act flatly banned the closed shop, where membership in the union was required as a condition of employment. It permitted a union shop, a less restrictive method of maintaining membership, but imposed severe obstacles to its creation. The law required a thirty-day waiting period to give newly hired workers the chance not to join the union; a union shop could only be negotiated if 30 percent of the workers petitioned for an election on this issue and if a majority of all eligible workers approved it; before holding an election union officials were required to sign an affidavit that the union was not communist; and state laws prevailed if they carried stricter provisions.

Taft-Hartley's union security provisions indicate what Hartley meant when he told the House, "there is more in this bill than may meet the eye." The "more" in the case of union security was a provision that stipulated employers need not accept a union shop even if workers voted for it; they were only required to bargain about the matter. More nefarious, the law's requirements for union security could be overridden by state laws prohibiting a closed shop, laws encouraged by the notorious Section 14(b) which made state "right to work" laws legal. The union security requirements were a sham, if not unworkable. The law created a national standard on union security but then proceeded to permit states to "outlaw completely all forms of union security and thus destroy the federal standard." All this was rather ominous since "right to work" laws were proliferating; by fall 1947, thirteen states had outlawed the closed shop. Most observers believed that Taft-Hartley's security provisions were mainly a threat to smaller, weaker unions. But not even the powerful steelworkers were immune. The steel companies were opposed to all but the loosest guarantee of membership, and the question of union security remained an issue until the 1952 steel strike.[43]

42. Herzog to President, July 1947, p. 11, OF 407, Taft-Hartley Bill 1947–48, HSTL.

43. Herzog to President, July 1947, pp. 1–4; Bakke to Clifford, June 14, 1947; "Union Security Provisions," August 23, 1948, Harold Enarson Papers, box 2, pp. 6–7, 12, 19–20, 25, HSTL; Harold Enarson, "Draft Statement on Amendments to Taft-Hartley," March 3, 1952, p. 8, Charles Murphy Papers, box 2, LMRA of 1947, HSTL; Spencer, "Bargaining with the Government," pp. 88–89.

The Taft-Hartley obstacle course for union security backfired in one respect: almost all votes on the issue resulted in strong majorities for a union shop, thus crushing conservative illusions about workers' desire for a closed shop. It also had little effect on hiring practices, according to insiders. Union security, however, was *the* hot issue before the NLRB. About two-thirds of all cases brought before the NLRB in late 1947 and 1948 pertained to the union security requirements. Outlawing the closed shop and erecting obstacles to the union shop led unions to search for other ways to ensure union security. The preferred device was a health and welfare fund, which solidified the loyalty of the rank and file and offered the union stability of membership because benefits were typically tied to the firm and, hence, the union.

Private social rights became a divisive issue between unions and management precisely because both unions and management were contesting for the loyalties of a work force formed, by and large, during World War II. Both black and white sharecroppers migrated to the factories of the North and the West Coast, and many women left the kitchen for the assembly line; union leaders were confronted with a more diverse work force, one that had not been through the organizing battles of the 1930s and that had become members of unions by virtue of government mandates rather than strikes.[44] Lacking the shared experience of organizing new unions, the loyalty of these new workers was up for grabs. Rather than create new plans, most unions demanded that existing corporate benefit plans be extended to union members on terms negotiated by the union. This amounted to disarming management in their ongoing struggle to gain the loyalty of workers, taking away one of the tools bosses had historically wielded to the detriment of labor organizers.

More significant, unions found that collectively bargained social rights provided an escape hatch from the threat to their security posed by Taft-Hartley. Fringe benefits obtained on union terms provided the "virtual equivalent" of a closed shop. Businessmen and their political allies in Congress were quite aware of this. The Ball report, a congressional assessment of Taft-Hartley one year after passage, concluded that union-bargained health and welfare funds provided not only a way of disciplining members but "a means of obtaining a condition closely approaching the closed shop now prohibited by the act." The Chamber of Commerce echoed Republican complaints, grousing that the "use of welfare plan demands as an organization device or as a substitute for the closed shop violates . . . precepts of cost, employee

---

44. Mike Davis, *Prisoners of the American Dream* (London, 1986), pp. 75, 77–78.

need, and the company's capacity to carry the plan."[45] Although management typically stated its opposition to negotiating fringes as an inability of reaching an agreement with unions on "actuarially sound" plans, their real objection was any hint of union involvement, on any basis. In his congressional testimony on the Taft-Hartley Act, Charles Wilson, the head of General Motors, told Congress: "Only by defining and restricting collective bargaining to its proper sphere can we hope to save what we have come to know as our American system and keep it from evolving into an alien form, imported from east of the Rhine. Unless this is done, *the border area of collective bargaining will be a constant battleground between employers and unions.*"[46]

The business strategy to weaken unions depended on undercutting the union's role as an intermediary between management and the workforce, and unilateral control over fringes was one way to weaken the union and build direct ties with workers. Employment relations departments were enlarged in the postwar period as managers revived the tools of 1920s welfare capitalism. Pensions and social insurance were combined with a variety of recreational and social programs, which were explicitly designed to win over workers and undermine the assumed radicalism of many unions.[47] Under these circumstances, it is not surprising that union leaders put private social rights on the bargaining table. They would have been foolish not to.

The Democrats' Dilemma: Unions or Welfare State?

The shift in union priorities during and after 1946 and the growth of unionized welfare capitalism is attributable to the exigencies of collective bargaining and union security. Thus the question of the relationship between unionized welfare capitalism and the welfare state was framed and decided as a matter of labor policy. Labor leaders consistently denied that there was any

---

45. Report of the Joint Committee on Labor-Management Relations, *Labor-Management Relations: Welfare Funds,* 80th Cong., 2d sess., p. 13; U.S. Chamber of Commerce, quoted in William Goldner, "Trade Union Structure and Private Pension Plans," *Industrial and Labor Relations Review* 5 (1951), p. 67.

46. Quoted in Harbison and Dubin, *Patterns of Union-Management Relations* p. 57.

47. Ibid., pp. 69–70; Elizabeth Fones-Wolf, "Industrial Recreation, the Second World War, and the Revival of Welfare Capitalism, 1934–1960," *Business History Review* 60 (1986): 242–43, 250–53; Harris, *Right to Manage,* pp. 170–71.

real conflict between their collective bargaining strategies and the future of public social welfare in America. Democrats knew otherwise. Harry Truman had warned that "the basic approach [to security] should be through a comprehensive public program of old-age, survivors, and disability insurance, rather than through a multiplicity of unrelated private plans, which would inevitably omit large numbers of the working population and treat others unequally."[48] Truman's statement obscured a fundamental truth of the postwar era: unions could not have succeeded in negotiating a private welfare state without the aid of the Democratic party. Unions lacked the power to compel companies to bargain in good faith over health and welfare funds. John L. Lewis's hardball tactics put the UMW at the forefront of unionized welfare capitalism and made the rest of the labor movement envious but did little to ensure businessmen's acceptance of collective bargaining of private social protection for the wider labor movement. On the contrary, his actions mobilized business against bargaining over fringes. Democrats were left with the difficult task of defending unions' right to bargain while they were trying to launch new public social policies and liberalize social security.

Mine owners launched a furious assault against union health and welfare funds when the Republican-controlled 80th Congress convened. One hard-headed mine owner warned of impending labor strife unless something were done, characterizing the UMW health and welfare fund as "coerced exaction typical of the broad band of coerced demands not related to wages and working conditions . . . [a strategy] now on the agenda of every central union in a program of sweeping encroachment on the earnings and functions of ownership and management, with no limitation whatever except the conscience of the union dynasty." Republicans responded by attempting to outlaw health and welfare funds. Taft-Hartley was as much about unionized welfare capitalism as anything else.[49]

Democrats did what Lewis could not. They first turned back the Republican assault on union health and welfare funds; then they made such bargaining legal in the NLRB's *Inland Steel* case of 1948 and legitimized the practice with the decision of the president's Steel Board in 1949. At each moment Democrats faced a wrenching dilemma. James Murray and other liberal proponents of universal public social welfare were well aware of the implications of health and welfare funds for their cause but thought they

48. *Public Papers of the Presidents of the United States: Harry S. Truman, 1950* (Washington, D.C., 1951), p. 72.

49. "New Strike Looms Coal Official Says," *New York Times,* February 12, 1947.

had to protect a union's right to bargain over them. Truman opposed private pensions, believing they would hinder efforts to liberalize social security and lead to an inequitable welfare state; but he could not very well oppose Philip Murray and the CIO, to whom he was indebted for victory in 1948.

The Democrats actually had little choice. Republicans and their business allies were always more hostile to unions than to the welfare state. For both sides the issue was control and influence in the workplace. The political struggle over unionized welfare capitalism was driven by the question of union security and influence just as union strategy was. Both the Case bill, antilabor legislation which failed to pass Congress in 1946, and the Taft-Hartley Act contained provisions that made employer contributions to a union health and welfare fund an unfair labor practice. House Republicans were not shy about the target of their animus—Lewis and the UMW—and portrayed the issue as one of abuse of power. The House majority report on Taft-Hartley said: "Certainly, it is not in the national interest for union leaders to control these great, unregulated, untaxed funds derived from exactions upon employers. The clause forbids employers to conspire with unions to mulct employees, without their consent, of huge amounts that ought to go into the worker's wages." Lewis was but a convenient target for Republicans intent on weakening unions. Banning health and welfare funds was akin to restoring injunctions, outlawing the closed shop, and facilitating state "right to work" laws—in short, it was a key element of the business agenda to contain unions. Democrats understood all this. Robert Wagner remonstrated in the Senate debate that the exclusion of pensions and social insurance from collective bargaining gave employers control over matters that should not be subject to the "power of industrial absolutism."[50]

Unionized welfare capitalism was a partisan issue that led to one of the more surreal debates in the United States Congress. If the opposing parties behaved with all loyalty toward their constituent groups, they found themselves arguing against their long-standing interests. The liberal Claude "Red" Pepper attacked the contradiction in the Republican position: "surely those who object to a national health insurance program should not object to a policy of providing for the welfare of the workers in an industry by collective bargaining agreement between management and employees engaged in the industry." Republicans assumed they could have both a weakened labor movement and no welfare state. Democrats had to follow a more tortuous

50. *Legislative History of the Labor Management Relations Act, 1947,* 2 vols. (Washington, D.C., 1959), 1:320–21; Senate, *Congressional Record,* April 11, 1947, p. 998.

path: Pro-welfare state liberals such as Adam Clayton Powell and John F. Kennedy defended union health and welfare funds in the House Minority Report by invoking anti-welfare-state rhetoric. "Provisions which deny employees and organizations the opportunity to make voluntary provisions against illness and insecurity," they said, "can only increase reliance upon the State. . . . The majority fails to appreciate the serious implications of their proposals and their invitation to unrestricted Government control of almost every aspect of normal life."[51]

Intransigent House Republicans inevitably had to defer to cooler heads in the Senate, and in the end Congress passed a law that regulated rather than banned health and welfare funds. Congress could have decided to exclude private social protection from collective bargaining altogether, but did not. The Senate bill, which prevailed, left intact language in the Wagner Act that permitted collective bargaining over "other conditions of employment," but made employer contributions to health and welfare funds legal only if the funds were jointly managed and the money was deposited into a trust. The law did succeed in circumscribing union control of the funds, but it provoked labor conflict rather than stability, as Taft had assured his colleagues would be the case. The reason had to do with the other provisions of Taft-Hartley which, as we have seen, inspired unions to make pensions and health and welfare funds contested terrain.

Republicans set out to destroy health and welfare funds in 1948. The issue figured prominently in hearings scheduled to evaluate the operation of Taft-Hartley, although the law had been in effect less than a year when the hearings commenced. Democrats undercut the Republican strategy when the NLRB, dominated by a four-to-one prolabor majority, ruled in favor of steel unions in the *Inland Steel* case and declared that private pensions were equivalent to wages and thus legally within the scope of collective bargaining. This was quickly followed by the *W. W. Cross* case, which permitted bargaining over social insurance. What interested contemporary observers was that the NLRB could have decided the case on narrow grounds without ruling on the broader question of whether pensions came under the Wagner Act's definition of "conditions of employment." But what the Republicans had been unable to settle in 1947 and wanted to settle in 1948, the NLRB decided. *Inland Steel* was a preemptive strike launched by Paul Herzog, a New York lawyer with solid New Deal credentials and strong labor ties. The

---

51. *History of Labor Management Relations Act*, p. 370; *Congressional Record,* May 7, 1947, p. 1306.

NLRB decision and its subsequent ratification by the courts opened the door to bargaining over social rights and left legislative derailment as the only way to shut down unionized welfare capitalism. Businessmen fumed during the hearings, union representatives made but a token appearance, and the Ball report castigated union health and welfare funds for a multitude of sins, but any possibility of outlawing unionized welfare capitalism was closed when the balance of power in Congress changed after the 1948 election.

The *Inland Steel* decision did not establish the legitimacy of collectively bargained social rights; it merely made them bargainable. What truly opened the flood gates and shattered corporate resistance was Truman's Steel Board. Appointed in July 1949 as a fact-finding board to recommend a settlement for the steel strike, the board surprised almost everyone by turning down the steelworkers' request for a wage increase but accepting the union's demand for pensions and social insurance. The Board concluded

> that all industry, in the absence of adequate Government programs, owes an obligation to workers to provide for maintenance of the human body in the form of medical and similar benefits and full depreciation in the form of old-age retirement—in the same way as it does now for plant and machinery. This obligation is one which should be fulfilled by enlightened business management not when everything else has been taken care of but as one of the fixed costs of doing business—one of the first charges on revenues before profits.[52]

Philip Murray could not have asked for more. He may have lost a wage increase, but he gained something far more important. Remarkably, the board incorporated the CIO theory of bargained social rights, almost word for word, into the steel strike settlement and gave it the imprimatur of the White House. The steel industry was outraged but also genuinely surprised. The big companies resisted settling while the union, predictably, embraced the report. Murray got more or less what he wanted when the companies did settle, and the autoworkers quickly followed suit and pressed similar demands on the automakers. The war was over.

The Steel Board report must be understood from the perspective of union bargaining strategies and the solidification of the tie between unions and the Democratic party in the late 1940s. Union bargaining strategies, particularly Murray's, were predicated on provoking federal involvement in labor disputes under the well-founded belief that federal intervention would tilt the

52. *Report to the President of the United States on the Labor Dispute in the Basic Steel Industry* (Washington, D.C., 1949), p. 55.

balance of power their way. Unlike Lewis, who abandoned Roosevelt and the New Deal, Murray put labor's future in the hands of New Dealers and carefully crafted his bargaining strategy accordingly. The success of the USW's three major postwar strikes—1946, 1949, and 1952—depended on presidential intervention, which Murray correctly calculated would work to their advantage. Bargaining in the steel industry unfolded according to a stylized format, with labor demanding and receiving federal assistance in overcoming the resistance of steel executives and all parties understanding that steel would be allowed to take a hefty price increase at the end.[53]

The Steel Board example highlights Murray's strategy. The union was at an obvious disadvantage in 1949: steel prices were falling and the industry was cutting back production. Moreover, the union was trying to reopen the question of pensions, which the industry maintained was closed by a prior agreement. The steel companies made it clear they were willing to take a strike on the question of pensions, the one demand about which the USW was unwilling to compromise. On the eve of the strike, Murray took the one action calculated to insure favorable federal intervention: he instructed union officers to comply with the Taft-Hartley requirement to sign an affidavit that they were not communists. This action was tied directly to the union strategy to gain pensions and social insurance. The reason goes back to the *Inland Steel* case, when the NLRB decided to make bargaining on pensions conditional on compliance with the affidavit requirement. The USW resisted and went to court, where they eventually lost. Signing the anticommunist affidavit signaled the acceptance of the NLRB quid pro quo.[54]

Truman's willingness to support a policy that ran counter to his own judgment was the result of concerted efforts to patch up the union-party alliance, which was in some jeopardy at the end of the war. Labor leaders had been soured by Truman's reconversion policies and his preemptive actions

---

53. Frederick H. Harbison and Robert Spencer, "The Politics of Collective Bargaining: The Postwar Record in Steel," *American Political Science Review* 48 (1954): 705–20; Ronald W. Schatz, "Philip Murray and the Subordination of the Industrial Unions to the United States Government," in *Labor Leaders in America*, ed. Melvyn Dubofsky and Warren Van Tine (Urbana, 1988), pp. 246, 251–55.

54. Spencer, "Bargaining with the Government," pp. 92, 114–19, 121–22. It was common knowledge in the press that the NLRB was using pensions as a tool to get unions to comply with Taft-Hartley's anticommunist provision. The *Chicago Daily News* reported on March 18, 1948, that it was understood in "labor circles in Washington that the board will use this case as a lever to force compliance by Philip Murray and the steelworkers union with all the requirements of the Taft-Hartley Act." Paul Herzog Papers, box 5, Speeches, folder no. 1, 1947–50, HSTL.

during the 1946 strike wave. Clark Clifford advised Truman he had to renew "the administration's working relationship with progressive and labor leaders," arguing that "no moment will ever be better for the President to make political capital out of the present frustration of the labor movement."[55] Truman acted on this advice and vetoed Taft-Hartley, held regular meetings with Murray and other labor leaders throughout 1948, and tailored the administration's legislative strategy to union needs. The Steel Board, then, was quite clearly the product of an alliance between a Democratic White House and the labor movement, and it produced a settlement that favored the agenda of labor elites.

Labor in the Welfare State

Unionized welfare capitalism was borne of a fear for the future viability of unions as political and economic institutions. The business assault on unions at the end of the war, rather than roadblocks to the welfare state thrown up by conservatives, made fringe benefits a collective bargaining issue that unions could not ignore. Labor leaders surely saw pensions and social insurance as a way to expand the pay envelope, and they used these programs to increase their bargaining options. But Taft-Hartley turned the issue into a question of union security, and unions acted accordingly. What remains is to assess the implications of this development for labor's relationship to the welfare state.

Did unionized welfare capitalism lead labor unions to turn their backs on the welfare state? In one respect, no. Katherine Ellickson, one of several national AFL-CIO officials involved with social insurance in the postwar years, recalled that CIO leaders of the late 1940s were men "who sincerely believed that the labor movement could not build its own welfare without consideration of the welfare of the whole working group, and [they] felt that the labor movement had a mission to do things for the nation as a whole."[56] There is overwhelming evidence of labor's advocacy of policies and programs dedicated to the economic well-being of all low-income and working citizens, whether union members or not. Union leaders stood for an aggressive fiscal policy and the indiscriminate use of federal spending as a way of countering unemployment. They favored increased spending for agricultural subsidies

55. Clifford to President, November 19, 1947, p. 21, Clifford Papers, box 2.
56. Katherine Ellickson, Columbia University Oral History Collection, pt. 4, Labor, p. 89.

throughout the postwar period, even when the Farm Bureau opposed it.[57] During the Eisenhower years the AFL-CIO social security department operated as an adjunct to the Democratic party and the social security administration, and it took over the "spearheading job in the field of social insurance and rallying the allies that it could muster for these improvements."[58] Outside the South, the labor movement became the organizational arm of the Democratic party, and with the formation of the Committee on Political Education (COPE) in the late 1950s, committed itself to transforming the party by recruiting low-income and African-American voters in the North and by purging the enemy, southern Democrats.[59]

But if the AFL-CIO leadership and prominent labor elites took an expansive view of their responsibilities toward working men and women, individual unions were not always willing to do so. Unionized welfare capitalism changed the incentives for union political action and undercut efforts to enact public social policies. This was nowhere more apparent at the time than in the campaign for national health insurance. The labor movement was one of the chief backers of the Committee for the Nation's Health (CNH), an umbrella organization lobbying for national health insurance. The CNH relied extensively on the labor press and the CIO in organizing its campaign in 1949.[60] Yet one labor leader admitted at the time that "the benefits workers get under the health and welfare plans are so much greater than those we have dared to include in the health insurance bills that it has become an anomaly for us to continue to favor compulsory health insurance."[61] Union leaders, in fact, only intended to wait and see if health insurance legislation was enacted by January or February of 1949, before pursuing "demands for private funds full blast."[62]

Structurally, the advent of unionized welfare capitalism meant that the labor movement was pulled in two directions by its role as an arm of the Democratic party and its form as a loose federation of unions dedicated to pursuing their own interests. The CIO's success in unleashing collective

57. Karen Orren, "Union Politics and Postwar Liberalism in the United States, 1946–1979," *Studies in American Political Development* 1 (1986): 219–28.

58. Ellickson, Oral History Collection, p. 88.

59. J. David Greenstone, *Labor in American Politics* (New York, 1970), chaps. 8, 10.

60. Monty Poen, *Harry S. Truman versus the Medical Lobby* (Columbia, Mo., 1979), pp. 84, 159.

61. Quoted in Edwin E. Witte, "Organized Labor and Social Security," in *Labor and the New Deal,* ed. Milton Derber and Edwin Young (Madison, Wisc., 1957), p. 271.

62. Stark to Jones, November 26, 1948, RG 51, ser. 39.14a, no. 821, NA.

bargaining for social rights made local union officials the administrators and protectors of welfare fiefs whose fiduciary responsibilities were usually not conducive to militant political action. The creation of private welfare states in unions deepened the bureaucratization of union organizations that began during the war. Administering the contract was often more important than negotiating it; class struggle, one might say, was reduced to bureaucratic struggle. Whatever the appeal of the idea that the labor movement represented all workers, whether organized into unions or not, it did not penetrate far below the national office. In union locals what mattered were the needs of the members, not any obligation to the unorganized.

Labor unions acted both as a force serving the interests of all workers—a "social democratic equivalent," as J. David Greenstone put it—and as interest groups.[63] This dichotomy defined the potential and limits of union politics after 1950. On issues of union security or of manifest interest to union members, the AFL-CIO could move with alacrity and dedication. Medicare is a case in point. Unions were largely uninterested in national health insurance after 1950, even though the AFL-CIO continued to support it, but they were vitally interested in health insurance for the elderly. Retired workers were not covered by private plans, and a universal public plan, although it also obviously benefited many nonunion citizens, relieved union families of an enormous financial burden. Nelson Cruikshank believes that labor viewed Medicare as a substitute for national health insurance, much as they had viewed private, bargained health plans.[64] However, on many other issues, such as housing, civil rights, and the poverty program, national support and aspirations rarely translated into local enthusiasm. Housing reformers, for example, found they could depend on the support of labor elites in national campaigns, but individual unions were rarely seen when the battle shifted to cities and towns.[65]

A common lament of labor historians is that unions sacrificed a capacity both to control their fate and to resist the encroachments of employers on workers rights. Unions were swaddled in high wages and private welfare programs, but they gave up control of investment decisions and stifled worker insurgency on the shop floor. Unions clearly paid a heavy price for the bargaining victories of the 1940s. But the key point is not that they tied their

63. Stanley Aronowitz (*Working Class Hero: A New Strategy for Labor* [New York, 1983]) was perhaps the first to point this out (see pp. 41–43).

64. Cruikshank, Oral History Collection, p. 15.

65. Richard O. Davies, *Housing Reform during the Truman Administration* (Columbia, Mo., 1966), pp. 124–28.

fate to businesses; all unions did, both in Europe and in America. Even if unions had been successful in acquiring some influence over investment, which European unions also failed to accomplish, they were not about to repeal the laws of capitalist development or curb the ability of owners to invest their capital elsewhere. What mattered was that after the 1940s the labor movement lost its political capacity to mobilize workers on behalf of the broad, inclusive social policies needed to protect them against economic dislocation. Union members remained loyal to the Democratic party, favoring such liberal welfare initiatives as the expansion of social security, but by virtue of the way they were organized into the American welfare state, they had few incentives to support any extension of social policies to those left out of it. As a consequence, unionized welfare capitalism eroded the basis for a biracial working-class coalition.

Unions succeeded in building comprehensive and equalitarian private welfare programs that narrowed the gap between skilled and unskilled workers and extended benefits to nonunion white-collar workers, though at the cost of manufacturing jobs. Black workers paid the price for this trade-off. John L. Lewis, for example, presided over a 50 percent decline in employment during the 1950s in the bituminous coal-mining industry, but black miners took the brunt of this change; their employment declined by 73 percent.[66] The coal-mining industry was not unique; black workers were disproportionately affected by automation and plant closures in the meat-packing, chemical, and tobacco industries. Black workers were left, by and large, outside the union-built private welfare systems. But when the opportunity arose in the 1960s to enact broad-gauged public policies that would rectify this exclusion, labor elites found themselves leading a Potemkin army.

66. Darold T. Barnum, "The Negro in the Bituminous Coal Industry," in *Negro Employment in Southern Industry,* ed. Herbert Northrup and Richard L. Rowan (Philadelphia, 1970), p. 26.

CHAPTER FIVE

The Color of Truncated Universalism

Every effort is being made [by opponents of the civil rights movement], short of using racial terms, to get over the idea to America at large that Negroes are the welfare chiselers. In our eyes here at the NAACP, this is first of all a racial smear and second a battle between conservatives and liberals. They keep talking about "migrants." They emphasize "people who come to our town to get relief." Every attempt is made to identify such persons as Negroes.

—ROY WILKINS

Peter Baldwin has argued that social policies contain elements of risk and fortune that determine how social classes and groups respond to demands for change and that shape beliefs about legitimate and illegitimate, deserving and undeserving beneficiaries.[1] Universal coverage was prized by European social democrats largely because it implicated all classes in the future of the welfare state and made a shared burden of a political necessity. No group of Americans has understood the political necessity of universalism better than African Americans. Black trade unionists and civil rights leaders were among fiercest proponents of the Third New Deal, but their hopes were subverted with the failure of the Democratic legislative agenda during the 1940s. The resulting fragmented pattern of social provision, truncated universalism, failed to establish a common interest among citizens in the welfare state and further divided blacks from whites. This chapter examines the implications of this legacy for the relationship of white workers, southerners, and African Americans to the U.S. welfare state.

Truncated universalism juxtaposed overlapping public and private social policies for the middle class with racially stigmatized policies for the poor. This welfare state primarily served working-age white citizens. Non-means-tested payments to the middle class rose dramatically between 1940 and 1960, increasing from 2 to 7 percent of the GNP. This growth occurred mainly in

1. Peter Baldwin, *The Politics of Social Solidarity* (New York, 1990), pp. 10–21.

social policies for men and women in their prime working years: veterans payments, housing subsidies, unemployment, and survivor's benefits made up two-fifths of all payments to individuals (including employee benefits) and almost half of all public payments.[2] Combined with private pensions and health care, these elements of public social provision created an umbrella of social protection rivaling anything European welfare states had to offer in the 1950s. American autoworkers were at least as well off as German autoworkers.[3]

This expansion of social provision to the middle class took place amid a massive migration of black and white sharecroppers to northern cities. The war-induced prosperity offered African Americans opportunities for employment and occupational advance and blurred somewhat the racial segmentation of the New Deal welfare state, but it did not eliminate the racial distinctions attached to federal policies. Postwar employment changes were disadvantageous to black workers, as was the economic stagnation of the 1950s. Persistent labor-market discrimination undermined the access of both black men and black women to social insurance while relegating them to means-tested public assistance or general assistance. Whites assumed that welfare and public housing were the exclusive domain of poor African Americans. Once again relief was seen as the "main occupation" of black people. The inversion of Myrdal's vicious circle that occurred with the implementation of New Deal social policy remained, but it received a new twist. To the notion of indolent blacks lounging on relief was grafted an image of sexually promiscuous, greedy African American women who produced children for their own profit at the expense of white taxpayers, an image that revived racist stereotypes dating from the period of slavery.[4]

The advent of truncated universalism rearranged the political stakes of social policy for Republicans and the contending factions of the Democratic party coalition. Republicans, white southerners, and white workers readily accommodated themselves to the new order, working to expand middle-class social polices. Republicans embraced social security; the electoral ben-

2. Author's calculation.

3. Hugh Mosley, "Corporate Social Benefits and the Underdevelopment of the American Welfare State," *Contemporary Crises* 5 (1981): 139–54.

4. Melissa J. Miller, "Effects of Stereotype Thinking on the American Welfare System" (Senior thesis, American Studies, University of California, Santa Cruz, 1987); see also Wahneema Lubiano, "Black Ladies, Welfare Queens, and State Minstrels," in *Race-ing Justice, En-Gendering Power: Essays on Anita Hill, Clarence Thomas and the Construction of Social Reality,* ed. Toni Morrison (New York: 1992), pp. 323–63.

efits to them were undeniable, but they also saw the program as an alternative to more costly public assistance. Southerners maneuvered, as they had since the late 1930s, to recast grant-in-aid formulas so as to redistribute federal funds below the Mason-Dixon line where a burgeoning white southern middle class used the money to gild a racially segregated welfare state. Labor elites sought to fashion new policy alternatives while individual labor unions demanded larger benefits at the bargaining table and union members embraced the attributes of a middle-class lifestyle.

African Americans faced politically instigated attacks on Aid to Dependent Children (ADC) and public housing. Writing on public housing policy in New Orleans after the racially charged 1960 gubernatorial election, Forest E. La Violette observed, "public housing is one instance of the general problem that Negroes . . . make disproportionate use of services for low-income groups; consequently the expansion of such services is affected by the general atmosphere surrounding Negro-white relations and the political situation affecting Negroes."[5] With the emergence of the civil rights movement, massive white resistance in the South, and unease with black migration in the North, the politics of race and social policy were entwined. Roy Wilkins recognized that the racial stigmatization of putatively neutral social policies such as ADC and public housing jeopardized not just the economic well-being of migrating sharecroppers but the civil rights movement itself. African American political leaders found themselves increasingly unable to balance demands for race and class unity within the Democratic party.

Truncated universalism reproduced the racial stratification of the New Deal by overlaying the de jure distinction between social insurance and public assistance established by the 1935 Social Security Act with a de facto distinction based on race. Thus racial distinctions replaced the class rhetoric of New Deal social policy as the fault line in the American welfare state during the 1950s. How and why did this happen?

The Politics of Welfare Purges and Middle-class Social Policies

For most Americans at mid-century, the idea of the welfare state was remote. A 1949 Gallup poll reported that two-thirds of those interviewed did not know what was meant by the term "welfare state." Yet those same Americans had

---

5. Forest E. La Violette, "The Negro in New Orleans," in *Studies in Housing and Minority Groups,* ed. Nathan Glazer and Davis McEntire (Berkeley, Calif., 1960), p. 120.

clear views about social policies. They defined the appropriate domain of the welfare state as a spare safety net, believing that society has an obligation to "assist people who are in distress" but no "duty to provide assistance permanently."[6] This view gradually replaced the bold universalism of the early New Deal and war years and emerged full-blown in the 1950s. From the late 1930s through the 1950s, public opinion surveys revealed widespread dislike for guaranteed income schemes (that is, the obligation to provide everyone a minimal standard of living), mistrust of people on relief or welfare, and an aversion to policies that might redistribute income. These opinions were combined with a grudging acceptance of a governmental obligation to provide assistance when no other means of support was available.[7]

The realm of public social protection that people actually embraced after World War II was much larger and far more generous than their opinions suggested. Social security, veterans programs, income payments to farmers, and the mortgage interest deduction are all conspicuous examples of the discrepancy between the public's stated preference for a minimal welfare state and the array of publicly provided social benefits it supported. Each program provided a nonmarket transfer to an identifiable clientele, and in each instance the payments supplemented market income. Yet each was defined and justified in terms that obscured the welfare characteristics of the policy. For example, widespread acceptance of the notion that OASI taxes were a payment into an annuity hid its welfare elements, namely, its progressive benefit schedule and guaranteed minimum benefit. Farm support payments were understood to be business subsidies necessary to sustain agriculture, not income support payments for downtrodden farmers.[8]

The politics of America's postwar welfare state reflected this dichotomy, displaying an admirable generosity toward veterans and the elderly, while reverting to harsh policies characteristic of traditional poor laws. Middle-class social policies were popular and incrementally expanded. During the

6. Herbert McClosky and John Zaller, *The American Ethos: Public Attitudes toward Capitalism and Democracy* (Cambridge, Mass., 1984), p. 274.

7. Michael E. Schiltz, *Public Attitudes Toward Social Security, 1935–1965* (Washington, D.C., 1970), pp. 98, 111, 152, 158–61; Hazel Erskine, "The Polls: Government Role in Welfare," *Public Opinion Quarterly* 39 (1975): 257–74.

8. The National Resources Planning Board excluded farm payments from the definition of public aid; *Security, Work and Relief Policies* (Washington, D.C., 1942), p. 10. The Office of Management and the Budget does not classify agricultural support payments as an income transfer, but the Brookings Institution has seen fit to do so; see *Setting National Priorities: The 1973 Budget,* ed. Charles Schulze et al. (Washington, D.C., 1972), pp. 195–97.

doldrums of Republican rule, the eligibility rules and benefits of innumerable social welfare laws were liberalized and new policies were added, notably disability insurance in 1956 and a federal supplement for unemployment insurance in 1958. ADC and public housing, on the other hand, came under unrelenting political attack as the welfare rolls rose amidst prosperity after the war. Initially triggered by state and local investigations, postwar welfare purges culminated in a national furor by 1952. The *Saturday Evening Post* captured the gist of the onslaught, editorializing, "it's time to ask how come direct relief to individuals in a boom costs twice as much as it did during the economic blizzard."[9] These alternate patterns of consensus and conflict set the stage for the racialization of social policy during the 1950s.

Veterans programs are the best illustration of the fortune of middle-class social policies. Public opinion polls of the late 1940s reported broad public support for extensive aid to veterans.[10] Even though they were eventually eclipsed by OASI, veterans programs were at the heart of the postwar welfare state and propelled the growth in social spending through the mid-1950s. Congress repeatedly liberalized benefits by extending the time veterans had to utilize readjustment benefits, increasing educational allowances, and virtually guaranteeing any veteran a home loan. Veterans payments made up 21 percent of federal outlays and 65 percent of transfer payments in 1950. By 1960, veterans payments had declined both relatively and absolutely, but they remained significant, amounting to $5.4 billion in Eisenhower's last budget.

Veterans programs were administered with exceptional regard for the distinctive and separate status of veterans. "The philosophy," observed the authors of an early study of the G.I. Bill, "seems to be one of treating allowances as a staggered bonus of which the veteran is encouraged to take advantage, and the administration of the program is characterized by extreme liberality."[11] What this meant was abundantly clear in the case of "52–20" benefits, which guaranteed unemployed veterans twenty dollars a week for a year. Benefits were higher, on the average, than unemployment compensation throughout the postwar period, and eligibility standards far looser. A Budget Bureau report discovered the rejection rate for unemployment compensation in Arkansas was nine times that for "52–20" benefits; and in Texas

9. *Saturday Evening Post*, November 5, 1949, p. 10.

10. George H. Gallup, *The Gallup Poll: Public Opinion, 1935–1946* (New York, 1972), 1:460–61, 531.

11. U.S. Bureau of the Budget, "Field Study Assignments, No. 12 1/2," Readjustment Allowance Program, VA, April 17, 1945, p. 3, RG 51, ser. 39.20a, box 9, NA.

only two veterans' claims were rejected, compared to seventy-four unemployment claims, during January and February of 1945. Readjustment allowances were treated as an entitlement, and there were no clear-cut guidelines for determining when veterans did or did not have good cause for rejecting work. Eligibility rules for unemployment compensation were not only more specific but were applied more rigidly, with the consequence that nonveterans were more likely to exhaust their unemployment benefits. It is not surprising, then, that more veterans received "52–20" benefits than nonveterans received unemployment compensation shortly after the end of the war.[12]

Other veterans programs were administered in much the same way. Income thresholds were applied so loosely as to be nonexistent. "Existing policies and procedures for assuring compliance with the income and dependency provisions of the law," the Budget Bureau concluded, "are largely a formality and ineffective."[13] Veterans' compensation was not subject to a means test and the legal definition of a service-connected disability was quite liberal. At one point even venereal disease, an obvious hazard of war, was considered a service-connected disability for which veterans deserved compensation. Two-fifths of all veterans receiving disability in the early 1950s were only 10 percent disabled. Such generosity was justified by the VA as needed compensation for "minor wound scars" and "pain and suffering," though most of the cases involved minor disabilities that did not result from combat.[14]

Poor women receiving welfare were treated very differently. In the spring of 1960, the Louisiana Legislature ordered the state welfare department to remove from the ADC rolls any woman who had ever received a welfare payment and given birth to an illegitimate child. About 31,000 families were purged from the rolls, 95 percent of them African American. Less than a year later, Joseph Mitchell, city manager of Newburgh, New York, issued a thirteen-point proclamation requiring newcomers to the city, single moth-

12. Ibid., pp. 10, 12; Mitchell to Garber, June 3, 1946, RG 51, ser. 39.27, box 11, folder no. 55, NA; President's Commission on Veterans' Pensions [hereafter Bradley Commission], *Readjustment Benefits: General Survey and Appraisal* (Washington, D.C., 1956), p. 60.

13. Labor and Welfare Division to The Director, BOB, April 1, 1953, p. 2, ser. 52.1, gray box, folder R9–1, NA.

14. Bradley Commission, *Veterans' Benefits in the United States: Findings and Recommendation* (Washington, D.C., 1956), pp. 175–76. It is worth noting that these minor disability cases accounted for about 24 percent of total outlays for veterans compensation, but 57 percent of the case load.

ers, and "able-bodied" workers to meet new eligibility criteria. Expressing his ire with rising welfare rolls, Mitchell said that the time had come to "get tough" with lazy welfare recipients and announced plans that imposed work requirements for women on ADC, denied aid to mothers of illegitimate children, opened up records of recipients for inspection, and stipulated that new applications must contain a statement that the individual had come to the city looking for work, not welfare.

The public was wildly in favor of the Newburgh plan. Senator Barry Goldwater, then planning a presidential campaign, endorsed it, saying that he would "like to see every city in the country adopt the plan." Gallup polls revealed that 85 percent of those persons interviewed favored requiring work in place of relief, 74 percent agreed with Mitchell's plan to make ADC applicants prove they were looking for a job, and about the same number thought absent fathers should be tracked down and made to pay the costs of raising any child they fathered out of wedlock. The public was equally harsh toward poor mothers. Only one in ten supported additional welfare payments for newborn children, and most advocated far more draconian remedies.[15]

There was little in either the Newburgh or Louisiana plans that had not already been proposed in innumerable state legislatures or discussed in various reports and legislative hearings. The welfare purges began during 1947–48 with public attacks in sixteen states. The charges have a familiar and contemporary ring. A New York Budget Bureau report said that "the welfare department appears to have no standards of morality for relief recipients but condones immorality and even abets it." In Baltimore, the Commission on Governmental Efficiency and Economy reported: "it certainly appears that the welfare policies have had the practical result of condoning and in effect encouraging dependence upon the government, idleness, pauperism, desertion, illegitimacy, dishonesty and irresponsibility."[16] The purges were a politically motivated reaction to the rapid rise in the public assistance rolls at the conclusion of the war. The ADC caseload trebled in the fifteen years after World War II, rising from 256,000 families in 1945 to almost 800,000 families in 1960 (see table 7). After dropping during the war, the caseload increased one and a half times, peaking in 1950, and then stagnated for the rest of the decade. This spike in the caseload motivated antitax

15. *New York Times,* July 21, 1961, sec. 1, p. 12; Gallup, *Gallup Poll,* 2:1731.

16. Donald S. Howard, "Public Assistance Returns to Page One—I," *Social Work Journal* (1948): 49, 51; see also Blanche D. Coll, *Saftey Net: Welfare and Social Security, 1929–1979* (New Brunswick, N.J., 1995), pp. 176–77.

Table 7. ADC caseloads by region, 1945–1960

	United States	South	North Industrial	Mid-Atlantic	Border	New England	North Central	Pacific	Mountain
Percentage change in caseloads									
1945–60	210%	204%	113%	194%	108%	166%	82%	716%	170%
1945–50	155	196	72	169	178	135	170	502	102
1950–55	−5	−10	−16	−24	−37	−7	−44	3	132
1955–60	28	14	48	44	18	22	21	31	31
1950–60	21	2	24	9	−25	13	−32	35	213
Number of children receiving ADC (per 1000 population)[a]									
1940	26	17	30	24	30	18	20	26	43
1950	26	30	20	22	41	23	20	22	31
1960	32	37	22	27	53	29	22	32	30
Percentage of ADC mothers working									
1958		35%	11%	5%	11%	8%	16%	8%	9%
Nonwhite		48	10	5	17	8	10	8	6
White		20	12	4	6	2	20	4	9

Sources: The Book of the States (Lexington, Ky., selected years); Department of Health, Education and Welfare, Bureau of Public Assistance, *Illegitimacy and Its Impact on the Aid to Dependent Children Program* (Washington, D.C., 1958), table 8.

[a]Children 16 years and younger.

groups and opponents of the New Deal to launch attacks on ADC and general relief.

One of the earliest and most important attacks began in Baltimore and was the brainchild of the Commission on Governmental Economy and Efficiency, an organization dominated by tax-sensitive real estate interests that had campaigned against relief throughout the 1930s. This investigation became the model for investigations in New York and Detroit.[17] Local opposition to public assistance and relief acquired national political significance in the conservative political atmosphere of the early 1950s. Along with corruption and weakness toward the "communist threat," charges of welfare fraud and abuse were invoked in both the 1950 and 1952 elections as examples of Democratic misrule. Republican acceptance of the welfare state did not extend to public assistance. The governor of Illinois, up for reelection in 1956, made welfare the focus of his budget cutting program. His politically minded advisers added a proposal to increase the residency requirement from one to three years to deter immigrants and reduce the rolls.[18]

Although fraud was the most visible charge of initial probes, it was quickly overshadowed by illegitimacy as the chief evil of welfare, with otherwise staid national publications reporting on the squalor of deadbeat husbands and unwed mothers, the latter of whom were often reputed to be working as prostitutes on the side while collecting taxpayers' money. When it was reported that up to 60 percent of residents in some counties were on relief, the governor of Tennessee commented that all too many Tennesseeans were "having babies just to qualify them for relief."[19] The rise of illegitimacy as an issue, it is well known, began with changes in the marital status of ADC mothers after 1939. Women whose loss of income was due to death of the father declined from 37 percent to 7 percent of the ADC caseload between 1940 and 1960, while divorced, separated, and unmarried women rose from 36 to 67 percent of all cases.

Punitive policies designed to limit eligibility and benefits were the main

17. Benjamin H. Lyndon, "Relief Probes: A Study of Public Welfare Investigations in Baltimore, New York, Detroit, 1947–1949" (Ph.D. diss., University of Chicago, 1953), pp. 37, 55–58, 120, 251–54; L. C. Gibson to O'Neill, May 25, 1951, p. 3, RG 51, ser. 39.14a, box 22, folder no. 176, NA.

18. Phyllis R. Osborn, "Aid to Dependent Children—Realities and Possibilities," *Social Service Review* (1954): 159–60; Edward Banfield, *Political Influence: A New Theory of Urban Politics* (New York, 1961), p. 70.

19. *Newsweek,* March 12, 1951, p. 25. See also Hilda C. M. Arndt, "An Appraisal of What the Critics Are Saying about Public Assistance," *Social Service Review* 26 (1952): 464–75.

accomplishment of those bent on purging the ADC rolls. In 1946 only one state made employment an official requirement of ADC (Louisiana); by 1956, seventeen states had such requirements, including eight of the eleven southern states.[20] The Michigan state legislature imposed a "potential employment" policy: if a single mother refused to take a job, her potential earnings could be deducted from her check, though an exception could be made if there was no one to care for the children. Limits on the amount of property mothers could possess and on the timing of property transfers were also used to restrict eligibility and reduce the welfare rolls. These laws got tougher over the decade. Twenty-two states had no property limits for ADC in 1946; by 1953 only Kentucky was without such a requirement. The number of states with no regulations governing transfer of property dropped from thirty-four in 1950 to fourteen in 1959. Both of these rules could be expected to deny aid to many single mothers and deter those in need from applying.[21]

Laws based on assessments of a mother's moral worth and the father's status were the most visible tools used by states to purge the welfare rolls. Many states initially sought simply to deny aid to mothers with illegitimate children. Eighteen states followed this practice, dropping it only when it became clear that the federal government would cut off welfare funds on grounds of discrimination. Southern states, practiced in the art of evading the Fifteenth Amendment's nondiscrimination requirement with poll taxes and other devices, redefined so-called suitable-home laws to exclude those with "substitute" parents or "illegitimate" children.[22] Many states simply declared poor mothers ineligible if there was a substitute parent present: a "boyfriend," an "uncle" or, in the eyes of some lawmakers, any available man. By 1962, twenty-four states had "man-in-the-house" rules or other rules designed to snag would-be or surrogate husbands. All eleven southern states passed such laws, mostly during the late 1950s. Outside of the South, such laws were typically characteristic of northern industrial states.[23] Finally, some states

20. These data are drawn from U.S. Department of Health, Education and Welfare, Social Security Administration, *Characteristics of State Plans under the Social Security Act, Old Age Assistance, Aid to the Blind, Aid to Dependent Children—General Provisions,* Public Assistance Report no. 50 (Washington, D.C., 1946, 1953, 1956, 1962). Author's coding and tabulation. See also, Mimi Abramovitz, *Regulating the Lives of Women* (Boston, Mass., 1988), pp. 322–28.

21. *Characteristics of State Plans,* selected years; Kirsten Gronjberg, "Mass Society and the Extension of Welfare, 1960–1970" (Ph.D. diss., University of Chicago, 1972), p. 338, table 63.

22. Winifred Bell, *Aid to Dependent Children* (New York, 1965), pp. 71–75, 93–99.

23. Gronjberg, "Mass Society and the Extension of Welfare, 1960–1970," pp. 306–9, table 57.

used the 1950 Notification of Law Enforcement Officials (NOLEO) amendment to the Social Security Act as an instrument of welfare repression. This
law required states receiving public assistance funds to notify law enforcement authorities if aid was given to a child who had been deserted or abandoned by a parent. Many states used the law to limit eligibility. Nineteen
states required legal action as a condition of eligibility, and another fourteen
states made it a necessity for the continuation of aid. Only one-quarter of
states did not make legal action a prerequisite for aid, merely requiring that
a notice be sent to prosecutors. Altogether, two-thirds of states used NOLEO
as a weapon in the ongoing welfare purge.[24]

What effect did the purges have? By some accounts very little. Kirsten A.
Gronjberg, who found no relationship between eligibility laws and ADC
caseloads, argued that changes in eligibility were largely symbolic, a view
Winifred Bell shared in her assessment of southern uses of suitable-home
laws.[25] In fact, those states with the highest caseloads (mostly in the South)
had the strictest eligibility rules. In some southern states the growth of the
ADC rolls during the 1950s (Mississippi and North Carolina, for example)
exceeded that of most northern states. By 1960, 3.7 percent of children aged
sixteen or younger received benefits in the states of the former confederacy,
compared to 2.2 percent in the industrial Midwest and 2.7 percent in the
states of New York, New Jersey, and Pennsylvania. The most important effect of the purges, in both the North and South, is also the most obvious:
many poor, eligible women were discouraged from applying because of the
stigma attached to ADC. Public assistance for poor mothers never came
close to meeting the obvious need. The take-up rate, an estimate of the proportion of eligible families who actually receive ADC, was 33 percent in the
early 1960s.[26]

Caseloads declined by one-quarter in northern industrial states and by almost two-fifths in border states in the early 1950s. (See table 7.) Some of
this decline was due to the economic boom accompanying the Korean War;
but caseloads also declined because of the purges. In northern states that got
tough, such as Michigan, eligibility rules appear to be the most important

24. Maurine McKeany, *The Absent Father and Public Policy in the Program of Aid to Dependent Children* (Berkeley, Calif., 1960), pp. 74–82.

25. Kirsten A. Gronjberg, *Mass Society and the Extension of Welfare, 1960–1970* (Chicago, 1977), p. 54; Bell, *Aid to Dependent Children*, p. 95. Bell found that Georgia social workers rarely invoked the suitable-home policy to deny aid and that it accounted for only 10 percent of discontinued grants.

26. Edward Berkowitz, *America's Welfare State: From Roosevelt to Reagan* (Baltimore, 1991), p. 118.

factor in explaining the fall and rise of the caseload over a twenty-five-year period. Michigan's "potential employment" policy had greater effect on caseloads than employment rates did.[27] Nor were southern states all of a piece. Arkansas pursued draconian policies, reducing the rolls by 60 percent during the decade; Florida's suitable-home law, which preceded the Louisiana purge by two years, resulted in a dramatic, if temporary, reduction in caseloads; and caseloads were reduced in Georgia and some other southern states.[28] Moreover, southern states were far more successful in enforcing work requirements than were northern states. Thirty-five percent of southern ADC mothers were reported at work compared to less than 10 percent in the rest of the nation; there was little difference between states with or without employment policies, indicating the significance of regional differences (see table 7).

Southern states actually faced conflicting incentives, which explains why strict eligibility requirements coincided with high caseloads. Although federal aid formulas encouraged large caseloads, rural landowners and suburban housewives had an interest in maintaining a low-wage workforce. Federal relief, after all, had been used since the 1930s as a replacement for furnishing sharecroppers and managing labor flows between harvest and planting season. One prominent former federal official publicly suggested that the demand by southern white suburban matrons for household help was behind the hostility to ADC. This demand for low-wage labor was reinforced by a presumption, dating from the period of slavery and undoubtedly strong in the South, that black women belonged in the workforce.[29] This presumption helps explain the higher proportion of nonwhite ADC mothers working in the South compared to other regions of the country (table 7).

27. Hugh Spall and Edward McGoughran, "AFDC in Michigan during the Twentieth Century," *Review of Social Economy* 2 (1974): 73.

28. Robert T. Lansdale, *The Florida Suitable Home Law: A Statistical Analysis of 17,999 Aid to Dependent Children Cases Affected* (Florida State University, 1962), pp. 116–17.

29. Wilbur Cohen, "Trends in Public Welfare Legislation" (paper presented to the regional meeting of the American Public Welfare Association, April 29, 1955), quoted in Lansdale, *Florida Suitable Home Law,* p. 3; Gwendolyn Mink, *The Wages of Motherhood* (Ithaca, N.Y., 1995), pp. 142–43; Frances Fox Piven and Richard Cloward, *Regulating the Poor: The Functions of Public Welfare* (New York, 1971), pp. 124–25, 128, 133–44. It is unclear whether rural landowners manipulated ADC. Richard F. Bensel and M. Elizabeth Sanders show that that southern landowners used the federal surplus food program rather than ADC to control farmworkers. See "The Impact of the Voting Rights Act on Southern Welfare Systems," in *Do Elections Matter?* ed. Benjamin Ginsberg and Alan Stone (New York, 1986), pp. 56–57.

This split in the politics of the welfare state had very different implications for whites and African Americans. The welfare purges coincided with dramatic changes in the racial composition of ADC and public housing. Both programs were used by whites in northern and southern cities to absorb black migrants and mitigate economic dislocation. On the other hand, the expansion of public and private social policies underpinned the prosperity of the white working and middle classes. Together, the welfare purges and the distributive effects of "hidden" social policies reproduced the racial stratification of the New Deal.

The Rise of the Truly Advantaged

The postwar white middle class came to worship, as Jonathan Rieder has characterized it, the "spontaneity of the marketplace, the pluck of bootstrapping, and the sacredness of middle-class advantage," whereas in reality, they were beneficiaries of advantages dispensed by federal bureaucrats.[30] Social insurance, veterans, and employee benefits, along with FHA guaranteed mortgages were of marginal benefit to the poor of both races. Truncated universalism entailed a horizontal expansion of social protection, which enfolded into the welfare state much of America's newly self-conscious middle class: young veterans, many of them from working-class backgrounds; union members; owners of small businesses; professionals and corporate managers. These recipients of federal largess displayed an unalloyed sense of entitlement. Most veterans, for example, were strongly disposed to think they deserved favored treatment, although they were somewhat more cautious in their claims than the veterans organizations. Two-thirds or more veterans believed they should receive entitlements, ranging from low-cost loans and insurance to education benefits and free medical care for service-related injuries, and over half thought they were entitled to government-subsidized job training. Similarly, support for social security was quite high throughout the decade, although there was some carping about the adequacy of benefits. Yet it was always understood that an adequate retirement income was an individual responsibility.[31] The much-discussed notion of a classless so-

---

30. Jonathan Rieder, *Canarsie: The Jews and Italians of Brooklyn against Liberalism* (Cambridge, Mass., 1985), p. 117.

31. Bradley Commission, *Veterans in Our Society* (Washington, D.C., 1956), pp. 127, 137; Charles Brain, "Social Security at the Crossroads" (Ph.D. diss., University of Pennsylvania, 1989), p. 150.

Table 8a. Total cash transfers by income class, 1949–1958 (percentage of households receiving a transfer)

	1949	1951	1957	1958
All households	28%	22%	26%	32%
Lowest income quintile	38	36	48	55
Second income quintile	36	22	33	40
Third income quintile	28	18	18	24
Fourth income quintile	23	14	20	23
Highest income quintile	15	12	13	15

Table 8b. Distribution of transfer payments by income, 1950 and 1960 (percentage of households receiving a transfer)

	Below median income		Below one-third	
	1950	1960	1950	1960
All households	54.0%	49.0%	33.0%	28.0%
Money income	27.0	22.0	11.0	8.0
Social insurance	84.3	68.7	75.0	45.2
Public assistance	99.8	89.1	95.0	78.5
Veterans payments	54.5	46.0	24.2	22.0
Farm payments	31.4	32.7	16.0	14.0

Sources: (Table 8a) 1950 *Survey of Consumer Finances,* pt. 3, "Distribution of Consumer Income, 1949," *Federal Reserve Bulletin* (August 1950): 11; *1952 Survey of Consumer Finances,* pt. 3, "Income, Selected Investments, and Short-Term Debt of Consumers," *Federal Reserve Bulletin* (September 1952): supp. table 12; *1958 Survey of Consumer Finances,* "The Financial Position of Consumers," *Federal Reserve Bulletin* (September 1958): supp. table 5; *1959 Survey of Consumer Finances,* "The Financial Position of Consumers," *Federal Reserve Bulletin* (July 1959): supp. table 5. *(Table 8b)* Morgan Reynolds and Eugene Smolensky, *Public Expenditures, Taxes, and the Distribution of Income* (New York, 1977), tables B-1, B-2.

ciety at mid-century had some resonance only because New Deal universalism had been sublimated to middle-class individualism.

There is abundant evidence that the social policies of the 1950s were mainly of benefit to the middle class. Consider first the distributive effects of income transfers. The proportion of households receiving an income transfer during the 1950s increased for all income quintiles, rising from 22 percent in 1951 to 32 percent by 1958 (the slightly higher proportion of households receiving a transfer in 1949 is due to veterans payments). (See table 8a.) The greatest increase came in the bottom two quintiles; increases in the top three quintiles were far more modest. Such data lend credence to those who argue that the public transfer system of the 1950s had its most noteworthy effect on the poor.[32] But data on who receives transfers yield

32. Mark Stern, "Poverty and Family Composition since 1940" in *The "Underclass" Debate: Views from History* (Princeton, N.J., 1993), ed. Michael B. Katz, pp. 230–38.

no information on how much different income classes receive from public transfers. Table 8b provides some partial evidence for the contention that middle-class citizens were the principal beneficiaries of transfer payments.

By distinguishing between four transfer payments—social insurance, public assistance, veterans benefits, and farm support payments—we find that between 1950 and 1960 households in the bottom one-third of the income distribution received a declining proportion of all four transfer payments.[33] Veterans and farm support payments helped mostly middle-class beneficiaries throughout the postwar period. Social Security, on the other hand, provided greater help to the middle class as the program expanded; over four-fifths of social insurance payments were distributed to families below the median income in 1950, compared to two-thirds in 1960. Significantly, the share of social insurance payments received by the bottom one-third of households dropped from 75 to 45 percent. It is not surprising that this distribution shifted upwards; people retiring had higher incomes and most of those who were added to Social Security in the 1950s were drawn from the top half of the income distribution.[34] There is also evidence that the distribution of benefits became less progressive during the decade; the ratio of replacement rates for low-wage recipients to high-wage recipients declined from 1.67 in 1945 to 1.45 in 1965.[35] Poor, elderly households continued to get proportionately higher benefits after 1950, but the many fat benefit increases of the decade mainly aided middle-income citizens.

More revealing, perhaps, are data on the distribution of private health insurance. Between 1953 and 1958 access to voluntary health insurance did not change appreciably for families with incomes below three thousand dollars, while it measurably improved for all other families. Health insurance coverage rose from 71 to 79 percent for those families in the middle third of the income distribution, and for those in the top one-third it rose from

33. More detailed breakdowns, between OASI and unemployment compensation for example, are not available for this period. These results are only slightly skewed by the differing thresholds used to measure low income (33 percent in 1950 and 28 percent in 1960). By looking at the bottom 38 percent (the only other classification available from published data), it can be shown that the magnitude is affected, but not the upward shift in payments.

34. The vast majority of 20 million workers Congress added to OASI were clearly middle class: 35 percent were self-employed, and the rest were civil servants, employees of nonprofit organizations, and professionals. Farmworkers accounted for just 13 percent of those added.

35. Robert Meyers, *Social Security,* 3d ed. (Homewood, Ill., 1985), p. 335.

Table 9. Group and nongroup hospital insurance by income, 1953 and 1958 (percentage of households)

	Family income				
	Under $2,000	$2,000–$3,499	$3,500–$4,999	$5,000–$7,499	$7,500 and over
1953					
Group	41%	67%	79%	79%	73%
Nongroup	62	37	25	25	36
1958					
Group	42	65	82	87	77
Nongroup	59	37	22	20	27

Sources: Odin W. Anderson, *Family Medical Costs and Voluntary Health Insurance* (New York, 1956), table A-5; Odin W. Anderson, Patricia Collette, and Jacob J. Feldman, *Changes in Family Medical Care Expenditures and Voluntary Health Insurance* (Cambridge, Mass., 1963), app. C, table 102.

80 to 86 percent.[36] A more revealing measure of middle-class advantage is the relationship between family income and whether a household had access to group (employer provided) or nongroup (indvidually purchased) insurance. Unionized welfare capitalism was strongly biased against low-income families in the 1950s. The majority of very low-income families, if they had hospital insurance at all, purchased it themselves. (See table 9.) But more than three-quarters of middle- and upper-income families were the beneficiaries of group health insurance. In fact, these well-off families, unlike low-income families, were less likely to purchase their own health insurance by the end of the decade.

The growth of truncated universalism was a key factor in the development of the postwar middle class, as an examination of the distribution of veterans' benefits reveals. Combined with the horizontal expansion of other public and private benefits, veterans' benefits fostered interclass mobility and compensated for the holes in the public safety net. By comparing income and home ownership of veterans and nonveterans, one can see the dramatic gains accruing to the returning soldiers of the 1940s. (See table 10.) Between 1948 and 1955, the incomes of veterans aged 25 to 34 rose relative to those of nonveterans. Income advantages were reinforced by differences in possession of assets. Most veterans had more liquid assets than nonveterans,

36. Odin W. Anderson, *Family Medical Costs and Voluntary Health Insurance* (New York, 1953), table A-4; Odin W. Anderson, Patricia Collette, and Jacob J. Feldman, *Changes in Family Medical Care Expenditures and Voluntary Health Insurance* (Cambridge, Mass., 1963), table 96.

Table 10. Income of veterans and nonveterans, 1948–1955

	25–34 years old				35–44 years old			
	1948		1955		1948		1955	
	Veteran	Nonveteran	Veteran	Nonveteran	Veteran	Nonveteran	Veteran	Nonveteran
Income quintile								
Lowest	7.8%	11.8%	4.3%	11.8%	6.8%	8.9%	3.9%	8.9%
Second	17.5	20.5	10.0	20.9	14.3	14.8	9.6	16.6
Third	33.4	25.4	26.7	33.7	27.7	24.9	25.2	25.4
Fourth	26.1	23.8	41.3	27.6	25.2	25.6	40.0	31.2
Highest	15.2	18.5	17.7	5.9	26.1	25.8	21.3	18.1
Median income	$2,734	$2,692	$4,330	$3,294	$3,045	$3,046	$4,483	$3,946
Median liquid assets	$399	$174	$279	$166	$710	$433	$412	$424
Home ownership	32%	32%	45%	34%	40%	47%	61%	61%

Sources: U.S. Bureau of Census, *Current Population Reports*, "Consumer Income," ser. P-60, 1948, no. 6 (February 1950), table 12; 1955, no. 23 (November 1956): table 3; President's Commission on Veterans' Pensions, *Veterans in Our Society*, Staff Report 4 (Washington, D.C., 1956), table 10.

though this difference appears to even out with age. Veterans of all ages made substantial gains in home ownership compared to nonveterans between 1948 and 1955, almost entirely through the heavily subsidized mortgage programs run by the Veterans Administration.

The gains made by veterans were a consequence of readjustment benefits and also probably of the veterans' preference awarded to applicants for public sector jobs. Veterans were disproportionately concentrated in high-paying occupations; compared to nonveterans, they were substantially more likely to be professionals, managers, or skilled workers. Of those veterans who occupied professional or managerial positions, 40 percent had been sales workers before the war, 30 percent operatives, 28 percent service workers, and 29 percent unskilled laborers. The Bradley Commission attributed the upward mobility to readjustment benefits: "veterans who used GI training benefits were in general more likely to shift into new occupational fields than those who did not take training, and more likely to shift into the higher-paid occupations."[37]

While younger veterans gained access to the highest paid, most influential positions in American society, older veterans received pension benefits that overlapped with existing public social policies, and made up for the relatively low benefits of Social Security. Congress loosened eligibility criteria for non-service-connected pensions after the war, and many veterans pulled down two pensions. A Veterans Administration survey in 1954 indicated that almost one-half of the veterans of the two world wars and the Korean War also received OASI benefits.[38] At a point when many retirees were either excluded from OASI benefits or received very low benefits, veterans' pensions often made the difference between a degraded, improverished old age and a dignified one. But this was not the whole story. Many well-off veterans receiving non-service-connected pensions evaded income requirements to qualify. In order to receive a pension, the income of a married veteran could not exceed $2,700 a year ($1,400 for single veterans). The law required veterans to report all sources of income, including interest, dividends, and annuities in addition to wages. Enterprising but morally unscrupulous veterans simply shifted their stocks, bonds, and other tangible

37. Bradley Commission, *Readjustment Benefits,* pp. 78, 111. The Bradley Commission found that 40 percent of preservice laborers who used training and educational benefits made it into professional jobs, but only 23 percent of those who did not use readjustment benefits became professionals (see pp. 96–97). Some of this, of course, may be due to the veterans' preference, not education.

38. Bradley Commission, *Veterans' Benefits in the United States,* pp. 363–64.

assets to their wife's name and collected the pension. A GAO survey ordered by Congress found that 17 percent of veterans receiving a pension exceeded the income threshold when their spouse's income was counted. The combined net worth of one-fifth of the beneficiaries was above $10,000, no minor sum in the 1950s.[39]

Nowhere were the effects of veterans' policies more apparent than in the South. Veterans' programs were a significant source of income for southerners. Although only one-fifth of the nation's veterans lived in the South during the 1950s, the eleven confederate states received 35 percent of veterans' dollars for readjustment benefits, disability compensation, and pensions. Average payments for readjustment benefits were one-third higher in the South than in other regions, and overall per capita veterans' payments were highest in southern states, averaging forty-nine dollars compared to about thirty-nine dollars for industrial states. Southern veterans were voracious consumers of readjustment benefits and non-service-connected pensions. Fifty-one percent of all southern veterans were enrolled in educational and training programs, compared to an average of about 41 percent in all other regions.[40] The average annual rate of payment for non-service-connected disability pensions was 32 percent higher than payments for service-connected disabilities ($720 compared to $545), reflecting a much higher participation rate in non-service-connected programs in the South than elsewhere. One explanation for this, offered by the Bradley Commission, is that low incomes in the South allowed more southern than northern veterans to qualify.[41]

The southern advantage in readjustment benefits derived not only from high participation rates but also from southern leniency. Southern veterans used readjustment benefits much longer than other veterans; the median number of weeks for receipt of such benefits was twenty-three in the South, but only fifteen in the rest of the nation. The proportion of veterans who used readjustment benefits for thirty-five weeks or more was 35 percent in the South, 25 percent in the Northeast, 19 percent in the North Central region, and 20 percent in the West. Moreover, southerners were twice as likely to exhaust their benefits.[42] In a region noted for its hostility to the welfare

39. *Survey of Financial Condition of Veterans Receiving Non-Service-Connected Disability Pensions,* House Committee Print no. 30, 86th Cong., 1st sess. (Washington, D.C., 1959), p. 2, and tables 3, 8.

40. Bradley Commission, *Readjustment Benefits,* pp. 316–17.

41. Ibid., pp. 337, 353.

42. Ibid., pp. 345–46.

state, southerners proved extraordinarily willing to take advantage of what was offered.

Veterans' payments were strikingly redistributive. They reduced relative differences in state per capita income by 5 percent in 1949, compared to a reduction of 1 percent in 1939. One study reported that veterans' payments accounted for 7 percent of income in Alabama, Arkansas, and Louisiana, and 9 percent in Mississippi.[43] Along with the redistributive effects of federal spending for defense and public works, veterans' programs were the progenitor of a new southern middle class.

The Persistence of Racially Stratified Social Policies

Black political leaders were infuriated by the self-righteous, harsh attitudes expressed by whites toward poor mothers during the welfare purges of the 1950s, especially by the "get tough" policy adopted in Newburgh, New York. Lester Granger, executive director of the National Urban League, told local Urban League affiliates that Newburgh was "the Louisiana and Mississippi plan more smartly handled, with obvious race bias muted and with a profession of concern for the welfare dollar." These factors, he went on, "make the Newburgh proposition palatable for persons who do not know what the score really is." The score in the North as well as the South, most black political leaders believed, was that the attacks on welfare were undertaken with the express intent of derailing the civil rights movement. These events, commented Whitney Young, Jr., of the National Urban League, "should . . . dramatically alert even the most naive that racism and the struggle for first class citizenship are far more than regional phenomena and are not always accompanied by overt symbols and signs." The NAACP strongly denounced Mitchell's plan, saying in a press release that the relief plan "could establish a relief pattern injurious to Negroes and others caught up in the national population shift to Northern cities and towns."[44]

Granger, Wilkins and others were not deluding themselves about the threat posed to the civil rights movement by the welfare purges. The Louisiana purge grew out of white opposition to racial integration; the Newburgh plan reflected white unease with black migration and the opportunism of parti-

43. Howard G. Schaller, "Veterans Transfer Payments and State per Capita Incomes, 1929, 1939, and 1949," *Review of Economics and Statistics* 35 (1953): 326–27.

44. Lester Granger to Executive Secretaries, July 25, 1961, p. 2, and *Columbus Dispatch*, September 7, 1961, NUL Papers, ser. 1, 1960–1966, box 47, folder "1962 Public Welfare Situation," LC; NAACP Press Release, July 1, 1961, NAACP Papers, Group 3, box 144, folder "New York, Newburgh, 1960–1962," LC.

san competition in the North. In both cases, whites focused on the concentration of African Americans on the welfare rolls and in public housing. Even though both programs are "universalistic" in the sense that all eligible recipients must be accepted, both came to be seen as—and to some degree actually became—policies designed to ameliorate if not reverse the poverty of African American families. The racial identification of these two policies derived from the mutually reinforcing effects of labor-market discrimination and the response by white politicians to black migration.

During the early years of the war, blacks, especially outside the South, were admitted to ADC at higher rates than whites, and between 1942 and 1948 the number of black families receiving ADC increased by 46 percent.[45] Throughout the 1950s the proportion of black families on the ADC rolls continued to rise rapidly even though the overall growth of the program stagnated with the purges. Almost all of the *relative* growth of African American families on the ADC rolls took place prior to the Great Society, not during and after it. By 1961, 40 percent of the ADC caseload was composed of black families, up from about 14 percent in 1939. In some regions of the country the proportion was much higher: black families made up 59 percent of the caseload in northern industrial states, 45 percent in the mid-Atlantic states (New York, Pennsylvania, and New Jersey), and 57 percent in the South (see figure 5). In many big northern cities the rates were extraordinarily high: in Chicago, for example, it was estimated that 91 percent of the caseload was nonwhite, and in northern cities of 50,000 people or more the proportion was 85 percent.[46] Similarly, the proportion of non-whites in public housing rose from 37 percent of total occupants in 1948 to 48 percent in 1957. In big cities, public housing was a program for blacks; 75 percent of all occupants in Chicago were black, and in Detroit 90 percent of all applications were submitted by black families. These families were also very poor.[47]

45. Elizabeth Alling and Agnes Leisy, "Aid to Dependent Children in a Postwar Year," *Public Assistance Report*, no. 7 (Washington, D.C., 1950), pp. 6–8.

46. Greenleigh Associates, *Facts, Fallacies, and Future: A Study of the Aid to Dependent Children Program of Cook County, Illinois* (New York, 1960), pp. 1, 36–7. Over half of all black families receiving ADC lived in cities of 250,000 or more inhabitants compared to one-sixth of white families on ADC. This pattern was more characteristic of the North than the South. U.S. Department of Health, Education, and Welfare, Welfare Administration, "Study of Recipients of Aid to Families with Dependent Children, November–December 1961: National Cross Tabulations" (August 1965), table 32.

47. Robert M. Fisher, *Twenty Years of Public Housing: Economic Aspects of the Federal Program* (New York, 1959), p. 165; Davis McEntire, *Residence and Race* (Berkeley, Calif., 1960), p. 329.

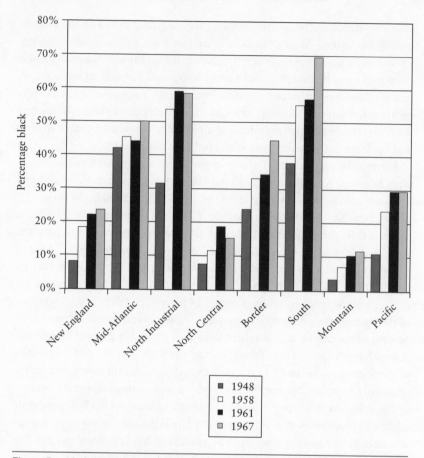

Figure 5. Black AFDC participation rates by region, 1948–1967. *Sources:* Department of Health, Education, and Welfare, Social Security Administration, *Characteristics of Families Receiving AFDC* (Washington, D.C., selected years).

Both ADC and public housing were deployed by politicians to manage postwar economic and racial dislocations. Many northern politicians viewed welfare as an expedient device to cope with the economic plight of a growing African American population. The *Greenleigh Report* on Chicago found that "the problem of ADC in Cook County cannot be separated from the problem of lower class Negroes." Attitudes toward the program were synonymous with attitudes toward blacks, though the report noted a dearth of overt hostility. In Baltimore, whose postwar welfare purge became a model for other cities, the reform-minded Greater Baltimore Committee supported an autonomous welfare department, "as it seems to be perceived as serving the needs of blacks, primarily." Welfare was also seen as a cheap way to placate blacks, especially in cities with district or ward elections.[48] In both Baltimore and Chicago, black council members routinely sought and obtained support for welfare, which white members viewed as a matter of concern only to the black community. Chicago politicians were not beyond manipulating welfare for electoral purposes. The black vote was decisive to Richard J. Daley's victory in the 1955 mayoral election, but this did not translate into any appreciable patronage; rather, welfare and public housing benefits were used to maintain the electoral tie between the white machine and black wards. In Baltimore, on the other hand, Democrats were reluctant to attack welfare out of concern that it would alienate liberal, mainly Jewish, support.[49]

Public housing was transformed into a bastion of Jim Crow by business interests, who used the program to remove black families from choice downtown properties, and by white opposition to integration. During and after the war, black participation in public housing was limited by quotas that were a consequence of segregation. After the war, the federal urban renewal program was used in both North and South to build urban ghettos. Plans to raze slums and rebuild city centers to attract fleeing white suburbanites necessitated removal of poor black migrants, and "planners saw the promotion of more public housing for the black families they wanted to displace as a necessary component of their redevelopment schemes."[50] White resistance, often violent, ruled out integration through dispersal of public housing, a measure advocated by liberals in many cities. Public housing became a racially identified program because it offered city officials a flexible way to respond to business demands for urban renewal while avoiding the wrath of fearful whites. Chicago was the archetype; other big cities followed suit, and cities with relatively low levels of segregation, such as Philadelphia, created highly contained ghettos from scratch.[51]

48. Robert Lieberman, "Race and the Organization of Welfare Policy," in *Classifying by Race,* ed. Paul Peterson (Princeton, N.J., 1995), p. 183. See also Steven P. Erie, *Rainbow's End: Irish-Americans and the Dilemmas of Urban Machine Politics, 1840–1985* (Berkeley, Calif., 1988), pp. 166–67.

49. Greenleigh, *Facts, Fallacies, and Future,* p. 33; Banfield, *Political Influence,* pp. 73–77; Sharon Krefetz, *Welfare Policy Making and City Politics* (New York, 1976), pp. 170–72; William Grimshaw, *Bitter Fruit: Black Politics and the Chicago Machine, 1931–1991* (Chicago, 1992), pp. 100–101.

50. Harold M. Baron, "Building Babylon: A Case of Racial Controls in Public Housing" (mimeo, Center for Urban Affairs, Northwestern University, 1971), p. 37.

51. Arnold Hirsch, *Making the Second Ghetto* (New York, 1983); John F. Bauman, *Public Housing, Race, and Renewal* (Philadelphia, 1987).

The racial transformation of public housing was completed by the adoption of policies that either excluded eligible whites from public housing or funneled them into separate housing programs. For example, cities acted to create separate, and segregated, projects for the elderly; given the absence of separate funding, space for the elderly came at the expense of poor blacks, who were often forced out of their own housing. As new housing policies were created, they were turned to the advantage of whites. In fact, before 1968, most housing policies were racially stratified: public housing was allocated to minority families, while subsidized ownership programs were allocated to white families.[52]

At the same time, black families were underserved by public social welfare programs; they received less than they needed or were entitled to than poor white families. In 1960, 80 percent of illegitimate nonwhite children did not receive ADC, compared to 20 percent of illegitimate white children. In the rural South access to public assistance was limited to eligible whites. In Georgia, for example, poor counties with "small black populations received higher welfare expenditures, whilst counties with large black populations in similarly poor socioeconomic conditions did not have as much spent on them." Public housing never reached more than a fraction of those in need. Just 59,000 families of all those displaced by urban renewal from 1950 to 1971, or 19 percent of the total, were relocated in public housing. Blacks were the chief beneficiaries, but two-thirds of black families displaced by slum clearance projects and eligible for public housing were unable to gain access.[53]

The combination of a racially stratified system of social provision and the deprivation of the black poor occurred because of widespread labor-market discrimination and economic changes (automation and productivity bargaining) that reproduced the racially competitive labor markets that had existed in the 1930s. Black workers did make economic gains during the immediate postwar period and this, along with legislative changes in coverage, brought

52. Heywood Sanders, "The Politics of City Redevelopment" (Ph.D. diss., Harvard University, 1977), pp. 358–60; Baron, "Building Babylon," pp. 67–68; Eugene Meehan, "The Rise and Fall of Public Housing: Condemnation without Trial," in *A Decent Home and Environment: Housing Urban America*, ed. Donald Phares (Cambridge, Mass., 1977), p. 22; Robert Gray and Steven Tursky, "Locational and Racial/Ethnic Occupancy Patterns for HUD-Subsidized Family Housing in Ten Metropolitan Areas," in *Housing Desegregation and Federal Policy,* ed. John M. Goering (Chapel Hill, 1986), pp. 235–51.

53. Lora S. Collins, "Public Assistance Expenditures in the United States," in *Studies in the Economics of Income Maintenance,* ed. Otto Eckstein (Washington, D.C., 1967), pp. 132–33; John Offord, "State Welfare Expenditures and the Geography of Social Well-Being in the US State of Georgia, 1950–1970," Occasional Paper no. 21, Dept. of Geography, University of London (January 1983), p. 18; Sanders, "Politics of City Redevelopment," pp. 353–55.

them under the protection of unemployment insurance and related social policies. Just over half of all black workers were covered by unemployment compensation in 1960, although their coverage lagged behind that of white workers and the gap between black and white workers actually widened over the 1950s (see table 11). Yet the integration of blacks into the postwar middle-class welfare state remained precarious.

Black workers were not excluded from middle-class social policies by overt discrimination. Their access to middle-class social benefits was undermined by discrimination in labor and housing markets, segregated, inferior education, and changing economic fortunes. Black women were doubly disadvantaged. Not only was their access to middle-class policies undermined by labor-market discrimination, but they remained statutorily excluded from unemployment compensation. Nationally, 49 percent of working African American women in 1960 were employed as agricultural laborers or domestic workers, both of which remained uncovered by unemployment insurance. In the South, 60 percent of black women were affected by these occupational exclusions. Only 10 percent of white women, on the other hand, were employed in these jobs.[54] For most black women, the situation had not progressed much beyond the New Deal.

The experience of black veterans is illustrative of how Jim Crow and discrimination undermined their access to social policies. Black veterans received G.I. Bill benefits at rates equal to whites in all regions of the country, and were slightly more likely to be the beneficiaries of education and readjustment benefits (table 11). Over half of black veterans participated in more than one readjustment program, compared to 44 percent of white veterans.[55] But African Americans received less than their "fair share" of veterans benefits because they were historically underrepresented among the veteran population; black men had been much more likely than white men to be disqualified from military service during World War II, as a direct consequence of their segregated, inferior education and poor health.[56] Nor did black veterans receive the same occupational and educational lift as did white veterans. At all income thresholds, black World War II and Korean War veterans did not earn as much by 1970 as white veterans, nor did they

54. United States Bureau of the Census, *U.S. Census of Population: 1960,* subject report, *Industrial Characteristics,* PC(2)-7F (Washington, D.C., 1963), table 3.

55. Veterans Administration, "Benefits and Services Received by World War II Veterans under the Major Veterans Administration Programs," pp. 13, 20, RG 51, ser. 39.20a, box 9, NA.

56. The black rejection rate from the armed services was substantially higher than the rate for whites: 48 percent compared to 28 percent. Lewis B. Hersey to Samuel Rosenman, 1945, Samuel Rosenman Papers, box 1, folder "Health Speech #1," HSTL.

Table 11.   Coverage and effects of unemployment insurance and veterans programs by race

Estimated percentage of workers covered by unemployment insurance				
	1940	*1950*	*1960*	*1970*
White	56%	60%	69%	74%
Black	33	47	54	67
Difference (White advantage)	+23%	+13	+15	+7

Percentage who received veterans' benefits as of 1950				
	Total G.I. Bill	Education	Readjustment	Loans	Multiple benefits[a]
White veterans	73%	43%	52%	13%	44%
Nonwhite veterans	75	49	61	5	51

Cumulative earnings for 1970 income thresholds				
	$23,000	*$13,000*	*$10,000*	*$7,000*	*$4,000*
World War II veterans					
White	5.5%	23.2%	43.9%	71.9%	87.8%
Black	0.5	3.9	12.7	40.4	68.2
Korean War veterans					
White	4.3	24.7	49.3	78.1	92.9
Black	0.8	6.1	15.2	44.2	73.4

Years of education completed			
	College	*1–3 yrs. of college*	*High school*
World War II veterans			
White	15.2%	26.7%	57.9%
Black	6.0	13.3	30.9
Korean War veterans			
White	18.3	32.6	71.5
Black	10.1	23.3	52.3

Sources: Dorothy K. Newman et al., *Protest, Politics, and Prosperity* (New York, 1978), tables 7, 8; Veterans Administration, "Benefits and Services Received by World War II Veterans under the Major Veterans Administration Programs" (August 1950), pp. 13, 22, 27, 33, 38–39; Wayne J. Villemez and John D. Kasarda, "Veteran Status and Socioeconomic Attainment," *Armed Forces and Society* 2 (1976): tables 2, 3.

[a]Veterans who received more than one benefit at the same time.

advance as far educationally. White and black veterans were advantaged relative to nonveterans, but black World War II veterans were less prosperous than white nonveterans of the same age. It is not difficult to see why.

Black veterans experienced a noticeably different homecoming than white veterans. Shut out of the American Legion in the South and elsewhere and confronted with pervasive labor-market discrimination, black veterans encountered greater difficulty finding jobs than did returning white soldiers. The National Urban League estimated that some 17,000 Georgia veterans lost benefits because they were excluded from local American Legion posts. One early report indicated that less than 7 percent of black veterans received on-the-job training through readjustment programs, and as a consequence they remained in the "52/20 clubs" much longer.[57] Labor-market discrimination virtually nullified blacks' access to veterans' benefits. A series of reports from local NUL branches in the late 1940s reveal that employers would not accept black applicants; their files were put in the inactive pile, and sooner or later black applicants gave up using the U.S. Employment Service office. The Seattle branch wrote,

> we would consider the Washington State Employment Service (WSES) interpretation of racial employment practices in our community negative. This is evidenced most through its attitude to its Negro clientele. If inference is to be taken from this, the WSES condones the practice of exclusion of Negroes by employers in the community who make discriminatory work orders without any representation on behalf of the market when there are skilled Negroes available to supply the needs of the employer.[58]

Similarly, in Detroit, 35.1 percent of all job placement orders received by the Michigan state employment service in 1946 contained discriminatory clauses; this increased to 44.7 percent in 1947.[59]

Despite such labor-market discrimination, blacks made gains in manufacturing employment during the fifteen years after the war. But the gains in

57. Julius Thomas, "Adjustment of Negro Veterans: A Report of the Adjustment Problems of Negro Veterans in Fifty Cities" (1946), p. 3, NUL Papers, ser. 4, box 19; Charles Bolte, "The Negro Veteran," p. 13, NUL Papers, ser. 4, box 19, folder "American Veterans Committee, 1945–47"; Thomas to Kerns, February 8, 1945, NUL Papers, ser. 4, box 19, LC.

58. Woodland to Jefferies, December 15, 1948, NUL Papers, ser. 4, box 18, folder "USES, 1946–48," LC.

59. Thomas J. Sugrue, *The Origins of the Urban Crisis: Race and Inequality in Postwar Detroit* (Princeton, N.J., 1996), p. 94.

the number of black workers employed in manufacturing masked changes in the economic terrain confronting them. Black workers faced costricting economic conditions. Because they remained concentrated in low-skill, low-wage jobs, they confronted growing competition from white workers who had been displaced from agriculture. At the same time, black workers were unable to find and keep full-time, high-wage employment because of shrinking demand for unskilled labor and corporate decisions to automate or relocate plants. The Eisenhower years were a turning point. There is evidence of an "upward shift in Negro unemployment beyond the level accounted for by over-all demand or increases in white structural unemployment" during the decade.[60] As automation and relocation sharply limited black economic opportunity in the North, the rate of agricultural modernization in Iowa, Illinois, and similar states fed a growing stream of white migrants to the city. The North Central region, which had contributed only 6 percent of the reduction in agricultural employment during the war years, accounted for 28 percent of farm job loss during the Eisenhower years. In the cities ringing the Great Lakes a growing economic contradiction was apparent: swelling numbers of black migrants faced an influx of white migrants, diminishing economic opportunities, and the slowest postwar growth rates in employment. It was altogether much too reminiscent of the 1930s.[61]

The net result was to erode blacks' access to permanent, full-time work, and thus the basis for their integration into the core of the American welfare state. By one measure, blacks rose from 18 percent of urban jobless in 1950 to 28 percent in 1960.[62] Unemployment for black men rose from about one-and-a-half times to over twice that of white men, and the sharpest divergence between black and white unemployment rates appeared among men in their prime working years. For males 25–34 and 35–44 of years age, the black unemployment rate was almost three times that of whites (see figure 6). If one takes account of those who had dropped out of the labor force, the jobless rate was even higher.[63]

Black women were similarly affected. The unemployment rate for black

60. Eleanor G. Gilpatrick, *Structural Unemployment and Aggregate Demand* (Baltimore, 1966), p. 205. For an analysis of the effects of automation and plant closings on blacks in Detroit, see Sugrue, *Origins of the Urban Crisis*, pp. 143–46.

61. Charles Killingsworth, *Jobs and Income for Negroes* (Ann Arbor, Mich., 1968), pp. 39–40.

62. Stern, "Poverty and Family Composition," pp. 237–38.

63. Killingsworth, *Jobs and Income for Negroes*, p. 30. After adjusting for "hidden unemployment," Killingsworth calculated the unemployment rate for black males aged 25–34 years was four times that of whites.

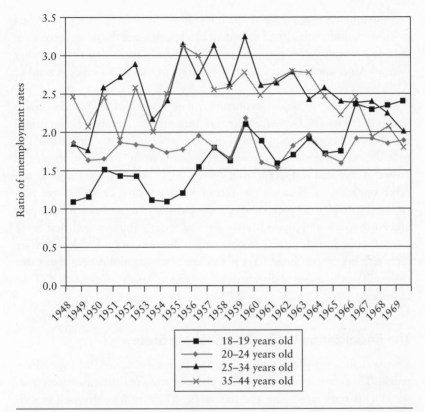

Figure 6. Ratio of black to white male unemployment rates by age, 1949–1969. *Source:* U.S. Bureau of Labor Statistics, *Handbook of Labor Statistics: 1970,* BLS Bulletin, no. 1666 (Washington, D.C., 1971), tables 68, 71.

females was almost twice that of white females, and since white females had average unemployment rates almost one-and-half-times those of white males, the result was that there was almost no difference in unemployment rates between black females and black males in the 1950s. Moreover, even though black women had higher labor-force participation rates, enormous numbers of white women, mainly between the ages of 35 and 55, entered in the labor market. The labor-force participation rate of white women 35–44 years of age rose by 63 percent between 1940 and 1960, compared to 24 percent for black women. Furthermore, white women had a different occupational profile than black women.[64] Whites were two-and-half-times as likely to

64. U.S. Bureau of Labor Statistics, *Handbook of Labor Statistics: 1970,* BLS Bulletin no. 1666 (Washington, D.C., 1971), tables 68, 71; William Julius Wilson and Kathryn M.

be in manufacturing jobs and much less likely to be in service jobs. When one also considers that over half of all black women in the labor force were outside unemployment compensation, it is hardly surprising that so many African-American women found themselves, from time to time, in need of ADC benefits.

That welfare was linked to unemployment was a widely shared assumption at the time. The *Greenleigh Report,* for example, assumed a clear causal relationship between employment discrimination and attachment to ADC rolls: "discrimination in employment was found in this study to have a greater direct and indirect impact on the ADC program than almost any other single factor, because it results in desertion, divorce and unwed parenthood with all their social and economic costs." The authors of the report argued that fair employment laws were necessary and asserted that those states that had made efforts to combat job discrimination had low welfare rates and lower spending.[65] Yet it was not black unemployment that came to dominate the political debate over welfare; it was the racialization of the caseload.

The Racialization of the Dual Welfare State

Race was the ever-present subtext to the political discourse of the welfare purges. The postwar jump in the ADC caseload attracted instant scrutiny from the Florida state legislature and the public. Their ire was "focused specifically on the mounting cost of welfare programs with particular criticism for ADC because of the large percentage of Negroes in this recipient group. . . . This upturn was viewed in absolute not relative terms. It contributed to the movement that led to the passage of the Suitable Home Law in 1959."[66] Elsewhere coded language conveyed unmistakable meanings. One *Saturday Evening Post* exposé of "welfare fraud" managed to avoid mentioning race, but practically every picture accompanying the story was of black women and children. A fixation on black migrants coming north to take advantage of generous welfare payments dates from the 1930s. The New York City welfare report of the late 1940s revived the charge and gave it currency in the postwar period, suggesting that the liberal relief benefits "granted in New

Neckerman, "Poverty and Family Structure," in *Fighting Poverty: What Works and What Doesn't,* ed. Sheldon H. Danziger and Daniel H. Weinberg (Cambridge, Mass., 1986), p. 246, table 10.4.

65. Greenleigh, *Facts, Fallacies and Future,* pp. 48–49.

66. Lansdale, "Florida Suitable Home Law," p. 114.

York City has and will continue to encourage migration . . . of people without any visible means of support, including those whose sole purpose is to receive public assistance."[67] The perils of migration also surfaced in other cities and were allusively linked to illegitimacy and the African American family.

Often this allusive language was discarded for direct verbal assaults. The Chicago welfare director compared "public assistance with the Poor House Over the Hill" and testily added, "unfortunately there are not cotton plantations in Chicago in which Negroes might be put to work." He was sharply criticized, but his views were not atypical. Chicago suburbanites and Republicans could be heard to voice antiblack welfare rhetoric, but among Democrats such language was muted for fear of alienating black voters. Corruption was tied to relief in Chicago's 1955 mayoral election; voters challenged Richard J. Daley's Republican opponent to indicate what he would do about "public housing . . . mixing races . . . [and public] relief to the thousands who come from the south to live on the tax payers of Chicago."[68]

The most explicit attacks came from conservative politicians intent on exploiting racial fears and concern over rising welfare expenditures, who fused race, sex, and welfare by depicting black unmarried mothers as "women whose business is having illegitimate children." They defined the issue less as a matter of welfare "dependence" than as welfare "corruption," a problem of "black women, sex, and money," that was portrayed, Rickie Solinger points out, as "a direct financial loss for whites."[69] In Newburgh, conservatives directly implicated federal policy as the progenitor of illegitimate black children. The NUL reported that "*The Truth Seeker,* a Negrophobic smear-sheet" appeared on the streets of New York City, headlining "UNCLE SAM: BLACK BASTARD BREEDER SUPREME—Unwed Negro Mothers Battle New Orleans, Mississippi, and Newburgh, New York."[70]

These racial polemics were national, but the political forces behind this process differed in the North and the South. Welfare purges in northern

67. Paul Molloy, "The Relief Chiselers are Stealing Us Blind," *Saturday Evening Post* (September 8, 1951): 32ff.; Lyndon, "Relief Probes," pp. 137–38.

68. Banfield, *Political Influence,* pp. 65, 70–71; Frank Valadez, "Americans Some: Racial Identity and the Politics of Culture in Chicago since the Second World War" (Paper presented to the Social Science History Association, October 1994, Atlanta, Ga.), p. 15.

69. Rickie Solinger, *Wake Up Little Susie: Single Pregnancy and Race before Roe v. Wade* (New York, 1992), pp. 29, 42.

70. National Urban League, "The Newburgh Plan," pp. 3–4, NUL Papers, ser. 1, 1960–1966, box 47, folder "1962 Public Welfare Situation," LC.

states were driven by electoral politics and mounting suburban hostility to rising welfare rolls. Although many northern states tolerated large and growing caseloads, they also faced pressure to contain the cost of ADC. Incipient antipathy toward rising welfare burdens, nourished by conservative or opportunistic politicians, contributed to an impulse to purge the rolls or lower benefits. As always, antipathy to taxes found a ready outlet.

Newburgh, New York, is the perfect illustration of this dynamic. When Joseph Mitchell unveiled his policy, the local cost of welfare was 14 percent of the municipal budget and rising. In New York, municipalities carried one-quarter of relief costs, and New York was one of seven states that had no residency requirement for ADC. Neither Mitchell nor his chief ally on the city council made any secret of their belief that taxes were going up because black migrants were moving to Newburgh "without any means of support and demanding and receiving support from our welfare department."[71] The city of Baltimore, on the other hand, avoided the welfare battles brewing at the end of the decade by shifting the fiscal burden to the state. A 1961 amendment to a state law, the brainchild of a state fiscal adviser, set a 10 percent limit on local welfare costs and reduced the local share in Maryland from 19 to 8 percent between 1960 and 1963. Janet Hoffman, the amendment's author, was partly motivated by the belief that as the state's population changed there would be increased hostility toward welfare, and she wanted to lessen Baltimore's fiscal burden for ADC before residents realized they were footing the bill.[72]

Hoffman minimized the electoral incentives to exploit welfare in the city of Baltimore, but her stratagem may have only shifted the controversy to the state legislature. The Maryland state legislature launched an investigation of ADC in 1960, and similar investigations were underway in at least five other northern states. New Jersey, a state with relatively liberal eligibility rules and benefits, established a state investigative committee in 1962 which proceeded to excoriate black families and rail about the "amoral existence of many ADC recipients." The Maryland state commission indignantly denied that taxes were an issue, yet its report subscribed to all of the racial stereotypes and polemics then suffusing antiwelfare rhetoric throughout the country.[73]

71. Joseph P. Ritz, *The Despised Poor: Newburgh's War on Welfare* (Boston, 1966), p. 22.

72. Krefetz, *Welfare Policy Making*, pp. 92–93, 150–52, table 10.

73. *Report of the Commission to Study Problems of Illegitimacy among the Recipients of Public Welfare Monies in the Program for Aid to Dependent Children* (Annapolis, Md., 1961), pp. 17–19; New Jersey State Legislature, Welfare Investigating Committee,

In the South, it was the race-baiting politics of white resistance to integration after *Brown v. Board of Education* that fueled attacks on welfare recipients. The Louisiana purge was the direct result of such electoral politics in a post–New Deal setting. All of the candidates in Louisiana's 1960 gubernatorial election advocated industrialization and low taxes, and they more or less accepted the generous old-age pensions, school lunches, and education budget that was the legacy of Governor Earl K. Long, Huey Long's brother, while campaigning to hold the line on segregation. But one of the candidates, William Rainach, a founder of the Louisiana White Citizen's Council and the most strident segregationist in the primary, upped the ante, saying the state should maintain "old age pensions and cut off aid to the parents of illegitimate children." Rainach, whose campaign slogan was "segregation, economy, and responsibility," said he proposed denying payments to unwed mothers in order to reduce "wasteful" expenditures.[74] Rainach lost the primary, but both the remaining contenders picked up much of his platform, including the animus toward ADC. Jimmy Davis, the eventual winner, repeatedly berated women welfare recipients, popularizing the idea that they were a threat to taxpayers' pocketbooks.

The Louisiana election showed that politicians could be neopopulist on most economic issues, yet remain staunch segregationists. Rainach, Davis, and others resembled those pro–New Deal southerners, like Theodore Bilbo, who combined a virulent racism with pork-barrel politics. But even erstwhile liberals and reformers such as DeLesseps Morrison, a former mayor of New Orleans, adopted racist appeals. The 1960 Louisiana campaign was not the first in which such appeals were made; in fact, it was reminiscent of Herman Talmadge's electoral appeals of the early 1950s. Talmadge had combined a program for economic modernization with white supremacy and built an urban-rural coalition that provided roads and services for businesses and suburbanites and gave patronage to rural counties. Both interest groups had been assuaged with strident attacks on poor black women. Following Talmadge's election, the Georgia legislature had enacted harsh, punitive welfare policies.[75]

Legislative Report on the Aid to Dependent Children Program in New Jersey (Trenton, N.J., 1963), pp. 1–2, quoted in Robert Lieberman, "Race and the Administration of Social Policy, 1935–1965" (Paper presented to the Social Science History Association, Baltimore, 1993), p. 23.

74. Glen S. Jeansonne, *Race, Religion, and Politics: The Louisiana Gubernatorial Elections of 1959–1960* (Lafayette, La., 1977), pp. 59–60, 62.

75. Numan V. Bartley, *The Rise of Massive Resistance* (Baton Rouge, La., 1969), p. 42.

Black families were singled out in the postwar purges, at least in the South. In Georgia, for example, cuts in ADC caseloads were concentrated in urban counties, where the number of families on the rolls declined by 33 percent over the 1950s. Since the ADC caseload had a rural tilt in the South (71 percent of white recipients and 42 percent of black recipients lived in rural areas) but the proportion of black families on ADC in southern cities was three times that of white families (30 percent compared to 13 percent), poor urban, black families suffered most. A similar pattern is apparent in Alabama, Arkansas, and Louisiana: disproportionate cuts were made in urban areas where black families accounted for the bulk of the caseload. And in Florida the suitable-home law was administered in a way that smacked of egregious racial discrimination.[76]

Race clearly mattered in the welfare purges, but one might object that middle-class hostility to ADC might have been driven by resentment toward a means-tested program. Blacks may have been singled out, but poor white women suffered as well. The best evidence that race, not means tests, was behind the purges comes from the way the poor elderly were treated, especially in the South. At the same time states cracked down on ADC mothers, they loosened eligibility criteria for Old Age Assistance (OAA) and raised benefits substantially. Senior citizens had received significantly higher benefits than single mothers since the late 1930s, a trend that accelerated after the war. Between 1950 and 1960 the OAA caseload dropped by 15 percent, but states continued to raise benefits; many even indexed OAA benefits to inflation.[77] States also acted to loosen eligibility criteria, often because they had difficulty enforcing any limits. Lien laws were one of the most potent devices used to reduce the old-age rolls since most elderly were loath to mortgage their property or personnel possessions to the state. Measured by removal of property liens, there was a substantial liberalization of OAA laws throughout the country, and the biggest shift took place in the South. In 1946,

76. Author's calculations based on data from Piven and Cloward, *Regulating the Poor,* source table 2; U.S. Department of HEW, Bureau of Public Assistance, "Characteristics and Financial Circumstances of Families Receiving Aid to Dependent Children—Late 1958," *Public Assistance Report,* no. 41 (1960): tables 2–3. Robert T. Lansdale found that in Florida 90 percent of all cases in which there was a question about the suitability of the home were cases involving black families. Put another way, 16.2 percent of white families were investigated by social workers because of questions about care and supervision of children rather than the "moral environment" of the home, compared to just 3.5 percent of black families, *Florida Suitable Home Law,* p. 75.

77. Labovitz to Jones, December 26, 1951, p. 3, RG 51, ser. 47.3, box 62; Martz/Stark to Alger/Labovitz, June 23, 1952, RG 51, ser. 39.14, box 22, folder no. 175, NA.

there were only five states that did not allow liens; by 1953, there were six-teen. The number of southern states without property liens increased from two to eight, most of them in the deep South.

Many southern states converted old-age assistance into an entitlement. Over 40 percent of southern senior citizens received an OAA payment in 1950, modest though it was, compared to a national average of 22.5 percent. Georgia, Arkansas, Mississippi, and Texas all provided old-age pensions to almost half of resident senior citizens but paid very low benefits. Louisiana, on the other hand, was distinctive even among southern states, giving three-quarters of all people over 65 years of age a pension that paid nine out of ten recipients over 80 percent of the fifty dollar maximum benefit.[78]

What made southern generosity toward the elderly so distinctive was southern harshness toward single mothers. A Budget Bureau report dryly noted that in Louisiana, "relatively rigid standards as compared with OAA cases are applied to the determination of income and resources for ADC cases."[79] Louisiana was by no means unique; throughout the South dis-parate treatment of the elderly and families relying upon ADC was appar-ent. In Georgia, for example, at the same time that the legislature decided to convict mothers with illegitimate children of fornication or adultery, it changed OAA policy to disregard the first fifty dollars of income when de-ciding on qualification for assistance and to allow elderly recipients to have up to eight hundred dollars in cash for unexpected expenses.[80] Average monthly payments to the elderly increased at a much faster rate in the South than nationally, while average monthly payments to ADC families grew more slowly, and in some cases there was actually a decline in average monthly payments.[81] The ratio of per capita payments for OAA to ADC remained high in the South, while declining elsewhere. In the deep South these ratios were extraordinarily high in 1960: 6.4 in Alabama; 6.7 in Arkansas; 4.1 in Louisiana; 3.4 in Mississippi and Georgia; and a whopping 8.2 in Texas. These were the same states that adopted some of the harshest policies to-ward ADC mothers in the late 1950s.

A final piece of evidence demonstrating disparate treatment is the way

78. Michael L. Kurtz and Morgan D. Peoples, *Earl K. Long: The Saga of Uncle Earl and Louisiana Politics* (Baton Rouge, La., 1990), pp. 55–56, 130–31, 197.

79. Ferebee/Martz to Rufus Miles, July 7, 1950, p. 5, RG 51, ser. 39.3, box 125, folder no. 831, NA.

80. *Public Welfare* 16 (1958): 97, 182.

81. Robert T. Lansdale, "The Impact of the Federal Social Security Act on Public Wel-fare Programs in the South," *Research Reports in Social Science* 4 (1961): 34–35.

Table 12. Relatives' responsibility laws for OAA and ADC, 1955

	South	Non-South
NOLEO law—ADC	(N=11)	(N=37)
Send notice only; eligibility not affected	18%	27%
Legal action required for continuation of aid	27	29
Legal action as a condition of eligibility	45	37
Alternatives to legal action permitted	9	5
Relatives' responsibility—OAA	(N=11)	(N=40)
Children not required to contribute	55%	28%
Court action possible but aid not contingent	27	45
Eligibility and payments based on ability to pay	18	28

Sources: (NOLEO [*Notification of Law Enforcement Officials*]) Maurine McKeany, *The Absent Father and Public Policy in the Program of Aid to Dependent Children* (Berkeley, 1960), pp. 74–82. (*Relatives' responsibility*) Elizabeth Epler, "Old Age Assistance: Plan Provisions for Children's Responsiblity for Parents," *Social Security Bulletin* (April 1954): 7.

southern states approached the problems of children's financial responsibility for elderly, poor parents, on the one hand, and the failure of husbands to pay child support, on the other. During the 1950s most states enacted relative responsibility laws for the elderly and laws implementing the NOLEO amendment for ADC mothers. Examination of table 12 reveals that southern states were much more likely to adopt the most lenient version of the relative responsibility law but the harshest version of the NOLEO amendment. A majority of southern states, compared to less than one-third of nonsouthern states, neither required children to contribute to their parents well-being nor made children's ability to contribute a reason for denial of aid. But almost half of southern states made legal action by a single mother a condition of ADC eligibility, compared to slightly more than one-third of nonsouthern states.

The Distributive Consequences of Truncated Universalism

In a letter to Charles Diggs, a friend and member of Congress, Roy Wilkins confessed his fear that the furor over welfare would undermine African American claims for equal rights and opportunities. Wilkins steadfastly defended ADC but worried that any defense of single mothers with children born out of wedlock "would be regarded by the Negro's opponents as an admission on our part that our people are not yet worthy of the status we demand for them."[82] Wilkins was obviously right about the threat. It was

82. Wilkins to Diggs, n.d. [July 1961?], NAACP Papers, ser. 3, box 145, folder "Government/Cities," LC.

no accident that William Rainach defended segregation by vilifying black women or that Joseph Mitchell ended up as a paid organizer for the segregationist White Citizens' Councils after resigning as city manager of Newburgh. To many white Americans, ensconced in their burgeoning affluence and convinced of their rectitude and individual responsibility, the spectacle of Newburgh and Louisiana confirmed dearly held prejudices.

Wilkins's admissions to Diggs are revealing for what they suggest about the post–New Deal color line. The racial stratification of the U.S. welfare state began, I have argued, during the depression with the inversion of Myrdal's vicious circle; it was then institutionalized by the failure of the Democratic party and unions to build a comprehensive welfare state and by persistent labor-market discrimination and welfare purges of the postwar period. At the same time that expanding private and public social policies contributed to the well-being of many middle-class households, ADC and public housing were used by public officials to manage urban economic change and the migration of black sharecroppers. Both programs, although statutorily color blind, acquired a racial identification that was politically exploited by white southerners intent on preserving Jim Crow and by northern politicians exploiting whites' unease over black migration. Prior to the Great Society and the black revolt of the 1960s, federal social policy had already become racially marked. The welfare state was defined as much by black and white as it was by rich and poor.

The inversion of Myrdal's vicious circle confronted African American political leaders with a bitter dilemma. As victims of America's pervasive racism, blacks turned to the available public remedies for their poverty. This made African Americans among the most resolute and staunch defenders of a welfare state and of programs of obvious benefit to the poorest among them. This explains why Lester Granger wrote local NUL affiliates in the wake of Newburgh, urging them not to "wait for uninformed, reactionary or ill-motivated influences to precipitate a crisis, but [to] move promptly to alert local leadership to the full implications of Newburgh's actions, so that some kind of protection can be set up to guard against what now threatens to be a disastrous blow at welfare standards throughout the country."[83] Yet labor-market discrimination and the absence of inclusive social policies put blacks in the position of defending the very programs that allowed white Americans to cultivate the most invidious prejudices. What is most significant

---

83. Granger to Executive Secretaries, Local Affiliates, July 25, 1961, p. 2, NUL Papers, 1960–1966, ser. 1, box 47, LC.

about the racial reconstruction of American social policy in the postwar period is that it allowed white Americans to sublimate white advantage in the welfare state to black dependence and individual failure.

It is difficult to determine how widespread the animus toward racially marked welfare programs was in the 1950s. It appears to have been concentrated in the South and in those northern cities experiencing the brunt of African American migration. Nor, until Newburgh, could one say that the issue of race and welfare attracted national attention. But in countless legislative hearings, in the comments of those responsible for administering welfare programs, and in the statements of politicians and other officials, there is unmistakable evidence that racial distinctions and a racialized narrative that built on the images and rhetoric of the 1930s were applied to federal social policies.

African American political elites proved unable to balance the tension between race and class within the Democratic party. Racial apartheid in the South with its segregated system of social provision and pervasive labor-market discrimination precluded such a balancing act. After the failure of the Third New Deal, black leaders concentrated on challenging the use of federal funds to prop up segregation and the discriminatory implementation of federal social policies. African Americans did not abandon the agenda integrating race and class that they had formulated at the end of the 1930s. For most black leaders, whether trade unionists like William Townsend or civil rights leaders like Roy Wilkins and Lester Granger, the problem remained one of finding remedies for both black unemployment and labor-market discrimination. Yet it was clear that class antinomies could never be transcended without first dismantling Jim Crow and overcoming African Americans' political and economic exclusion.

The opportunity to undo the racial stratification of federal social policy appeared as the civil rights movement became more militant in challenging Jim Crow and the Democrats returned to power. How and why Great Society liberals responded to these challenges are the questions to which we must now turn.

PART III

REINVENTING THE NEW DEAL

CHAPTER SIX

The Political and Economic Origins of the Great Society

Unless we have more jobs, the cost of eliminating discrimination will mean the loss of a job by someone else. . . . It will be a hollow victory if we get the "whites only" signs down, only to find "no vacancy" signs behind them.
— WILLARD WIRTZ

The expenditure proposals in this budget are ample to satisfy our most pressing needs for governmental services, but the broad economic stimulus needed to carry our economy to new high ground in production, income, and employment will not come principally from Government outlays. . . . The primary impetus needed to move our economy ahead should come . . . from an expansion of the private sector rather than the public sector.
— LYNDON B. JOHNSON

As political argument, Lyndon Johnson's 1964 budget message was persuasive, leading to the passage of the 1964 Kennedy-Johnson tax cut and ushering in the ascendance of Keynesian economics. As political forecast, it was seriously misleading, for Johnson is hardly remembered as a president who restrained the growth of government. Johnson was, as Charles Schultze, his budget director, once remarked, the last New Dealer; but if the Great Society could be said to have completed the New Deal, it also departed from the assumptions of New Deal liberalism and proceeded to build a redistributive welfare state.

The Democratic party policy agenda of the 1960s may have lacked the social democratic vision of the Third New Deal, yet it nevertheless aspired to render America's capitalist order more humane, if not more equalitarian. The 1959 report of the Senate's Special Committee on Unemployment Problems (the Clark Committee) set out a bevy of recommendations, many of which became law and partially remedied some of the New Deal's more egregious flaws. The Clark committee's agenda was composed mainly of policies that would appeal to broad constituencies: full employment, national standards for unemployment insurance, health care for the elderly, and aid to education. To these programs the Kennedy-Johnson liberals added an inventory of job training, social service programs, and policy innovations such as the War on Poverty and the Model Cities program. Taken together, these new programs formed the core of a policy strategy whose main objective was redistribution to the poor and disadvantaged, an objective which had specific legal and political meanings in the 1960s.

Much of the liberal agenda was an attack on truncated universalism, an attempt to reorder the priorities of federal agencies, reallocate federal resources from middle-class to poor citizens, and patch up the holes in the federal safety net—impulses most clearly signified by the War on Poverty. Yet the Great Society was framed as a particular kind of redistributive welfare state: it was intended to redistribute opportunity rather than money, through provision of educational, social, and employment training services that would enable individuals to take advantage of economic opportunities or would compensate for undeserved economic losses (for example, unemployment arising from automation or trade fluctuations). This idea provided the rationale for practically all of the Kennedy-Johnson social legislation from 1962 to 1966, leading to both the creation of new service programs and the expansion and redirection of existing programs.[1]

Great Society liberals did not challenge the core assumptions of the American welfare state, the middle-class devotion to stable work and its relation to contributory social insurance. Rather they believed social policies should be of greater benefit to those on the margins of American society, though what they meant was changing the poor to fit the welfare state. In a cabinet report written toward the end of Lyndon Johnson's presidency, Labor Secretary Willard Wirtz explained the assumptions of Great Society liberalism: "The point . . . is that the nation should be receding from a tendency to become a 'welfare' state by making more of its citizens increasingly self-supporting at the same time that it embarks on a new era of guaranteed and universal social and economic rights of the kind that reinforce the individual's opportunity to become self-supporting."[2] The problem, Wirtz and Johnson assumed, was one of remedying poverty and unemployment among particular groups: the young, blacks, and individuals in depressed areas. Although there was no consensus, most Great Society liberals assumed the solution was a full-employment policy—the intended result of the massive tax cut President

1. Federal outlays for service programs reached almost $7 billion by 1970, increasing from less than 1.0 percent of GNP in 1960 to 1.6 percent (author's calculation).
2. "Report on Workers and the Welfare State," September 1968, p. 30, Joseph Califano Papers, box 8, LBJL.

Kennedy proposed in 1963—and "a federally led [antipoverty] effort . . . with special emphasis on prevention and rehabilitation" based on employment training and education that would render a "welfare state" less necessary.[3]

Cash and in-kind transfers or publicly provided employment were ruled out, even though in internal debates Wirtz himself was inclined to remonstrate about the need for jobs. LBJ, Schultze has said, "was never big on [cash] transfers. Therefore, we could never get him interested in reforming welfare or beefing up welfare. . . . He was strictly a man with a lot of compassion, but from the '30s. We used to joke and say [he] would give his left arm for the deserving poor."[4] Means-tested cash transfers did become part of the Great Society, partly because the War on Poverty unleashed grassroots protest and mobilized political activists who successfully campaigned for loosened state eligibility rules and access to public transfers as a right. In this chapter and the next, I consider why liberal democrats in two successive presidential administrations chose to build a redistributive state and why they chose a policy strategy based on the redistribution of services rather than any of the other alternatives considered and rejected, such as family allowances and a revived WPA.

Great Society liberalism was formed in the midst of a shattering racial crisis that precipitated policy changes and influenced their implementation and impact. The moral claims of Martin Luther King Jr., and the civil rights movement were combined with a fear of impending social disorder, signified by barely literate youths on the loose in big cities, and these provoked an assault on the inadequacies of federal social policy and impelled policymakers to devise remedies. Yet these remedies were assiduously crafted to avoid the appearance of benefiting only blacks. The service strategy, I argue, originated during the Kennedy administration as a set of policies designed to *avoid* introducing race into the political landscape. Northern Democrats from Senator Joseph Clark to John F. Kennedy understood that any policy appearing to be of specific or great benefit to African Americans acquired instant liabilities in Congress. Legislative strategy and politics were still governed by a southern veto on the question of race and by Republican willingness to play the race card. By 1963, however, demands by civil rights protesters for racial equality in the North as well as the South compelled

3. Walter Heller to Theodore Sorenson, December 20, 1963, box 1, Legislative Background, Economic Opportunity Act, WHCF, LBJL. See also *Economic Report of the President, 1964* (Washington, D.C., 1964), chap. 2.

4. Author's interview with Charles E. Schultze, November 1984 [hereafter Schultze interview].

Kennedy to act, and the service strategy became one prong of the administration's response to the impending racial crisis.

The racial politics of the early 1960s explains why Kennedy and his advisers acted; it does not explain why they choose a fiscally conservative set of policies that retargeted existing programs on black ghettos and reallocated federal funds. What does explain these decisions are the economic and political realities of federal tax and budgetary policy. In the 1960s, as in the 1930s, liberal aspirations were mediated by race and money. But whereas southern defense of Jim Crow and labor-market discrimination were the underside of Roosevelt's fiscally circumscribed social policies, in the 1960s federal tax and budget policy formed the crucible in which Kennedy's and Johnson's responses to America's racial crisis were forged. Neither Johnson nor Kennedy set out to reshape the relationship between the public and private sectors, and both men designed their policies and made budget decisions so as to preclude extensive intervention in private labor markets and to avoid a greatly expanded public sector. As Johnson told the Business Advisory Council (BAC) just prior to leaving office, the idea was to "bake a bigger pie each year; a pie with more and bigger slices, including some for a direct attack on our neglected social problems."[5] The engine of social renewal was the 1964 Kennedy-Johnson tax cut, which was crafted not only for short-run recovery but also for long-term economic growth. But passage of the tax cut was contingent on limiting federal spending, leaving redistribution of federal resources as the only viable way to rectify existing inequities in America's pattern of social protection.

The significance of the War on Poverty has less to do with the political impact of community action than its role in the genesis of a strategy for reallocating federal funds and altering the priorities of federal agencies. The War on Poverty was the leading edge of a budgetary and policy strategy employed throughout the 1960s that used new funding to leverage existing resources in an effort to reorder federal social policy.

Race and Federal Social Policy before the War on Poverty

The nexus of race, social policy, and tax and budget policy that formed the Great Society began in the tangled politics of domestic policy during the three

5. *Public Papers of the Presidents: Lyndon Baines Johnson, 1968–1969*, Pt. 2 (Washington, D.C., 1970), pp. 1165–68.

years of John F. Kennedy's presidency. Unlike his successor, Kennedy did not take office with grandiose plans to remake America. His inaugural address preached sacrifice, his forays into domestic policy were tentative, even halting, and on the great issue of the day, civil rights, he temporized. Yet by the time of Kennedy's assassination, federal social policy had been put on the side of the African American struggle for racial equality and set on a redistributive path that Lyndon Johnson continued and extended. The crucial decision came in June of 1963, when in response to the violence of Birmingham and the spread of racial conflict to the North, Kennedy finally cast his lot with the civil rights movement, dedicated his administration to the passage of a new civil rights act, and fused a set of disparate legislative proposals and laws into a strategy for social renewal and racial equality.

Daniel Patrick Moynihan and others attribute the War on Poverty and the decision to expand federally subsidized employment and social services to the influence of professional reformers, either social workers or economists. This argument reduces the origins of the War on Poverty to an episode in intellectual history, slights the more obvious economic and political factors that both Kennedy and Johnson had to consider, and fails to explain adequately why the service strategy became so intimately connected to the question of racial equality. The influence of so-called reformers in the origins of the Great Society has been overemphasized. The main features of the service strategy were already in place by the time Robert Lampman, one of those often held responsible for the War on Poverty's "human capital" strategy, concluded that the blessings of economic growth would fall short, leaving the elderly, the disabled, and single mothers with children in the lurch.[6] Nor was the poverty program and the redistributive state it presaged the consequence of a presidential innovation undertaken to aggrandize presidential power and symbolize presidential action and mastery. Redistribution of services did not originate with LBJ's declaration of war on behalf of the poor.[7]

6. Lampman to Heller, June 10, 1963, Legislative Background to EOA of 1964, box 1, CEA Draft History, LBJL. Daniel P. Moynihan, *Maximum Feasible Misunderstanding: Community Action in the War on Poverty* (New York, 1970), chaps. 7–8; Margaret Weir, *Politics and Jobs: The Boundaries of Employment Policy in the United States* (Princeton, N.J., 1992), pp. 67–75; Carl M. Brauer, "Kennedy, Johnson, and the War on Poverty," *Journal of American History* 69 (1982): 98–119. All of these sources stress the intellectual assumptions of policymakers.

7. Lawrence Friedman, "The Social and Political Context of the War on Poverty," in *A Decade of Federal Antipoverty Programs,* ed. Robert Haveman (New York, 1977), pp. 31–36; Hugh Heclo, "The Political Foundations of Antipoverty Policy," in *Fighting*

Actually, the service strategy began with Kennedy's effort to *evade* the question of race by forging a political coalition cemented by social class and centered on ameliorative but technocratic social policies. Criticism of President Kennedy's failure to send civil rights legislation to Congress upon taking office prompted his aides to respond that blacks would be among the main beneficiaries of the administration's economic package of extended unemployment benefits and minimum wage legislation.[8] In fact, Democrats were deeply concerned about the social and economic implications of the postwar African American migration. "I have come to the tentative conclusion," Senator Joseph Clark, the chief proponent of employment training policies, announced, "that we have got to make some provision in this bill for this group of youngsters, many of them as young as 16, according to Dr. Conant, a very high percentage of them Negroes, who have no skill, and many of them no home, who are out of school, have no church affiliation, are just raw material for all kinds of trouble."[9] The massive movement of white and black workers from farm to city coincided with technological changes and a marked shift in investment from cities to suburbs. The resulting unemployment, along with evidence of rising numbers of divorces, desertions, and out-of-wedlock births, were linked by officials of the Kennedy Administration and legislators to idle, mischief-prone young males and collapsing families in the cities.

Administration officials assumed blacks did not fit into the economy that was emerging in the 1950s either because they lacked the necessary job skills or because they were disadvantaged by matriarchal, welfare-dependent families. They denied that racial discrimination was the chief obstacle to black economic progress. Arthur Goldberg, Kennedy's first Secretary of Labor, told the Senate Subcommittee on Employment and Manpower:

> The plain fact of the matter is that every statistic available to us indicates what Senator Prouty has just pointed to, and that is this: the higher the skill, the less discrimination operates. Discrimination operates now very

Poverty: What Works and What Doesn't, ed. Sheldon H. Danziger and Daniel H. Weinberg (Cambridge, Mass., 1986), pp. 312–40. Both Friedman and Heclo explain the poverty program in light of presidential politics. Both of these studies miss the poverty program's significance for fiscal and other social policies, a point elaborated below.

8. *New York Times*, March 6, 1961, p. 1.

9. U.S. Congress, Senate, Subcommittee on Employment and Manpower, Committee on Labor and Public Welfare, *Training of the Unemployed: Hearings on S. 987 and S. 1991*, 87th Cong., 1st sess., pp. 187–88. James Conant's book, *Slums and Suburbs* (New York, 1961), was frequently quoted in Congressional hearings.

often on the basis not of overt discrimination, but on the basis that people of minority groups do not have the skills, and it is difficult, often, to determine whether the cart comes before the horse, or the horse comes before the cart in this area.[10]

It was routinely assumed, moreover, long before Daniel Patrick Moynihan's famous report, that welfare dependency was tied to the structure of the black family. In responding to a presidential inquiry about the difficulties with AFDC in the District of Columbia, one high-level federal official repeated the conventional wisdom of the time: the problems stemmed mainly from "the preponderance of needy Negro families accompanied by housing shortages and the matriarchal family system."[11]

These assumptions remained a dominant tenet of federal social policy and political discourse even though they were an inadequate guide to the problems at hand. Goldberg was wrong, of course. Skilled black workers were subject to virulent discrimination; they were systematically excluded from craft jobs and skilled positions in mass-production industries.[12] Goldberg's statement is less a confession of ignorance than a description of political reality. The service strategy, and thus the foundation of Great Society liberalism, took shape as discrete legislative proposals were melded into a course of action for ameliorating racial inequality in a context of economic stagnation and structural change. But the liberal response was confined to the postwar accommodation between northern and southern Democrats. For liberal Democrats this meant keeping race off the political agenda, much as FDR had done.

Although Senator Joseph Clark recognized the disproportionate burden of economic change borne by African Americans, he intentionally downplayed the issue. During hearings on structural unemployment, he commented, "as a matter of draftsmanship . . . it seemed to me unwise to try to single out one race for priority of treatment. . . . I am not sure that you would not run into an awful lot of trouble on the floor, possibly even some

10. Senate, *Training of the Unemployed*, pp. 249–50.

11. Philip S. Hughes to Lee White, May 7, 1962, RG 51, box 43, NA. Hughes recommended "increased employment opportunities, housing and social service facilities," but he added that any solution "will also require increased effort by various Negro associations in programs designed to facilitate adaptation of change of Negro mores" (p. 4).

12. This was not a matter about which there was any lack of knowledge at the time. The NAACP, among other African American organizations, had gone to great lengths to make it known. See, for example, NAACP, *Racism Within Organized Labor: A Report of Five Years of the AFL-CIO* (NAACP Labor Department, 1961).

constitutional problem."[13] Kennedy was equally determined to avoid the question of race. An early decision not to submit a civil rights bill was based on a fear of provoking southern resistance to other proposals. "Suppose the President were to send up a dramatic message on civil rights," one of Kennedy's advisers taunted a reporter, "and alienate enough Southerners to kill his economic program in Congress. Would the Negro be better off or worse off? I think he'd be worse off."[14]

The Kennedy administration's nascent service strategy was stimulated by the economic stagnation and prolonged high unemployment of the late 1950s. It was composed of four legislative initiatives: the Manpower Development and Training Act (MDTA); the proposed Youth Opportunities Act; the 1963 Vocational Education Act; and the 1962 Social Security Amendments. These proposals derived from distinctive political impulses and were the project of particular interests, yet all were seen as solutions to the interlocking problems of unemployment and racial change. MDTA was a response to the plight of the victims of structural unemployment, which was commonly understood as a consequence of decline in the demand for unskilled workers because of technological changes in manufacturing. The Clark committee envisioned manpower training as a policy to manage a changing economy; it would retrain displaced blue-collar workers for new occupations. Even though structural unemployment mainly affected older workers, both Clark and Goldberg believed the policy would assist black and white migrants with the transition from farm to factory.[15]

Liberals were equally preoccupied with teenaged workers, who were estimated to be one-third of the unemployed and growing. Arthur Goldberg saw a rising tide of unemployed high-school dropouts who could not be absorbed into the labor force and told Kennedy that "their future outlook is extremely dark unless constructive plans and programs are developed to assist them."[16] Democratic senator Hubert Humphrey of Minnesota did just that, introducing legislation to create a Youth Conservation Corps and solve, in one blow, the problems of youth unemployment and impending social instability. The Kennedy administration was also developing programs to deal with the plight of unskilled youth through the reform of vocational education. Kennedy appointed a cabinet-level committee to develop recommen-

13. Senate, *Training of the Unemployed,* p. 116.
14. *New York Times,* March 6, 1961, p. 1.
15. Senate, *Training of the Unemployed,* p. 231.
16. Arthur J. Goldberg to President Kennedy, June 2, 1961, Myer Feldman Papers, box 29, JFKL.

dations. It reported that 21 million youths without a college degree would enter the labor market in the 1960s, when the demand for unskilled labor was "sharply diminishing." Humphrey's bill never passed Congress, but the administration's revamped vocational education policy did what his Youth Opportunities Act was intended to do. By shifting federal vocational education policy toward "out-of-work, out-of-school youths," the vocational education policy was transformed into a youth version of the MDTA.[17]

The final cog in the developing service strategy was the 1962 amendments to the Social Security Act. These amendments created law which tried to put "rehabilitation" rather than income maintenance at the center of the Aid to Families with Dependent Children (AFDC) program. Abraham Ribicoff, Secretary of the Department of Health, Education, and Welfare (HEW), appointed an ad hoc committee dominated by social workers to recommend reforms, telling Kennedy that the secret is "reorienting the whole approach to welfare from a straight cash hand-out operation to one in which the emphasis is on rehabilitation of those on relief and prevention ahead of time."[18] The welfare reforms presented to Congress that eventually passed were modest compared to the claims made by Ribicoff and others, but they did provide more federal money for social services and made two-parent families eligible for AFDC at the option of states.

All of these policies were modest. Ribicoff characterized the efforts as "fundamental" reforms that "can be done with very modest expenditures." The meager funding in all these programs was incommensurate with the perceived problems they were designed to remedy. Yet this ensemble of policies provided the beginnings of a new agenda while maintaining the course of conservative social reform John F. Kennedy was charting. They also afforded triumphs in an otherwise barren political landscape. The Youth Economic Opportunities Act succumbed to conservative opposition, but the other three legislative proposals encountered little resistance in Congress, passing by overwhelming majorities.

Kennedy's success depended on his subservience to the rules of political engagement established in the 1940s. Within Congress the racial impact of legislation remained a volatile issue, posing political difficulties for any policy that appeared to be aimed at blacks. Humphrey's youth bill was openly assumed to be a measure for stabilizing inner-city ghettos. Republicans

17. *Congressional Quarterly Almanac, 1963* [hereafter *CQ Almanac, 1963*] (Washington, D.C., 1964), pp. 202, 204.

18. Ribicoff to President, November 11, 1961, p. 2, Theodore C. Sorenson Papers, box 34, JFKL.

opposed the proposal in both the House and Senate, and they sabotaged the bill by playing on the racial fears of white southerners again and again. All twelve Republicans on the House Education and Labor Committee voted against it, and in the Senate Barry Goldwater and John Tower proposed antidiscrimination amendments to kill the bill. Adam Clayton Powell persuaded a majority of the committee to approve a bill, but the administration was "unable to round up sufficient Southern Democratic support for a program benefiting a large number of Negroes to override Republican opposition in the Rules Committee."[19]

Republican opposition to New Frontier domestic legislation could be overcome with southern votes when distributive formulas were tilted South, local control was upheld, and there was no "Powell" (antidiscrimination) amendment. The Kennedy administration was generally accommodating. An impasse over the Vocational Education Act was broken by distributing 90 percent of the funds on the basis of per capita income and increasing funds for Impact Aid to local school districts, both of enormous benefit to the South.[20] MDTA threatened to break this mold, but the administration compromised. Ribicoff formulated the welfare amendments with a conservative-liberal coalition in mind, much as Senate Democrats worked to entice Republican support for MDTA and the Youth Economic Opportunities Act. Many Republicans could be convinced to support services as an alternative to more interventionist policies, and at least in the case of MDTA they put their stamp on the legislation.[21]

Republican and southern Democratic willingness to bring up race remained an ever-present problem for Kennedy. Carl Albert, a Congressman from Oklahoma, warned JFK that southern Democrats were suspicious that federal programs would be used to promote integration and this was jeopardizing much of their program, even funds for mass transit. In a meeting to plan the administration's response to civil rights demonstrations, JFK told his advisers that any new proposal appearing to target funds on northern ghettos would be defeated in Congress.[22] Kennedy himself consistently

19. *CQ Almanac, 1963*, pp. 514, 517. *Congressional Quarterly* reported that the administration did not push the bill because a strong supporter, Alabama Democrat Carl Elliott, could not have supported a program that benefited "mainly Negroes" without endangering his reelection (p. 516).

20. Irving Bernstein, *Promises Kept: John F. Kennedy's New Frontier* (New York, 1991), pp. 171–72; *CQ Almanac, 1963*, p. 202.

21. The final bill passed by Congress was written mainly by Charles Goodell, a Republican congressman from New York.

22. Phone transcripts, Civil Rights, June 1963, item 22 2–4, June 12, 1963, POF, JFKL; Tape Recordings of Meetings, June 1, 1963, tape 90.3, POF, JFKL.

stressed that neither blacks nor whites could escape unemployment and both deserved help. And when Walter Heller suggested the poverty program to Kennedy, he told the president that "having mounted a dramatic program for one disadvantaged group (the Negroes), it was both equitable and politically attractive to launch programs specifically designed to aid other disadvantaged groups."[23] Yet by the time Kennedy decided to go ahead with the poverty program, he had already rejected Heller's advice and linked federal social policy to the brewing racial crisis.

Civil Rights and the Great Society's Service Strategy

Kennedy's eloquent June 1963 civil rights message revealed the decisions that all but insured the service strategy would become an integral part of a policy designed to alleviate racial inequality. Referring to jobless rates of 20 percent or more among black youths and to protests in Philadelphia over black unemployment, the president laid out a three-pronged strategy: economic growth fueled by the tax cut introduced the previous January; a civil rights bill to attack racial discrimination; and legislative proposals that would redirect the service strategy toward the black ghettos of the North. Kennedy proposed changes in MDTA that would lower the age out-of-work youths were eligible for training allowances to sixteen years from between nineteen and twenty-one years, increase the amount of the training allowance, expand eligibility, and add literacy training and relocation assistance.[24] The Vocational Education Act was revised by increasing the set-aside for special programs for youths with educational or socioeconomic handicaps from 5 to 15 percent, broadening the scope of these projects, and increasing the funding for work-study, which was really an income allowance during training. Similar changes were added to the pending Youth Economic Opportunities Act. All these changes encountered little difficulty in Congress. As a result, MDTA and vocational education were shifted toward the so-called hard-core unemployed, a term that by 1964 was a code word for young, inner-city black males. The service strategy was refashioned into a tool to cut the knot between race and class.[25]

---

23. Walter Heller, "Confidential Notes on Meeting with the President," October 21, 1963, p. 2, Walter Heller Papers, box 6, JFKL.

24. John F. Kennedy, "Special Message to the Congress on Civil Rights and Job Opportunities," June 19, 1963, *Public Papers of the Presidents: John F. Kennedy, 1963* (Washington, D.C., 1964), pp. 485, 488–89.

25. *CQ Almanac, 1963*, pp. 519, 525. Wirtz told Congress that increased funds for training allowances would allow a major expansion in number of youths served, of whom

Kennedy could no longer avoid addressing black poverty, unemployment, and labor-market discrimination for two reasons. Rising African American militancy and protest in the North was the most immediate. One indication that things had changed was when black legislators reversed themselves in the fight over the vocational education bill and opposed a Republican-sponsored "Powell amendment" that would have denied funds to segregated vocational education courses. The fight against this amendment was led by Augustus Hawkins, elected in 1962 from a district in south central Los Angeles. He argued that the defeat of the bill would "deprive more Negroes of needed training than even whites."[26] Hawkins's concern was echoed by many black leaders and protesters at the time. Whitney Young Jr., president of the National Urban League (NUL), warned Kennedy and Congress that the nation faced a "tinder-box of racial unrest" about to explode in northern cities. Sounding what would become an African American tocsin, Young said blacks were "struggling beneath the mounting burden of automation, overcrowding, and subtle discrimination."[27]

Most black political leaders believed there was a connection among discrimination, automation, and unemployment, reviving fears of the rampant job competition with whites and of renewed displacement of black workers similar to what had occurred during the depression. Blacks made up a disproportionate share of the long-term unemployed in the early 1960s and had borne, in many respects, the brunt of the 1950s automation crisis. The Urban League discovered extraordinarily high African American unemployment rates in a fifty-city survey in the fall of 1961—including 39 percent in Detroit and 20 percent in St. Louis—and Roy Wilkins pointed out that one-third of all black workers were unemployed sometime during 1961.[28] For Wilkins the problem was clear:

> As for our old bottom layer of unskilled workers, the new machines are tossing them to one side. . . . Part of the blame for this must rest with certain labor unions which have either restricted or denied membership to Negroes and thus have placed them at the bottom of the scale as far as seniority and skills are concerned. Thus, they have been vulnerable to au-

a large proportion would be African American (U.S. Congress, Senate, Subcommittee on Employment and Manpower, Committee on Labor and Public Welfare, *Manpower Retraining: Hearings,* 88th Cong., 1st sess., p. 16).

26. *CQ Almanac, 1963,* p. 205.

27. *New York Times,* June 10, 1963, p. 1.

28. Guichard Parris and Lester Brooks, *Blacks in the City* (Boston, 1971), p. 405; Roy Wilkins, Speech to 53rd Annual Meeting of NAACP, January 2, 1962, p. 3, NAACP Papers, Group 3, Administrative Files, Roy Wilkins Speeches, LC.

tomation. The Negro man with little knowledge and no training is finding a shrinking market for pure muscle.[29]

Automation and "subtle" discrimination were thus linked, providing the
fulcrum for black protest in the North.

Wilkins made unemployment and labor-market discrimination key priorities for the NAACP's 1963 agenda, focusing the attack mainly on the
racial practices of unions: outright exclusion, segregated locals and seniority systems, and exclusion from apprenticeships. Craft unions were the main
target, but the practices of the United Auto Workers and other industrial
unions also came under NAACP scrutiny. Young's statement capped a tu-
multuous month of protest as the civil rights movement traveled north.
While Martin Luther King Jr., and masses of demonstrators battled Bull
Conner in the streets of Birmingham, demonstrations over unemployment
and housing discrimination erupted in numerous cities from Philadelphia
to Los Angeles. Until 1963, just 10 percent of all protest incidents occurred
in the North, but that spring the number of northern protests rose dramatically, accounting for 28 percent of all incidents.[30]

Black protest in the North was a product of both spontaneous revolt and
organized mobilization. Inspired by the rising militancy and the popularity
of Malcolm X's nationalistic appeals, moderate civil rights leaders launched
campaigns against job and housing discrimination. The Congress on Racial
Equality (CORE), which had been most active in the southern civil rights
movement, began to organize demonstrations in northern cities and shifted
from protesting housing discrimination against middle-class blacks to agitating over jobs. CORE also became more militant, targeting the discrima-
tory practices of banks, insurance companies, and labor unions as well as
retail stores.[31] The NAACP campaign focused on Philadelphia, where local
demonstrators were protesting the absence of black workers in municipal
construction projects and in craft unions. NAACP officials threatened to
picket the whole city, and only relented when the city government agreed to
some token hiring.[32]

29. Roy Wilkins, Speech at Spellman College, Atlanta, Ga., March 16, 1961, p. 8,
NAACP Papers, Group 3, Administrative Files, Roy Wilkins Speeches, LC.
30. Doug McAdams, *Political Process and the Development of Black Insurgency, 1930–
1970* (New York, 1982), p. 152.
31. August Meier and Elliot Rudwick, *CORE: A Study in the Civil Rights Movement,
1942–1968* (New York, 1973), pp. 187–94, 200–201.
32. *New York Times,* November 25, 1962, p. 1; *New York Times,* May 16, 29, June
1, 9, 1963.

With the 1963 March on Washington, black agitation in the North merged with the southern civil rights movement. Martin Luther King Jr. believed the march could "arouse the conscience of the nation over the economic plight of the Negro." Organized by A. Philip Randolph and Bayard Rustin, one of the key advisers of Martin Luther King Jr., the March on Washington articulated much of what northern protesters had been agitating about for a year or more—demands for public works, a higher minimum wage, and an end to labor-market discrimination. Rustin conceived these demands as a vehicle to revive the incipient biracial working-class coalition of the 1930s.[33] Yet with the eruption of protest in the North, the debate over what it would take to achieve racial justice and equality of opportunity radically changed.

This shift in the debate was not the work of Malcolm X but of one of the most unlikely figures in the civil rights movement, Whitney Young Jr., who, upon taking charge of the Urban League, had proved more adept at milking corporations for donations than articulating new directions for the civil rights movement. In 1963, sounding like a black nationalist, Young made the notion of reparations for past injustices the subject of political debate. Searching for ways out of the deepening predicament facing northern blacks, Young publicly asked whether job quotas could not be seen as compensation for racial discrimination. He discarded this idea after criticism from other civil rights leaders and from outsiders. Instead, Young resorted to the idea of a "crash" program in education, housing, and employment modeled after Harry Truman's Marshall Plan.

Central to Young's Marshall Plan was the notion of indemnification, by which he meant "realistic compensation (not necessarily in money alone) and realistic reparation for past injuries." Young insisted that he was not advocating preferential treatment, saying at one point that what the Urban League wanted was a "special effort," not "special privileges." Most of the elements of his plan were modest in scope, asking for fair treatment and nondiscrimination and even insisting on African Americans' responsibility to do their part. Young's policy statements were not especially remarkable for the time—he advocated job training, including allowances, and the usual litany of urban policies, including urban renewal, public works, and education. Yet the direction Young was charting for the Urban League in 1963 was potentially radical, comparable only to the efforts of Lester Granger and T. Arnold Hill who worked to align the Urban League with the labor move-

33. David Garrow, *Bearing the Cross: Martin Luther King, Jr., and the Southern Christian Leadership Conference* (New York, 1988), pp. 278, 281, 284, 288.

ment in the 1930s. The difference is that Young was responding to the incipient, explosive militancy of the northern ghettos. Despite its appearance as a mainstream remedial program, Young's ten-point plan departed radically from conventional political discourse by challenging the accepted meaning of equality of opportunity. The basic definition of equality of opportunity, the Urban League stated in its Marshall Plan, "must be broadened and deepened to include recognition of the need for special effort to overcome serious disabilities resulting from historic handicaps." Young argued that three hundred years of preferential treatment for whites left a legacy that could not be righted simply by applying "equal weights." It would take a massive effort to correct the injustices of the past.[34]

Black disenchantment with Kennedy's lethargic response to the civil rights struggle in the South and black anger over unemployment in the North raised fears of social instability compelling the administration to act. There is ample evidence that black protest in the North had a decisive impact on Kennedy and his advisers, who believed that timely action was necessary to prevent radicalization of the civil rights movement. The president underscored the need for urgent action in a phone conversation with James H. Davis, governor of Louisiana. "It isn't just Jackson," Kennedy said. "It's Philadelphia, and it's going to be Washington D.C. this summer, and we're trying to figure out what we can do to put this stuff in the courts and get it off the streets because somebody is going to get killed." Kennedy solicited ideas from his cabinet in early June and, in a wide-ranging discussion with his advisers, considered increased funding for the Accelerated Public Works program and job training as possible responses to black anger in the North.[35]

Black protest was not the only reason why Kennedy's initial policy strategy unraveled. It had also become clear by the spring of 1963 that ameliorating the effects of "automation, overcrowding, and subtle discrimination" with the service strategy while avoiding a confrontation with the racism endemic to American society would prove impossible for Kennedy or anyone else. The deeply rooted racial bias at the core of the American welfare state rendered Kennedy's color-blind, technocratic social policies unworkable. In

34. "The National Urban League's 'Marshall Plan' Proposal," July 3, 1963, NUL Papers, pt. 2, ser. 1, box 38, LC; Whitney Young Jr., "Should There Be 'Compensation' for Negroes? 'Domestic Marshall Plan,'" *New York Times Magazine*, October 6, 1963, p. 129.

35. Phone transcripts, Civil Rights, item 21A, June 3, 1963, POF, JFKL. See also *Los Angeles Times*, July 6, 1984, p. 1; Transcript of Meeting, June 1, 1963, tape 90.3 POF, JFKL; *New York Times*, June 2, 1963, p. 8E; Kennedy to Secretaries Wirtz and Celebrezze, June 4, 1963, Sorensen Papers, box 30.

a report submitted to the Kennedy administration, Roy Wilkins documented the obstacles that would subvert any attempt to use the new federal services to reduce black unemployment. The United States Employment Service (USES) and the Bureau of Apprenticeship Training (BAT), for example, were intended to be the backbone of the MDTA, largely because the Department of Labor and the White House thought they could meet the challenges of re-training displaced workers more effectively than the ossified state vocational agencies. But the one thing the USES and BAT had in common with voca-tional education was their subservience to the racial status quo. Retraining efforts in companies with black workers typically failed in the South when the only option was segregated training facilities.[36]

The problem was not restricted to the South, however. Wilkins pointed out that "even in areas where open discrimination is not practiced, dis-criminatory job orders are accepted and discriminatory referrals are made [by the USES]. Reports have been received of 'gerrymandering' of districts serviced by employment offices in order to maintain *de facto* racially segre-gated facilities."[37] State employment agencies' ties to business made them reluctant to recruit or recommend blacks to employers disinclined to cross the color line. BAT's close relationship to skilled craft unions, then under harsh fire from the NAACP for unremitting discrimination, made it seem unlikely that many blacks would benefit from MDTA. Wilkins, in fact, had been informed by a member of his staff, "we have had difficulties in con-nection with the existing manpower training program because of segrega-tion and the assignment of colored applicants to training in less desirable trades."[38]

The question of whether MDTA could be implemented free of racial bias was one of the first issues to confront the administration. Since the admin-istration had ducked the question of a Powell amendment, Kennedy's ad-visers had to decide whether to issue a nondiscrimination regulation. Fear-ful that a nondiscrimination regulation would lead Congress to refuse to

36. Bernstein, *Promises Kept*, p. 165.

37. Wilkins/Aronson report, August 29, 1961, p. 29, Feldman Papers, box 5. See also U.S. Civil Rights Commission, *Employment: 1961 Commission on Civil Rights Report*, bk. 3 (Washington, D.C., 1961), pp. 114–21.

38. J. Francis Pohlhaus to Wilkins, January 10, 1964, NAACP Papers, pt. 3, Admin-istrative Files, box 147. NUL officials voiced similar concerns; Whitney Young Jr. to Arthur A. Chapin, July 12, 1962, box 54, Young to Wirtz, March 15, 1963, box 17, NUL Papers, pt. 2, ser. 1, LC. See also Jill Quadagno, "Social Movements and State Transfor-mation: Labor Unions and Racial Conflict in the War on Poverty," *American Sociological Review* 57 (1992): 621–22.

appropriate funds and USES offices to refuse to participate, the Labor Department and HEW argued against an explicit policy. Hobart Taylor of the Civil Rights Commission, who was in favor of an explicit policy, said that blacks were already excluded from vocational education and USES and the administration could not afford to let MDTA operate that way. But the problem of racial bias went beyond the question of a nondiscrimination pledge. Taylor was also concerned that an obscure provision of the legislation, section 202(d), requiring persons selected for training to have a "reasonable expectation of employment in the occupation for which the person is to be trained" would be used to exclude blacks.[39]

Taylor's fears were real enough since HEW had already issued such a requirement for vocational education, but the administration apparently had agreed not to push the issue and had an understanding to that effect with the appropriations committee. Other officials feared any change in policy would jeopardize funding for MDTA and kill the pending amendments to the Vocational Education Act.[40] Taylor wrote Lee White, Kennedy's chief adviser for civil rights, that he could not believe section 202(d) was an issue. Apparently it was, and it seemed likely that if allowed to persist, it would be used to exclude African Americans from the program. Taylor's dilemma makes clear how deeply the color line was embedded in the American welfare state. It also revealed just how difficult it would be to use putatively universalistic policies, such MDTA, to assist African Americans.

Kennedy's response was quite tepid, given the brewing upheaval and the limits to his service strategy, but it had profound consequences. Kennedy decided to focus civil rights legislation on the public accommodations title; to request statutory authority for the President's Equal Opportunity Committee, which was charged with enforcing nondiscrimination pledges for federal contractors; and to retarget service programs. Kennedy, thus, jettisoned the more expansive dreams of northern liberals and the civil rights movement. He also evaded the question of job discrimination and black unemployment. The proposed civil rights bill did not contain an employment discrimination title, which was left out because of a fear that any title resembling a Fair Employment Practices Commission would unite Republicans and southern Democrats in opposition and a belief that employment discrimination was less salient to the civil rights movement's political aims than

39. Taylor to Lee White, March 1963, p. 3, Lee White Papers, box 20, JFKL.

40. Samuel V. Merrick to Secretary of Labor, March 25, 1963, White Papers, box 20. Merrick was chief consul to the Senate Labor Committee.

desegregation of public accommodations. The service strategy was regarded as compensating for, even substituting for, the absence of an employment discrimination title. In this respect, it was politically expedient. Kennedy made a trade-off between a law prohibiting labor-market discrimination, which was later added in Congress, and a modest expansion and retargeting of job training and vocational education services.

Kennedy and the men around him had convinced themselves that a service strategy was an indispensable undergirding for the civil rights bill. It was widely believed that without economic progress the struggle for civil rights would reach a dead end. Willard Wirtz told Congress that "it becomes increasingly clear as we get into this matter [of civil rights] that there is no separation of the problems of fair employment and full employment." Hubert Humphrey made the connection between civil rights and the service strategy a matter of policy when he said that civil rights legislation was needed but there would still be a problem if blacks were unequipped to get and hold jobs. By linking job training and other services to civil rights, Kennedy implicitly recognized the quandary of the civil rights movement: the futility of civil rights without social rights, of granting the right to enter a desegregated restaurant to people who could not afford the price of a cup of coffee.[41]

The significance of Young's Marshall Plan was less in the melioristic remedies it offered than in its claim that civil rights without compensation was futile. By making compensation an issue, Young had exposed the tension between a civil rights movement morally anchored in the vision of a color-blind society and the realities of a racially stratified society. The question then, as now, was what to do about this contradiction. Young's harshest critic, Kyle Haselden, editor of the *Christian Century,* accepted the premise of Young's plan, pointing out that "even though all racial bars were removed, most Negroes could not, in a free and impartial society, compete on equal terms with most white people for jobs and preferments," but he rejected Young's conclusion.[42] Haselden argued for a domestic "point four plan" that would be based on need rather than race, echoing the social democratic rhetoric of civil rights leaders like Bayard Rustin. The emergence of black nationalism,

41. U.S. Congress, Senate, *Manpower Retraining: Hearings,* 88th Cong., 1st sess., p. 18; *The New York Times,* June 19, 1963, p. 1. SNCC also began to worry about the question of economic justice in 1963 (Clayborne Carson, *In Struggle: SNCC and the Black Awakening of the 1960s* [Cambridge, Mass., 1981], p. 167).

42. Kyle Haselden, "Should There Be 'Compensation' for Negroes? Parity, Not Preference," *New York Times Magazine,* October 6, 1963, p. 128.

which influenced Young's Marshall Plan, would make difficult any revival of the biracial, class-based coalition that Haselden and Rustin preferred. John F. Kennedy rejected this alternative.

The approach to black unemployment adopted by Kennedy and his advisers remained affixed to the rather expedient assumption (given their efforts to suppress discussions of race) that the economic plight of northern blacks was not fundamentally a matter of racial discrimination but rather resulted from their lack of job skills. Willard Wirtz told Congress that one-fifth of the unemployed (a group in which blacks were disproportionately represented) had less than a grade-school education but few of them received any assistance under MDTA. Wirtz repeatedly insisted that antidiscrimination legislation was fruitless without training.[43] Evidence of appallingly low levels of literacy among northern blacks uncovered by the Budget Bureau buttressed such arguments. The Budget Bureau did a study of alternative remedies for "hard-core unemployment" in the summer of 1963, sending investigators to Detroit, Pittsburgh, and New York. They discovered, to their surprise, quite high levels of illiteracy among welfare recipients and resistance among local officials to anything but job training. The New York report concluded that "none of the groups had much enthusiasm for public works or made work programs as potential solutions for hard core unemployment. It was a general consensus that more education, vocational training, and on-the-job training were the preferred approaches to the problem."[44]

Whatever its justification, Kennedy's policy strategy clearly had discernible political advantages. A federal social policy founded on provision of job training and education to northern blacks not only fit with the reigning assumptions of policy discourse, but it also avoided conflict with another key Democratic constituency, labor unions. The problem the administration faced emerged clearly when Charles Schultze, then deputy director of the Budget Bureau, explored the possibility of using the Accelerated Public Works program as an interim solution to hard-core unemployment until the tax cut took hold. Schultze's staff reported that local officials in three big cities believed that public works projects could not be readily given to the hard-core unemployed because of the opposition of unions. Labor unions in Detroit monitored a work program for welfare recipients to be sure they were not doing tasks that could be done by union members, and in New York City

43. Senate, *Manpower Retraining: Hearings,* pp. 16, 24; Press conference, January 6, 1964, *Weekly News Digest,* U.S. Department of Labor, NUL Papers, pt. 2, ser. I, box 17.
44. Turen to Schultze, August 6, 1963, "New York City," p. 4, RG 51, ser. 61.1a, E3–2/1, first grey box, NA.

local officials rejected a work program because of a "conviction that the highly and strongly unionized labor pattern which exists in the area would be an unsurmountable inhibition."[45] Kennedy was careful to avoid the impression that his policies were intended to benefit only African Americans, saying that lack of job skills was not restricted to African Americans and that the administration would explore programs for the long-term unemployed "among both white and nonwhite workers."[46] But his policy decisions effectively retargeted existing social policies on downtrodden, unskilled black workers and their families.

For all practical purposes Kennedy declared the War on Poverty in June 1963. From that moment on there was a clear link between racial equality and federal social policy. Many of the features of Great Society liberalism that were so prominent later, and indeed the War on Poverty itself, were contained in the policy course Kennedy set for the country that summer.

The Political Economy of the War on Poverty

Kennedy's legacy went beyond joining the service strategy to civil rights. He also put federal social policy on the redistributive path that in Lyndon Johnson's hands became the hallmark of Great Society liberalism and the basis for the transformation of the American welfare state. Yet Kennedy's choice was a pale form of redistribution: retargeting existing programs and reallocating resources solely *within the public sector* rather than redistributing jobs or income more generally.

This choice was hardly inevitable; Kennedy and, subsequently, Johnson had other options, and neither was immune from political pressure to pursue them. Labor leaders and prominent northern liberals, such as former Michigan governor G. Mennen Williams, lobbied hard for the creation of massive new programs in education, housing, public works, and work relief. George Meany, president of the AFL-CIO, urged the president to press Congress for $2 billion for the Accelerated Public Works program "to provide a significant job-creating program." And some of Kennedy's advisers advocated reviving "WPA type work relief" programs. Willard Wirtz told Kennedy the real problem was a shortage of jobs, not a need for more train-

45. Ibid.
46. Kennedy, "Message on Civil Rights and Job Opportunities," June 19, 1963, pp. 488–89.

ing, and the danger was "that many [blacks] would be trained, but unemployed."[47]

None of these polices was seriously considered. Schultze's staff told him that a work program that could reach 10 percent of the hard-core unemployed would cost $1.5 billion annually and was out of the question. Kennedy's CEA debated the merits of cash transfers for the poor during this period but rejected them because "a politically acceptable program must avoid completely any use of the term 'inequality' or of the term 'redistribution of income or wealth.'" Whitney Young Jr. pressed the case for a Marshall Plan in the cities in a December meeting with President Johnson, but the president ignored him. Johnson greeted a proposal for an expanded but costly public employment program with such an icy response that one adviser recalled, "I have never seen a colder reception from the president. He just—absolute blank stare—implied without even opening his mouth that [Sargent] Shriver should move on to the next proposal." In rejecting these proposals, Kennedy and Johnson defied civil rights leaders, liberal democrats, and organized labor.[48]

The retargeting of programs and redistribution within the public sector accounts for much of the policy change that was later hailed as the Great Society. It was, however, the War on Poverty that first extended this strategy beyond the programs affected by Kennedy's June 1963 civil rights message. Many of the president's advisers understood the poverty program to be broadly redistributive, even though they shied away from such language. Charles Schultze, for instance, advocated using a "redistributive" political logic, noblesse oblige—which he thought had more political cachet than narrow self-interest—as a way of convincing Congress to concentrate resources where they were needed most.[49] But redistribution in the sense of transferring

47. Meany to President, May 23, 1963, box 29, folder no. 43, Legislation, GMMA; Wilbur Cohen to Sorenson, June 10, 1963, Wirtz to President, June 10, 1963, Sorenson Papers, box 30.

48. Schultze to Labor and Welfare Division, October 14, 1963, Labor and Welfare Division to Schultze, November 6, 1963, RG 51, ser. 60.3a, box 4, NA; Brauer, "Kennedy, Johnson, and the War on Poverty," p. 108; Lampman to Heller, June 10, 1963, Legislative Background to EOA of 1964, box 1, CEA Draft History, LBJL; Nancy Weiss, *Whitney M. Young, Jr., and the Struggle for Civil Rights* (Princeton, N.J., 1989), p. 148; "Poverty and Urban Policy" (Conference Transcript of 1973 Group Discussion of the Kennedy Administration Urban Poverty Programs and Policies, June 16–17, 1973, Brandeis University), p. 287, JFKL.

49. Charles E. Schultze, "Some Notes on a Program of Human Conservation," November 2, 1963, RG 51, ser. 61.1a, R1–6, box 80, pp. 3–4, NA.

resources from rich to poor was less important to the planners of the War on Poverty than the capacity to reallocate federal resources. Most accounts of the War on Poverty take the creation of community action as the decisive innovation. Community action, as many have made clear, was ill understood by those framing the policy and subject to varying interpretations. Yet whatever the ambiguities besetting the idea, the concept of community mobilization was not central to those planning the program.[50] At issue was not decentralization or community participation, although there were ardent proponents of this approach, but rather centralized fiscal control and the reallocation of federal resources.

The structure of the program Lyndon Johnson sent to Congress in March of 1964 was unique: it allocated money to a new agency, located in the executive office of the president, and drew heavily on the resources of other agencies. The bill proposed about $500 million in expenditures for Community Action and other new programs and another $400 million or so for existing categorical programs. From the outset, administration planners had assumed that for a "small (e.g., under $500 million) increment to the budget plus some redirection of existing programs, we can mount a meaningful attack." The initial proposal contemplated liberalizing existing programs (increasing AFDC benefits, for example), retargeting existing programs "already aimed in part or whole at ameliorating or eliminating poverty," and concentrating resources on designated areas.[51] The responsibility of the new poverty agency was to fuse these three elements by centralizing control of federal spending across cabinet agencies. For this reason, planners resisted putting the Office of Economic Opportunity in a cabinet department.

The initial plan contained two provisions indispensable to centralized control over financial resources. One provided authority for the president to waive "certain restrictions on the use of funds," allowing administrators to bypass congressional restrictions in order to direct money to the poor. The second provision gave the president authority to take money from existing appropriations and reallocate it to the poverty program. One planner noted that this augmentation of presidential power "clearly raises some questions

50. In fact, as Paul Peterson and J. David Greenstone make clear, mobilization of the poor by the Office of Economic Opportunity is much better understood as a product of a federal agency in search of a constituency ("Racial Change and Citizen Participation: The Mobilization of Low-Income Communities through Community Action," in Haveman, ed., *Decade of Federal Antipoverty Programs*, pp. 247–48, 253–56).

51. William Capron to Walter Heller, December 5, 1963, Legislative Background to EOA of 1964, box 1, CEA Draft History.

in that existing programs would lose control over those funds handled directly by the Council. In its crudest terms, a Congressman could visualize program funds destined for his District scooped up and put into a poverty program."[52] The alternative of simply giving the funds to existing agencies was clearly rejected. Elements of the idea of reallocating existing federal expenditures toward the poor remained in the final proposal, and it was not completely eliminated even by a furious assault by federal agencies and the bureaucratic inclinations of a task force Johnson had created to plan the program. Despite its political fate in the War on Poverty, this idea survived as the leitmotif of a broader fiscal strategy that would govern future decisions over federal social policy.

Why did Kennedy and Johnson choose to retarget and redistribute services? Their resistance to greater spending reflected the imperatives of their fiscal policy, a Faustian pact they had made in the name of economic growth. Both presidents pinned their hopes for social renewal on the promise of the 1964 tax cut and tailored their social initiatives accordingly. The War on Poverty was thus mortgaged to the tax cut. Kennedy decided on a tax cut and a deficit in order to turn fiscal drag into a fiscal dividend. His economic advisers thought that current tax rates were too high to stimulate real growth in GNP, but if taxes were cut, the resulting economic growth would yield increased tax revenues and a dividend that was virtually up for grabs. Walter Heller assured Kennedy, whose announcement of the tax cut was blasted by John Kenneth Galbraith as "the most Republican speech since McKinley," that he had made a good deal. Those, like Galbraith, who wanted more spending for social needs, Heller wrote, should realize that the fiscal dividend generated by a tax cut will get them to "our government program goals."[53]

Kennedy's economic advisers made their Faustian pact for economic growth willingly; the president went along reluctantly. His decision was due more to the perceptible erosion of business confidence than to the lectures and supplications of his chief economic adviser.[54] But like Faustus, Kennedy

52. "Anti-Poverty Program," p. 4., n.d., Sorenson Papers, box 59, folder "1964 Legislative Program." The author of the quote is not identified; presumably it is Sorenson. Heller to Sorenson, December 20, 1963, Legislative Background to EOA of 1964, box 1, Heller/Gordon to Cabinet Secretaries, June 6, 1964, RG 51, ser. 60.3a, box 4, NA.

53. Herbert Stein, *The Fiscal Revolution in America* (Chicago, 1969), p. 421; Heller to Kennedy, December 16, 1962, p. 4, Sorenson Papers, box 31.

54. Stein, *Fiscal Revolution in America*, pp. 411, 415; Ronald F. King, *Money, Time, and Politics: Investment Tax Subsidies and American Democracy* (New Haven, Conn., 1995), pp. 180, 211–12.

had to pay the devil. Lucifer in this case took the form of an elderly but ferocious senator from Virginia, Harry Byrd. Conservative opposition, particularly in the Senate, focused on the fearful specter of deficit spending in the administrative budget, the sum of federal expenditures excluding trust funds, which was an economically meaningless but politically important realm. Building support for the tax cut required a fiscally conservative course of action in the budget, and Kennedy obliged. The tax cut submitted to Congress in early 1963 called for a net reduction of $10.2 billion in corporate and personal income taxes. Kennedy cut his fiscal year 1964 budget, and the administration estimated that federal outlays would be just under $99 billion, more than $3 billion lower than initially planned. Yet Kennedy not only had to give up budgetary resources for his tax cut; he had to give up his fiscal dividend and thus any liberal hopes for social renewal. For conservatives both the size and the duration of the looming deficit was an issue. Kennedy had to agree to use the revenues generated by the tax cut to reduce the deficit. Kermit Gordon, Kennedy's budget director, formally agreed to this fiscal bargain in a letter to Jacob Javits, the Republican senator from New York: "The transition deficit is to be reduced by holding any necessary increase in expenditures to an amount substantially below the accompanying increase in revenues." Kennedy reiterated this commitment to Wilbur Mills in August.[55]

Kennedy and his aides were clearly talking out of both sides of their mouths, telling liberal allies they had only to wait for the fiscal dividend, while reassuring conservative opponents that deficit spending would be contained.[56] The decision to give up the fiscal dividend was not frivolous. The alternative was expenditure cuts to offset the tax cut, an action which Heller feared and Kennedy opposed. Gordon realized the full dimensions of the dilemma facing the administration while planning the fiscal year 1965 budget: even a modest increase in outlays over the current year, at best $2 billion, would violate all the commitments made to Congress. No wonder Kennedy turned down requests for public employment projects and the CEA suppressed any thought of enlarging cash transfers!

55. Gordon to Javits, May 25, 1963, RG 51, ser. 61.1a, E3–2, first grey box, NA; "Letter to Chairman on Tax Reduction," House Ways and Means Committee, August 21, 1963, *Public Papers of the Presidents of the United States: John F. Kennedy, 1963* (Washington, D.C., 1964), pp. 637–39.

56. The administration was equally duplicitous toward conservatives. They knew that the deficit in the administrative budget would reach $17 to $20 billion, depending on economic conditions, and that the budget would not run a surplus anytime soon. Smith to CEA, December 3, 1962, pp. 2–3, Kermit Gordon Papers, box 11, JFKL.

Harry Byrd extracted further expenditure cuts in the fiscal year 1965 budget from Lyndon Johnson, much to the discomfort of the CEA. LBJ recognized what sort of deal would have to be made with the Senate to pass the tax cut. As Gardner Ackley recounted, Johnson "thought that you could get the tax cut, but there was one absolutely essential requirement, and that was to reduce budgeted expenditures and hold the budget below I think it was 100 billion dollars." Johnson's undersecretary of the treasury, Henry Fowler, warned him that "a budget figure for fiscal 1965 well in excess of the fiscal 1964 spending level estimate might weaken support of the tax bill from business and financial sources." LBJ accepted the fiscal trade-off needed to pass the tax bill. But it meant that if he was going to fight a War on Poverty, he would have to fight it on the cheap.[57]

LBJ proposed expenditures in the administrative budget (excluding trust funds) of $97.9 billion for fiscal year 1965, a good $3 billion or more below the budget figure Kennedy's advisers had originally discussed. LBJ's first budget held estimated outlays lower than even the fondest hopes of conservatives (actual outlays that year were only $96.5 billion), while reallocating a small portion of federal spending to social welfare. In addition to the $1 billion set-aside for the War on Poverty, LBJ increased funds for manpower training, education, and other service programs. Johnson launched his attack on poverty by shifting priorities within a conservative budget.

Those planning the War on Poverty recognized the breadth of the attack they were contemplating. A real war on poverty, they understood, would include liberalized cash transfers, especially social security and AFDC, more money for job training programs, education, health care for poor families, and social services. Yet these aims were set aside for a more limited and confined demonstration program. The key players, Heller and Schultze, were trying to accommodate both budgetary constraints and the propensity of Congress for horizontal distribution—to spread the butter among numerous congressional districts. Schultze, who occupied a pivotal place in the gestation and emergence of the Great Society, had been soured by his experience with the Area Redevelopment Act (ARA), and once a public employment scheme had been ruled out he was looking for a way to funnel limited federal resources to poor people. Schultze believed the problem of poverty

57. Gardner Ackley, Oral History, September 16, 1980, p. 5, LBJL. See also Heller's notes: "Troika Meeting with President Johnson," November 25, 1963, Heller Papers, box 7; Douglas Dillon to President Johnson, December 6, 1963, with attached memo from Henry Fowler, LE/FI 5–7, box 51, WHCF, LBJL. See also Weir, *Politics and Jobs,* p. 73.

was mainly one of inner-city ghettos and Appalachia, and in both cases he believed that precise targeting of federal resources was necessary to avoid the waste and inefficiency of the ARA. He and Heller devised a scheme to attack poverty by scouring the budget for usable programs (they had identified some 35 pending programs, besides currently existing ones, by early December) and developed a mechanism to concentrate the resources on designated areas.[58]

Lyndon Johnson's December decision to expand the program beyond a small demonstration program intensified the demand for retargeting and centralized budgetary control over poverty-related programs in other federal agencies. In their memorandum to agency heads early in January 1964, Gordon and Heller instructed them to indicate which of their existing programs could be redirected to the poverty effort in addition to proposing new activities that could be undertaken, either under existing law or through new legislation. The $500 million of new money in the poverty budget had been divided between operational programs that the poverty agency, it was assumed, would manage and money that would be used to supplement agency budgets. The latter was "enticement" money, or "glue money" as Schultze called it, and was intended to diminish agency opposition.[59]

Though they later denied it, the intention of Johnson's key budget and economic advisers all along was to achieve a greater degree of centralized control over agency budgets. The initial draft of the poverty legislation prepared by the Budget Bureau contained two key provisions that gave the poverty administrator sweeping powers to use funds appropriated to other agencies and even, in some instances, direct control over other funds. Schultze and Gordon were thinking of a financial plan that could be used to retarget funds, to shift money from low priority to high priority programs. The draft bill contained language permitting the president to reallocate funds *prospectively:*

58. Schultze, "Some Notes on a Program of 'Human Conservation,'" pp. 1–3; Schultze to Director, December 14, 1963, RG 51, ser. 61.1a, R1–6, box 80, NA; Charles Schultze, Oral History, March 29, 1968, pp. 40–41, LBJL; Schultze interview. William Capron, one of the main planners, has said: "Because of the budget situation . . . there wasn't going to be a lot of new money. We were groping for some way to make the existing money in the budget focus. And it was for this reason that the community action notion struck us as very attractive" ("Poverty and Urban Policy," Brandeis transcript, p. 144).

59. Heller/Gordon to Secretaries of Agriculture, Commerce, Labor, HEW, Interior, and HHFA, January 6, 1964, RG 51, ser. 60.3a, box 4, HEW 1962–69, NA; Schultze, Oral History, p. 43, LBJL; Schultze interview.

Funds appropriated for other Federal programs in the fields of health, education, housing, vocational training and rehabilitation, manpower development and training, mental health and mental retardation, and other fields related to the purposes of this Act . . . may be designated [by the president] for use by the department or agency to whom the funds were appropriated in conjunction with or support of programs carried out by the Administrator under this Act. . . . The administrator shall specify the amounts of funds appropriated for each such program which shall be made available to him from time to time for purposes of this Act.[60]

Resistance from agency heads, particularly Wilbur Cohen and Willard Wirtz, and concern on Capitol Hill that Johnson was creating a "poverty czar" forced Gordon and Schultze to back down. Cohen wrote, "we are . . . deeply concerned, if we understand section 513 correctly, with this attempt to authorize one Federal agency to use funds which were appropriated to other Federal agencies for other Federal programs." HEW preferred voluntarism, asking for a statement in the bill enjoining federal agencies to help carry out the poverty program. Wirtz was similarly riled by the apparent power grab, though he was more concerned to do away with the notion of an independent poverty agency altogether and concentrate the effort in existing cabinet departments. Schultze faced opposition even within the Budget Bureau.[61]

It is unlikely that Congress would have approved such sweeping powers for a presidential assistant, the title proposed for the director of the Office of Economic Opportunity (OEO). As an alternative, Schultze proposed leaving control of some of the programs with the agencies but giving the poverty director some authority to approve the use of the funds. This compromise was further diluted by giving the Department of Labor absolute control over one program, the Hometown Youth Corps (later renamed the Neighborhood Youth Corps). Yet Schultze's defeat was not absolute; the OEO administrator still retained sufficient power to influence the allocation of funds.

Most accounts of the genesis of the War on Poverty have concluded that Heller's and Gordon's grand scheme was subverted by the Shriver task force, which abandoned Community Action for operational control of their own

60. "Poverty: Draft Bill," Schultze subject files, February 24, 1964, RG 51, 61.1b, box 71, NA; Schultze to Shriver, February 3, 1964, RG 51, ser. 61.1b, box 118, NA.

61. "I believe this is an undesirable authority," a member of Schultze's staff wrote, "and that it would be impossible to estimate an amount for any fiscal year which would be appropriate for this purpose." Pfleger to Schultze, February 26, 1964, RG 51, ser. 61.1b, box 71, NA; "Poverty: Draft Bill," Schultze subject files, NA.

programs, and then that it degenerated into a constituency-based program no different from farm subsidies or water projects.[62] Yet almost all observers agree that Shriver all too willingly gave up the authority he had. David Hackett, who presided over the President's Committee on Juvenile Delinquency and is often given credit for the idea of community action, recalled that he told Shriver that the choice was between spending $500 million or "having an influence over all the domestic spending that had to do with cities and urban problems."[63] Nevertheless, the War on Poverty changed the allocation of federal resources. Schultze believed that part of the problem they faced was the unwillingness of federal agencies to confront the realities of poverty in urban ghettos. Part of the rationale for the poverty program, he has said, "was deliberately to put some heat on the federal agencies," which meant shifting MDTA, Vocational Education, USES, and other like-minded agencies away from a historically lower-middle-class or working-class clientele toward the so-called hard-core unemployed. Despite the absence of strong financial control, Schultze recalled that "in two or three years those agencies had to revamp themselves completely. It made a difference in housing. It made a difference all over the place because they were in competition with OEO which was, at least for the time being, popular."[64]

Toward the Great Society

The fate of the Great Society was cast by the Kennedy-Johnson policy innovations of the early 1960s. A redistributive path was added to the residue of a proto-social-democratic policy agenda dating from the 1940s. This approach did not mean redistribution of either income or jobs; it meant redistribution of opportunity. As I have shown, redistribution of public services was chosen over other modes of intervention because of the way in which race and class determined the policy options and responses. Race became attached to federal social policy as the Kennedy administration, facing African American protesters in the North and South, sought to break the knot of racial and class disadvantage by underpinning civil rights with federal social policy. The service strategy was a dead end without jobs, however, and here

---

62. Moynihan, *Maximum Feasible Misunderstanding*, pp. 82–90; John Bibby and Roger Davidson, *On Capitol Hill: Studies in the Legislative Process* (New York, 1967), pp. 231–37.

63. "Poverty and Urban Policy," Brandeis Transcript, pp. 301–2; for additional evidence, see pp. 258–62, 285–87.

64. Schultze interview.

the administration put its faith in the tax cut. If social policy acquired a racial cast, the tax cut displayed a class bias in the name of economic growth. To assuage the opposition of business and congressional conservatives, the administration had to agree to pay for capital-intensive tax cuts with tight budgets and an agreement to use the fiscal dividend for debt reduction. Thus, while the racial conflict of the early 1960s dictated the direction of federal social policy, the tax cut confined it to reallocation of public resources.

Neither the lure of constituent politics nor presidential designs on re-election appear to have had much to do with the policy choices of this period. In retrospect, it is astonishing that electoral politics, particularly worry over the allegiance of black Democrats, had so little to do with the outcome.[65] But African Americans were solidly aligned with the Democratic party at the time in cities such as Chicago and were being mobilized on behalf of the Democratic party in other states, notably Michigan. Evidence of African American electoral instability that could be assuaged with patronage rather than a civil rights bill is hard to find. Nor is there any evidence that either Kennedy or Johnson crafted the service strategy or the War on Poverty with its vote-getting potential in mind.[66] There is impressive evidence, on the other hand, that up until the summer of 1963 Kennedy and Johnson sought to avoid policies that singled out African Americans. And even after they were forced to acknowledge race, they proceeded cautiously.

Oddly, the electoral assumptions of the time were just the opposite of those usually assumed to motivate citizens and politicians. The themes of sacrifice, obligation, and charity—symbolized by the rediscovery of poverty in an age of affluence—permeated the discourse of policymakers and were assumed to have a political cachet. Kennedy had initially rejected the idea of a tax cut as inconsistent with calls for sacrifice made during the campaign.[67] Much of this rhetoric was pressed into the service of the cold war,

65. Frances Fox Piven and Richard A. Cloward argue that the War on Poverty was used to shore up the loyalty of blacks. See *Regulating the Poor: The Functions of Public Welfare* (New York, 1971), chap 9.

66. Many of the officials who were instrumental in planning the War on Poverty and drafting the legislation deny that mobilizing black voters was a concern or even a topic of discussion. See "Poverty and Urban Policy," pp. 162–63, 191–95. William Grimshaw notes Chicago's problems with black voters began after passage of the War on Poverty and was motivated by the racism of the Chicago Democratic party (*Bitter Fruit: Black Politics and the Chicago Machine, 1931–1991* [Chicago, 1992], pp. 117–22, 228–29 n. 4).

67. One of Kennedy's economic advisers believed that Kennedy explicitly rejected "old-style Democratic liberalism" because it would not pay off electorally (*CEA Transcript: Discussion of Economic Advisers to President Kennedy*, p. 49, JFKL).

but much spoke to tangible injustices. The civil rights movement made the questions of fairness, rectification of past injustices, and obligations to the poor unavoidable. Martin Luther King Jr., not John F. Kennedy or Lyndon Johnson, set the tone for the political discourse of the era. Johnson's decision to go ahead with the War on Poverty was surely motivated by what he assumed would be its political appeal in this context and by his own penchant for visible symbols of legislative accomplishment. It also fit with his judgment of what was needed. Robert Kennedy thought that racial protest was mainly about desegregation of public facilities, whereas Lyndon Johnson worried about black unemployment, job training, desperate youths, and the rise in welfare rolls.[68]

But given Johnson's desire to complete the New Deal and the heady rhetoric of 1964 and early 1965, was he really serious about limiting the growth of the public sector? Did he really have to adhere to the pact implicit in the tax deal? In an early discussion of the tax cut, Johnson is reported to have said that "once you have the tax cut you can do what you want just like Eisenhower did. Eisenhower talked economy and then spent."[69] Whatever his ultimate intentions, LBJ consistently pursued a conservative budget strategy, which was entirely in line with the constraints imposed by the 1964 tax cut. The modest efforts at redistribution initiated by Kennedy became the core of Lyndon Johnson's legislative strategy. Johnson successfully used it to launch many new programs, but his efforts would set in motion distributive struggles within the welfare state.

68. F. R. Kappel to Business Council, July 17, 1963, p. 2, White Papers, box 19. Johnson made a strong pitch at a meeting with Kennedy and his staff on June 1, 1963, for training and education programs (Transcripts of Civil Rights Meetings, tape 90.3, POF, JFKL).

69. Stein, *Fiscal Revolution in America*, p. 453.

CHAPTER SEVEN

Building a Redistributive State

The absurd battle between defense and the cities arises because we insist on rather stable tax rates and hence on a relatively constant federal share of our national product.

— ARTHUR OKUN

[There were] terrific pressures to move all of the employment programs back away from the hard-core unemployed to the middle class kids. . . . The HEW constituencies were basically trying to get ahold of the OEO money and put it back into the normal distribution system. It really was astonishing to me how weak the constituency was for the real poverty programs.

— JAMES GAITHER

Lyndon Johnson presided at one of those rare moments when the American political system opens up, and the normal barriers to political change fall away. The 1964 election gave Johnson the political muscle he needed to realize his ambitions; his economic advisers told him that his dreams were affordable and, perhaps more interesting, consonant with what they thought necessary to sustain economic growth after passage of the 1964 tax cut. The election left LBJ with an impregnable congressional majority: 68 Senate seats, a gain of two, and 295 House seats, a gain of 38. It broke the back of the conservative coalition; northern Democrats replaced more conservative Republicans, and the Democrats who were defeated were mostly southern. Johnson had, at least temporarily, ideological majorities comparable to those enjoyed by FDR in 1934–35.[1]

Johnson's victory came at a moment when the civil rights movement had finally shattered American complacency, unleashing new aspirations that evoked both hope and rage. Many within the administration were more concerned with dangers than the opportunities. Richard Goodwin told

---

1. Milton C. Cummings Jr., "House Nominations and Elections," in *The National Election of 1964*, ed. Milton C. Cummings Jr. (Washington, D.C., 1966), pp. 241–43, 247–48, 251.

Johnson, "my own feeling is that ferment is growing and we may well be in for a series of explosions even if the civil rights bill goes through," reasoning that the civil rights bill would raise, not satisfy, expectations. Douglas Cater, another White House aide, warned: "Negro leadership is being pushed hard by a more radical element. Some of the leaders like Bayard Rustin have been heard to predict that a little violence this summer might be a healthy thing."[2] Johnson was advised to "denounce violence, but recognize frustration" and stress the relevance of the administration's social policies to the future of African Americans. But Lyndon Johnson was prepared to do more. While Martin Luther King Jr. defined the moral commitments of the era, Johnson prepared to translate them into political reality. In his first State of the Union address after the election, Johnson heralded a new order of continued prosperity, opportunity for all, and enrichment of the quality of life.

Yet the most distinctive feature of Lyndon Johnson's Great Society was less its expansive vision than its political and fiscal restraint. The budget introduced in January 1965 portrayed a more circumscribed vision of the new order, and for all the hoopla, the legislative package was indebted to conservative political strategies of an earlier day. The Great Society was predicated on redistributive politics in which liberal reform was disciplined by fiscal conservatism. This logic dictated the shape of the Great Society: retargeting federal resources, reforming old-line agencies, and providing broad publicly funded transfers only for the elderly. None of this, I should note, depended on budgetary constraints arising from escalation of the Vietnam War. On the contrary, the tentative steps toward redistribution taken in 1963 were marshalled by LBJ into a full-blown reform strategy before Vietnam had escalated. When the war required money, it merely intensified the administration's efforts at redistribution while starving many programs for funds.

According to Daniel Patrick Moynihan, the political conflict unleashed by the community action program was to blame for erasing the political opportunities that had opened up after John F. Kennedy's assassination and Johnson's victory over Barry Goldwater. But it was not the political turmoil of the War on Poverty that foreclosed Johnson's opportunities; it was the fiscal choices he made. Arthur Okun of the CEA saw the artificiality of the choice between guns and butter when a tax increase was not even discussed. His assessment was closer to the mark than Moynihan's vituperative but misguided fusillade at the War on Poverty. By uniting liberal reform with fiscal

2. Goodwin to President, May 4, 1964; Cater to President, May 1964, Ex HU 2, box 2, WHCF, LBJL.

conservatism, Johnson could feed his voracious appetite for legislative victories and manage conflicting political and economic imperatives—he could reconcile his Great Society, his fiscal policy, and eventually his war. But this choice meant that programs designed to remedy poverty were, at best, quite limited, and the fiscal and political logic that shaped redistributive social policies ultimately undermined the Great Society itself. Johnson's fiscal conservatism thwarted any chance of attacking poverty, for any group other than the elderly, with broad, cross-class social policies that permit redistribution without stigmatization. His policies fostered distributive conflict.

Redistributive policies inevitably entail middle-class backlash. At least, that is the lesson of the history of European social policies. Where social renewal was led by middle-class agitators who accepted the need to go beyond de facto means-tested policies, the transition to inclusive policies covering individuals from different social classes has been accomplished without conflict. Where governments have sought to amend non-means-tested policies by including the excluded, however, the results have been catastrophic.[3] This situation in America was no different, and the Great Society came to be engulfed by distributive conflicts. These conflicts were of two kinds. There were conflicts arising out of institutional rivalries as the administration tried to target funds for services to the poor while Congress tried to spread funding across congressional districts, and there were generational disputes which pitted advocates of OASI growth against advocates of services and transfers for the nonelderly. James Gaither, a presidential aide who was at the center of these conflicts, believed that opposition to targeting funds on the poor nearly destroyed the Great Society.[4] Such conflict mocked Johnson's vision of a just society and undermined any pretense of joining liberal reform to fiscal conservatism.

Why did LBJ decide to fasten liberal reform to fiscal conservatism? His decision, made when he enjoyed large congressional majorities waiting to do his bidding, invites comparison with Roosevelt's behavior in similar circumstances during the fall and winter of 1934–35. Like Roosevelt, LBJ sought to inaugurate new departures in social policy under cover of conservative budgetary and fiscal policies. LBJ's fiscal year 1966 budget was less deceptive than FDR's fiscal year 1936 budget with its fiction of temporary spending, but it had the same purpose: reconciling demands for social

---

3. Peter Baldwin, *The Politics of Social Solidarity* (New York, 1990).

4. Author's interview with James Gaither, January 21, 1985 (hereafter cited as Gaither interview).

justice with the imperatives of capital accumulation. Johnson remained bound to the political assumptions underpinning the 1964 tax cut, which required limiting the growth of the public sector relative to the private. The political boundary guiding decisions about federal social policy was set forth by Johnson's 1964 task force on economic growth. All but abandoning Kennedy's promise to plow the fiscal dividend into debt reduction, the task force told Johnson: "With defense outlays constant, we could expand total Federal nondefense expenditures by more than 60 percent over the next 4 years without raising the size of the administrative budget relative to the full-employment GNP to be expected by that time." The task force stated that this judgment, written after Johnson's landslide electoral triumph, was a measure of the freedom of action that policymakers had "without expanding the relative size of Federal spending"; it was not meant to be an estimate of political feasibility.[5] It was also, however, an indication of the fiscal imperatives that would constrain policymakers in the future and consign social policy to a redistributive path.

Liberal Reform and Fiscal Conservatism

In 1964, there was extensive political support for broad, all-encompassing social policies and a new effort to complete the New Deal agenda, not merely a narrowly framed war on poverty or a redistributive state. Horace Busby, one of Johnson's closest and most conservative advisers, explicitly warned him that he courted a middle-class backlash when he decided to fight a war on poverty.[6] Simultaneously, the labor movement was pushing hard for broad-based policies to bolster Johnson's war on poverty. Writing to Lyndon Johnson to proclaim his support for the antipoverty bill, George Meany cautioned, "a program that is too narrow, a program that is not based on solving the root causes of poverty in America would, it seems to us, delay rather than accelerate the full impetus of the campaign you have undertaken."[7] Some of labor's proposals were clearly self-interested and would have had only marginal consequences for the poor—increased public-works spending for example—but all of the proposals would have benefited most

5. "Sustaining American Prosperity," Task Force Report to the president of the United States, November 17, 1964, p. 10, Bill Moyers Papers, box 4, LBJL.

6. Horace Busby to President, December 30, 1963, WE-9, box 25, WHCF, LBJL.

7. Meany to President, March 6, 1964, Legislative Files, box 29, no. 24, GMMA; see also "Waging War Against Poverty," Statement by AFL-CIO Executive Council, February 21, 1964, NAACP Papers, pt. 3, ser. A, box 331, folder "War on Poverty 1964," LC.

Americans, whether union members or not. Nor did African Americans necessarily see the war on poverty as of exclusive benefit to them. Martin Luther King Jr., in particular, thought the object should be to attack both white and black poverty. Speaking before the NAACP Legal Defense and Educational Fund, he said, "the economically deprived condition of the Negro will remain unless the Negro revolution builds and maintains alliances with the majority white community, alliances with a basic goal: the elimination of the causes of poverty."[8]

Bold and sweeping proposals also came from within the administration. Johnson set fourteen secret task forces to work, instructing them to pursue solutions to domestic problems without reference to cost or political opposition.[9] The task forces produced a legislative program consisting mostly of liberal-labor social policies that dated from the 1940s. But if this agenda was dedicated to completing the New Deal, it was less a call to reconstruct the American welfare state than to patch its obvious holes. Johnson not only rejected Busby's advice to embrace the middle class rather than the poor; his advisers and task forces also rejected Busby's assumption of a beleaguered middle class. "If there is a single unifying 'goal' involved here," wrote the Task Force on Income Maintenance in its report, "it is 'to make provision for those who got left out' of the nation's increasing prosperity and who therefore require special assistance."[10] The logic of this agenda, in keeping with the moral claims of the civil rights movement, was to include those citizens who by dint of racism or economic misfortune were excluded from America's welfare state.

Inclusion of those left out of truncated universalism did not require redistributive policies, as the Task Force on Income Maintenance made clear in its proposal for a Tax Adjustment Allowance. The idea was to give an additional two hundred dollars per year through the tax system to families with insufficient income to claim personal exemptions or the standard income tax deduction. The advantage, members of the task force believed, was that the money could be provided directly to families in need without applying a means test, and since it was a tax expenditure, "the payments could appropriately be classified, under a change in the revenue legislation,

8. David Garrow, *Bearing the Cross: Martin Luther King, Jr., and the Southern Leadership Conference* (New York, 1988), p. 326.

9. William E. Leuchtenberg, "The Genesis of the Great Society," *Reporter*, April 21, 1966, pp. 37–38.

10. "Report on the Recommendations of the Income Maintenance Task Force," December 1, 1964, p. 2, Moyers Papers, box 99, folder "Legislative Program," bk 4.

as 'tax refunds' (and thus directly reduce revenues) rather than expenditures."[11] The task force's logic was predicated on reversing one of the perversities of truncated universalism: the use of reverse means tests that granted benefits only to those families *above* an income threshold. The task force's target was America's de facto family allowance. The federal income tax laws acknowledged the burdens of raising a family, and the tax adjustment allowance "would make this recognition meaningful for those families in the poverty area whose income falls short of the taxable level."[12] Similar criticisms were leveled at other federal programs by Johnson's task forces, and many of their remedies were similarly expansive.

What is more, the Great Society was affordable—or so LBJ was told by his advisers. His Task Force on Economic Policy believed the economy would need an added boost in the coming year if the path toward full employment were to be maintained. The task force wanted "a *minimum* of nearly $9 billion" ($7 billion plus slated increases in cash transfers) in fiscal stimulus for fiscal year 1966, to be achieved through a combination of expenditures and tax cuts.[13] Similarly, LBJ's chief panel of economic advisers, the troika of treasury secretary (Douglas Dillon), director of BOB (Kermit Gordon), and chair of CEA (Gardner Ackley), advised the president that continued economic growth would require a boost after mid-1965 with some combination of tax cuts and/or increases in nondefense spending. Independently, the CEA warned that without additional fiscal stimulus the unemployment rate could not be reduced below 5 percent. In December 1964, the troika asked for an additional $3 billion in fiscal stimulus over and above a proposed excise tax cut and increase in social security payments "as the near-term budgetary price-tag of a full employment program."[14]

In making these recommendations, Johnson's economic advisers went to some lengths to defend spending and argue against the political logic of the 1964 tax cut while they conformed to the fiscal limits established by that decision. If federal outlays could not be increased relative to GNP, neither, they argued, should tax cuts have priority nor should there be an arbitrary

11. Cater to Moyers, November 3, 1964, p. 7, Moyers Papers, box 4, folder "Task Force"; "Report on the Recommendations of the Income Maintenance Task Force," p. 7.

12. "Report on the Recommendations of the Income Maintenance Task Force," p. 7.

13. "Briefing Paper on Sustaining Prosperity," December 1, 1964, p. 6, Moyers Papers, box 99, folder "Legislative Program," bk. 4.

14. Ackley to President, December 13, 1964, Economic Troika to President, December 7, 1964, Ex BE 5–4, box 32, WHCF, LBJL; Dillon to President, December 4, 1964, BE 5, box 23, WHCF, LBJL.

ceiling on federal expenditures. Most members of the Economic Policy Task Force thought "there is a good case at this time for placing increased emphasis on expenditures, in combating fiscal drag, in order to respond adequately to the backlog of pressing social wants." Recognizing the "symbolic political importance" of the $100 billion threshold in the administrative budget, the task force nevertheless urged LBJ to cross this Rubicon because an "expansionary budget for FY 1966 *requires* a substantial administrative budget deficit."[15]

Clearly, choice was not foreclosed for Great Society liberals. The administration lacked neither bold plans for social renewal nor political muscle. But Lyndon Johnson defied his economic advisers and decided upon a budget and thus a legislative agenda that depended on reallocating federal resources and retargeting existing programs. In late November 1964, Johnson requested that "each agency head make a searching review of his agency's activities and transmit to him a statement of desirable reforms in ongoing programs . . . which would help to free funds in the 1966 and subsequent budgets to meet more urgent requirements." Kermit Gordon had warned LBJ in August that he could hold 1966 outlays below the magic $100 billion level only by sharply reducing defense expenditures, holding the line on the poverty program, or going after popular but low-priority programs. Johnson told his cabinet that the Great Society would require both new ideas and "*reforms* in existing programs."[16] The president made his political logic quite clear, saying:

> The Great Society will require a substantial investment. This means: that *as a nation* we cannot afford to waste a single dollar of our resources on *outmoded* programs . . . [and] that *as a government* we must get the *most* out of every dollar of scarce budget resources, reforming old programs and using the savings for the new programs of the Great Society.[17]

15. "Briefing Paper on Sustaining Prosperity," December 1, 1964, pp. 7, 11; "Sustaining American Prosperity," Task Force Report to the President of the United States, November 17, 1964, pp. 5, 8–9, 14, Moyers Papers, box 4, folder "Task Force." The task force stressed the investment potential of spending, arguing somewhat perversely that "primary reliance on tax cuts may involve a somewhat larger public debt in each year of the 1960s than would greater reliance on expenditure programs" because tax cuts may not provide as much lift for the economy.

16. Kermit Gordon to Agency Heads, November 23, 1964, including president's statement on "The Great Society," WE 9, box 25, WHCF, LBJL; Gordon to President, August 22, 1964, EX FI 4, box 21, WHCF, LBJL.

17. President's statement on "The Great Society" in Gordon to Agency Heads, November 23, 1964.

LBJ steadfastly refused to cross the Rubicon in his second budget, holding outlays in the administrative budget to $100 billion and reallocating funds from defense, agriculture, veterans, and commerce programs to the Great Society. Overall, the consolidated budget (the administrative budget combined with the trust fund budget) was slated to increase by $6 billion, of which $3 billion would pay for Medicare and an increase in social security. Johnson proposed to increase the administrative budget by $2 billion while increasing funds for social welfare programs by $3 billion.

Johnson ruthlessly turned down requests for more federal dollars for Great Society programs, which dismayed his economic advisers. Gardner Ackley led a charge in late December to get Johnson to add $2 or $3 billion to the budget, knowing it would push outlays in the administrative budget above the $100 billion threshold. LBJ told his advisers he would do it if they could convince labor and the Business Advisory Council (BAC) of the need. The CEA failed to convince the BAC, which was always more concerned about growing social programs than large deficits (something that LBJ probably knew), and the budget stayed where it was.[18] LBJ also summarily turned down a public employment program for an estimated 600,000 unskilled workers, mainly in big cities. He had asked his budget director, Kermit Gordon, to come up with a plan to do something about hard-core unemployment, and Gordon responded with a program to put eligible individuals in needed public-service jobs. Gordon told LBJ this would reduce the unemployment rate from 5 to 4.5 percent in 1965, but Johnson ignored him.[19]

Reallocation and retargeting were at the center of LBJ's strategy for launching the Great Society. His first two budgets effectively trebled budget authority for discretionary Great Society programs while trimming defense spending and other domestic spending. Table 13 presents the changes in discretionary budget authority requested in the president's budget between fiscal year 1964, Kennedy's last budget, and fiscal year 1966, the Great Society budget.[20] Changes in budget authority measure presidential decisions to launch or retrench government programs; they are one of the best gauges of a president's long-term policy intentions. While Kennedy paid only slight attention to budget authority, reflecting his own preoccupation with fiscal policy and his troubles with Congress, LBJ shaped the allocation of budget

18. Gardner Ackley, Oral History, September 16, 1980, pt. 1, pp. 27–28, LBJL.
19. Gordon to President, January 13, 1965, Ex LA 2, box 6, WHCF, LBJL.
20. The table excludes all entitlements funded by general revenues and thus portrays presidential intentions with regard to controllable federal spending or spending requests subject to approval by the appropriations committees.

Table 13. Changes in budget authority for discretionary federal spending, 1964–1969

	President's budget		Congressional budget		
	Request ($ billions)	Change from previous budget	Appropriation ($ billions)	Change in president's budget	Change from previous appropriation
Total Great Society					
FY 1965–66	$4,643	231%	$4,156	–9%	220%
(Annual average)		85		–4.5	80
FY 1967–69	2,258	34	1,898	1.5	27
(Annual average)		11		0.5	14
Total budgets	6,901	343	6,054	–7.4	247
(Annual average)		40		–1.5	40
All other domestic					
FY 1965–66	–976	–2.3	6,418	16	16
Annual average)		–1.2		7.9	7.9
FY 1967–69	7,119	16	820	–4.0	4.6
(Annual average)		7.5		–1.6	1.5
Total budgets	6,143	14	7,238	11	21
(Annual average)		4.1		2.2	4.1
Antipoverty					
FY 1965–66	1,836	215	1,452	–7	186
(Annual average)		83		–3.3	69
FY 1967–69	2,060	74	1,260	–31	46
(Annual average)		23		–10	22
Total budgets	3,896	456	2,712	–37	232
(Annual average)		47		–7.5	40
Education					
FY 1965–66	2,563	399	2,541	–1.8	406
(Annual average)		124		–1	125
FY 1967–69	43	1.4	309	42	21
(Annual average)		0.8		14	7
Total budgets	2,606	405	2,850	40	427
(Annual average)		50		8	54

Source: Budget of the United States Government (Washington, D.C., selected fiscal years).

authority to his own ends. Like Eisenhower, who reduced budget authority in order to shrink the growth of federal programs, Johnson manipulated it in order to reallocate federal resources while behaving as a fiscal conservative.[21]

In his first two budgets, LBJ increased budget authority for discretionary, nonentitlement Great Society programs by a total of $4.6 billion.

21. David C. Mowery, Mark S. Kamlet, and John P. Crecine, "Presidential Management of Budgeting and Fiscal Policymaking," *Political Science Quarterly* 95 (1980): 405, 410, 423.

This category includes antipoverty and employment training programs ($1.8 billion), education ($2.6 billion), and economic development programs ($200 million). Defense and other discretionary spending was reduced by almost $7 billion, or by about 6 percent. Education, employment training, and other service programs that made up the core of the Great Society's service strategy rose from 4.5 percent of civilian budget authority in fiscal year 1964 to 13.6 percent in fiscal year 1966. During this period, Congress accommodated the president, giving him substantially what he wanted for Great Society programs but rejecting cuts in other domestic spending. LBJ's Great Society budget requests were trimmed by 4 percent over two years, almost all of that in 1965; in the rest of the civilian discretionary budget, Congress increased budget authority by an average of 8 percent. Appropriations for Great Society programs rose by an average of 80 percent compared to 8 percent for other discretionary spending.

It was a conservative beginning, striking in light of LBJ's working legislative majorities. What motivated the president to reject the advice of his economic advisers and mortgage most of the Great Society to a fiscally conservative budget? The answer lies in his desire to assuage the fears of conservatives, both inside and outside Congress, while providing leverage for reform. His fiscal year 1965 budget strategy had proven successful, despite Congress's refusal to trim non–Great Society civilian spending, and earned him the respect of conservative Democrats. Commenting on Johnson's social welfare budget that year, Congressman Fogarty, chair of the Appropriations Subcommittee for Labor, HEW, and related agencies, said, "the action of this committee does not so much reflect a liberal attitude as it does a recognition that the 1965 budget was one of the most conservative that has been submitted to Congress in recent years."[22]

Fiscal conservatism, on one interpretation, may have been a strategy for budgetary expansion. Charles Zwick, LBJ's budget director during his last year in office, commented:

> The legislative technicians, and I include in there the President and [Joseph] Califano and Wilbur Cohen, were of the school that you take what you can get and run. Then they would come back and say, "Oh, just start it with five million or ten million, a foot in the door." And if you look at the HEW program, it's just loaded with little bitty programs. Some of them we haven't funded, but most of them we put a little bit in and then they come back and start working.

22. Gordon to President, April 23, 1964, FI 4, box 21, WHCF, LBJL.

In this respect LBJ's legislative strategy was similar to one honed to perfection over the years by the social security administrators—the use of incremental additions to expand and transform programs, or "salami slicing," as Wilbur Cohen called it.[23] There is no doubt that Johnson was a canny legislative tactician and that he was often guided by institutional constraints. For example, the administration followed a cautious political strategy with Medicare; its health care initiative did not depart from the King-Anderson bill that had been the object of legislative combat throughout the Kennedy years, leaving it to a conservative Ways and Means Committee to make the bill more generous. Yet it is doubtful that LBJ's budgetary decisions can be explained solely by reference to his legislative strategy. Incrementalism as a legislative strategy only makes sense from a position of weakness, when advocates of policy change lack a substantial legislative majority. Such a situation confronted social security administrators after the conservative coalition came to power in the late 1930s. Johnson, on the other hand, faced a Congress in which he had a clear liberal majority.

Nor does "salami slicing" quite describe Johnson's budgetary strategy in early 1965. What distinguished it from incrementalism was LBJ's politically bold ambition to reshape the federal budget and embark on a redistributive path. Redistribution was a recurring theme during LBJ's first year in office. Johnson laid out his aims to reporters prior to the election, saying that the administration was trying to reduce programs for the "'haves' . . . in every way we can in order to give to other new programs for . . . the 'have-nots'— and we will take from the ones that can be reduced over to the ones that need to be started. . . . I am trying to follow the policy that if I am going to have a new venture, then I have to have some way whereby I can find the money for that, rather than just adding to what we spend."[24] The fiscal year 1966 budget message clearly anticipated a rising trajectory of welfare spending and a modest decline in other governmental functions. LBJ was less interested in spending the fiscal dividend than hewing to an unwritten

23. Charles Zwick, Oral History, pt. 2, December 1, 1969, pp. 16–17, LBJL; Wilbur Cohen, Oral History, December 8, 1968, p. 10, LBJL. Charles L. Schultze thinks that Johnson was driven by the need for legislative victories and rarely concerned himself with the long-run fiscal consequences. Nevertheless, Schultze agrees that Johnson's political and budgetary calculations allowed him to expand the welfare state while behaving as a fiscal conservative (Schultze interview; also see Charles L. Schultze, Oral History, pt. 2, pp. 27–28, LBJL).

24. *Public Papers of the Presidents of the United States: Lyndon B. Johnson, 1963–1964*, vol. 2 (Washington D.C., 1965), p. 1198, also vol. 1, p. 344; and "Remarks of the President to the Press," January 8, 1964, Diary Back-Up, box 3, LBJL.

boundary. Here he modified the political logic underpinning the expansion of post–World War II welfare states and opted, within the federal sector at least, for something like a zero-sum strategy.

What must be explained is why Johnson combined a conservative budgetary strategy with a politically risky policy of redistribution. One possible explanation is that LBJ was hedging his bets on Vietnam. If Johnson's budget estimates entailed any legerdemain, it was in the defense budget. Vietnam was an unstated element in the budget proposals, but it is not clear that this influenced LBJ's budget decisions or that it dictated his preference for redistribution. Gardner Ackley has said that Vietnam was not a factor in planning the fiscal year 1966 budget.[25] The policy decisions of late 1964 continued to adhere to the political logic of the 1964 tax cut, especially the understanding between Kennedy and businessmen and fiscal conservatives that federal spending would be limited. LBJ combined liberal social policies with conservative budgetary policies mostly as a way of managing businessmen and their allies, not only recalcitrant legislators.

All of LBJ's decisions assumed the significance of business confidence and the necessity of putting reform on a fiscally conservative path. Harry McPherson, who served Johnson in both Congress and the White House and knew him well, recalled that the president "believed very strongly that what mainly had to be done was to stimulate the economy, and [to do that] you had to generate confidence in the business community that you were going to do the thing right."[26] This effort began almost immediately. One of the first things Johnson did upon taking office was to canvass business leaders' support for the pending tax cut. A poll revealed that Johnson had greater support among business leaders than Kennedy had. Most believed that Johnson, unlike his predecessor, was a fiscal conservative: he would cut taxes and restrain federal spending. LBJ cultivated the allegiance of industrial and financial chieftains by reassuring them of his intention to hold spending below Kennedy's budget and adhere to the $100 billion threshold. He had each of his cabinet officers reveal exactly where the cuts would fall.[27]

Johnson's landslide election victory did little to diminish his concern to gain the confidence of businessman. His economic advisers tried to reassure him that adding money to the budget would not "lead to a loss of confi-

25. Ackley, Oral History, p. 26.

26. Author's interview of Harry McPherson, November 1984 (hereafter cited as McPherson interview).

27. "Survey of Businessmen," January 21, 1964, Ex BE 5, box 23, WHCF, LBJL; Kim McQuaid, *Big Business and Presidential Power* (New York, 1982), p. 226.

dence and a run on the dollar." But Johnson was well aware that most businessmen were opposed to more spending. In the meeting he called between his advisers and the members of the Business Advisory Council, one businessman opposed to spending bluntly said, "I think we ought to forget about the deficit and think about the economy."[28] Johnson went out of his way to reassure businessmen. In a speech to the National Industrial Conference Board, a corporate-sponsored research organization, in early February 1965, he said: "The Great Society is not a welfare state—nor is it a spending state. Its object is to give the individual identity and purpose and self-esteem—not to impose upon him an oppressive paternalism." Business opposition to the Great Society was not widespread. The U.S. Chamber of Commerce was the most vocal in denouncing the new programs, but most businessmen responded to Johnson's charm with tacit if not reluctant acceptance.[29]

McPherson explicitly compared Johnson's pursuit of business support to FDR's efforts during the depression to convince skeptical businessmen that his reform program was necessary. The comparison is apt. Just as FDR minimized the tax burden on businesses in 1934–35 to finance work relief, LBJ sought to minimize short-term deficits and a rising ratio of federal spending to GNP—and he publicized this fact. Johnson announced in his Great Society budget message that, even with the new programs, federal expenditures would decline as a proportion of GNP, dropping to "less than 15 percent."[30] LBJ's economic advisers knew this was a consideration that would make a difference. When Schultze and others lobbied LBJ for a tax increase in the summer of 1966, they told him that federal spending was rising as a proportion of GNP and was providing his political enemies with ammunition. Johnson always preferred large increases in social security, which came out of the trust fund budget and did not appear as an addition to the deficit. Similarly, Medicare would not affect the deficit and would be financed by a payroll tax that businesses could pass on to workers and consumers. Within the administrative budget, Johnson ruthlessly retargeted and reallocated funds and started new programs with "budgetary wedges," programs created with large authorizations but small appropriations.[31]

28. Ackley to President, December 13, 1964; Ackley, Oral History, p. 28.

29. *Public Papers of the Presidents of the United States: Lyndon B. Johnson, 1965,* vol. 1 (Washington, D.C., 1966), p. 204; "Big Federal Budget Fails to Stir Outcry from Executives," *Wall Street Journal,* February 2, 1965.

30. *Budget of the United States Government: FY 1966* (Washington, D.C., 1965), p. 9.

31. Mark S. Kamlet and David C. Mowery, "Budgetary Side Payments and Government Growth: 1953–1968," *American Journal of Political Science* (1983): 648, 652. The

LBJ's fiscal logic put much of the Great Society on a trajectory that constrained its possibilities for growth. The federal share of GNP declined as the Great Society was launched, dropping from 19.2 percent in fiscal year 1964 to an average of 18.2 percent in Johnson's first two budgets (fiscal years 1965 and 1966).[32] Given the tax cut and a consensus on restricting the budget to a constant proportion of the GNP, any growth in existing programs or creation of new programs had to come either out of the anticipated fiscal dividend or from cuts in other programs, a prospect made palatable only by sustained economic growth. But growth served as a political lubricant, not as the vehicle for a larger public sector. The Faustian pact Kennedy and Johnson made on behalf of economic growth meant that policymakers would always have to choose not only between guns and butter but also between different kinds of butter. Middle-class welfare such as social security and Medicare would increasingly compete with new service programs. One of Johnson's aides, Douglas Cater, described the full measure of the administration's predicament when he told Bill Moyers, who was coordinating secret task forces in preparation for the 1965 legislative agenda, that the Income Maintenance Task Force had produced recommendations estimated to cost $4 billion annually over the next ten years or "two-thirds of the total increase in Federal revenues under present tax rates."[33] Whatever the administration's inclinations, so long as income and corporate tax increases or larger deficits were ruled out, there would not be much money for social problems.

Social policy was molded to the structure of Johnson's budget. Both new and old social programs were shaped in light of fiscal constraints and the redistributive imperative; broad-based entitlements, such as family allowances, were rejected in favor of narrowly framed, means-tested policies. The administration's decisions were predicated on redistributing scarce resources to those in need. This process began with the legislative accomplishments of 1965 and intensified with the escalation of the Vietnam War and the urban

term "budgetary wedges" is Kamlet and Mowery's. Schultze, Ackley, and Secretary of Treasury Henry Fowler wrote Johnson that the increase in expenditures between the FY 1966 and FY 1967 budgets "would set a post-Korean record and increase the ratio of Federal expenditures to GNP" (Troika to President, August 22, 1966, FI 4, box 23, WHCF, LBJL).

32. Federal outlays as a proportion of GNP began to rise only with the impact of the Vietnam War expenditures (*Historical Tables, Budget of the United States Government, Fiscal Year 1986* [Washington, D.C., 1985], p. 1.2[1]).

33. Cater to Moyers, November 3, 1964, Moyers Papers, "Task Force," box 4.

revolts of the late 1960s unleashing distributive conflict that vitiated the antipoverty strategy of Great Society liberalism.

The Dubious Triumph of Retargeting

The retargeting strategy transformed existing programs and changed the political calculations regarding new policies. Federal agencies acquired larger budgets and new clienteles. For example, manpower training (MDTA) was amended both in 1965 and 1966 to augment its antipoverty objectives. A sharp shift toward disadvantaged workers—youth, handicapped people, older workers, and racial minorities—was accompanied by provisions that increased the time limit on training allowances from 52 to 104 weeks, raised the basic training allowances, and allowed trainees to undertake up to twenty hours of outside work per week. Sixty-five percent of training funds were reserved for hard-core unemployed.

The administration also gave hefty funding increases to vocational education and the Vocational Rehabilitation Administration, and it specified that they serve a new clientele. Congress required states to target 40 percent of vocational education funds for the education of the "physically handicapped and the disadvantaged and for post–high school courses." To the list of beneficiaries for vocational rehabilitation, Congress added, at the administration's request, the mentally disabled, which, in the political lexicon of the time, was understood to mean the poor.[34] Previously, the agency had served a physically disabled, low-income population with more or less stable work histories. In 1965, the vocational rehabilitation regulations were rewritten to include persons with "behavioral disorders characterized by deviant social behavior or impaired ability to carry out normal relationships with family and community which may result from vocational, educational, cultural, social, environmental, or other factors." As an administrator later said, "I can't imagine anyone raised in a ghetto without needing our services." The administration pressed this change on unwilling state agencies.[35] There was widespread support in Congress for these policy initiatives.

The Elementary and Secondary Education Act of 1965 (ESEA) and Model Cities provide compelling evidence of how political expediency combined with the fiscal and ideological force behind redistribution to shape new social

34. *Congress and the Nation, 1965–1968*, vol. 2 (Washington, D.C., 1969), pp. 736, 741–42.

35. Garth Mangum and Lowell M. Glenn, *Vocational Rehabilitation and Federal Manpower Policy* (Ann Arbor, 1966), pp. 6, 8, 12–13, 22.

policies. Aid to education, which had been part of the Democratic party agenda since the 1940s, was the most significant policy to acquire a redistributive label. Originally a general education program to provide a federal subsidy for school construction and teachers' salaries, the proposal had been perhaps the most conspicuous legislative failure since World War II. It went nowhere in the Kennedy administration because of resistance among northern Democrats to the funding formula and controversy over the constitutionality of public aid to parochial schools. The impasse was finally broken when HEW secretary John Gardner and Francis Keppel, commissioner of the Office of Education, abandoned a general aid bill and proposed a policy that distributed money to poor children in virtually all school districts. Keppel assumed that such a package would be politically irresistible in Congress; "it is not easy," Keppel told Moyers, "to oppose a combination of the existing impacted areas program and an added program for the poor."[36] This reformulation turned the original bill inside out, creating a program of institutional aid to school districts under the guise of aid to poor children. Title I, the largest component, provided a federal subsidy to school districts based on the number of low-income children.

The retargeting of service programs amounted to an effort to strip money from existing departments and commit it to new endeavors. This strategy reached its apogee with Model Cities. A grandiose effort to rebuild the nation's cities, model cities was attractive to Johnson in the wake of the Watts riot of August 1965 as a way to address urban problems without busting the budget. Walter Reuther of the United Auto Workers, who first suggested the idea to the president, saw Model Cities as a way to rebuild cities' physical fabric and rejuvenate social life. The White House had visions of a Marshall Plan for the cities. But the underlying reality that fixed the program's development was succinctly captured by Joseph Califano, who told LBJ that with Model Cities, "the president will be the great provider, as well as the great economizer."[37]

The creators of the Model Cities program proposed to reconcile LBJ's desires to be the "great provider" and the "great economizer" through a

36. Francis Keppel, "Memorandum on Education Program and Message," p. 6, attached to Celebrezze to Moyers, December 1, 1964, Moyers Papers, box 99, folder "1965 Legislative Program."

37. Reuther to President, May 13, 1965, Haar to Goodwin, June 9, 1965, Califano to President, October 9, 12, 1965, p. 5, all in Legislative History: Model Cities, box 1, LBJL; also Bernard J. Frieden and Marshall Kaplan, *The Politics of Neglect: Urban Aid from Model Cities to Revenue Sharing* (Cambridge, Mass., 1975), pp. 35–41.

straightforwardly redistributive scheme: participating cities were to be given a "priority" claim to money in other federal programs "to the maximum extent authorized by existing legislation"; and an additional pot of money, estimated at $2.3 billion over five years, would supplement the money siphoned off from other agencies. The proposal called for commingling all relevant funds in a "common account."[38] It was a clever scheme, reminiscent of Schultze's and Heller's ambitions for the war on poverty, though far bolder, and certainly attractive to a president seeking to avoid large appropriations for a new program, yet it went nowhere. In the final legislation, Congress stipulated that HUD had no authority to single out federal grants-in-aid for use in the Model Cities Program. Nevertheless, the program retained a claim, albeit a weak one, on the resources of all federal agencies.[39]

Retargeting proved to be a dubious policy strategy. Redistributing resources to the poor ran afoul of congressional propensities to disperse funds across districts. This tendency is inevitable in a fragmented political system with weak political parties, where legislative coalitions must be assembled piecemeal, provision by provision. The practice did not begin in the 1960s, but the dynamics were altered then. Since the 1930s, as we have seen, Democrats had to rig funding formulas in order to buy southern support for social policies. After 1964 they continued to use the same tactics, but also found it necessary to buy off Republican or suburban Democratic opposition with concessions. This had two notable consequences: limited resources were spread thinly, diminishing programmatic capacity; and programs were rendered more vulnerable. Congressional opposition to Johnson's social policies was motivated as much by the question of who got what as by ideological animus toward the Great Society.

Model Cities emerged from Congress as more of a program to aid cities than a policy to concentrate resources on a few of the most severely impoverished neighborhoods in the country. Congress increased the number of eligible cities and inserted language that included small cities. Republican Senator John Tower of Texas further dispersed funding by successfully amending the bill to limit a state's share to 15 percent of the congressional

38. "Proposed Programs for the Department of Housing and Urban Development," December 1965, pp. 5–6, 14, 18, Harry McPherson Papers, box 20, LBJL.

39. Michael March to Hughes, January 25, 1966, Legislative History: Model Cities, box 2, LBJL. March explicitly noted that the authority being requested for HUD "would parallel the authority which OEO has now for setting priorities." Frieden and Kaplan, *Politics of Neglect*, pp. 42–43, 48, 50–51, 53, 60–64.

authorization. At the same time, Congress reduced funding substantially.[40] The program passed Congress only because the administration finally agreed to increase the number of eligible cities and to reward key supporters and opponents with grants. Faced with a difficult legislative battle in 1967, the administration deliberately allocated Model Cities planning grants with congressional votes in mind. Of the 48 grants approved, 44 went to the districts of members of Congress who voted the right way the first time.[41]

The Elementary and Secondary Education Act is perhaps the most egregious illustration of the pitfalls of redistributing economic opportunity by reallocating federal resources. The notion that poverty could be mitigated or opportunity redistributed through retargeting services was a dubious presupposition sustained only by the administration's blind faith in the efficacy of education. But even if the policy had been viable, Johnson never committed sufficient resources to make a difference. In a memo strongly critical of the Keppel/Gardner approach of attacking poverty indirectly with aid to schools, the Budget Bureau estimated that $5 to $10 billion would be required, not the $1 billion actually appropriated. Congress raised authorized spending for the program to almost $3 billion annually, but appropriations, with the administration's agreement, remained flat.[42]

Aiding poor children with limited funds was made worse by distributive conflict set in motion by the administration's strategy. The policy more nearly resembled a universal entitlement to school districts than a categorical aid program to poor children. Title I distributed money to 95 percent of the school districts in the country, and it included aid for school libraries, supplementary educational centers, and state departments of education. Pressures in Congress rapidly mounted to add money and programs to ESEA, little of it for the poor. Congress was mainly interested in altering the Title I formula and adding provisions that would have converted ESEA into a general aid to education program. Southern Senators, aided by Representative Edith Green, an Oregon Democrat, were joined by Republicans wanting to cash in on the Great Society. They launched a campaign to peg allocation of

40. Frieden and Kaplan, *Politics of Neglect*, pp. 59–60.

41. Califano to President, July 10, 1967, EX LG, box 2, WHCF, LBJL. The White House kept elaborate tallies of the voting records of members of Congress who represented applicant cities.

42. Gordon to Johnson, cited in Julie Roy Jeffery, *Education for Children of the Poor* (Columbus, Ohio, 1978), p. 73. Johnson was told by his budget director that it was "unlikely that such an approach would effectively provide sufficient funds in many districts to accomplish significant results." *Congress and the Nation 1965–1968*, vol. 2, pp. 711–12.

ESEA funds to the national, rather than state, average expenditures per pupil, which benefited southern and rural states. Congress added $250 million dollars to Title III, which funded innovative education programs, and stipulated that it be used to remedy "suburban crowding" and de facto segregation.[43] And a Senate subcommittee boldly added language that would have permitted ESEA funding for the education of all handicapped children regardless of income-levels within the district.

Schultze strongly objected to the Senate amendment because it would dilute federal funding for "any one child," and, he added, "if the handicapped are able to secure the favorable treatment which the amendment would allow, it would become increasingly difficult to head off further attempts in later years to make Title I a 'general aid' program."[44] The administration was able to limit the use of ESEA funds to just 15 percent of the handicapped but lost on the aid formula and allocation of Title III funds. ESEA's fate was characteristic of many federal programs. But, just as Schultze predicted, resources for the poor were diluted as beneficiaries were added while appropriations stagnated. Spending per child for ESEA declined from $210 in 1966 to $173 by the end of Johnson's presidency.

Congressional opposition to the War on Poverty was motivated more by antagonism to Johnson's efforts at retargeting than by ideological conviction. While Republicans offered amendments designed to weaken, if not kill, the Office of Economic Opportunity (OEO), congressional Democrats proceeded to earmark funds for specific programs. In 1966 the House Education and Labor Committee doubled funds for the Neighborhood Youth Corps and increased the authorization for Head Start; funds for the Community Action Program (CAP) were reduced. The committee preferred tangible programs for their districts to the amorphous flexibility of CAP agencies. Congress, in fact, readily substituted education funding for community action (and later Model Cities). Congress increased budget authority for education programs by an average annual rate of 8 percent, most of this coming in the last three Johnson budgets. Funding requests for social services other than community action were trimmed slightly, while LBJ's requests for community action and Model Cities were reduced by an average of one-third (see table 13).

43. Ralph Huitt to Cater/Wilson, March 29, 1966, "Education and Secondary Education Act of 1966," p. 2, Henry Wilson Papers, box 13, folder "Education," LBJL; Huitt to Cater/Wilson, February 18, 1966, EX FA2, box 6, WHCF, LBJL; Cater to President, June 22, 1966, Douglas Cater Papers, box 15, folder "Memos 6/66," LBJL.

44. Schultze to Cater, August 1, 1966, RG 51, ser. 61.1a, box 199, folder R7–10, NA.

The losers, of course, were the poor. ESEA, Johnson's pride and joy and the crown jewel in the administration's redistributive state, did little for the poor, at least initially. Federal audits disclosed that Title I money benefited all children rather than only poor children. Since the money was passed out directly to school districts—bypassing states and counties—with little federal control over how the money was spent, federal dollars were substituted for local dollars. Much of the money was siphoned off from compensatory educational programs and used to fund activities for middle-class school children. Of the children receiving Title I services, one-fifth in big-city urban schools and half in suburban schools were not poor.[45] Perversely, Johnson's policy strategy was insufficiently funded to achieve its goals or to create a policy with a durable cross-class coalition, while a substantial portion of the money was diverted to middle-class constituencies.

Distributive Conflict within the Welfare State

Rather than redistribute opportunity, Great Society liberals could have simply redistributed money. This option was never really ruled out, despite the failure to make income redistribution part of the War on Poverty legislation. Both Kennedy's and Johnson's advisers recognized the necessity of new or expanded cash transfer policies. The 1964 Income Maintenance Task Force was asked to provide "an across-the-board appraisal of the structure, role, and interrelationships" of transfer policies, including aid to poor children, in-kind benefits (health care, food), coverage and level of benefits in OASI and disability insurance, and unemployment compensation.[46] Schemes to transform AFDC into a more general aid program or to replace it with a negative income tax flourished in the 1960s, but the Johnson administration did not set out to revive means-tested policies. Great Society liberals were well aware of the political advantages of broad, inclusive transfer programs—"a program for the poor is a poor program," Wilbur Cohen liked to quip—and they flirted with universalistic social policies for citizens other than the elderly. The Budget Bureau recommended to Kennedy upon his taking office that he replace AFDC with a subsidy to general assistance and link it to unemployment compensation, a radical step that would have folded

45. Jeffrey, *Education for Children of the Poor*, pp. 127–28; Allen J. Matusow, *The Unraveling of America: A History of Liberalism in the 1960s* (New York, 1984), p. 223.
46. "Task Force Issue Paper: Income Maintenance," p. 3, Moyers Papers, box 94, folder "Task Forces on the 1965 Legislative Program."

AFDC into a broad-based, non-means-tested entitlement.[47] Family allowances were actively considered. And with its proposals for financial aid for higher education and housing subsidies, the administration sought to develop a network of policies covering both the middle class and the poor.

Decisions made by the Johnson administration extended, rather than altered, truncated universalism. With the adoption of Medicare, the Democrats finally succeeded in constructing a seamless web of social protection for all the elderly. For working-age citizens, the story was decidedly different. Johnson remained intransigently opposed to cash transfers for the poor and ambivalent about the expansion of food stamps. Non-means-tested transfer policies that embraced diverse income classes either were rejected by the administration (more because of the brutal logic of LBJ's budgetary policies than anything else) or failed. Johnson's advisers were unable to convince the president to liberalize AFDC. They constantly toyed with modifications to the program such as national benefits standards, but never proposed any major changes to Congress. The one time they slipped a request for a national requirement to add unemployed parents to AFDC into the 1968 budget message, Johnson erupted at Schultze: "You didn't clear that with me. . . . It looks like your bluff's being called and if you're gonna' look like a fool that's too bad. I will not do it."[48] AFDC caseloads exploded because of court decisions and actions by states to loosen eligibility and increase benefits, not because of presidential or congressional decisions to expand the program.[49]

Food stamps, the main alternative to cash transfers (as liberals clearly recognized), remained moribund until embraced by the Nixon administration. Enacted in 1964, the program served fewer people than the policy it was intended to replace, the 1930s surplus commodity program. Counties that shifted from surplus commodity distribution to food stamps experienced a 40 percent decline in participation. Johnson refused to expand the program despite a CBS television documentary exposing widespread hunger in

47. David E. Bell to Sorenson/Feldman, January 24, 1961, pp. 2–3, Myer Feldman Papers, box 27, folder "Aid to Dependent Children," JFKL.

48. Schultze interview; *The Budget of the United States, FY 1968* (Washington, D.C., 1967), pp. 29, 135.

49. For relevant explanations of the rise in AFDC caseloads, see Frances Fox Piven and Richard Cloward, *Regulating the Poor* (New York, 1971), chaps. 9–10; Kirsten Gronjberg, *Mass Society and the Extension of Welfare, 1960–1970* (Chicago, 1977); and Martha Davis, *Brutal Need: Lawyers and the Welfare Rights Movement, 1960–1973* (New Haven, Conn., 1993).

America, skillful agitation by Senate liberals, protests and vociferous lobbying by advocates for the poor, and a full-scale effort by his aides to persuade him to propose major changes in eligibility and coverage. His staff argued for an additional $465 million, and when LBJ turned them down, they
come back with a proposal for $285 million. Johnson turned them down
twelve times. As usual money was at the root of matters: any expansion of
food stamps would have exceeded the budget and jeopardized the tax sur-
charge Johnson desperately wanted, by then, to pay for his war. But neither
was Johnson convinced of the need; the bedrock of the administration's social policy remained redistribution of social services.

Medicaid was the noticeable exception to this pattern. The reason for
this is that Medicaid was understood as the entering wedge of a broader
health insurance program. The administration believed that extending a
means-tested health program for the elderly (the Kerr-Mills policy) to cover
poor children and the medically indigent was but one step on the road to
universal access. Future policy decisions required "ascertaining the degree
of success realized by the private sector in meeting the needs of the remainder of the population, and then developing public programs to assist the
next most neglected or disadvantaged group."[50]

A social policy that might have met the needs of the poor while satisfying
the middle class was precluded by fiscal limits to expansion of the welfare
state, namely the budget and tax policies guiding decision making. Cross-
class cash transfer policies for people other than the elderly, such as Moynihan's family allowance, were taken off the table early. The 1964 Income
Maintenance Task Force had little to say about universal versus means-
tested policies, but the 1965 task force was instructed to explore alternatives
to public assistance: a negative income tax or a non-means-tested transfer
payment. The task force recommended a negative income tax after deciding
against family allowances. These deliberations were among the most serious
discussions of alternatives to means-tested and targeted social policies
during the Johnson years. LBJ's policy advisers concluded that family allowances were expensive but ineffective policies for distributing money to
poor families. They estimated that only one-fifth of the total outlays for a
family allowance would go to poor families, regardless of the total amount
spent. The only way to raise the proportion going to the poor, the task force
report argued, was by replacing the six hundred dollar personal exemption

50. "Policy Issues Raised by Recommendations in Proposed Health Message," December 1964, Moyers Papers, box 99, folder "Legislative Program," bk. 4.

for each child in the federal income tax with a family allowance. This step, of course, would have obviated the political advantages of an inclusive, non-means-tested cash transfer, since middle- and upper-income families would lose more than they would gain. For the usual fiscal reasons, the task force preferred to bridge the gap between middle-income and poor families with a combination of tax subsidies and income allowances. "Such a program," they noted, "avoids passing the money through the Federal budget and keeps the level of taxes lower."[51]

With the escalation of the Vietnam War, the question of whether to advocate broad or targeted transfers was rendered moot and replaced by a demand to create redistributive policies. To manage the enormous budgetary pressures it faced and the angry opposition within the Democratic party to its war policies, the administration schemed to convert middle-class transfers into targeted programs for the poor. This strategy precipitated distributive conflict within the welfare state and exposed the fiscal logic governing the Great Society. In one instance, LBJ tried to retarget the National School Lunch Program, a subsidized food program that benefited a broad but mainly middle-class constituency and that consequently enjoyed ample congressional support. LBJ's Child Nutrition Act of 1966 tied budget cuts in the Special Milk Program, a juicy subsidy for dairy producers, with expansion of school food programs for poor children who were underserved. A Congress more concerned with protecting agricultural subsidies than with feeding poor children rejected the plan.[52]

Another, and more interesting, illustration of the administration's quandary was the internal debate over raising social security benefits for the poor elderly. Johnson successfully did so, but at an enormous cost, which was widely believed within the administration to jeopardize related social policies for the nonelderly. Both the White House and HEW officials, mainly Wilbur Cohen, wanted to raise social security benefits in 1965 and again in 1967; LBJ publicly pledged to raise social security benefits during the 1966 election campaign. But there were deep differences over how to do this. HEW preferred large increases in benefits and a corresponding rise in the

51. Ackley to Califano, September 20, 1965, "Report of the Task Force on Income Maintenance," p. 10, Joseph Califano Papers, box 26, folder "Task Force on Income Maintenance," LBJL; Califano to Ackley August 5, 1965, RG 51, 60.3A, box 56, folder "Public Assistance Task Force," NA.

52. McPherson to Phillip S. Hughes, September 1, 1965, McPherson Papers, box 15; Nick Kotz, *Let Them Eat Promises: The Politics of Hunger in America* (Englewood Cliffs, N.J., 1969), pp. 57–64.

taxable wage base, in effect, a tax increase.[53] Within the White House, the CEA and Joseph Califano's domestic policy staff vigorously opposed Cohen's gambit; they wanted to couple modest benefit increases with major changes in the OASI benefit formula. More than verbal sparring was involved in this colloquy; the dispute revealed deep differences over the nature of the redistributive state that Great Society liberals thought they were building.

Central to the dispute was the issue of whether social security should be used to redistribute income to the poor. Social security bureaucrats since the 1930s had fought hard to protect OASI's contributory principles and quash any legislative proposal that smacked of redistribution. Wilbur Cohen, true to this legacy, told the members of Johnson's 1966 Income Maintenance Task Force, "people at the top contribute the most, and [we] should pay them at least as much as they contribute." Cohen accepted the generally held stipulation that social security benefits should be tilted to the poor but preferred to do it with a substantial increase in the minimum benefit and a large across-the-board benefit increase. The White House staff opposed this for the same reason they had dropped other proposals for large, universal income maintenance programs: too little would reach the poor. Since most of the CEA's proposed increase would go to the poor, this would circumscribe how much other recipients could receive.[54] For Ackley, Califano, and others, the issue was straightforwardly one of distributive conflict: social security competed with other social programs, and a substantial rise in OASI benefits could only be had either by cuts in outlays for other social welfare programs or by "increases in the government share in GNP (which has been notably constant in recent years) to which there may be public resistance." Ackley pointedly posed the dilemma to LBJ, telling him that $3 billion in new spending might be used for a social security benefit increase, little of which would go to the poor, or for radical improvements in public assis-

53. Cohen to President, March 16, 17, 1966, WE 6, box 15, WHCF, LBJL.

54. Comments by Wilbur Cohen from a meeting of the 1966 Income Maintenance Task Force, handwritten notes taken by James Gaither, James Gaither Papers, box 85, folder "Income Maintenance Part I," LBJL; "Report of the Task Force on Income Maintenance," November 21, 1966, pp. 33, 56–57, FG 600, WHCF, LBJL; Gardner Ackley, "Basic Issues in Income Maintenance," November 29, 1966, WE 6, box 15, WHCF, LBJL. It is worth pointing out that the CEA thought there was little redistributive gain in raising the minimum OASI benefit because it had its biggest impact on new entrants such as farm workers or domestics. The only way to get more of the money to the poor was to change the formula. Merton J. Peck to Califano, November 30, 1968, Gaither Papers, box 208, folder "Income Maintenance II"; Okun to President, July 28, 1968, EX LA 8, box 3, WHCF, LBJL. Peck was a member of the CEA.

tance. Johnson's Budget Bureau would have held OASI to a 10 percent increase and put the rest of the money into a national standard based on minimum needs for public assistance benefits.[55]

Taxes were at the root of this conflict. The Social Security Administration's proposal to raise the wage base was thought to be a direct threat to the growth of other social programs. Raising the wage base not only increased taxes for higher-income families, but it also gave them a claim to higher future benefits. The CEA astutely recognized that this imposed a double burden on the rest of the welfare state: higher future benefits for the elderly would consume resources that could not be allocated to poor children; and the resulting tax hikes "are likely to be at the expense of public willingness to pay personal income and other taxes."[56] Regressive payroll taxes took a larger bite from low- and middle-income workers, the very voters on which Democrats would have to depend in the future for innovations in social policy.

Wilbur Cohen won the battle, as he usually did. The administration requested a 15 percent across-the-board benefit increase and a hefty hike in the minimum benefit, though Congress reduced the size of the former. Social security policy was not redistributive during the Great Society. The benefit formula actually was regressive at the upper end, and the proportion of OASI benefits going to the pretransfer poor declined from 62 to 58 percent between 1965 and 1968.[57] As a member of the CEA observed at the close of the Johnson years, "because of continual increases in the contribution ceiling and the bias in the benefit calculation formula, the income class whose social security benefits have increased the most both recently and in the history of the program have been those with incomes over $650 per month" (approximately the median family income in 1968).[58] There is no doubt that the elderly poor reaped large rewards from social security policy during the 1960s, but they did so only because of massive increases in benefits, not because the program was made more redistributive.

55. "Report of the Task Force on Income Maintenance," p. 34; Ackley to President, October 13, 1966, EX WE6, box 15, WHCF, LBJL; March to Director, November 25, 1966, pp. 4–5, Califano Papers, box 63.

56. Ibid.

57. Robert D. Plotnick and Felicity Skidmore, *Progress Against Poverty* (New York, 1975), pp. 52, 54, tables 3.2, 3.3.

58. Peck to Califano, November 30, 1968, Gaither Papers, box 208. Peck said that benefits equaled "71% of the first $110 per month, plus 26% of the next $290, plus 24% of the next $150, plus 28% of the remainder up to the contribution ceiling" (emphasis in original).

Social Class and Redistributive Politics in the Great Society

The social policies of the 1960s did not lead to substantial growth of the public sector relative to the private. Between 1955 and 1975, federal spending as a proportion of GNP hardly changed, averaging between 19 and 20 percent. Federal resources were massively reallocated to social welfare programs from non-social-welfare activities. Outlays for social welfare rose from 35 to 59 percent of all federal expenditures by 1975.[59] By comparison, as European welfare states reached maturity, not only did social welfare spending consume a greater share of public sector resources, but government accounted for a much greater share of GNP.[60] European governments were able to finance broadly comprehensive social policies that added middle-class citizens to policies initially crafted for the poor.

The Great Society was of immeasurable benefit to many people: poverty rates were reduced, particularly among the elderly, and the lives of many poor people were improved by access to health care, education, and nutrition programs. Yet the legacy of Johnson's policy revolution for the American welfare state is more ambiguous. If the redistributive political logic underlying the Great Society allowed Lyndon Johnson to manage conflicting economic and political impulses, it was an inadequate footing on which to launch even modest proposals, and once the Vietnam War commenced, it all but precluded general rather than targeted policies and intensified the pressure to reallocate funds within discretionary programs. In the fiscal year 1967 budget, for example, the administration proposed to trade a $3.3 billion increase in Great Society programs for a $3.1 billion decrease in the budgets of NASA, Agriculture, Food for Peace, and the Atomic Energy Commission.[61]

Johnson's budget logic, coupled with the war, put Great Society liberals in the paradoxical position of siding with their enemies, advocating means-tested policies. For Republicans and conservative Democrats, means-tested policies with strict eligibility criteria subject to local control had been the nucleus of their vision of a welfare state since the 1940s. Given the fiscal

59. Henry J. Aaron, *Politics and the Professors: The Great Society in Perspective* (Washington, D.C., 1978), p. 13.

60. In 1960 the public sector in the United States made up 28 percent of GNP compared to an average of 31 percent in the main European welfare states. By 1975, the public sector absorbed 36 percent of GNP in the United States and 46 percent of GNP in Europe. Growth in the United States occurred largely in state and local government.

61. Schultze to President, January 14, 1966, p. 2, EX FI 4, box 22, WHCF, LBJL.

limits to social policy, the acceptance of a constant ratio of federal spending to GNP, and a refusal to countenance tax increases, Great Society liberals had few options other than defending policies targeted toward the poor. In fact, they were morally obligated to do so, since so-called universalistic or more inclusive policies invariably short-changed low-income families. Food assistance became a prominent cause among liberal Democrats in 1968 largely because it was seen as a politically viable strategy to increase assistance to the poor at a time of fiscal restraint and white backlash. Yet this meant the Great Society would find itself in the odd position of reinventing America's dual welfare state.[62]

Lyndon Johnson's effort to put America on a path toward a redistributive welfare state left a legacy of distributive conflicts. Vietnam obviously slowed down the growth of the welfare state in the 1960s and made it difficult to raise taxes. Johnson's dilemma was that any tax increase was likely to be coupled with severe cuts in his Great Society programs. Southern Democrats and Republicans kept the pressure on for significant cuts in the new programs as their price for a tax increase, and by April 1968 Johnson was reduced to telling congressional leaders, "we need a tax bill. . . . If there is anything I can do to get the Congress to vote on a tax bill I will do it."[63] Yet as Arthur Okun clearly understood, this conflict was a product of an unwillingness (and inability, perhaps) to breach an imaginary line between public and private. "In principle," he argued to one of his fellow compatriots in a beleaguered White House, "a greater proportion of the United States' total output could be transferred from the rich to the poor and from the private to the public sector without causing hardship to those from whom it is taken."[64]

Absent a tax increase or greater deficits, the fate of Johnson's Great Society hinged on the distribution of the fruits of economic growth, and the economy yielded a fiscal dividend, just as anticipated. But as Philip Hughes, a top budget official during the Johnson years, regretfully observed almost twenty years later, the fiscal dividend was diverted to social security.[65] This

62. *Congress and the Nation 1965–1968*, 2:587.

63. April 3, 1968, Tom Johnson's Meeting Notes, LBJL. For a sense of Johnson's predicament at the time, see Tom Johnson's notes on the November 20, 1967 meeting (Johnson to President, November 27, 1967, Tom Johnson's Meeting Notes).

64. Okun to Nimitz, June 3, 1968, Gaither Papers, box 51.

65. Interview with Philip S. Hughes, November 1984. I should note that Charles Schultze disagrees with the proposition that social security competed with other domestic social policies (Schultze interview). But that assumes there were no other constraints such as tax resistance, and there were many people in Johnson's White House who believed the future of the welfare state had been mortgaged to social security.

outcome only intensified the distributive conflicts engendered by the reallocation of federal resources. To little avail, Schultze waged guerrilla warfare
against congressional propensities to maximize the number of congressional
districts that benefit from federal programs; his conception of noblesse
oblige fared badly when it came to the distribution of scarce resources. Targeting could not survive the necessity of building and sustaining congressional coalitions, something Cohen understood better than Schultze. Given
the impossibility of raising the public share of the GNP, whatever resources
were allocated would be spread thinly. The middle class would exact its price,
whether through higher social security benefits or by claiming the lion's
share of federal largess.

In an angry memorandum written in response to one of Cohen's social
security initiatives, one of the Budget Bureau's most knowledgeable analysts
of social policy, Michael March, squarely confronted Lyndon Johnson's fiscal legacy. Cohen's proposal, he said, "adds to the tax burden of the middle
class people and will further augment the taxpayer's revolt, making it more
difficult to get revenues for socially meritorious programs." March's anger
was widely shared among White House staff, though Johnson's advisers are
not without culpability.[66] If they lamented the consequences of distributive
conflict, they also failed to acknowledge their own responsibility for the
progrowth economic strategy that left them bereft of the fiscal capacity to
meet the challenges they had assumed.

The distributive conflicts of the late 1960s mocked the facile assumptions
of 1963 and called into question both the service strategy and Johnson's
dual commitment to civil rights for African Americans and the promise of
economic advance for all people. Walter Heller recognized as much when
he pleaded with Johnson for a tax increase to finance the Vietnam War.
"Well-heeled private citizens and businesses—cashing in on government-
sparked prosperity—can afford the costs of Vietnam far better than the bare
bones budgets of our programs for the poor, the Negro, the unskilled, and
the undereducated," he wrote. "The idea that the poor and the Negro au-
tomatically get the benefits of a highly prosperous economy by way of a
'trickle down' of jobs and incomes is true to only a limited extent."[67] Just
how Johnson's fiscal strategy affected African Americans is the question we
now examine.

66. March to Director, December 18, 1968, Gaither Papers, box 208, folder "Income
Maintenance II." For other views see Peck to Califano, November 30, 1968, Gaither to
Califano, November 13, 1968, Gaither Papers, box 208.
67. Heller to President, December 21, 1965, C.F. WE, box 98, WHCF, LBJL.

CHAPTER EIGHT

"To Fulfill These Rights"

Until the Harlems and racial ghettos of our nation are destroyed and the Negro is brought into the mainstream of American life, our beloved nation will be on the verge of being plunged into the abyss of social disruption. No greater tragedy can befall a nation than to leave millions of people with a feeling that they have no stake in their society.

— MARTIN LUTHER KING JR.

To see the poverty of the slums and ghettoes [sic], . . . and then to report that what is needed is a "change in administrative emphasis" cheap enough that history's richest nation will buy it—is to wonder a little whether today's larger crisis is the poverty of the body of the poor or the poverty of spirit of the well-to-do? The right report to the nation might be that its moral obligation is to tithe itself on its incredible gross national product for just one year and clear out completely the human cess pools that have collected the cruel waste of a hundred years of racial bigotry.

— WILLARD WIRTZ

The Great Society's commitment to the liberation of African Americans culminated with Lyndon Johnson's declaration in his Howard University speech that removing the vestiges of slavery and Jim Crow required "not just equality as a right and a theory but equality as a fact and equality as a result."[1] Even though Johnson's speech is usually understood to have set a new standard for equality, it did not depart from the Kennedy administration's June 1963 understanding of the relationship between civil rights and social policies. In defining the meaning of the rights that African Americans had won after a decade of bitter struggle, Johnson grafted the idea of equality of opportunity onto the ameliorative social policies that his predecessor had invoked as a solution to the knot between race and class. Where Johnson departed from Kennedy was in his blunt indictment of racism as the ongoing

1. *Public Papers of the Presidents of the United States: Lyndon B. Johnson, 1965*, bk. 2 (Washington, D.C., 1966), p. 636. The speech was delivered on June 4, 1965.

cause of African American poverty and his rejection of facile comparisons between blacks and white ethnic groups. "Negro poverty is not white poverty," Johnson said; it is "solely and simply the consequence of ancient brutality, past injustice, and present prejudice."[2]

Written to chart the next step forward after the civil rights victories of 1964 and 1965, Johnson's speech endorsed compensatory policies. Indeed, it displayed remarkable affinities to the argument Whitney Young Jr. had made in support of the National Urban League's Marshall Plan. As Lee White, Johnson's special assistant for civil rights, told the president, the "remarkable legislative achievements" of 1965 would have a "profound impact on the lives of all Americans, but perhaps even more so on Negroes: the *housing, education, Medicare* breakthroughs, plus a doubling of the poverty program cannot help but lift the living standards of millions of Negroes over the long haul."[3] These hopes were rudely called into question by the explosion of the Watts ghetto in Los Angeles the day after White penned his memo. By fall, the administration's plan to "leapfrog" the civil rights movement was in a shambles. Watts revealed a rising, visceral anger within black America, as recently enacted and expanded social policies had had little tangible effect.[4]

Johnson's speech did not answer the question of whether blacks would find themselves "with a mouthful of civil rights and an empty dinner table."[5] Instead, it marked the breakup of the civil rights coalition and the onset of a bitter (and lasting) debate over the meaning of African American political participation and the relationship between race, poverty, and social policy. Violence in northern cities made the ghettos central to the question of racial equality in America. Conditions of life in the ghetto were marginally altered by the Great Society; African American poverty rates declined and economic opportunities opened up. But the Great Society was more a vehicle of political transformation than anything else. The War on Poverty, it is well known, became clearly identified with the African American cause and served as one of the main routes to black political incorporation in the 1960s. Sargent Shriver, director of OEO, reported in early 1967 that 58 percent of all beneficiaries (including those in the Head Start program) were black (about 3.5 million people), though the proportion of African Americans on the

2. Ibid., p. 638.

3. White to President, August 10, 1965, Ex HU2, WHCF, LBJL.

4. LeRoy Collins to President, August 1965, Long to O'Brien, August 30, 1965, Ex HU2/ST 2–12, box 25, WHCF, LBJL.

5. The quote is Whitney Young Jr.'s (*Washington Evening Star*, April 14, 1964, p. B19).

staff was much lower. More important, the commuity action program was a conduit for a new generation of black leaders, politicians, and administrators. The War on Poverty was controversial precisely for these reasons.[6]

Yet ghetto walls persisted, the question of black poverty remained unresolved, and political incorporation, many analysts believe, worked to the detriment of the civil rights movement and diminished future possibilities for eliminating poverty and remedying economic and racial inequalities. African Americans, Theodore Lowi argues, became the clientele of the War on Poverty: they gave up the morally legitimate civil rights struggle for the dubious right to a share of public pork. William Julius Wilson believes the Great Society undermined any possibility of reviving the biracial political coalition that appeared to be ascendant at the end of the New Deal by propagating "separate legal and medical systems—one public and predominantly black, the other private and predominantly white." Any capacity to reverse corporate disinvestment in cities, to address the need for full employment, and to design broad, comprehensive social policies was lost with the emergence of the black power movement and demands for community control. For with those two agendas came feckless bickering over representation and control of minor agencies in the ghetto. What was left was a residue of underfunded programs that collapsed amidst administrative chaos. Equally important, the War on Poverty's service programs inspired white hostility.[7]

The question of whether the Great Society undermined possibilities for a biracial political coalition based on common economic concerns cannot be answered from the vantage point of the late 1960s alone. Racially bifurcated social policies did not begin with the Great Society, nor did Johnson's programs precipitate the split between black and white workers. By the 1960s, white workers, white southerners, and blacks already had very different interests in federal social policy. The New Deal put blacks and whites on a different footing in the nascent welfare state by incorporating racial hierarchies into social policies. After the war, blacks' and whites' interests diverged when the income thresholds of New Deal welfare policies were superseded

6. Shriver to President, February 24, 1967, C.F. Subject Reports (OEO), box 129, WHCF, LBJL; J. David Greenstone and Paul Peterson, *Race and Authority in Urban Politics* (Chicago, 1977); Peter K. Eisinger, "The CAP and the Development of Black Political Leadership" in *Urban Policy Making*, ed. Dale Rogers Marshall (Beverly Hills, Calif., 1979), pp. 127–44.

7. Theodore Lowi, *The End of Liberalism*, 2d ed. (New York, 1979), p. 226; William J. Wilson, *The Truly Disadvantaged* (Chicago, 1987), p. 119; Ira Katznelson, *City Trenches* (New York, 1981), chaps. 5–8.

by an incipient racial polarization. From this angle, what is interesting about the Great Society is not that it led to race-specific policies, but that the color line embedded in federal social policy emerged more or less intact from the profound upheaval of the decade. Neither Johnson nor African American political leaders intended to create or perpetuate social policies that would divide blacks from whites.

Why did the Great Society fail to undo the racial bifurcation embedded in the American welfare state? Any answer must begin with analysis of the significance of racial conflict for the Great Society. It is usually assumed either that policymakers were driven to formulate racially biased social policies in response to ghetto violence and black demands for incorporation or that they were simply in the business of distributing patronage. Race, of course, was an omnipresent subtext to almost all discussions of social policy and had been so at least since the Kennedy administration fused civil rights and ameliorative social policies. But to interpret this relationship as a reprise of interest-group liberalism or a demand for race-specific policies is misleading.

What mattered for both policymakers and civil rights leaders was the necessity of breaking down the color line. Federal social policies were devised for "all disadvantaged persons," Attorney General Nicholas Katzenbach told Joseph Califano, but "would permit, and should permit, the concentration of these programs in areas in which the beneficiaries would be predominantly Negro."[8] This aim often required steps to ensure that African Americans would not be excluded. The phrase "maximum feasible participation," which became the legal justification for OEO's efforts to mobilize the poor, was inserted into the antipoverty bill out of a concern that white southerners would exclude southern blacks from the program.[9] Similarly, changes in manpower programs were undertaken partly to redirect the operations of the United States Employment Service, which was notorious for its history of aiding and abetting labor-market discrimination. The rewriting of vocational rehabilitation regulations to encompass ghetto residents was not due simply to the imperialistic aims of federal bureaucrats. It was part of the logic of redistribution, which was understood to mean overcoming the racial bias embedded in most federal social policies as well as expanding economic opportunity for the poor.

---

8. Memo of December 13, 1965 attached to "Civil Rights Program for 1966," p. 9, Harry McPherson Papers, box 21, folder "Civil Rights," LBJL.

9. Daniel P. Moynihan, *Maximum Feasible Misunderstanding* (New York, 1970), pp. 86–87.

Two interrelated factors reproduced the color line in federal social policy: the fiscal logic of the Great Society and white racism. The political and economic assumptions of the Great Society, not the logic of interest groups or distributive politics, meant that limited resources would be targeted toward specific constituencies, a process that was intensified as the Vietnam War drained off resources and race riots consumed the cities. Lyndon Johnson's redistributive strategy extended the constituent-based policies inherited from the New Deal and deepened the fragmentation of the state. In this context, the motivations and actions of blacks, white workers, and southerners were governed by a mixture of racial and economic interests defined by their divergent relationships to the welfare state. What were those interests, and how did they shape the political and economic outcomes of the Great Society?

The response of African Americans to the Great Society was governed more by the racial logic of federal social policy than by interest-group politics or black separatism. Gary Orfield points out that African Americans remained strongly committed to integration throughout the 1960s and rejected separatism.[10] But they joined to their preference for integration a widely accepted assertion of group solidarity, and they did so in order to annihilate the racially pernicious practices embedded in the welfare state. "Color-blind" implementation of federal policies, as we have seen with MDTA, was impossible so long as federal agencies and institutions were allied with groups dedicated to maintaining white superiority. The demand for political inclusion and control, which cut across normal divisions in black politics, was a radical assault on white privilege and on those governmental agencies and political practices sustaining the color line in the welfare state.

White resistance to integration was an underlying source of political opposition to the Great Society, as politicians and political groups sought to avoid any substantial breach of the color line. Nor did whites see the need for a biracial political coalition to rebuild the American welfare state. The flip side of black exclusion from social policies that served the middle class was white inclusion; most whites had no economic interest in a broader welfare state.

In short, the logic of African American incorporation in a society governed by deeply rooted beliefs in the rightness of racial stratification and the

10. Gary Orfield, "Race and the Liberal Agenda: The Loss of the Integrationist Dream, 1965–1974," in *The Politics of Social Policy in the United States,* ed. Margaret Weir, Ann Orloff, and Theda Skocpol (Princeton, N.J., 1988), pp. 319–22.

premises of Johnson's budget and policy strategy determined the shape and impact of federal social policy in the late 1960s.

Unraveling the Color Line: Black Politics in the Great Society

It is commonplace to portray the fracturing of the civil rights movement as a split between those who remained committed to the goal of integration and those who advocated separatism. Yet this dichotomy, a recurring one in African American politics, obscures what was at stake in the 1960s. The argument was less about alternative visions of the African American future—integrated or separate—than about the kind of political reforms and social policies needed to transform the conditions of African American life. It is with respect to this debate that African Americans decided how to respond to Great Society policies.

One of the ironies of the decade is that Martin Luther King Jr. occupied the radical end of the spectrum while Whitney Young Jr., better known as a denizen of the corridors of corporate America than as a ghetto militant, embraced the black nationalist agenda. Disillusioned by the war in Vietnam and the white hostility he encountered in his assault on segregation in Chicago, King went beyond his vision of an integrated society to connect race and class in a way that transcended the debate over black power and integration. He accepted neither black nationalism nor a facile belief in the power of a class coalition. Rather, he believed the civil rights movement could redefine the relationship between race and class by paving the way for a more inclusive form of social justice, which in turn would form the basis for integration. In an essay drafted just before his assassination, King wrote:

> The black revolution is much more than a struggle for the rights of Negroes. It is forcing America to face all its interrelated flaws—racism, poverty, militarism and materialism. It is exposing evils that are rooted deeply in the whole structure of our society. It reveals systemic rather than superficial flaws and suggests that radical reconstruction of society itself is the real issue to be faced. . . . Americans who genuinely treasure our national ideals, who know they are still elusive dreams for all too many, should welcome the stirring of Negro demands.[11]

---

11. Martin Luther King Jr., "A Testament of Hope," in *A Testament of Hope: The Essential Writings of Martin Luther King, Jr.,* ed. James M. Washington (New York, 1986), p. 315.

King's approach was indeed radical, envisioning a fundamental transformation of American society that affected whites as well as blacks.

Young's approach, though compatible with black power, was conservative by comparison. Deeply anguished over Martin Luther King Jr.'s assassination and the violence that erupted in its wake, Young told those attending CORE's 1968 convention: "The Urban League believes strongly in that interpretation of black power which emphasizes self-determination—pride—self respect—participation and control of one's destiny and community affairs." He received a standing ovation. Later in Dayton, Ohio, a black militant commented, "I can't give the League hell any more because it got fifteen jobs for my boys. I'm not calling them names any more. I'm calling them espionage agents for the black people!"[12]

Neither King nor Young abandoned integration, but in the debate over how to solve the problem of ghetto poverty they occupied opposite ends of a new fissure in African American politics, one that turned on the question of what inclusion in American society meant. This debate was every bit as significant as that among black intellectuals and political activists in the 1930s over whether racial oppression could be ended by aligning with the white working class.[13] Social class, as we have seen, became the essential element of black political agendas from the conservative Urban League's to the radical National Negro Congress's. A class alliance was seen as the only path that would adequately address the economic needs of African Americans. Bayard Rustin attempted to revive a biracial working-class coalition in the 1960s, but by then it was clear to many blacks that a class-based alliance which did not confront white racism would provide neither economic nor racial justice.

Two successive summers of rioting in northern and western cities suggested to Rustin a convergence of race and class. Watts was not a "race riot," Rustin commented, but an "outburst of class aggression." The worsening economic situation of African Americans could be reversed only with a coalition similar to the one that staged the 1963 March on Washington.[14] The

---

12. Nancy J. Weiss, *Whitney M. Young, Jr., and the Struggle for Civil Rights* (Princeton, N.J., 1989), p. 183; Guichard Parris and Lester Brooks, *Blacks in the City: A History of the National Urban League* (Boston, Mass., 1971), p. 463. Robert Allen argues that the black power movement was split between reform and revolutionary alternatives; see *Black Awakening in Capitalist America* (New York, 1969), pp. 46–50.

13. Adolph Reed Jr., *Stirrings in the Jug: Black American Politics in the Post Segregation Era* (Minneapolis, Minn., 1998) chap. 4.

14. Bayard Rustin, *Down the Line* (Chicago, 1971), pp. 114–15, 117–19.

vehicle to revive a biracial class-based coalition was the *Freedom Budget,* a $100 billion plan to fight poverty modeled on the social welfare agenda of the 1940s. The budget called for "decent and adequate wages," a guaranteed annual income for those who "cannot and should not work," massive investments in new housing, expanded access to health care and educational opportunities, environmental regulation, and a full-employment high-growth economy. Rustin believed that white resistance to black demands was a consequence of economic insecurity, and "as long as a psychology of scarcity and depression is abroad in the land, then just so long will there be a tendency for the organized to be wary of the unorganized, for the white unemployed to feel threatened by and hostile to the black unemployed." Similarly, greater access to housing for low-income families would dissipate the hostility of small homeowners, and improving the quality of education would diminish white opposition to integrated schools.[15]

There was little disagreement among civil rights organizations over Rustin's social welfare agenda. All of the major black civil rights organizations— SNCC, CORE, SCLC, NAACP, NUL—pledged their support for the Freedom Budget. Much of the Freedom Budget was similar to proposals submitted to the Johnson administration by black leaders after Watts. Those proposals advocated job creation and income maintenance schemes that would be available to all the poor, not just the black poor. The Freedom Budget was compatible with Whitney Young's domestic Marshall Plan, and the NAACP had advocated lowering unemployment to 2.5 percent at least a year before Rustin identified a 2 percent unemployment rate as an achievable goal. Even organizations committed to black power approved the goals of the Freedom Budget. The original manifesto of the Black Panther party subscribed to the full-employment, housing, and educational goals articulated by Rustin. And Wilfred Ussery of CORE, an outspoken advocate of black power, publicly endorsed a coalition of poor whites and blacks around federal poverty programs.[16]

What Rustin could not do was convince other civil rights activists that the Freedom Budget by itself was sufficient for black liberation. The message that Stokely Carmichael found in Watts was exactly the opposite of Rustin's interpretation. Echoing Du Bois's assessment of white workers in the 1930s,

---

15. Rustin to Community Leaders, n.d., p. 3, Bayard Rustin Papers, reel 12, folder "General Correspondence," microfilm ed., University Publications of America (Frederick, Md., 1988) [hereafter UPA].

16. Dona Cooper Hamilton and Charles V. Hamilton, *The Dual Agenda: Race and Social Welfare Policies of Civil Rights Organizations* (New York, 1997), pp. 141, 163–64.

Carmichael told a group of blacks in South Central Los Angeles, "the only reason [whites] suppress us is because we are black." He eschewed any notion of an alliance with white workers, arguing that black unity was necessary before entering into any political coalition. He told Rustin: "In regard to your statement that the only movement that is doing anything for Negroes is the labor movement, we would suggest that one of the major roadblocks to the freedom of the black people is the labor movement as it is presently constructed."[17] Militants like Carmichael were not alone in their skepticism about white workers' willingness to align themselves with the civil rights movement. Some blacks who worked in the trucking industry told one interviewer: "Chicago is the trucking center of the United States. The truck drivers are unionized. Yet you cannot find 40 Negro truck drivers. . . . The unions and especially the skilled craft unions, are among the worst offenders against Negroes."[18] Even the NAACP remained unconvinced that unity with the labor movement was possible. After the NAACP and AFL-CIO joined forces to lobby for the civil rights act, relations between them deteriorated over the implications of Title VII for seniority arrangements (a matter of concern to industrial unions as well as craft unions) and the refusal of building trades unions to open up apprenticeships.[19]

Rustin was strangely myopic when it came to the question of race and social policy. His analysis of racism was based on the black experience of vicious competition with whites for jobs during the Great Depression, which he assumed had continued even though the white unemployment rate by the mid-1960s was well below 4 percent. He attributed the persistence of white economic insecurity to the fear of automation, although there is no evidence that technological displacement was of great concern to white workers or that it accounts for the white racism of the 1960s. Rustin's argument for coalition politics, then, was based on the mistaken assumption that economic insecurity was behind racism in the 1960s. This idea led him to endorse public

17. Stokely Carmichael and Charles V. Hamilton, *Black Power: The Politics of Liberation in America* (New York, 1967), p. 44; Carmichael to Rustin, August 16, 1966, Bayard Rustin Papers, reel 13, folder "General Correspondence," UPA. Carmichael and Hamilton accepted the necessity of a biracial coalition of low-income workers but thought it was the responsibility of whites to encourage low-income whites to join in.

18. Carl Holman to Lee White, December 16, 1965, McPherson Papers, box 21, folder "Civil Rights."

19. Herbert Hill, "Black Workers, Organized Labor, and Title VII of the 1964 Civil Rights Act: Legislative History and Litigation Record," in *Race in America: The Struggle for Equality,* ed. Herbert Hill and James E. Jones Jr. (Madison, Wisc., 1993), pp. 267, 271–75. See also Jill Quadagno, *The Color of Welfare* (New York, 1995), pp. 61–75.

works spending as a way of remedying poverty, and he simply assumed that blacks would get their share of construction jobs funded by the federal government. The NAACP, in contrast, had no illusions about such putatively inclusive policies. Rustin's Freedom Budget assumed that a 2 percent unemployment rate would guarantee not just racial harmony but also an equitable distribution of resources. Equitable distribution, however, was the one thing he could not guarantee.[20]

African Americans widely assumed that unless they had genuine political influence and control over the implementation of social policies, then dismantling the ghetto or radically improving the lives of the poor would be impossible. There was profound doubt, if not cynicism, among African Americans about the benefits of federal policies. Many thought public housing was a fraud and adding to the stock of public housing would simply enrich developers and labor unions. Public assistance was deeply resented and regarded as a way to avoid coming to grips with black unemployment. Residents of Watts interviewed by a secret task force Johnson appointed to investigate the causes of the revolt said "welfare relief is rammed down our throats" and "the white power structure wants us to stay in our place, to be kept in poverty, in ghettos, uneducated, on relief." Some activists believed that local politicians manipulated welfare as a tool of political repression: "If you are on relief, they have their thumb on you, if you are in a public housing project, they have their thumb on you." The widespread assumption that federal social policies worked against black aspirations was not limited, it is important to underscore, to the black radicals of the 1960s. When an NAACP official said, "we must rescue the anti-poverty program from the social work profession and from the politicians who want merely a sterile and ineffective program that will mean little or nothing for the Negro community," he was expressing a principal conviction of African American politics.[21]

It was Malcolm X, not Bayard Rustin, who signified what was to become the maxim of black politics when he asked, "Why should white people be running all the stores in our community?" Malcolm X's preoccupation with the self-determination of ghetto neighborhoods anticipated both black power and the community control movement of the late 1960s, and his message re-

20. Rustin, *Down the Line,* pp. 188–89, 191.
21. William L. Van Deburg, *New Day in Babylon* (Chicago, 1992), pp. 114–15; "Report of the President's Task Force on the Los Angeles Riots, August 11–15, 1965," September 15, 1965, pp. 16–18, LBJL; Carl Holman to White, December 16, 1965, p. 4, McPherson Papers, box 21. *Washington Evening Star,* June 29, 1965, quoted in Sar Levitan, *The Great Society's Poor Law* (Baltimore, Md., 1969), p. 86.

verberated across African American political organizations. Although most African Americans rejected black separatism, they voiced a desire for a greater measure of control over their lives and within their communities.[22] Nor was black power the prerogative of the more radical black organizations of the time. Shorn of Malcolm's fiery rhetoric, the notion of community control was accepted even by the NAACP and the Urban League, which publicly endorsed it at the end of the decade while specifically repudiating the notion that it was separatist. Roy Wilkins, widely regarded as moderate or even conservative, understood this clearly. "The whole NAACP program," he said, "is about building group power . . . but not separate or black power. . . . We must be for change, yes. Reform, yes. Sharp alteration in methods, yes. Acceleration, most certainly so. But separation no."[23] Whitney Young Jr. and the Urban League went further. By the time Young addressed the CORE convention in 1968, the Urban League had already launched programs dedicated to building economic and political capacity in the ghetto. Labeled the New Thrust, the plan called for direct and militant intervention in ghettos and clearly rejected Bayard Rustin's call for a new coalition.[24]

For both the NAACP and Urban League and for many African Americans, the limited conception of social rights embodied in LBJ's Howard University speech was overshadowed by their assertion of actual, not just legal, political rights, and their drive to exert some degree of political control over the allocation and use of federal resources. Simply targeting resources to ghetto communities was unacceptable and regarded as tokenism by many. Aggressive efforts to seize control of programs established in the ghettos reflected the African American experience with the racially stratified welfare state of the 1940s and 1950s. Officials in both organizations worried that blacks would receive less than their fair share. Herbert Hill warned Roy Wilkins that "if new [poverty] programs are to be based upon the currently operating 'vocational training and educational services,' then this represents a very real danger as Negroes are traditionally excluded from training programs in the skilled craft organizations."[25] An Urban League official was

22. Angus Campbell and Howard Schuman, "Racial Attitudes in Fifteen American Cities," in *Supplemental Studies for the National Commission on Civil Disorders* (Washington, D.C., 1968), p. 19, table II-f; Van Deburg, *New Day in Babylon,* pp. 115–16.

23. Wilkins's statement is quoted in Thomas Blair, *Retreat to the Ghetto* (New York, 1977), p. xix.

24. Parris and Brooks, *Blacks in the City,* pp. 456–60.

25. Hill to Wilkins, nd., pp. 2–3, NAACP Papers, pt. 3, ser. A, box 331, folder "War on Poverty," 1964–65, LC; Parris and Brooks, *Blacks in the City,* p. 428.

keen to impress upon Peter Libassi, a special assistant to HEW Secretary John Gardner, that blacks wanted "full equality—and nothing less." He pointed out that

> Negroes have not shared equally in these programs in the past, as a result of deliberate exclusion; and it will take a deliberate effort to overcome this past exclusion. . . . [The] federal government is going to be held accountable in what it does or does not do in this area. . . . [The] key thing is service—what services Negroes are actually getting from these programs, in terms of dollars going to Negroes (i.e., education—new schools; hospitals). No one has done the kind of intensive evaluation to see who is reaping the benefits.[26]

The War on Poverty offered the leverage needed by civil rights organizations to control the operation of federal social policies at the grass roots. Blacks regarded the federal government's employment training programs as tokenism but thought that Model Cities, "with its built-in community involvement," was a significant step.[27] Clarence Mitchell, the NAACP's chief lobbyist, explained why the War on Poverty was so important to the civil rights struggle when Congress was considering whether to dismantle OEO and shift its functions to state vocational education departments or the U.S. Employment Service. If this were done, Mitchell told the House Education and Labor Committee, it would mean "we are going to shift Negroes out." He bluntly added, "the Employment Service would be the worst possible agency to which to give any of the functions of OEO."[28]

Both the NAACP and the NUL were successful in penetrating the poverty program and building links to other social policies, often at the expense of more militant leaders. Local NAACP branches were instructed to take the lead in organizing local poverty programs and to act as a "primary source of those who represent the Negro community." In the South, mobilization of NAACP chapters into the poverty program was crucial to circumventing white control of employment training programs and establishing an alter-

26. "Note on Conversation with Peter Labasse" (sic), NUL Papers, pt. 2, ser. 1, box 17, LC).

27. "Evaluation of the Concentrated Employment Program," p. 4, attached to the correspondence of Carey to Gaither, June 5, 1968, James Gaither Papers, box 17, folder "Concentrated Employment Project," LBJL.

28. United States Congress, House of Representatives, Hearings, Committee on Education and Labor, *Economic Opportunity Act Amendments of 1967*, 90th Cong., 1st sess., pt. 4, pp. 2975–76.

native system to distribute federal resources.[29] Urban League executives served on Community Action advisory boards in twenty-eight cities and often acted as paid consultants. NUL chapters also got into the business of organizing at the grass roots. In the 1930s, NUL Workers' Councils had sought to aid the creation of unions; local chapters in the 1960s enlisted in the welfare rights movement. The Newark, New Jersey, chapter established a welfare rights center, and in Fort Wayne, Indiana, the local chapter organized mothers to challenge local welfare officials in court.[30]

Civil rights leaders, from moderate to militant, were motivated more by an ambition to break down the color line in federal social policy and to overcome barriers to inclusion than they were by interest group politics. Although their political strategy led to gains in political influence and economic well-being, it came at considerable cost to the civil rights movement. In their struggle to influence the implementation of federal policies, black civil rights organizations became deeply enmeshed in the state, compromising their organizational capacity and independence. At the same time, they were blamed by white liberals for the failure of a biracial political coalition to emerge. African Americans found themselves trapped behind the color line in federal social policy, and their political strategy was turned against them.

The absorption of the civil rights movement into the welfare state was encouraged by federal officials who were looking for ties to African American political groups and hastened by Lyndon Johnson, who responded to black demands for political representation with public jobs. Johnson acted to preserve political stability, rather than merely to distribute patronage. Confronted by big-city mayors outraged by the political conflict unleashed by OEO's community action program, Johnson decided to quell demands for community control with jobs. When the furor over community action erupted, Schultze told Johnson that OEO's demands for representation of the poor had "got the wrong emphasis from the start. . . . We ought not to be in the business of organizing the poor politically." Schultze suggested the president order OEO to offer the poor jobs, which was something the mayors could live with, and Johnson agreed.[31]

The authors of this policy were, ironically, two of the most articulate advocates of the idea of community action and mobilization of the poor:

29. "The Anti-Poverty Program," p. 1, NAACP Papers, pt. 3, ser. A, box 331, folder "War on Poverty," LC; Quadagno, *Color of Welfare*, pp. 43–46.

30. House, *Economic Opportunity Act Amendments of 1967*, pt. 2, pp. 964–65; Parris and Brooks, *Blacks in the City*, pp. 453, 470.

31. Schultze to President, September 18, 1965, WE 9, box 26, WHCF, LBJL.

William Cannon, still ensconced in the Budget Bureau, and Richard Boone, who left OEO to head the Citizens Crusade for Poverty. It was Boone who fashioned the quid pro quo, telling Cannon, "if we back off of representation and elections, we extract in return payment to build up the 'subprofessional' aspect of CAP—to involve the poor through jobs in operating and influencing the Community Action Program." In a confidential memo written after Watts and as the furor over community action was erupting, Cannon explained the rationale to Schultze: "If we do not have programs like CAP, then we are going to have to resort to other and perhaps more costly and more authoritarian measures to contain the extreme fragmentation of urban life." CAP, he suggested, "is a conservative way of containing and controlling an inevitable change." To judge from the evidence that is available, jobs were explicitly wielded as a tool of co-optation. By the last year of Johnson's presidency, local antipoverty agencies were diverting money from community action to services. Funding for CAP agencies declined from 30 percent of the OEO budget in 1965 to 17 percent by 1969, while funding for OEO-sponsored employment training programs rose from 39 to 47 percent of the agency's budget.[32]

Blacks acquired a sizable share of the jobs generated by the new social policies. The organizational effects were less beneficial. Absorbed into the state, black nationalists ceased agitating for representation and began agitating for federal dollars. Both the NUL and CORE became heavily implicated as contractors within the Great Society. The NUL received an $8 million contract from the Labor Department in 1964 to train the hard-core unemployed, and in 1966 received $22 million in Labor and OEO grants. Though it retained its identity and autonomy, the National Urban League virtually became an organized constituent of the federal government. By 1972, 74 percent of its budget was derived from federal agencies.[33]

32. W. B. Cannon's notes on conversations with Richard Boone, September 25, 1965 and Cannon to Director, September 25, 1965, RG 51, ser. 60.11, box 5, NA; Wormser to Carey, October 10, 1968, RG 51, ser. 60.11, box 6, NA; Stanley H. Ruttenberg, *Manpower Challenge of the 1970s* (Baltimore, Md., 1970), p. 27, table 1; Bennett Harrison, "Ghetto Employment and the Model Cities Program," *Journal of Political Economy* (1974): 353–71. As I argued in Chapter 7, the decline in funding for community action was due to congressional decisions as well.

33. House, *Economic Opportunity Act Amendments of 1967*, pt. 2, pp. 991–93; M. T. Puryear to Executive Directors, July 16, 1963, pp. 2–3, NUL Papers, pt. 2, ser. 4, box 30, LC; Herbert H. Haines, *Black Radicals and the Civil Rights Mainstream, 1954–1970* (Knoxville, Tenn., 1988), p. 125. Haines notes that no other black organization received funds from the federal government.

Upon passage of the Voting Rights Act, CORE shifted from protest to community organizing in northern ghettos. This change of tactics and mission coincided with the collapse of its financial support from white liberals and its growing involvement with the War on Poverty. CORE turned to OEO to finance much of its community organizing in northern cities, as local CORE chapters got involved in various antipoverty and employment training projects. August Meier and Elliot Rudwick have argued that the War on Poverty was instrumental to CORE's eventual transformation into an arm of black capitalism. Key leaders were lost as local CORE members took jobs in antipoverty agencies, and as the chapters became involved with OEO, they lost their identity as independent organizations.[34]

Blacks and other minority groups acquired considerable leverage, though mostly at the local level or in interstices of the intergovernmental grant system. Incorporation fundamentally changed the logic of black politics, dissipating the radical thrust of the civil rights movement. Yet this outcome was not just a consequence of the logic of African American political demands or of the Johnson administration's success in co-opting the civil rights movement. Civil rights leaders never settled for a meager piece of the welfare pie, continuing their advocacy of more universalistic programs to address the causes of economic deprivation and insecurity. Nonetheless, blacks' inability to go beyond a foothold in the welfare state was, in at least equal measure, a consequence of whites' resistance to the Great Society and their own refusal to allow the ghetto to be dismantled.

White Opposition to the Great Society: The Two Faces of Labor Unions

White Americans may have been prepared to dismantle Jim Crow, but they were not prepared to integrate schools and housing, particularly in the North, or to collaborate with blacks in expanding the American welfare state. Their responses were governed both by a reluctance to relinquish the benefits, psychological and otherwise, of the color line and by sheer economic self-interest. Blacks' demands for desegregation, meaningful inclusion in antipoverty programs, and influence over Great Society policies at the local level provoked white resistance and flight. Calls for new and more inclusive social policies—guaranteed incomes, public employment, family allowances—were

---

34. August Meier and Elliot Rudwick, *CORE: A Study in the Civil Rights Movement, 1942–1968* (New York, 1973), pp. 335, 351, 353, 359–60, 362–64.

irrelevant to a white middle class and white union members already securely protected from the ills of industrial capitalism. Together economic self-interest and strong motivations to perpetuate racial privilege contributed to the racially bifurcated pattern in the distribution of social benefits lamented by so many contemporary writers and undermined any prospect for Bayard Rustin's ideal of a biracial, social-democratic coalition.

The possibilities for a political coalition in the 1960s between blacks and whites dedicated to far-reaching economic reform were distinctly limited. In a trenchant critique of Rustin, James Q. Wilson argued that the potential allies of blacks were either southern businessmen, who were more concerned with political stability than racial justice and were intent on placating discontent before it interfered with profits, or upper-middle-class northern reformers, who were ideologically committed to civil rights. Although both of these groups could be counted as allies and advocates of civil rights legislation, neither was interested in fundamental economic change.[35] But what about the labor movement? In spite of acrimony between unions and the civil rights movement, black leaders and labor elites did collaborate during the 1960s. For members of local unions, however, the idea of a new, biracial political coalition evoked only hostility or indifference. Rustin's vaunted coalition was confined to the leadership of the labor movement.

The AFL-CIO's Committee on Political Education (COPE) and its congressional lobby was at the center of the struggle to revitalize federal social policy in the 1960s. Acting on behalf of all working citizens, not just members of unions, labor leaders aggressively supported Johnson's efforts to complete Roosevelt's and Truman's work and often made the difference in crucial legislative battles. Union lobbying was necessary to passage of the 1964 Civil Rights Act, and labor's lobbyists provided the political muscle for the passage of Medicare and ESEA, for hikes in social security benefits, and for the defense of OEO and community action in 1967. COPE's efforts on behalf of the Democratic party went beyond lobbying to a broad-gauged campaign to recruit blacks and nonunion members into the Democratic party. Labor leaders sought to forge an alliance between black and white workers in the 1960 presidential election, and they claimed some of the credit for John F. Kennedy's election.[36]

35. James Q. Wilson, "The Negro in Politics," in *The Negro American,* ed. Talcott Parsons and Kenneth Clark (Boston, 1967), pp. 423–47.

36. J. David Greenstone, *Labor in American Politics* (New York, 1969); Alan Draper, *A Rope of Sand: The AFL-CIO Committee on Political Education, 1955–1967* (New York, 1989), pp. 69–79, 92–93.

National labor elites campaigned for Great Society policies for both economic and political reasons. They tended to be agnostic about specific social policies, acting mainly as advocates of greater social spending since they were convinced that high social spending brought full employment and tight labor markets. But they were not motivated merely by economic interests; much of what they did was of little immediate benefit to union members. The behavior of COPE and other labor leaders only makes sense, as J. David Greenstone argues, in a partisan context. Labor leaders ardently pursued a black-white political coalition precisely because they assumed blacks would inevitably elect prolabor liberals. In advance of the 1962 elections, James McDevitt, COPE's director, was advised, "we will have to bolster our Negro-labor alliance if any liberal candidate is to have a chance of reelection." State labor councils, with COPE's financial backing, invested heavily in recruiting black voters, especially in the South where state labor elites often acted as an arm of the civil rights movement.[37]

In order to succeed, COPE had to convince affiliated unions to put up cash and manpower on behalf of its voting and lobbying programs. But this was the one thing that COPE could not do. COPE's ardent pursuit of its goal of a black-white electoral coalition everywhere in the South was undertaken, often secretly, at considerable cost. Support for civil rights by state labor councils provoked a backlash by white union members. Many union locals dropped their affiliation with state labor organizations, and a wave of disaffiliations engulfed state labor councils in Arkansas, Mississippi, and Louisiana. Membership in Alabama's state labor federation declined from 93,800 to 55,546 between 1960 and 1965. As a result, state labor leaders in the South publicly denied their financial contributions to civil rights organizations, hoping to stanch the defections.[38]

COPE was indeed a "rope of sand," as Alan Draper acutely observes, an organization floating above rank and file union members with little ability either to reach or to mobilize constituent members of labor unions. If COPE and others in labor's hierarchy were motivated by their vision of the AFL-CIO as the core of a progressive black-white labor coalition, local unions were moved only by threats to their security or autonomy. COPE was able to mobilize local unions on behalf of a broader labor strategy only when union security was clearly at stake, as it was in 1964 when Goldwater's

37. Greenstone, *Labor in American Politics*, pp. 261, 352; Draper, *Rope of Sand*, p. 106.
38. Draper, *Rope of Sand*, pp. 112–14.

candidacy appeared to threaten union gains. COPE's difficulties stemmed, in part, from the decentralization of the American labor movement—the AFL-CIO was an umbrella for autonomous often warring unions—and from the success of unionized welfare capitalism in undercutting COPE's appeals to extend the welfare state.

There were two faces of the labor movement. National labor elites dedicated themselves to the liberal causes of the day, behaving as reform-minded, issue-oriented liberals, rather than grubby, narrow-minded interest-group leaders. COPE eschewed appeals to specific, tangible economic benefits in mobilizing supporters; rather it appealed to the collective interests of workers in social legislation or electoral reform. Down in the unions and in the locals, however, labor leaders remained dedicated to trade-union consciousness and utterly responsive to the demands of their immediate constituencies. This second tier of the labor hierarchy had little incentive to pursue a social-democratic agenda, since unions already administered privatized welfare systems. For similar reasons, COPE's welfare-state agenda proved unattractive among the rank and file. A survey undertaken by the AFL-CIO leadership in the wake of substantial Democratic losses in the 1966 off-year elections revealed that "union members do not readily identify with such labor union goals as better workmen's compensation, improved unemployment compensation, 14(b), or uniform minimum wage."[39] Economic self-interest rendered Rustin's dream of a biracial political coalition revolving around economic issues irrelevant to most whites.

Attempts to convince white trade unionists that registering black voters was crucial to defeating antilabor legislation also failed. Racial privileges always proved more compelling than class solidarity and served to perpetuate racially segmented social policies. Compelling evidence of how white racism undermined a coalition of black and white workers and contributed to the emerging pattern of racial bifurcation within the Great Society can be found in the implementation of LBJ's employment training programs.[40] In a study

39. Ibid., p. 127. I have drawn on Draper's work for this argument. See also Haynes Johnson and Nick Kotz, *The Unions* (New York, 1972), pp. 99–100.

40. "Evaluation of the Concentrated Employment Program," pp. 2, 4, attached to correspondence of Carey to Gaither, June 5, 1968, Gaither Papers, box 17, folder "Concentrated Employment Program." Apparently, white flight from integrated job settings was not uncommon in the 1960s. Herbert Northrup said of the auto industry, "Employers have found that when a department or plant becomes heavily Negro, whites no longer seek employment there. . . . As the percentage of Negroes approaches one half, new white worker applications decline and those who apply tend not to stay long" (*Negro Employment in Basic Industry* [Philadelphia, Pa., 1970], p. 105).

of the Concentrated Employment Project (CEP), a Department of Labor innovation designed to coordinate employment training programs in poor communities, investigators for the Bureau of the Budget discovered that poor whites refused to participate in programs with poor blacks.

> Discrimination and prejudice was found to be sometimes blatant, as in Birmingham, sometimes subtle as in Boston, but everywhere that we went it was one of the dominant influences on the program. Its influence came to bear most directly on development of jobs, job placements, community and business attitudes toward CEP and CEP enrollment. For example, racial antagonisms influence whether individuals (whites) will enroll in CEP (mostly black); whether businessmen (white) will be willing to offer good job opportunities to CEP graduates (mostly black); whether CEP graduates (mostly black) will accept jobs which they consider dead-end, low status, and low pay (blackman's or Negro jobs); and whether CEP as an institution can survive when it is viewed by the white community as another program for Negroes and by the Negro community as white tokenism. . . . The overwhelming proportion of enrollees are non-white— mostly Negro. This is partly because of the geographic areas selected, partly because the non-whites are generally more disadvantaged, and partly because disadvantaged whites are loath to enroll in a program they see as predominantly Negro.

The Budget Bureau's study documents what happened when federal social policies collided with underlying patterns of racial stratification. Not only did poor whites reject government social initiatives, but the labor movement had more or less abandoned employment training programs by the mid-1960s. Although unions had been instrumental in launching these programs, they never became organized constituents of them, according to Gary Mucciaroni. Stanley Ruttenberg, an AFL-CIO official and later an administrator of the training programs, explained that unions lost interest in the programs because they were more concerned with full-employment policies and some unions viewed manpower policy as a threat. "There was a feeling on the part of the building trades unions," Ruttenberg said, "that . . . any kind of governmental training program would interfere with their apprenticeship program and that wouldn't be good." Other unions thought the training policies might turn out to be subsidies for sweat shops or runaway employers.[41]

41. Gary Mucciaroni, *The Political Failure of Employment Policy, 1945–1982* (Pittsburgh, Pa., 1990), pp. 200–201; "Statement on MDTA," December 5, 1963, Legislation box 33, no. 2, GMMA.

The AFL-CIO and affiliated unions asserted a proprietary interest in manpower policies, but they were mostly concerned to prevent encroachment on labor's prerogatives. Andy Biemiller, the AFL-CIO's chief congressional lobbyist, convinced OEO and the Labor Department to pay the prevailing wage rate, adhere to the minimum wage, operate with unionized employers, and try to avoid displacing regular workers.[42] More controversial was union opposition to an effort to eliminate the requirement that training be offered only where graduates had a "reasonable expectation of employment" and to provide training whenever it would enhance an individual's employability. The NAACP and Urban League had long believed that this requirement facilitated discrimination, and with their support James O'Hara, one of the leading advocates of employment training in the House of Representatives, had proposed scrapping the requirement in 1966. Unions characterized this as a "prison labor" proposal, believing that it would only flood the market with surplus skilled labor and thus drive down wages and intensify job competition. The requirement remained in effect, with deleterious consequences for blacks enrolled in employment training programs.

Union disinterest effectively left antipoverty organizations or black interest groups in control of the employment training programs. In the apprenticeship outreach program, for example, 56 percent of all slots or indentures (about 15,000) went to two black organizations, the Urban League and the Worker's Defense League, a group funded by the A. Philip Randolph Institute. Unions, by comparison, controlled just under one-third of the slots.

A pattern of sharp racial bifurcation developed between different training programs. African Americans made up about 23 percent of the participants in on-the-job training (OJT) programs during the Kennedy-Johnson years, programs which were run by the Labor Department's Bureau of Apprenticeship Training. Yet blacks accounted for a much higher proportion of enrollees in the MDTA institutional component, averaging one-third of all participants. Overall, blacks were less likely to participate in skill training programs than in "employability development" programs that emphasized counseling and prevocational skills (learning to be at work on time). In fact, blacks and women enrolled in training programs "were heavily concentrated in programs having a limited emphasis on the acquisition and development of marketable occupational skills."[43]

42. Jill Quadagno, "Social Movements and State Transformation: Labor Unions and Racial Conflict in the War on Poverty," *American Sociological Review* 57 (1992): 621.
43. Charles Perry et al., *The Impact of Government Manpower Programs* (Philadelphia, 1975), pp. 21, 24, 152–53, 225.

Even when manpower programs were implemented by sympathetic unions, they served the racial status quo, a response that reflects the two faces of the labor movement. Nowhere was this more apparent than in the United Auto Workers (UAW), which was really two unions: one imbued with a zeal for reform and committed to the cause of racial equality, the other tethered to the business of protecting the rights and privileges of union members. While many unions remained indifferent if not hostile to the African American cause, the UAW became deeply involved with the civil rights movement. UAW officials financed civil rights organizations, participated in civil rights marches, were involved in the activities of civil rights organizations, took the lead in legislative advocacy for measures to redistribute opportunity and resources, and advanced proposals for organizing and funding antipoverty projects and community economic development in cities such as Los Angeles and Detroit.[44] Yet when faced with a choice between preserving established privileges and procedures within the workplace or promoting racial equality, the union temporized and acquiesced to demands of the predominantly white rank and file.

When UAW officials sought to upgrade blacks in the auto industry or to remedy the racial disadvantages of seniority systems, they tailored their reforms to the prerogatives of white workers. Programs to increase minority employment and break down black-white occupational distinctions were made voluntary and were subject to the approval of union locals, which in effect undermined them. According to Vernon T. Coleman, Jr., "local officials in decentralized plants were reluctant to accept minority programs, and many of the training and apprenticeship programs earmarked for the disadvantaged went to whites not blacks."[45] UAW officials aggressively sought on-the-job-training contracts from the federal government as part of their effort to incorporate black labor into the auto industry; they believed that training programs would expand job opportunities by upgrading the skills of existing employees and providing an avenue to recruit new black employees while avoiding the redistribution of jobs that affirmative action would require. At its peak, the UAW's OJT program had two thousand trainees and focussed on the hardest cases. But the strategy was self-defeating. Coleman concludes that although it "may have temporarily increased minority employment and job skills development, it also exacerbated black concentration

---

44. Vernon T. Coleman, "Labor Power and Social Equality: UAW Politics and Black Workers, 1960–1980" (Ph.D. diss., UCLA, 1984), pp. 116–25.
45. Coleman, "Labor Power and Social Equality," pp. 108–9, 186–88.

in declining plants" and thus reinforced the cycle of low-wage employment and unemployment in the ghetto.[46]

Most of the firms participating in the union-run program were small jobbers on the periphery of the auto industry. The jobs held by trainees were at the low end of the industry's occupational scale, offered little mobility, and were subject to frequent spells of unemployment. Because of white resistance, black trainees were placed in declining plants in the inner city rather than in new, suburban plants. Contracts with suburban plants usually stipulated that training slots would go to in-plant personnel. Nor could trainees count on a job when they finished. The union refused to waive seniority rules, which meant that new hires under OJT would be the first to be laid off. Although the UAW program did train some seventeen thousand poor people, OJT was undermined by the union's adherence to voluntarism and local control and its failure to suspend or at least modify work rules such as seniority that sabotaged successful training.[47] The UAW's failure went beyond its inability to place trainees in good jobs and assure their future employment; the one union that was overtly committed to the cause of racial equality ended up sustaining rather than diminishing the color line within the auto industry.

Preserving the Ghetto:
The Failure of the Great Society

White opposition to policies that would break down the color line was always a threat to Johnson's social policies. It imperiled his legislative ambitions just as it had stymied John F. Kennedy's. Such fears almost sunk the poverty bill. (One Georgia congressman, for example, told Bill Moyers "that the poverty bill was cooked up several months ago as another device to foster racial integration without regard for poverty."[48]) Equally significant it undermined his strategy for eradicating African American poverty.

Desegregation of cities and federal investment in the ghetto were understood as alternative strategies for renewal following the urban violence of the 1960s. John Kain, one of the first analysts to explore the implications of disinvestment in central cities for the black poor, believed that the economic decentralization of metropolitan areas combined with residential segrega-

46. Ibid., pp. 91–92, 96.
47. Ibid., pp. 95–96.
48. John W. Carley to Moyers, Bill Moyers Papers, box 39, folder "Poverty," LBJL.

tion to separate blacks from decent jobs. Any remedy for urban poverty that did not include desegregation was bound to fail, Kain argued. The alternative to dispersing the ghetto was federal economic investment, either through wage and investment subsidies to businesses or through community-based development corporations.[49] Senator Robert Kennedy, who introduced a package of wage subsidies and tax incentives to stimulate economic development in ghettos, was the most visible political proponent of investing in the inner city.

Johnson's advisers were thoroughly hostile to the idea of investing in the ghetto, and Kennedy's plan was regarded as a failure. Schultze wrote LBJ a scathing critique of the proposal, arguing that Kennedy's scheme would gild the ghetto: "It basically abandons the concept of mobility and integration for the concept of building up a black ghetto," and shifts the emphasis to subsidizing the unskilled, which was the opposite of the administration's current policy (or so Schultze presumed). "This approach," he warned, "carried the danger of subsidizing sweatshops in the ghetto."[50] The alternative was a housing desegregation policy that would dismantle the ghettos and an employment training policy that, as Willard Wirtz described it, would unite training with jobs, concentrate "substantial resources on slum areas in 29 cities," and reach 100,000 of the hard-core unemployed. Wirtz and others believed that if sufficient funds were targeted on specific geographic areas, commitments for jobs were obtained from private sector employers, and training and social services were linked to jobs, the administration could overcome the desperation and anger in the ghettos and provide a way out. Johnson willingly committed substantial resources to this effort, siphoning off funds from existing manpower and poverty programs.[51]

The debate over whether to gild or disperse the ghetto was stillborn, however, since white resistance to desegregation left the Johnson administration with what amounted to a de facto investment strategy that pumped needed

49. John Kain, "Housing Segregation, Negro Employment, and Metropolitan Decentralization," *Quarterly Journal of Economics* 82 (1968): 175–97; Bennett Harrison, *Urban Economic Development* (Washington, D.C., 1974).

50. Harding to Shriver, July 7, 1967, Schultze to Califano, July 12, 1967, RG 51, ser. 60.11, box 10, folder "Urban Slum Employment Program," NA.

51. Director of BOB to President, January 26, 1967, p. 2, RG 51, ser. 60.11, box 10, folder "Urban Slum Employment Task Force," NA; Wirtz to President, January 4, 1967, RG 51, ser. 61.1a, box 232, T2–1, NA; Gaither to Califano, December 11, 1967, LA 2, box 8, WHCF, LBJL; Califano to LBJ, January 11, 1968, LA 2, box 9, WHCF, LBJL. Funds earmarked for the Concentrated Employment Project increased from $97.5 million in 1967 to $495 million in 1969.

resources into urban neighborhoods yet was of little help as an avenue of escape. Until 1968 any attempt to tear down ghetto walls was subject to a racial veto. Congress avoided the question of housing discrimination in the 1964 Civil Rights Act by specifically exempting federal housing insurance and subsidies from Title VI, the universal Powell amendment, which prohibited the use of federal funds for discriminatory purposes (public housing and urban renewal projects were covered).[52] In the wake of the riots, Congress confronted the issue and, to the surprise of many in the administration, made erasure of the residential color line national policy. The 1968 Civil Rights Act was hobbled by weak enforcement provisions, which were the price of passage, but enactment of Johnson's landmark 1968 Housing Act provided the capacity—if it was combined with meaningful enforcement of the fair housing provisions of the new civil rights law—for government to diminish the residential color line.[53] Although the new housing law gave the Federal Housing Administration (FHA) the authority to extend housing subsidies and mortgage insurance to low-income individuals in riot-torn neighborhoods who were ordinarily denied loans because of their credit history—turning Johnson's rent supplements program into a subsidy for developers—the new policies only bolstered urban apartheid.

Production of subsidized housing exploded, but most of the new housing was built in the suburbs and occupied by white families. Mortgages for existing housing were concentrated in inner-city neighborhoods, and given almost entirely to black families. Similarly, most of the rental housing units in suburbs were in nonminority census tracts, and those in central cities were disproportionately in minority census tracts. The mortgage and rent subsidy programs operated in much the same way.[54] This was because the FHA acted as it always had, complaisantly and tacitly accepting the racist practices of the banking and real estate industries. There was virtually no change in the magnitude of residential segregation after passage of the 1968 Civil Rights Act. Measures of black housing segregation between 1970 and 1980 remained high in both northern and southern cities, and the rapid sub-

---

52. Douglas S. Massey and Nancy Denton, *American Apartheid: Segregation and the Making of the Underclass* (Cambridge, Mass., 1993), pp. 191–92.

53. Ibid., pp. 193–96.

54. U.S. Civil Rights Commission, *Home Ownership for Lower Income Families: A Report on the Racial and Ethnic Impact of the Section 235 Program* (Washington, D.C., 1971), pp. 15–26; Robert Gray and Steven Tursky, "Location and Racial/Ethnic Occupancy Patterns for HUD-Subsidized Family Housing in Ten Metropolitan Areas," in *Housing Desegregation and Federal Policy,* ed. John M. Goering (Chapel Hill, N.C., 1986), pp. 241–43, table 3.

urbanization of the burgeoning black middle class did not alter this pattern.[55]

The implementation of federal housing policy propped up ghetto walls, and the training programs did little to move individuals out of the dead-end, low-wage jobs. Evaluations revealed high turnover and, more importantly, that the training programs recycled people between low-wage jobs, unemployment, and training. Besides white resistance, flawed assumptions about the need for and efficacy of job training were to blame. Administrators had compelling incentives to push low-income ghetto residents into the sort of low-wage jobs they had always occupied rather than jobs with some possibilities for upward mobility. The "reasonable expectation of employment" requirement led administrators to search out low-wage employers with job vacancies. One study revealed it was those employers who had the most difficulty hiring workers that made the most use of CEP trainees. There was evidence of racial competition for high-wage, blue-collar jobs, and white workers were typically the victors. For many white workers the training programs were an avenue out of the syndrome of low-wage employment; for African Americans it was part of a ghetto merry-go-round. Black workers found upward mobility only in the rapidly expanding public sector.[56]

Willard Wirtz thought "it could prove the one ironic, historic blessing of America's slums that they collected her poor in such concentrations that they became the vulnerable target areas in the war against poverty."[57] But without an explicit effort to break down the color line in urban labor markets and provide some upward mobility, which is what critics meant when they called for "structural" remedies, money would merely be pumped into ghettos without changing anything. In the eyes of many of the recipients, the

55. Civil Rights Commission, *Home Ownership for Lower Income Families*, pp. 78, 84, 86; Massey and Denton, *American Apartheid*, pp. 63–66, 69–71, 77, 85.

56. Bennett Harrison, *Education, Training, and the Urban Ghetto* (Baltimore, Md., 1972), pp. 140, 143, 147–49; Peter B. Doeringer et al., *Low-Income Labor Markets and Urban Manpower Programs: A Critical Assessment* (Washington, D.C., 1972), p. 27; Stephen R. Weissman and Lynne G. Zucker, "External Constraints and Organizational Responses in Urban Social Programs: The Case of San Francisco's Concentrated Employment Program and Its Implications for Manpower Revenue Sharing," in *Restructuring the Federal System: Approaches to Accountability in Post-Categorical Programs* ed. Steven A. Waldhorn and Joseph Sneed (New York, 1975), p. 169. An evaluation of MDTA graduates in 1965–66 showed that whites were substantially more likely to gain employment in high wage jobs than blacks. The study also indicated that whites experienced greater wage gains than blacks. See *Manpower Evaluation Research Report*, no. 8 (U.S. Department of Labor, December 1968), pp. 21–23.

57. Wirtz to President, January 4, 1967, p. 4, RG51, NA.

training programs were just another "dole," a temporary source of income. This impression was not misguided. With the 1966 amendments, which shifted the program toward the poorest of the poor and extended the time period for training allowances, MDTA had been transformed into a surrogate income transfer policy. Policymakers had created a pipeline that allowed individuals to move through different training programs and get off and on the ghetto job-training–unemployment merry-go-round. Faced with the difficulties of training and placing motivated but unskilled people into jobs, administrators often "were content to stress the more immediate goal of providing income and work relief for the destitute."[58]

In retrospect, what is so startling about the 1960s employment policies is how they replicated the relief cycle of the 1930s. In both cases, federal social policies functioned to hold black workers off the labor market and to rigidify the racial bifurcation of urban labor markets. The success of the Johnson-Wirtz-Schultze strategy in 1967 depended on their ability to find viable private-sector paths out of the ghetto. The necessary business involvement failed to materialize, despite the administration's herculean efforts, and a mild recession at the end of Johnson's term scotched the policy. The failures of their policies, though, were apparent well before then.

Watts made the furious anger in the ghettos visible. The Detroit riot in July 1967 called the very premises of the Great Society's racial liberalism into question. In the wake of the violence, Willard Wirtz discovered a substantial number of unused job-training slots throughout the country, with especially high vacancy rates in cities experiencing riots. A survey of 48 cities revealed that 50 percent of OJT training slots and 60 percent of places in classroom training were unfilled. Wirtz, whose compassion for the poor is beyond doubt and who was one of the key architects of the Great Society's poverty strategy in the ghettos, rejected any claim that the riots were about unemployment. Acknowledging high black unemployment rates, Wirtz wrote Johnson that "the conclusion" then being drawn by African American leaders and liberals "that this problem can be met by 'more jobs' is a dangerous over-simplification." Wirtz argued that the problem was not the absence of jobs but a "lack of willingness or ability or both to do the jobs that are available." Although blacks in some cities were threatening to revolt over low wages, Wirtz went on to say:

> The more basic and serious problem is reflected in the increasing evidence of rejection of the training programs. . . . Thousands of training berths (in-

58. The quote is from Sar Levitan; cited in Robert Hall to Director, August 11, 1967, p. 2, RG 51, ser. 60.11, box 9, folder "Manpower Federal Coordination (1966–67)," NA.

cluding on-the-job-training) are now going unfilled. *Some* of this is administrative inefficiency in running the programs. *More* of it is individual unwillingness to meet this problem the hard way. So the cry is going up for guaranteed government jobs ("employer of last resort") or a negative income tax. Any compromise on this point is going to be wrong—for a long time. There is a real danger that the wrong answers which have crept into the welfare program will be turned to in an attempt to buy our way out of the civil rights revolution. It has got to be insisted that the jobs be earned. . . . The motivation problem is more critical today than the job development problem.[59]

Some of these vacancies resulted from administrative bungling or the forward allocation of training slots for later use. Yet there was evidence, just as Wirtz claimed, that the beneficiaries of the Great Society were rejecting its help. One study found that blacks saw the training programs "as a threat to their self-respect [and] as being defeating, useless, and humiliating." The administration decided not to make knowledge of unfilled training slots public, "fearful that it was politically risky and would open the effectiveness of the current programs to severe questioning."[60]

Evidence of the failure of the service strategy had little effect on administration policy. Public employment and guaranteed income schemes, the main alternatives to the service strategy, were rejected. Sargent Shriver advocated "public service jobs," minimum wage jobs such as paralegals and educational aides that would be available to anyone who wanted to work.[61] Liberal Democrats in Congress, who argued that the training programs were a blind alley filled with low-wage jobs, persisted in trying to create a public employment program under the aegis of OEO. Wirtz believed these would only perpetuate the problem and preferred a *"guaranteed job opportunity program"* in which training would be required. The White House, like

59. Wirtz to President, August 1, 1967, LA 2, WHCF, LBJL.

60. David Wellman, "Manpower Training for Low Wage Work," in *The Poverty Establishment,* ed. Pamela Roby (Englewood Cliffs, N.J., 1974), p. 129; Wirtz to President, August 10, 1967, Ex LA 2, box 60, WHCF, LBJL; H. Floyd Sherrod Jr. to Hardesty, September 8, 1967, Robert Hardesty Papers, box 3, LBJL. Sherrod was the Legislative Liaison Officer for the Department of Labor and Hardesty wrote press releases for the White House. The most severe problems were found in MDTA, but a Budget Bureau study argued the extremely high rate of vacancies was due to forward funding of training slots. They did not rule out, however, the possibility of rejection and, in fact, found some evidence of it. (Francis to Director, August 22, 1967, RG 51, ser. 61.1a, box 232, folder T2–1, NA.)

61. Robert Levine, "Second Description of the Public Employment Program," August 28, 1965, RG 51, ser. 60.11, box 9, folder "Manpower Federal Coordination, 1963–1965," NA; Kershaw to Califano, October 18, 1965, LA 2, box 7, WHCF, LBJL.

Wirtz, was loath to give up on the service strategy, which is why they invested so much in an effort to lure corporations into ghettos and why they waged such a fierce battle in 1967 to preserve OEO. James Gaither, Califano's chief deputy responsible for coordinating employment and income maintenance proposals, said, "we were clearly going the other way; it was much cheaper to get industry to train people for real jobs than to create jobs that we'd have to continue paying forever." The White House even rejected the idea of an emergency public employment policy triggered by unemployment rates, an idea Johnson suggested when he realized that a recession would subvert his employment training programs.[62]

Great Society liberals remained true to their version of racial liberalism. Unfortunately, rather than liberating the ghettos, their policies merely served to feed them, thus engendering not merely bitterness aroused by unfulfilled promises but resentment against the kind of jobs being offered—mainly low-wage jobs that white Americans had historically considered fit for African Americans. No wonder these programs could not fill their training slots![63]

Race, Rights, and Distributive Politics

Lyndon Johnson departed from the passive, ill-formed racial liberalism of the 1930s in his recognition of the legacy of white racism in America and his willingness to confront it openly. He committed himself to adding social rights to the civil and political rights already obtained, in effect, to completing the New Deal for African Americans. Yet the Great Society, though it improved the lives of many blacks, deepened the racial bifurcation at the core of the American welfare state. The ghetto, a system of social control, became both an appendage of the welfare state and a metaphor for it.

White racism and hostility to integration in the North is obviously a central element in any explanation of the persistence of racially coded social policies. Any possibility of reviving a biracial working-class coalition was chimerical, ruled out by economic and racial self-interest. Glib assertions that

62. Gaither interview; Gaither to Califano, December 2, 1968, Gaither Papers, box 230, folder "1969 Manpower Program." LBJ's economic advisers regarded the idea as potentially inflationary.

63. Yet when jobs with decent wages and some potential for mobility were available the response was quite different. The Budget Bureau's report on the training vacancies noted when three thousand new jobs were created in the auto industry, sixteen thousand people applied, and advertisements in the Philadelphia ghetto for five hundred city jobs attracted twenty-five hundred applicants (Francis to Director, August 22, 1967, p. 4, RG 51, ser. 61.1a, box 232, NA).

more universalistic policies would have cemented a broader and more durable political coalition are misleading. So long as whites were prepared to reject policies that benefited blacks or led to integration, there was little Rustin or anyone else could do.

Along with white racism, it was the fiscal strategy behind the Great Society that accounted for the triumph of a welfare state predicated on interest-group politics. Comprehensive social policies sufficiently large to obliterate all manifestations of race were never in the cards, and once the Vietnam War drained the federal treasury there was no way to avoid concentrating the limited resources on the ghettos. In a context where residential and labor-market discrimination endured, the service strategy merely reinforced segregated urban labor markets. Johnson's fiscal restraint, his deference to businessmen and investors, and his inability to raise taxes undermined his liberal reforms.

Unable to influence the direction of federal social policy, African Americans strove to acquire sufficient leverage over the implementation of the new policies to prevent their exclusion and to break down the color line in the welfare state. Regardless of their ideological views on black liberation, African American political activists shared a common belief in the need for broader social policies and most of them, at one time or another, lobbied for such policies. What they got instead was a racial liberalism predicated on redeeming American individualism for African Americans. The civil rights movement ensured that this new liberalism surpassed the tepid racial liberalism of the New Deal and confronted the reality of American apartheid. Although the Great Society's racial liberalism succeeded in delegitimizing publicly professed expressions of white superiority and in diminishing white support for racial separatism (at least as expressed in public opinion surveys), it failed because it did not dismantle the structural basis for America's system of racial stratification.

More than almost anyone else at the time, Martin Luther King Jr. recognized the limits to the racial liberalism of the Great Society. In his last presidential address to the Southern Christian Leadership Conference, King repudiated the ameliorative liberalism that Johnson made central to his Great Society and reversed Johnson's conception of the relationship between race and class. In a tone that was ironic rather than disdainful, King argued that both racial and economic justice depended on a measure of reform and social transformation that went far beyond anything Johnson ever contemplated. "We are called upon to help the discouraged beggars in life's marketplace," King said. "But one day we must come to see that an edifice which produces beggars needs restructuring. . . . Now when I say question the whole society, it means ultimately coming to see that the problem of racism, the problem of economic exploitation, and the problem of war are all tied together."[64]

Martin Luther King Jr. would not live to serve on behalf of the social revolution he envisaged, and Lyndon Johnson would leave the White House for Richard Nixon. Nixon's ascension heralded the rise of a dramatically different welfare strategy; he had every incentive to widen the growing breech between the races.

64. Martin Luther King Jr., "Where Do We Go From Here?" in *A Testament of Hope*, p. 250.

PART IV

BEYOND THE GREAT SOCIETY

CHAPTER NINE

Remaking the Great Society: Nixon's Gambit

What I am proposing is that the Federal Government build a foundation under the income of every American family with dependent children that cannot care for itself—wherever in America that family may live.

—RICHARD M. NIXON (AUGUST 8, 1969)

Be sure [the Family Assistance Plan is] killed by the Democrats and that we make a big play for it, but don't let it pass, can't afford it.

—RICHARD M. NIXON (JULY 13, 1970)

Richard Nixon is often said to have enlarged the Great Society. He advocated a guaranteed annual income, proposed national health insurance, and adopted a policy his presumably more liberal predecessor had refused to undertake—make food stamps cheaper and more accessible. Yet one should not assume the Republicans were interested in building a bigger (and more liberal) welfare state, although many people do make that assumption.[1] Nixon hardly thought of himself as continuing Johnson's revolution. Quite the contrary. Nixon's agenda embraced both expansion and contraction: enlarging and centralizing cash and in-kind transfers to individuals but cutting or dismantling Great Society service programs and consolidating categorical grants-in-aid into block grants, euphemistically labeled "special revenue sharing," in order to reduce federal outlays.

Nixon completed Johnson's redistributive state but altered its form. Federal social policy for all but the elderly was turned around toward means-tested transfer programs, while funding for services, the heart of Johnson's revolution, declined precipitously as a proportion of federal spending. Had it been enacted as envisioned, Nixon's gambit would have radically altered the relationship between the federal government and the states and cities; it would have replaced congressional control over programs with formula-

1. Joan Hoff argues for the liberal Nixon in *Nixon Reconsidered* (New York, 1994). Her account is largely limited to welfare reform and misleads about Nixon's intentions.

driven social policies; and it would have institutionalized policies that would limit the growth of the welfare state.

Taking office after a political and policy revolution, the Republican administration found itself in a situation similar to the conservative coalition of the 1940s: it faced a political movement with new ideas for the use of public authority and a Democratic majority in Congress. Old questions were reopened. Passage of Medicare, for example, made the absence of national health insurance more, not less, prominent, leading Senator Edward M. Kennedy to greet the new president with a legislative proposal for national health care. A right to employment was revived by liberal senators scheming for a way to extract from Nixon the public employment programs rejected by Johnson. Hunger in America became a legislative priority. The ensuing debate over hunger established an implicit right to a minimal standard of living for all citizens.

The Great Society created new constituents who made new demands.[2] Protest activities and federal social policies fed on one another in an escalating dance of demand and response. Community groups and social workers mobilized by the War on Poverty encouraged poor women to take advantage of changes in AFDC eligibility and the new federal poverty programs. This mobilization led to the formation of the National Welfare Rights Organization (NWRO), the only national organization explicitly representing the women receiving public assistance payments. Similarly, the Elementary and Secondary Education Act made school districts, teachers, and even librarians (who aligned themselves with book publishers) organized constituents of the federal government.

In Congress, Nixon confronted a Senate ruled by a cadre of liberal senators, of whom a near majority were progressives on social welfare issues. The Democrats' seven-seat majority was augmented by liberal northern Republicans such as Jacob Javits.[3] The Senate exuded a sweeping vision of postwar liberalism and was the incubator of countless proposals to liberalize the Great Society, but Nixon could often count on the House of Representatives to help him turn back liberal advances. There the conservative coalition had reemerged as an influential force after the 1966 and 1968 elections. It often gave Nixon the ability to sustain vetoes, even though he still confronted a

2. See, Jack L. Walker Jr., *Mobilizing Interest Groups in America* (Ann Arbor, Mich., 1991).

3. A. James Reichley, *Conservatives in an Age of Change* (Washington, D.C., 1981), pp. 84–85; Michael Foley, *The New Senate: Liberal Influence in a Conservative Institution, 1959–1972* (New Haven, Conn., 1980), pp. 68–69, 97, table 3.2.

strong liberal presence in the House committed to defending Great Society programs and adding to the welfare state.

Nixon responded to these forces just as Taft and the southern Democrats had; he devised a policy agenda dedicated to containing liberal dreams while exploiting the electoral potential of the welfare state. John Ehrlichman, a key aide in charge of domestic policy, described the administration's domestic policy strategy as "zig and zag." It included, he told Nixon, "some non-conservative initiatives deliberately designed to furnish some zigs to go with our conservative zags in the same way we have included [Daniel Patrick] Moynihan with our [Harry] Dents (rather than trying to recruit only those non-existent middle-of-the-roaders)."[4] Zig and zag was born of the fiscal threats and political opportunities confronting the new administration.

Alongside escalating claims on the national budget, the Great Society bequeathed Republicans political opportunities. Electoral backlash, the George Wallace vote, gave Republicans an opening. Republicans came into office intent on forging a new electoral coalition and were never content to merely gain a marginal advantage over the Democrats. Unlike the Reagan administration, which would use tax cuts and budget cuts to cement an electoral coalition, Nixon initially followed a course of action governed by the logic of expansion. Many of his proposals were devised to benefit obvious Republican constituencies or hive off (white) Democratic ones. Nixon blended the racial appeals of George Wallace with the old-time religion of Republican frugality while sponsoring policies that would add to the American welfare state. The beneficiaries of these policies, though, were not the poor, but middle-class suburbanites.

Nixon's room to carve out new policies for electoral purposes was limited by Lyndon Johnson's budgetary legacy. Alarmed by the potential growth of new social programs, Nixon's advisers searched for ways to rein in domestic spending and curb their long-run growth. The administration preferred means-tested transfer policies to broadly inclusive ones advocated by congressional Democrats, and if it could not eliminate service programs outright, it sought to convert categorical grants-in-aid to block grants, which was tantamount to putting a lid on spending. In this sense, Nixon acted in response to fiscal imperatives every bit as much as Roosevelt, Truman, and Johnson had, but was guided by a very different set of political calculations.

4. John Ehrlichman, *Witness to Power* (New York, 1982), pp. 214, 216. Dent had been an aide to Senator Strom Thurmond, and his appointment was taken as a sign of the administration's efforts to woo southern voters.

Together these imperatives, fiscal and political, led Nixon to a double-sided strategy for remaking the Great Society that embodied both expansion and contraction. Race and class were at the heart of the Republican agenda as they aimed to shift social policy toward middle-class white voters in a fiscally circumscribed welfare state. This was a bold undertaking that even in its failure had decisive consequences for the trajectory of federal social policy. Nixon further deepened the racial bifurcation of the welfare state while inviting its political exploitation.

Liberal Policies, Conservative Aims

Nixon first publicly set forth his agenda in August 1969. In a televised speech, he presented four specific proposals: an extraordinary plan to reform the welfare system; general revenue sharing for state and local governments; consolidation and decentralization of manpower programs; and reorganization of OEO. From these seeds sprouted a full-blown reform agenda a year-and-a-half later, which Nixon introduced as a plan "to reform the entire structure of American government so we can make it again fully responsive to the needs and the wishes of the American people."[5] To welfare reform and general revenue sharing, the administration added a federal health policy that would have reorganized the delivery of health care and increased access to health insurance and six special revenue sharing programs that converted categorical grants into block grants.

Nixon's gambit, his far-reaching and politically divisive plans to overhaul the Great Society, developed in two stages, reflecting a shift from more liberal policies (food stamps and the Family Asssistance Plan [FAP]) to more conservative policies (special revenue sharing). The first stage occurred during the initial eight months of the administration, when Nixon decided to propose FAP and when the trade-off between income-maintenance and Great Society services provided the solution to an impending budget crisis. The second stage, the development of special revenue sharing, began in late 1970 after a protracted battle with congressional Democrats over the budget. The transition from expansion to contraction was prompted by rising fears in the Nixon White House that George Wallace would run for president again (a possibility that changed their electoral calculations) and by a growing re-

5. *Public Papers of the Presidents of the United States: Richard M. Nixon, 1971* (Washington, D.C., 1972), p. 51.

alization they were confronted with an exploding budget that could not be contained in the usual way.

From the outset, Nixon's strategy was based on expanding means-tested transfers and slashing Great Society service programs. Federal transfers were the administration's lodestar. FAP, a scheme to replace AFDC with a national negative income tax, was the centerpiece of this effort. It would have doubled the number of families and individuals receiving a cash transfer by including the working poor; it would have established national eligibility and benefit standards; and it would have finished what Congress began, haltingly, with the 1967 amendments to the Social Security Act, namely, abolish the de jure distinction between employables and unemployables that had been established by Roosevelt's 1935 policy settlement. By adding work incentives to AFDC, Congress repealed the presumption of the original law that poor, single mothers should stay at home with their children. Under FAP, the attributes that made the poor either "employable" or "unemployable" would no longer matter; only family income would count.

The Family Assistance Plan foundered under attack from conservatives who thought the plan provided too much and from liberals who believed it provided too little. But this was not the only effort by the administration to shift federal social policy toward cash or in-kind transfers. After waffling in early 1969, Nixon proposed a $1 billion increase in funding for the food stamp program. Initially, he acted only after Senate Democrats successfully politicized the issue of "Hunger in America." News that Senator George McGovern was planning a large food stamp program with the support of southern senators prompted a Nixon aide to advise, "we must go on the offensive before we get bombed by these moves." Nixon wanted to counter with a limited "free food stamp program" and a big expansion of the surplus commodities program. When it became apparent that McGovern's Senate Select Committee on Hunger was preparing to embarrass the administration by revealing that Nixon refused to help starving children, Nixon approved changes in the food stamp program. Nixon had been trapped by the "politics of circumstances," as Nick Kotz described it.[6] But Nixon subsequently took the initiative and acted to increase food stamp allotments for individual families and to reduce purchase requirements. Combined with

6. Draft memorandum, April 14, 1969, Egil Krogh Papers, box 74, WHSF, NPMS, NA; Nick Kotz, *Let Them Eat Promises: The Politics of Hunger in America* (Englewood Cliffs, N.J., 1969), pp. 195–96, 211–14, 223.

passage of the food stamp amendments of 1971, these decisions resulted in a major expansion of the program and made it less a narrow policy to attack hunger than a broad cash equivalent for the poor.[7] When the 1973 amendments mandated food stamps in all counties, the program became a nationalized transfer system for the poor, realizing an objective sought by policy planners in the Johnson administration.[8]

Nixon did not stop with the negative income tax and food stamps. His administration proposed increasing housing assistance and even advocated changing the criteria for mortgage and rent subsidies in order to reach more of the poor. This caused one journalist to comment that the Republicans were now "on record in support of a comprehensive and expanded federal subsidy program of housing assistance for lower-middle and lower-income families."[9] Subsequent to the defeat of FAP, the administration continued to support replacing the adult public assistance programs with a nationally run cash transfer for poor elderly and disabled citizens, Supplemental Security Income (SSI). With respect to Social Security, Nixon disagreed with Congress only over how much benefits should be increased, not the desirability of the proposition. And it was Nixon, not the Democratic Congress, who first suggested indexing Social Security benefits to the rate of inflation. After FAP, the boldest transfer policy Nixon introduced was the 1971 health insurance scheme, which would have replaced Medicaid with a health insurance plan for the poor and created an employer mandate to cover catastrophic and preventative health care for blue-collar families. With these two plans, the administration assumed that health care coverage would be more or less universal.[10]

In contrast to Nixon's willingness to expand cash and in-kind transfers was his dislike of Great Society service programs and most categorical grants-

7. The 1971 amendments reduced the total amount of a family's personal contribution for food and thus left them with more money to spend on other goods. See Congressional Budget Office, *The Food Stamp Program: Income or Food Supplementation?* (Washington, D.C., 1977), pp. 8–9.

8. Johnson's advisers had thought of food stamps not as an emergency program but as an integral part of a *national* welfare system. "Federal food programs," a Budget Bureau staff paper argued, "should be regarded as 100 percent Federal grants to supplement local welfare systems and to correct local welfare disparities." See Zwick to Califano, November 8, 1968, p. 2, RG 51, ser. 61.1a, first grey box, T5–15, NA.

9. William Lilley III, "Best-Laid Plans Aren't Enough to Rebuild HUD Housing Program," *National Journal,* May 2, 1970, p. 924.

10. "Report of the Domestic Council Health Policy Review Group," December 21, 1970, p. 16, RG 51, ser. 69.1, box 114, R5–1, NA.

in-aid. "What we have to realize," he told a reporter, "is that many of the solutions of the '60s were massive failures. They threw money at the problems and for the most part they have failed and we are going to shuck off those programs and trim those programs that have proved simply to be failures."[11] The initial reason to squeeze services, however, was to free up money for transfers. Robert Finch, Nixon's Secretary of Health, Education, and Welfare (HEW), acknowledged as much in a March 12, 1970, memorandum to HEW staff. "While we were developing the (long-range) plan a strategy evolved for the administration's attack on the country's social problems. This strategy . . . stressed investment in income maintenance rather than services. . . . We realize that by adopting this strategy we would not be able to make additional high cost attacks on education and health problems."[12] In fact, the administration began trading services for transfers with the budget submitted to Congress in January 1970. The fiscal year 1971 budget proposed increasing domestic spending by $14.4 billion, most of which was for Social Security and Medicare. Of the $4.6 billion left over, almost three-quarters was allocated to social welfare, and most of this amount went into transfers, leaving room for only modest increases in services. The money reserved for services was allocated to manpower and education programs that presumably served the poor, such as Title I of ESEA. Other Great Society programs were held down, and overall, a study by the Brookings Institution concluded, the administration had made a decision "against additional large sums for the major education and health programs."[13]

All of the core Great Society service programs were sharply cut by 1974, and some were phased out with the passage of the special revenue sharing block-grant programs. The Model Cities Program, for example, rapidly disappeared once it was folded into the Community Development Block Grant Program (CDBG). These developments coincided with the dismantling of the original poverty program and the dispersal of its functions to other federal agencies. The attack on OEO was one of the administration's first priorities. Nixon told Republican congressional leaders in a March 1969 meeting that "OEO has the worst collection of creeps we can find in any government agency."[14] The administration initially attempted to spin off

11. *National Journal*, December 16, 1972, p. 1913.

12. *National Journal*, September 5, 1970, p. 1906.

13. Charles Schultze et al., *Setting National Priorities: The 1971 Budget* (Washington, D.C., 1970), p. 16.

14. Meeting with Republican Leadership, March 6, 26, 1969, pt. 2, 69–3-2, 69–3-25, *Papers of the Nixon White House*, ed. Joan Hoff-Wilson (Washington, D.C., 1987).

Table 14. Discretionary spending and transfers in the Johnson and Nixon administrations: average annual change in budget authority

	President's budget requests		Congressional action, 1969–1974	
	Johnson's budgets	Nixon's budgets	Change in Nixon's budget requests	Congressional appropriation
Great Society	40.3%	7.5%	24.3%	13.1%
Antipoverty	46.7	7.3	15.0	15.3
Education	50.0	8.5	39.4	11.5
Social services	84.0	−4.7	9.1	5.6
Work training	71.5	12.0	24.7	23.1
Health services	28.1	10.0	7.3	12.0
Other domestic	4.1	8.1	20.1	28.2
Transfers	13.3	21.9		
Means-tested cash	14.8	18.0		
Food	22.4	49.5		
Housing	11.6	33.3		

Source: *Budget of the United States Government* (Washington, D.C., selected fiscal years).

OEO programs into cabinet departments, and then resorted to severe budget cuts to eliminate local community action agencies. Frank Carlucci, Nixon's OEO Director in 1971, bragged, "we're starting to cut the strings between the federal government and local community action agencies." The fiscal year 1972 budget proposed significant cuts in OEO, folding Community Action into one of the special revenue sharing programs. The scope of the proposals surprised Carlucci, who complained to his superiors in the White House, "FY 1972 has been advertised as a *transition* period for CAAs to revenue sharing, not a *phase-down*." The assault on OEO culminated with a decision in 1973 to zero it out; but by this time the agency's strings had already been cut.[15]

Republican distaste for service programs and preference for transfers is evident in their budgetary choices. Under Nixon, budget authority for Great Society discretionary spending increased by an average of about 7.5 percent, compared to the 43 percent annual jump during the Johnson years (see table 14). There were sizable increases in Nixon's budgetary requests for some Great Society programs but these were largely expedient, intended to mollify opponents of revenue sharing in fiscal year 1972 and to buy congressional solicitude in fiscal year 1975 when Nixon was on the ropes over Watergate.

15. Carlucci to Weinberger, March, 15, 1971, RG 51, ser. 69.1, box 104, R1–2, NA; John Iglehart, "Conflict over Future Role for OEO Leaves Agency without Clear-Cut Mission," *National Journal*, September 11, 1971, p. 1869.

These aggregate figures conceal the way in which the Nixon administration was reconfiguring Great Society service programs. Overall, Nixon's budget requests cut discretionary poverty services (Model Cities, OEO, and other agencies) by an average of 7.5 percent, with large cuts in fiscal years 1972 and 1974. Education and work-training programs fared somewhat better, as Nixon requested, on average, 10 to 11 percent increases in funding. Budget authority for transfers grew much faster on Nixon's watch, rising at an average annual rate of 22 percent compared to 13 percent under LBJ. Not surprisingly, the biggest increases over Democratic budgets were for food stamps and housing subsidies, though Johnson bears responsibility for a share of the housing outlays. The rapid rise in housing subsidies during Nixon's first four budgets stemmed from the 1968 Housing Act. But Nixon did nothing to reverse the trend, and if anything, George Romney accelerated the expansion of housing aid.[16]

The Republican social policies of the early 1970s satisfied many liberal aims. FAP, for example, would have established national eligibility and benefit standards for public assistance and extended coverage to all two-parent families, goals of social welfare liberals since the 1940s. Nixon intentionally appropriated liberal rhetoric, yet his social policies were not merely a Republican version of Great Society liberalism, even though they often seemed so to some of his more conservative economic advisers—Arthur Burns, aghast at Nixon's decision to go ahead with FAP, thought it breached the Republican party's tradition of fiscal conservatism. In important respects, however, Nixon and his aides repudiated what they understood to be the core of the Great Society.

Republicans justified their policies as enhancing individual freedom, restoring local democracy, and imposing administrative rationality. Freedom had two faces for Republican reformers. One was revenue sharing, the freedom for local governments to decide how to allocate federal resources. In his 1971 State of the Union address, Nixon framed his reforms as a revolt against federal power: "The idea that a bureaucratic elite in Washington knows best, what is best for people everywhere and that you cannot trust

---

16. Comparing budget authority for transfers is perilous, because such budget requests are normally estimates of anticipated spending rather than a request to appropriations committees. Since the federal government agrees to pay a portion of public assistance costs, outlays depend on state and local decisions about eligibility and benefits. Nevertheless, presidents and Congress can take steps to hold down public assistance spending. Moreover, when an administration decides to alter the scope of a program, as in the case of food stamps, requests for budget authority represent meaningful choices.

local governments is really a contention that you cannot trust people to govern themselves. This notion is completely foreign to the American experience."[17]

The other face of freedom was social welfare transfers. In a wholly novel interpretation, the administration depicted transfers as complementing revenue sharing and block grants by shifting "control" away from social workers and other bureaucrats to individuals. Transfers were a further blow against governmental encroachment, as Nixon told a White House Conference on Food, Nutrition, and Health:

> Our basic policies for improvement of the living conditions of the poor are based on this proposition: that the best judge of each family's priorities is that family itself, that the best way to ameliorate the hardships of poverty is to provide the family with additional income—to be spent as that family sees fit. . . . The task of government is not to make decisions for you or anyone. . . . Our job is to get resources to people in need and then to let them run their own lives.

The bedrock of the administration's approach was a transfer system that would replace food stamps, Medicaid, and housing subsidies with dollar bills.[18]

Nixon's hostility to bureaucrats made him receptive to market solutions such as negative income taxes, and he regarded FAP as a way to remove meddlesome social workers and downsize public bureaucracies. Daniel Patrick Moynihan's retrospective account of the fate of the Family Assistance Plan put the administration on the side of the angels: against bureaucratic inefficiencies and redistribution to the middle class, failings that were the inevitable result of Johnson's service strategy. Rather than "tax factory workers to pay school teachers" as Johnson presumably did, Nixon would embrace the radical idea of direct income redistribution. Both Nixon and Moynihan saw the social welfare bureaucracy as dominated by Great Society liberals, a source of never-ending pressure to expand social programs.[19] This perspective had racial implications since the agencies under attack were those manned by

---

17. *Public Papers of the Presidents: Richard M. Nixon, 1971*, p. 55.

18. *Public Papers of the Presidents: Richard M. Nixon, 1969* (Washington, D.C., 1970), pp. 981–82; Herbert Stein, *Presidential Economics: The Making of Economic Policy from Roosevelt to Reagan and Beyond* (New York, 1984), p. 144.

19. Daniel P. Moynihan, *The Politics of a Guaranteed Income* (New York, 1973), p. 55; Nicholas Lemann, *The Promised Land: The Great Black Migration and How It Changed America* (New York, 1992), pp. 211–12.

middle-class African Americans that served ghetto communities. In the process of emasculating the War on Poverty and the Great Society's service strategy, however, a completely liberal idea that most Americans had been hostile to since the 1930s—a guaranteed income and nationalization of cash transfers—was linked with conservative notions of free markets and efficiency. The idea of equality of opportunity, more consonant with the beliefs of average citizens, was depicted as big government.

Although the "new federalism" was couched in the language of decentralization and opposition to bureaucratic paternalism, its actual effects went far beyond these stated goals. Block grants had less to do with freedom than limiting future spending. Special revenue sharing would have distributed federal aid to state and local governments for general purposes, such as community development or employment training, and allowed local officials wide discretion on how the money was spent. It would also, however, have changed the rules of distributive politics in Congress from a process in which constituencies and congressional committees establish funding levels and make programmatic changes to one in which politicians merely debate alternative funding formulas, rather than decide on the goals and aims of federal policies. By folding categorical programs into a block grant and allocating the money by formula to states and cities, special revenue sharing reduces the role played by local program constituencies at the national level and minimizes political pressure to increase spending. In this scenario, these constituencies must compete with each other for funds at the state and local level in a zero-sum game.

The Republicans preferred policies that reduced the federal government's responsibility for delivery of services, giving it mostly funding obligations. They also preferred policies that diminished congressional discretion. The object here was not so much to circumvent Congress, though the administration proved adept at that, as it was to change the way in which federal social policy was made. Besides revenue sharing, indexing of social security payments is an example. Automatic adjustment of OASI payments would forestall congressional temptation to raise benefits every election cycle. "These automatic adjustments," Nixon told Congress, "are interrelated and . . . taken together they will *depoliticize,* to a certain extent, the Social Security system and give a greater stability to what has become a cornerstone of our society's social insurance system."[20] What Nixon and his advisers

20. *Public Papers of the Presidents: Richard M. Nixon, 1969,* p. 742 (emphasis added).

preferred was a welfare state governed by impersonal formulas rather than public debate or congressional deliberation.

The Logic of Ballots: Race, Class, and the New Republican Coalition

It is not immediately obvious why Nixon expanded transfers. Although the administration initially had accepted food stamps in order to outmaneuver the Democrats, the logic of party competition did not lead inevitably to adoption of an income maintenance policy. Competing with the Democrats was problematic, as Nixon learned quickly with food stamps. The Democrats always outspent the Republicans on food stamps, and the administration always settled for better benefits and higher levels of spending than they wanted. Rather than competing with the Democrats to see who could best assist the poor, the Republicans devised policies that included Republican constituencies, looked for ways to appeal to other groups historically hostile to the Republican party, and tried to contain the growth of the welfare state. This thread links three otherwise dissimilar policies: FAP, health insurance, and revenue sharing. Each of these policies was undertaken to remedy identifiable problems, such as the supposedly perverse incentives of AFDC and an impending fiscal crunch facing state governments. At the same time, each would have altered the boundaries of social policy by adding new beneficiaries to the welfare state. FAP brought the working poor into the welfare state, effectively doubling the AFDC caseload; the health insurance scheme added workers excluded from either Medicaid or employer-provided insurance; and revenue sharing, in both its general and special incarnations, made local governments hitherto outside the ambit of federal grants-in-aid beneficiaries.

All three policies were predicated on reversing what Nixon and his aides regarded as the explicit racial targeting of social policy by Democrats, which they assumed was a key source of social and political instability. The issue of race was a consuming preoccupation for both Moynihan and Nixon. Moynihan's typically apocalyptic memoranda to Nixon set the tone for the administration's deliberations, at one point blaming poor African Americans for the collapse of New York City's social fabric. "A large segment of the [Black and Puerto Rican] population is becoming incompetent and destructive," Moynihan told Nixon. "Growing parasitism, both legal and illegal, is the result; so also is violence."[21] Moynihan believed the existence of a large

21. Moynihan to President Elect, January 9, 1969, p. 3, RG 51, ser. 69.1, box 122, R4–3, NA.

lower-class population, which was no different from earlier lower-class residents of big-city slums except for the color of their skin, had undermined the civil rights revolution. Middle-class blacks and black militants used the persistence of black poverty as "proof that the national commitment is flawed, if not indeed fraudulent, that the society is irredeemably 'racist.'" In venting their own hostility toward white America, they provoked a massive counter-reaction.[22]

Early discussions of the Model Cities program are an important indication of the administration's thinking about race and social policy. Model Cities was considered nothing more than a transfer to disadvantaged black neighborhoods that had rioted. An investigative committee reported to the White House Council on Urban Affairs that almost three-quarters of the residents of Model Neighborhoods were African American and recommended rescinding regulations that restricted the program to geographical areas containing no more than 10 percent of a city's population. This change would permit cities to spread Model Cities resources throughout their jurisdiction. This was necessary, the committee reasoned, in order to move "away from policies which have the effect of polarizing a community and toward policies that even-handedly meet the problems of all disadvantaged persons, white and black."[23]

The attraction of alienated white Democratic constituencies who were potential Republican voters and the reversal of racial targeting were crucial to the political logic of health insurance, general revenue sharing, and FAP. The main beneficiaries of all three programs were white and middle-class constituencies. Nixon's health plan was aimed at blue collar workers and lower-middle-class families excluded from medicaid and employer-provided health plans; revenue sharing was pointed at suburban (mostly white) cities; and FAP, the administration calculated, would have mainly benefited poor people, both whites and blacks, in the South. One should avoid oversimplifying the administration's reasons for adopting these policies, but in each case the distributive and constituent implications were important.

The health plan grew out of a report prepared for George Schultz, then Secretary of Labor, by Jerome Rosow, who transformed a modest proposal to scrap Medicaid for a health plan attached to FAP into a complicated health policy for blue-collar workers without insurance. Rosow's report depicted

22. Moynihan to President Elect, January 3, 1969, p. 5, RG 51, ser. 69.1, box 122, R4–3, NA.

23. Report of the Committee on Model Cities of the Council for Urban Affairs, April 7, 1969, pp. 1–2, 6–7, pt. 2, 69–4-6, A03, *Nixon Papers*, ed. Hoff-Wilson.

America's blue collar workers as forgotten citizens, children of immigrants trapped in low-status jobs, who "are most exposed to the poor and the welfare recipients. . . . Yet they are excluded from social programs targeted at the disadvantaged. . . . As taxpayers, they support these programs with no visible relief—no visible share." These workers faced an economic and social squeeze: they were encumbered with "heavy family responsibilities" but found themselves in jobs with little upward mobility and received paychecks steadily eroded by inflation.[24]

Rosow failed to provide a specific agenda, but his report galvanized Nixon, who ordered every member of the Domestic Council to read it. After a wide-ranging discussion of domestic policy, Nixon instructed aides to "proceed with some initial implementation of the Rosow blue collar report even if it is only symbolic," and to investigate the possibility that voluntary health insurance could be offered to blue-collar workers.[25] The plan Nixon eventually decided upon was estimated to extend health insurance to an additional 150 million persons (part-time, seasonal, and self-employed workers, such as domestics, were excluded). Even though the scheme sharply segregated the poor and unemployed from other beneficiaries, it would have drawn many (white) blue-collar workers into the safety net.[26]

General revenue sharing, the leading edge of Nixon's new federalism, would have drawn many new cities into the federal money machine. Congressional Republicans were first attracted to the idea of sharing federal revenues with local governments as a weapon in their campaign to derail the Great Society. By the time Nixon took office, revenue sharing, like welfare reform, became an issue partly because of a perceived fiscal crisis among state and local governments. But general revenue sharing had little to do with a fiscal crisis in the cities; it was really about distributive politics. Nixon's 1969 plan made all general-purpose local governments, some thirty-eight thousand eligible for federal revenue sharing. Most other plans then under consideration limited aid to cities with populations of fifty thousand or more. The revenue sharing formula was fashioned to reward identifiable Republican constituencies, especially northeastern and midwestern suburban towns,

24. Jerome Rosow to Secretary of Labor, April 16, 1970, p. 7, pt. 2, 70–8-16, A03, *Nixon Papers,* ed. Hoff-Wilson.

25. John R. Brown III to Shultz, September 26, 1970, RG 51, ser. 69.1, box 130, folder T2–6, NA; handwritten notes of Domestic Council Meeting, August 27, 1970, Edwin T. Harper Papers, WHSF, box 9, folder "Meetings of Domestic Council," NPMS.

26. Charles Schultze et al., *Setting National Priorities: The 1972 Budget* (Washington, D.C., 1971), pp. 228, 231–32.

many of them irritated by increased welfare spending. Nixon's gift to local governments would have provided about half as much aid to big cities as the alternatives. Congress, not surprisingly, amended the formula to funnel more aid to Democratic constituencies without fundamentally altering the distributive thrust of the legislation.[27]

FAP is a more complicated case than either health insurance or revenue sharing, yet it too was attractive partly because of its political potential. Welfare reform was on the agenda when Nixon took office, mostly because governors and mayors were complaining about the cost of rising caseloads. John Lindsay, Mayor of New York, told Nixon: "The reason [welfare] is a hot political issue is that it has such terrific impact, not in the South but in the North. The message about the inequities of the burden is beginning to get through to the northern middle class taxpayer."[28] The administration was initially inclined to make some modest changes in public assistance rather than scrap AFDC for a cash transfer for both working and nonworking poor family heads. Nixon made the question of a guaranteed annual income central to the administration's discussion of welfare reform when he decided to make the working poor part of any scheme.

Nixon's decision to add the working poor was rarely challenged by the foes of a guaranteed annual income within the administration; in fact, it was accepted by some. Robert Mayo, Nixon's first budget director and, along with Arthur Burns, a major opponent of FAP, had a deep aversion to the idea of a guaranteed income for poor families and to increasing the number of families on the rolls, but he was genuinely concerned with the plight of the working poor. Mayo was unable to find a way to craft a policy that improved upon AFDC and that also included the working poor. Arguments against FAP usually attacked issues of cost or were based on an ideological aversion to extended income maintenance of any kind. Most of Nixon's cabinet were bothered by the sheer increase in the number of beneficiaries. Vice President Agnew spoke for many when he asked Nixon during the Cabinet debate, "isn't it possible to fix the deficiencies of the present system—with regard to work incentives and day care—without adding . . . 13 million people to the rolls?"[29]

27. Samuel Beer, "The Adoption of General Revenue Sharing: A Case Study in Public Sector Politics," *Public Policy* 24 (1976): 142, 148; David R. Tarr and Harley H. Hinrichs, "Nixon Revenue Sharing Plan Faces Major Obstacles in Congress," *National Journal*, December 20, 1969, p. 408.

28. Minutes, Council for Urban Affairs, Meeting of May 26, 1969, p. 3, pt. 2, 69-5-25(1), A03, *Nixon Papers*, ed. Hoff-Wilson.

29. Memorandum from Jim Keogh, Cabinet Meeting, August 12, 1969, p. 5, pt. 2, 69-8-3, A03, *Nixon Papers*, ed. Hoff-Wilson.

Agnew had a point. Why did Nixon agree to bring the working poor under a national income maintenance scheme? FAP was intended by its authors to remove inequities between male- and female-headed families and diminish the incentives to break up families. There were certainly less expensive ways to do this, such as making two-parent families eligible for AFDC by requiring all states to adopt AFDC-UP. Most explanations of Nixon's decision focus on his desire to scoop the Democrats with a significant issue or on the belief among many within the administration that FAP was a solution to a growing "welfare crisis." But neither of these explanations are satisfactory. The Democrats could have been scooped with less expensive alternatives, which was precisely the point that Arthur Burns kept making in the internal debate. Nor was it clear how FAP would resolve the welfare crisis, partly because there was no agreement either about what caused the crisis or what FAP would do. Nixon certainly believed that FAP would eliminate social workers, and this was undoubtedly one of his reasons for agreeing to add 10 million new persons to the rolls. Yet one participant has commented that the final bill "did not properly reflect the president's aversion to social workers, and his desire that the bill put income and therefore greater independence in the hands of poor people themselves."[30] Nixon's own statements reveal dissatisfaction with AFDC but little else. He answered Agnew's question by telling the Cabinet, "the welfare road we have been on is the wrong road. It is a total disaster. I don't want to patch it up; we must move in a new direction."[31]

What does seem clear is that most members of Nixon's inner circle, including Moynihan, assumed that FAP was a way to overcome racial hostilities. Moynihan actually had little to propose in the way of concrete solutions to the problem of black poverty. He told Nixon that the "Negro lower class must be dissolved," by which he meant transformed into a stable working class population of "truck drivers, mail carriers, assembly line workers," but how that was to come about was left unstated.[32] What Moynihan did do was convince Nixon and his aides that welfare reform was the proper instrument to restore social stability and end racial turmoil. The way to do this was to bring poor whites under a national guaranteed annual income. Just as the Model Cities regulations were changed to make white neighborhoods eligible for federal aid, inclusion of the working poor in FAP was

30. Vincent J. and Vee Burke, *Nixon's Good Deed: Welfare Reform* (New York, 1974), p. 89.
31. Quoted in ibid., p. 8.
32. Moynihan to President Elect, January 3, 1969, pp. 8–9.

explicitly predicated on adding a group that was largely white (about 70 percent of the working poor were white) to a program in which the caseload was (mistakenly) thought to be increasingly African American or Puerto Rican. "Discrimination against the working poor is a critical source of racial divisiveness," Robert Finch informed Nixon. "[FAP] eliminates that and gives poor whites help under a system in which poor blacks are now close to a majority."[33]

One of the most explicit statements of the administration's desire to use FAP to mitigate racial antagonisms can be found in a draft message on welfare reform presented to the Council on Urban Affairs. In describing the onset of a "cycle of welfare dependency," the draft message characterized AFDC recipients as "the elite of the poor" because they were among the 40 percent of poor who actually received a cash transfer. The significance of this fact was boldly stated: "The way the welfare system has developed, with ever greater economic cleavage between welfare recipients and the working poor, is leading the country toward greater racial division." The advantage of FAP, the message went on to argue, was not only that it would raise the living standards of many poor families or remove incentives to break up a family, but it would transcend the racial bifurcation of AFDC and "reduce the mounting and unfortunate racial tensions which an increasingly Black welfare caseload has been fostering." The political consequences of the divergence between AFDC recipients and nonrecipients was one of the main reasons Mayo believed the administration had to find a way to include the working poor.[34]

Willard Townsend's fears of what would happen if white workers believed they had to support blacks on relief had now penetrated the White House. "The bitterness of the urban white worker," Arthur Burns wrote Nixon, "who feels he is supporting Negroes on relief as a result of the machinations

33. Finch to President, April 30, 1969, John Ehrlichman Papers, WHSF, box 40, folder "Welfare Proposals and Commentary," NPMS, NA; Theodore R. Marmor and Martin Rein, "Reforming 'The Welfare Mess': The Fate of the Family Assistance Plan, 1969–1972," in *Policy and Politics in America*, ed. Allan P. Sindler (Boston, Mass., 1973), pp. 12–13. Marmor and Rein say that changing the racial composition of AFDC was one of key aims of Worth Bateman, a federal bureaucrat who designed the plan.

34. Meeting of the Council for Urban Affairs, April 21, 1969, Presidential Message to the Congress on Welfare, Draft No. 3, April 18, 1969, pp. 4–5, 10, pt. 2, 69–4-20, *Nixon Papers*, ed., Hoff-Wilson; Mayo to President, May 7, 1969, RG 51, ser. 69.1, box 21, folder R3–4, NA. The message was probably written by Moynihan though that is not clear. But this was not only Moynihan's view; many people accepted this rationale for including the working poor.

of vote-hungry politicians, is a social and political fact of first-rate importance."[35] But changing the racial composition of AFDC in the interests of political stability dovetailed with another reason to adopt FAP: the obvious political advantages, perceived by some of Nixon's advisers, to adding 13 million mostly white poor people to the rolls. Finch argued the best thing the administration could do to assuage the anger of the "forgotten man," by which he meant the white working poor, was FAP: "We could really do something for these people . . . and it should have a tremendous beneficial political impact to the administration." Nixon himself subscribed to this view, telling Bob Haldeman and John Ehrlichman, "it is the weakness of virtually all our programs that we keep talking to minorities (urged on by the Establishment) and overlook our greatest potential," by whom he meant white skilled and unskilled workers.[36] Burns and others scoffed at this and remained unconvinced that the plan was good politics and fiscally responsible. Burns in particular doubted whether it would minimize racial tensions, assuming that FAP would inflame rather than mitigate the anger of the northern white working class.

The political advantages of health care and revenue sharing for the Republicans were readily apparent; in the case of FAP they were more ambiguous. There were many reasons to support the policy: it would have removed inequities in the distribution of cash; it might have tended to minimize incentives to form single-parent households; and it would have raised the living standards of many people. In one sense, FAP was indebted to the logic of expansion. Indeed, there is some evidence for the proposition that Nixon was not averse to using FAP, like other social policies, to build an electoral coalition.[37] Yet, unlike the other policies, FAP contained obvious political liabilities which go far toward explaining its demise.

Burns's surmise that FAP would not sit well with Republican-leaning white workers and would be politically counterproductive was confirmed when one of Nixon's political operatives reported strong opposition among rank-and-file union members. FAP's implications for the "southern strategy" were also problematic. Had FAP passed, it would likely have turned the South

35. Burns to President, May 26, 1969, Ehrlichman Papers, WHSF, box 39, folder "Welfare Book."

36. "Comments on Dr. Burns' Memorandum of July 12," July 14, 1969, Ehrlichman Papers, WHSF, box 38, folder "FSS 1969"; Nixon is quoted in Stephen E. Ambrose, *Nixon: The Triumph of a Politician, 1962–1972* (New York, 1989), p. 293.

37. Jill Quadagno reaches a similar conclusion (see *The Color of Welfare* [New York, 1994], p. 123).

topsy-turvy. FAP was tailored for northern constituencies, but it would have had its largest monetary effects in the South. In the North, it benefited primarily the working poor, but in the South, it benefited *all* the poor. In some southern counties upwards of 50 percent of the residents would have been eligible. This was not a policy calculated to woo southern, white, middle-class voters.[38] It could also be expected to arouse the antipathy of northern liberals. The most conspicuous losers in the FAP sweepstakes were northern welfare mothers, the constituents of the National Welfare Rights Organization. They received no increase in benefits and would have been subject to ever more restrictive work policies.

Nixon eventually backed away from the plan. By the spring of 1970, he had reason to worry about his appeal to angry southern Democrats and white, blue-collar workers because George Wallace was gearing up for another run at the presidency. The specter of another Wallace candidacy and FAP's cost weakened Nixon's resolve. Nixon recognized he would get into a bidding war with Democrats over FAP just as he had with food stamps. The Republicans were also appalled by the prospective costs of a work requirement, without which the bill would not pass. Too many people were being classified as "employable" by Congress, they had concluded, and this "will create a powerful force for massive public sector jobs." This was the last thing the administration wanted.[39]

With the exception of general revenue sharing, Nixon's efforts to use transfer policies to attach disgruntled Democrats to a new Republican majority failed in Congress or were stillborn. Yet by 1970 the administration had already begun to shift course. Pouring over polling data that revealed that for the first time people outside the South hated big government, Nixon mused to his staff: "When they think about big government they are talking about big government in Washington. People do not like Feds from Washington pushing them around—*they are not of us.*"[40] Nixon had initially sought to exploit racial divisions that were tearing at the New Deal coalition by appealing to those whites he believed were left out of the Great

38. Ibid., pp. 128–31; Richard Armstrong, "The Looming Money Revolution down South," *Fortune*, June 1970, pp. 66ff.

39. Handwritten notes on a meeting of the Welfare Reform Group, March 2, 1971, Harper Papers, box 67, folder "Welfare Reform," WHSF, NPMS; Dan T. Carter, *The Politics of Rage: George Wallace, the Origins of the New Conservatism, and the Transformation of American Politics* (New York, 1995), pp. 374, 398–99.

40. Handwritten notes on Domestic Council Meeting, August 27, 1970, p. 2 (emphasis in original).

Society. This put Nixon in the position of supporting liberal policies. Exploiting the increasing antipathy to "big government" was not only more consonant with the administration's fiscal priorities; it would also prove to be politically powerful when the notion of big government was linked to the suggestions that racially targeted programs for the poor were unfair and wasteful and that black demands were unreasonable. When tied to race, fiscal conservatism could be used to turn white Democrats against the New Deal.

Asymmetrical Budgets and Uncontrollable Social Policies

The liberal face of the Nixon administration coexisted with a more conservative core devoted to contraction. Despite the administration's apparent willingness to spend, the Republicans pursued a consistent policy of budget restraint throughout the first four years. Only in the fiscal year 1972 budget did the administration propose stimulative spending policies.[41] Nixon framed his policies in light of three factors: a deteriorating economy (rising inflation and the erosion of the U.S. position in the international economic order) a budget subject to the proliferating demands of the newly organized constituents of an expanding welfare state, and his own commitment to defense spending.

Republicans were always guided by conservative preferences for means-tests and work incentives, not an expansive vision of the welfare state. Their social policies were designed with rigid boundaries in mind: public social policies were targeted narrowly on poor or very poor people; middle-class social policies were typically privatized, as exemplified by health insurance which divided the poor and the nonpoor, while imposing discrepant burdens and benefits on each. Nor did the administration ever pass up an opportunity to target spending. For example, Nixon boldly introduced a bill that would have increased housing subsidies by $100 million annually while consolidating some fifty categorical programs, in effect, eliminating them. This bill actually increased subsidies by targeting more of the money on the poor families, which meant that for the first time many of them became eligible for home ownership subsidies. Since housing assistance to moderate-income

41. M. Mark Amen, "Macroeconomic Policy under Nixon," in *Richard M. Nixon: Politician, President, Administrator,* ed. Leon Friedman and William F. Levantrosser (Greenwood, Conn., 1991), pp. 210–13.

families was reduced, the deeper subsidy for poor households did not increase budgetary totals.[42]

Nixon's preference for narrowly targeted social policies conflicted with the ambitions of Senate liberals to create income transfers and policies that straddled social classes. Eliot Richardson, by then Secretary of HEW, complained, "our liberal opponents . . . are advocating alternatives that could only have the effect of diluting scarce resources."[43] Senate liberals, acting more like social democrats than they ever did under Lyndon Johnson, resented targeting. They responded to FAP by introducing a family allowance. "In all candor," stated John Brademas, majority whip in the House of Representatives, "I resent being told I have to trade off middle-income bodies against low-income bodies. What I don't understand is why we can't help both."[44] Generosity was scarcely the only motivation. Confronting a conservative Republican president rather than an ambitious liberal one, Senate Democrats included more working-class and middle-class families as beneficiaries so as to inoculate social programs against budget-cutting opponents.

At stake in the battles between Nixon and the Democratic congress were issues of cost and program expansion. In rejecting national health insurance, for example, the administration proposed an alternative plan that combined publicly subsidized health insurance with reorganization of the delivery system in order to control the proliferating demands of newly organized constituents and potentially large increases in federal outlays.[45] The main effort to contain spending, however, concentrated on federal domestic discretionary spending (though the administration under congressional prodding also cut defense spending substantially in its first two budgets). The decision to cut service programs and consolidate categorical grants—to trade services for transfers—initially arose as a response to short-run budget constraints on the administration's ability to put its own stamp on federal policy. Moynihan identified categorical grants as the chief budgetary threat to Nixon's

42. Mayo to Ehrlichman, March 17, 1970, RG 51, ser. 69.1, box 110, folder R4–1/1, NA.

43. John K. Inglehart, "Budget Report/HEW Dept.: Largest Federal Spender Seeks to Funnel More Money to the Poor," *National Journal*, January 29, 1972, p. 169.

44. Ibid., p. 170.

45. Report of the Domestic Council Health Policy Review Group, December 21, 1970, p. 16, RG 51, ser. 69.1, box 114, folder R5–1, NA. This strategy was also true for FAP. Even though FAP would have increased spending on cash transfers for the poor and near poor, it would also have limited *future* benefit increases by states through elimination of automatic federal reimbursement of state expenditures. In other words, FAP contained both a minimum benefit and a ceiling on federal outlays to states.

ambitions, warning that the budget had to be protected from congressional inclinations to increase Great Society programs across the board each year: "If your extra money goes down the drain, I fear in four years' time you really won't have a single distinctive Nixon program to show for it all." Moynihan's worry was echoed by Robert Mayo, who wrote Finch, "we must start now to redirect the Government's activities along the lines of our own objectives, reducing and removing programs where we can."[46]

By the summer of 1970, Nixon's advisers believed they faced "an intolerable FY 1972 deficit" and a federal budget that was careening out of control. Ehrlichman was informed that an Office of Management and Budget (OMB) estimate of agency budgets "far exceeds the resources we expect to have available under present tax laws for FY 72." The CEA believed that the budget process had become "asymmetrical"; that is, "it permitted deficits when the economy was below full employment but did not require surpluses when the economy was in an inflationary state."[47] Asymmetry in the budget process aroused concern within the administration because it meant the public sector was growing at the expense of the private sector. The budget crisis provoked a wide-ranging discussion within the White House about the size of government and what to do about it. Nixon made the matter clear, telling his assembled staff and cabinet members:

> We need to take a hard look at percent of government expenditures as a total of GNP. We are in real trouble when people are working more for the government than for themselves. We ought to think explicitly how high a percent of GNP ought to go through government and what the implications of that are. This relates directly to the question of how high taxes ought to go.[48]

To put Republican vexations over the size of the federal government into perspective, we should compare them to Roosevelt and Johnson. Both of these presidents confronted the dilemma of building a welfare state while sustaining economic growth. This meant they crafted their policies with one eye on the confidence of investors. FDR did this by emphasizing that deficits were temporary and minimizing taxes, which led to a temporary and lim-

46. Mayo to Finch, January 23, 1969, RG 51, ser. 69.1, box 20, folder R1–1, NA. Similar letters were sent to other cabinet secretaries.

47. Herbert Stein, *Presidential Economics* (New York, 1984), p. 170; Edwin Harper to Flanigan, June 2, 1970, Harper to Ehrlichman, July 7, 1970, Harper Papers, box 12, folder "Budget FY 1971," WHSF, NPMS.

48. Handwritten notes on Domestic Council Meeting, August 27, 1970.

ited work relief policy, decentralization of public assistance, and a preference for contributory social insurance. Johnson solved the dilemma by redistributing federal resources. The loss of business confidence is a short-run
phenomenon, however, and both Democratic presidents expected that their
policies would be sustained by their successors and thankful constituents.
Both men negotiated the dilemma between capital accumulation and social
rights by choosing policies that minimized the immediate conflict but permitted some future growth. For Republicans the issue was how to put the
genie back in the bottle. It was not a question of dismantling the welfare
state so much as reining it in.

Nixon's initial efforts to cut domestic spending and change congressional
priorities ended in a bitter stalemate. Congressional opposition precluded
a straightforward trade-off between transfers and services, and by mid-
1970, with their general revenue sharing bill buried in committee and while
facing what they regarded as a fiscal crisis, the administration began planning to introduce a much more comprehensive revenue sharing program.
What Nixon's planners had in mind was canceling domestic programs in exchange for general revenue sharing. The Revenue Sharing Working Group,
set up to plan the effort in the fall of 1970, stated the goal as "termination
of categorical grant programs to cut [the] size and spending of the Federal
Government."[49] They produced a long memorandum which identified $15
billion in domestic programs that might be folded into revenue sharing or,
more accurately, phased out, of which $4 billion or about 26 percent, was
concentrated in social welfare programs. The prime candidates slated to
disappear were the usual Great Society suspects: social services, OEO, manpower training, and vocational rehabilitation.

The idea of a grand trade-off of categorical grants for revenue sharing
was stillborn. Ehrlichman told Nixon that "virtually all think the dramatic
deep cuts and the shift to Revenue Sharing (without any strings) are too
much." What Nixon's advisers advocated instead was a more moderate approach, namely, shifting from categorical grants to block grants, or special
revenue sharing, because they anticipated political opposition. Raymond
Price told Nixon, in one of the many memoranda the president received on
the subject, that the change would be too abrupt and politically disruptive.
Kenneth Cole (as well as Price and others) made the case that special revenue sharing was only a way station, arguing that by moving categorical

49. Domestic Council, chart no. 7, 1971, n.d., John Ehrlichman Papers, pt. **4, no. 19,**
pp. 36–43, *Nixon Papers,* ed. Hoff-Wilson.

grants into block grants with few strings, they could eliminate many federal employees while avoiding political problems. It was Cole who suggested combining block grants with income maintenance. "Trying to reverse the trend of 30 years of government in six months will be next to impossible to sell to the people," he told Nixon; block grants would provide an "orderly transition" to the future.[50]

Special revenue sharing was adopted for political reasons with a clearly defined economic goal: to reduce federal spending and curtail the long-run growth of the public sector. Unlike the administration's general revenue sharing proposal, which would have stimulated state and local spending, special revenue sharing was intended to facilitate the substitution of federal for state and local revenues. The evidence on this point is clear. The initial formula for special revenue sharing would have required "maintenance of effort" and stimulated state and local taxation. This "would have the effect," the Revenue Sharing Working Group noted, "of making a national determination that the public sector is too small—a policy that may be inconsistent with the Administration's objectives."[51] While some of Nixon's advisers thought "maintenance of effort" provisions were necessary, they were widely regarded as contrary to the administration's policies. George Schulz, by then Nixon's Director of OMB, believed that a maintenance of effort clause was "contrary to the approach and theory of special revenue sharing."[52] He pointed out to Nixon that, "so long as there is no maintenance of effort provision included in the block grant, that grant has the identical impact of revenue sharing," that is, it facilitates substitution. Another key adviser, Peter Flanigan, argued that if bloc grants were designed to "free up equivalent amounts of State or local funds . . . a very impressive amount of money could be disbursed in this manner without increasing federal expenditures." And finally, Ehrlichman was forced to admit in a press conference that special revenue sharing without a matching requirement could mean the federal government was subsidizing local tax cuts since revenue sharing replaced local expenditures. The political benefits of this were obvious. Nixon typically remonstrated in meetings on domestic policy about

50. Price to President, December 12, 1970, pt. 4, no. 19, pp. 81–85, Cole to President, December 18, 1970, pt. 4, no. 19, pp. 87–90, *Nixon Papers*, ed. Hoff-Wilson.

51. William Niskanen to Weinberger, December 2, 1970, p. 15, RG 51, ser. 69.1, G4–5, NA.

52. Nathan/Harper to Ehrlichman, March 27, 1971, RG 51, ser. 69.1, box 78, G4–5, NA.

the need for his staff to sell revenue sharing as a way of reducing local property tax burdens.[53]

That Nixon and his budget makers were disturbed by the prospect of unrelenting and uncontrollable growth in the federal budget is no surprise. Paradoxically, though, what they feared was the growth of discretionary spending, not transfers, which the administration was quite willing to fund, as we have seen. Why is it that a conservative administration agitated by the growth of social welfare spending would choose to expand transfers and make domestic discretionary spending—even then, the smallest component of government—the object of their animus? The answer lies in their understanding of the source of budgetary pressures. Casper Wienberger, deputy director of OMB and a passionate opponnent of categorical programs, formulated the problem as one of run-away service programs. Wienberger thought "the local functional bureaucracy, working with its federal counterpart and with private lobby groups, form a formidable pressure bloc to seek higher appropriations each year," a belief Nixon shared.[54]

The Model Cities program was a prime example of the problem. It was never regarded as an open-ended transfer or entitlement for cities; funding depended upon what Congress appropriated. But it had the same capacity as other Great Society programs to create demand, and inevitably a backlog of needed but unfunded projects would emerge. The view of the Nixon White House was summed up by a White House official who said of Model Cities, "the program generates the recognition of billions of dollars of needs and provides legitimacy for funding them. Mayors can say, 'We were told to plan and document, now fund us.' In sum, the program creates very scary demands from a budgetary point of view." The White House and HUD officials early recognized Model Cities' potentially expansionary effects. Transferring service programs into block grants, in addition to outright dis-

53. Shultz to President, December 18, 1970, pt. 4, no. 19, pp. 57–58, Flanigan to President, December 19, 1970, pt. 4, no. 19, pp. 78–79, *Nixon papers,* ed. Hoff-Wilson; transcript of press conference, February 26, 1971, Charles Colson Papers, box 108, folder "Revenue Sharing," WHSF; Minutes of Domestic Council, June 8, 1971, Harper Papers, box 9, folder "Materials on Domestic Council," WHSF, NPMS.

54. Weinberger to Nixon, December 17, 1970, pt. 4, no. 124, pp. 37–40, *Nixon Papers,* ed. Hoff-Wilson. On entering office, Nixon described himself as the "outsider" facing an alliance of congressmen, lobbyists, and federal bureaucrats, who "provided a built-in constituency in favor of an ever bigger federal government" (quoted in Kim McQuaid, *Big Business and Presidential Power* [New York, 1982], p. 260).

mantling of them, demobilized constituents or put them under the thumb of elected officials and Nixon-created regional offices.[55]

Demand and need often combine in categorical grants to drive up federal outlays. Need of course is in the eye of the beholder and lends itself to expansionary strategies. A backlog (unsatisfied demand, if one likes) is an opportunity for growth because, as Aaron Wildavsky ruefully observed, "Nobody loves a backlog. The very use of the term suggests that there is an obligation to do something about it."[56] What the administration sought—and found with special revenue sharing—was a way to break the link between need and demand. OMB put the matter succinctly in an analysis of the federal water and sewer program:

> So long as the water and sewer program is kept alive, there will be strong political pressure on the Administration to increase funding for it. With applications coming in at the rate of $1.2 million per year, *no* funding level within reason will remove these pressures. However, by folding the program into Urban SRS, the Administration could respond to these pressures more effectively by arguing that the entire amount of shared revenues— $2 billion, $2.4 billion whatever—is available for water and sewer *if* that's how the localities want to use it.

Special revenue sharing, then, was devised not as a gift for state and local governments nor to bring order to the presumed anarchy of domestic programs. It was a response to the budgetary pressures facing the administration and augured a leaner federal government.[57]

The Denouement of Nixon's Gambit

Nixon's ambitious agenda was greeted with silence or disdain by Congress. Most of his major programs never received a full hearing in Congress. Yet

55. William Lilly III, "Model Cities Faces Uncertain Future despite Romney Overhaul," *National Journal,* July 11, 1970, p. 1475; Floyd Hyde to George Romney, February 8, 1969, RG 51, ser. 69.1, box 22, R4–3, NA. Robert J. Waste of San Diego State University first suggested to me the significance of the regional offices.

56. Aaron Wildavsky, *The Politics of the Budgetary Process,* 4th ed. (Boston, Mass., 1984), p. 115.

57. Staff Paper, "HUD's Basic Water and Sewer Facilities Grant Program," RG 51, ser. 69.1, box 111, R4–1/1, NA. For another account, to which I am indebted, see Heywood T. Sanders, "Renewing the American City III: The Demise of Urban Renewal and the Shift to Block Grants, 1968 to 1974" (paper presented to the Fourth National Conference on American Planning, Richmond, Va., November 1991), pp. 7–9, 13.

Nixon significantly altered the trajectory of federal social policy, and his victories, modest though they were, had a profound impact. He succeeded in shifting federal social policy toward transfers, which grew at an average annual rate of 25 percent during his time in office. Republicans were less successful in squeezing services initially. Congress sharply modified Nixon's budget requests, raising budget authority by an average of 25 percent (see table 14). The Democrats reversed Nixon's efforts to cut discretionary poverty services and doubled his proposed budget authority for work-training programs. Nixon's assault on Great Society services also faltered because the administration was unable to control some expenditures during the first two or three years. For example, prior commitments for Model Cities only appeared as outlays during the early 1970s. Nor could the administration control the run-away growth of the public assistance social services program, which had grown to $1.5 billion by the end of 1973.[58] Consequently, service programs grew at a rate of 11.5 percent annually and outlays increased from $6.9 billion at the end of the Johnson administration to $11.4 billion in 1974. In real terms, however, Nixon succeeded in sharply slowing the growth of Great Society service programs.

The Republicans fared better with their revenue sharing proposals, although they never came close to realizing the grand aims of their 1971 scheme. Only two special revenue sharing programs were created: the Community Development Block Grants (CDBG) and the Comprehensive Training and Development Act (CETA). CDBG worked much as anticipated, breaking the link between demand and budgetary claims. Between 1975 and 1980, CDBG funding was flat in constant dollars, a sign of effective budgetary stasis.[59] Political conflict turned on changes in the funding formula and the extent of federal control over state and local decisions. CETA was not effective in controlling spending, mainly because Nixon and his advisers had to agree to a permanent public employment program as part of it, which drove up federal expenditures.

Nixon's legacy is far more significant than his modest legislative achievements would suggest. If the reforms in food stamps and creation of the Supplemental Security Income program achieved a goal that had been dear to liberals since the 1940s, the fiscal burden of the welfare state provoked a search for new policies that had, as Nixon realized at the time, enormous political implications. Nixon made the fiscal implications of federal social

58. For an account of the social services program see Martha Derthick, *Uncontrollable Spending for Social Services Grants* (Washington, D.C., 1975).

59. Sanders, "Renewing the American City III," p. 19.

policy salient at the same time that he turned special revenue sharing to his political advantage. Special revenue sharing was invented as a device to redistribute aid to Republican constituencies while restraining the growth of the public sector by substituting federal for local dollars. Debate no longer centered on programs and need but on funding formulas. But because 80 percent of the money in urban revenue sharing, for example, was allocated to cities with a population of fifty thousand or more, the program was horizontally redistributive, encompassing white, middle-class, suburban constituencies. In reversing Johnsonian concern for targeting limited resources to impoverished ghetto communities, Nixon, with help from Congress, spread limited aid across a larger number of beneficiaries. The implications of this were made evident when the Nixon administration and the Democratic majority in Congress finally agreed on a public employment policy as part of CETA. The original aim of this policy—reducing ghetto unemployment—had become remote. Jacob Javits's quite serious comment from the senate floor indicates just how remote: "Think of the horrors and the sufferings in the aerospace industry now, in both the States of Washington and California."[60]

The class bias underlying Nixon's shift to contraction merged with a growing Republican penchant for exploiting racial divisions. The Republican search for policies that would benefit old constituencies and add new ones was partly justified as a way of ending racial divisions thought to be a consequence of the Great Society. Yet Nixon's social policies, in the end, did little to remedy the racial bifurcation of federal social policy; indeed, they entrenched it more deeply. In the guise of reducing racial tensions, the Republicans sought to add white voters to the beneficiaries of 1960s social policies while trying to delegitimize black demands and limit blacks' control over programs such as Model Cities. By suggesting that the so-called racial targeting of the Great Society was unfair to whites (Johnson, it should be remembered, opposed expansion of AFDC, which was regarded as the heart of the problem), the Nixon administration reinforced white resistance to black demands and intensified the racial divisions over social policy.[61] At a time when the fiscal costs of social policy had come to be called into question, Nixon's policy strategy set the stage for Republicans to exploit the white political backlash against the Great Society and taxation.

60. Quoted in Roger Davidson, *The Politics of Comprehensive Manpower Legislation* (Baltimore, Md., 1972), p. 85.

61. In some cases the administration acted directly to foment racial tension. Nixon's affirmative action policies, especially the Philadelphia Plan, are a case in point. See John D. Skrentny, *The Ironies of Affirmative Action* (Chicago, 1996).

CHAPTER TEN

The Ghetto in the Welfare State: Race, Gender, and Class after the Great Society

The important point is that the people on welfare receive this money and immediately transfer it into the hands of, for the most part, absentee landlords. . . . This is a form of conduit colonialism, with the poor serving as the *conductors* of resources from one segment of the economy to another. If the welfare family is to be identified as a "welfare recipient," then it is quite proper to identify the landlords, merchants, and loan sharks as "welfare beneficiaries."

—CHARLES V. HAMILTON

Richard Nixon failed to remake the Great Society, but his policies changed the distribution of resources and benefits of federal social policies. The Republicans substituted transfers for services, and converted many of the new federal social programs such Model Cities and employment training into locally run block grants, curtailing the targeting of federal resources that was the hallmark of the Johnson years. Coupled with the utter failure to dismantle the ghetto after passage of the 1968 Civil Rights Act, Nixon's policies deepened racial divisions within the welfare state and left the black poor stranded on urban reservations, tethered to the rest of society through conduit colonialism, to use Charles Hamilton's apt phrase.

Significantly, these changes occurred as racial divisions within the country eroded support for the welfare state. Middle-class tax revolts signaled a backlash against the burdens of the welfare state; the most alienated and angry whites believed that "blacks, the poor and the wealthy are in some ways sources of threat and have undue access to political favoritism." George Wallace's racially coded incantations about lazy welfare recipients convinced many people that the Great Society undermined the work ethic. Such attitudes were exploited by conservative politicians willing to play the race card.[1]

---

1. Donald I. Warren, *The Radical Center: Middle Americans and the Politics of Alienation* (Notre Dame, 1976), pp. 21, 30, 49; Dan T. Carter, *The Politics of Rage* (New York, 1995), chaps. 10–11, esp. pp. 344–48.

The legacy of Nixon's policies combined with white backlash made racial, rather than class, divisions crucial to political conflict over social policy. A racially stratified welfare state persisted after the civil rights revolution and shaped the politics of retrenchment that culminated in the tax revolts of the late 1970s and Ronald Reagan's election. It is not obvious why the racially bifurcated social policies that began in the 1930s, when African Americans were generally excluded from middle-class social policies and relief was substituted for jobs, should have persisted after the 1960s. Labor-market discrimination and Jim Crow were the two pillars underpinning the color line in federal social policy. But after the civil rights revolution, black enfranchisement and federal antidiscrimination laws eroded these props to racially bifurcated social policies. The Voting Rights Act provided incentives for southern black leaders to demand public services, and white politicians reciprocated. The universal Powell amendment—Title VI of the 1964 Civil Rights Act—outlawed discriminatory use of federal funds. And some observers thought that Title VII, which outlawed employment discrimination, resulted in an apparent "convergence" of blacks' and whites' economic positions and "a virtual collapse in traditional discriminatory patterns in the labor market."[2]

Leaving aside the early, hyperbolic assessments of Title VII, it is clear that the decade or so after the passage of the civil rights laws did witness a narrowing of racial differentials in occupations, educational attainment, and earnings, even though stark differences between blacks and whites in family incomes and unemployment rates remained. Many people drew the conclusion that the civil rights laws had solved the problem of caste discrimination and replaced race with social class as the arbiter of African Americans' destiny. The identifiable group status that was a consequence of Jim Crow gave way to a widening class schism among blacks, "up for some members of the group and down for others," as Daniel Patrick Moynihan put it. That race remained salient to the question of who got what in the welfare state and to the conflict over social policy was, Moynihan and others assumed, because of the breakdown of the African American family.[3]

This entire line of argument is misleading. Race remained central because black economic progress continued to depend on federal social policy, as it

2. Richard B. Freeman, "Changes in the Labor Market for Black Americans, 1948–1972," *Brookings Papers in Economic Activity* (1973): 67.

3. Daniel P. Moynihan, "The Schism in Black America," *Public Interest,* no. 27 (Spring 1972): 6, 15. Also see William J. Wilson, *The Declining Significance of Race* (Chicago, 1978).

had since the 1930s. Where social policies for the elderly were concerned, racial differences were submerged. Whether Social Security and Medicare were regarded as earned rights or as a generational compact, all had a stake in these two policies—young and old, white and black, men and women. In the rest of the welfare state, however, both middle-class and lower-class blacks continued to be tied to the public sector in a way that white men and women were not. African American economic improvement in the 1960s depended initially on public expenditures as much as on affirmative action policies. With the political leverage gained through the civil rights movement and urban uprisings, blacks used public power to transform their lives through provision of jobs and access to education, employment services, and cash transfers. For nonelderly white Americans, the welfare state was indirect (tax breaks and subsidized loans), private (union or corporate health plans and pensions and indexed wages), and tied to social insurance (survivor's benefits or unemployment compensation). This pattern applied to women as well as men, although women's direct participation in the welfare state far exceeded that of men (partly because women outlive men) and women were affected by the gender bias of federal social policy.

Racially stratified social policies also persist as a consequence of the distributive effects of Nixon's policies and the intensification of residential segregation. Reynolds Farley and Walter R. Allen posed the pertinent questions when they tried to explain why black unemployment rates remained twice those of whites and why the labor-force participation rates of black men had declined sharply, even though there had been a substantial narrowing of the gap in earnings and occupational standing between blacks and whites. What if, they asked,

> instead of expanding support programs, there had been a strong federal push to eliminate those practices that keep blacks at a disadvantage by isolating them from whites. . . ? Would the ratio of black to white unemployment rates be 2 to 1, and would black family income lag far behind that of whites if federal efforts had ensured that black and white children obtained identical educations by attending the same schools and that black families wishing to leave a deteriorating central city for the suburbs had been able to do so as readily as white families?[4]

Farley and Allen preferred to disperse the ghetto rather than gild it. By the 1970s, though, after most politicians, including many liberals, had abandoned

4. Reynolds Farley and Walter Allen, *The Color Line and the Quality of Life in America* (New York, 1989), p. 357.

the cause of residential desegregation, the real question was whether there would be public investment in ghetto communities and what form it would take. Wirtz, Schultz, and others rejected policies they thought would gild the ghetto, but the service strategy they adopted was a de facto investment strategy. Any assessment of what has happened to the urban poor since the Great Society must examine what has happened to public investment in the ghetto after 1974, after Nixon. This question is rarely considered in contemporary post-mortems of the Great Society or studies of urban poverty.[5]

In the post–civil rights welfare state, transfers became the mainstays of deteriorating inner-city economies, the salve for an otherwise meager livelihood, but about the only source of public investment available. The problem is not, as all too many people believe, that transfers became more readily available and induced bad behavior; people too easily forget just how pervasive poverty was before the growth of Medicaid, AFDC, and food stamps. Rather, the problem is that little else was done in poor communities. Public investment in jobs, education, and neighborhoods was diminished at the same time that corporate disinvestment sucked jobs out of ghetto communities. Transfers replaced public and private investment, and perversely became the basis for a racially loaded narrative about the debilitating effects of federal welfare policies and the bankruptcy of the Great Society.

Abandoning the Ghetto: The Distributive Legacy of Nixon's Gambit

Two distinctive trends in the distribution of social benefits characterize the post–civil rights welfare state for the nonelderly.[6] There is, first, a widening gap in the distribution of public payments between middle-class citizens and poor citizens. Transfers for both groups expanded, but over the 1970s, the value of transfers for the middle class increased while the value of those for

5. William Julius Wilson has nothing to say in *The Truly Disadvantaged* (Chicago, 1987) or in *When Work Disappears: The World of the New Urban Poor* (New York, 1996) about the changing distribution of federal resources in the communities he studied. Similarly, Christopher Jencks ignores distributive patterns in the allocation of public resources and the effects for different groups of poor in *Rethinking Social Policy* (New York, 1993).

6. The experience of the elderly is quite different, of course. After the large benefit increase of 1972, social security became the most effective transfer program in reducing poverty, and by the mid-1980s, according to one study, it reduced income inequality more than the tax system or any other public program. See U.S. Bureau of Census, *Measuring the Effect of Benefits and Taxes on Income and Poverty: 1986*, ser. P-60, no. 194-RD-1 (Washington, D.C., 1988), pp. 6–7, 11–12.

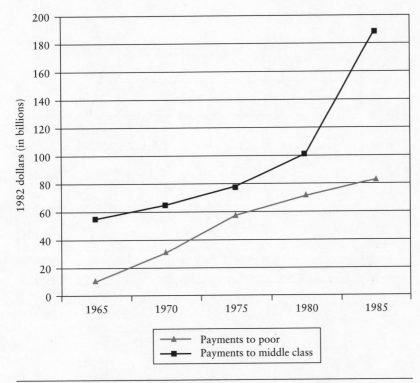

Figure 7. Federal payments to nonelde.ly citizens, 1965–1985. Middle-class payments include tax expenditures (fringe and income tax benefits only), social insurance, and veterans' benefits. Payments to the poor include AFDC, food stamps, and housing subsidies. *Source: Budget of the United States Government* (Washington, D.C., selected fiscal years).

the poor diminished (see figure 7). The steep rise in the real value of federal benefits for middle-class families is almost entirely a consequence tax expenditures for fringe benefits (such as exclusion of payments to health plans) and tax benefits (such as the mortgage interest deduction). The real value of transfer payments to the poor, on the other hand, declined sharply by the mid-1970s. The decline in AFDC payments was steep, it began in the late 1960s as caseloads rose, and it was not offset by food stamps. The combined value of the AFDC/food stamps package in 1984, Robert Moffitt calculates, was only slightly higher than the value of AFDC in 1963. Taking the two programs together, the maximum amount paid to a family of four with no other income was $505 per month, compared to a maximum monthly payment of $483 for AFDC in 1960. In fact, the combined AFDC/food stamp/

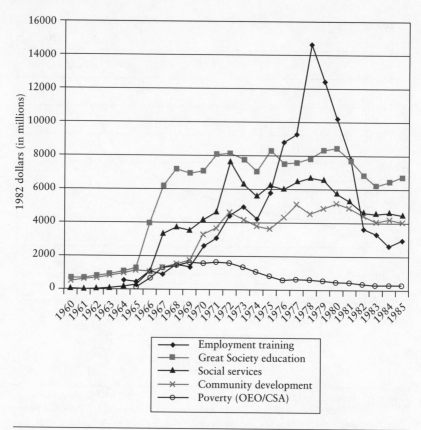

Figure 8. Outlays for Great Society service programs, 1960–1985. *Source: Budget of the United States Government* (Washington, D.C., selected fiscal years).

Medicaid package was only 39 percent higher than the AFDC benefit of 1960—not an exceptionally large increase. Nor did the growth of food stamps compensate for differences in AFDC benefits among the states, as many liberals assumed it would. States, in all regions but the West, Moffitt convincingly demonstrates, substituted food stamps for AFDC on a dollar for dollar basis.[7]

These trends in the transfer system coincided with the stagnation of funding for the Great Society service programs. (see figure 8.) For most programs spending peaked toward the end of Nixon's first term and then stabilized or

7. Robert Moffitt, "Has State Redistribution Policy Grown More Conservative?" National Bureau of Economic Research Working Paper No. 2516 (Cambridge, Mass., 1988), pp. 6–9, 13, 28–38.

declined in real terms because of the administration's success in containing Great Society spending. The only exception is the Comprehensive Employment and Training Act (CETA), which grew quite rapidly during the 1974–75 recession before declining after 1978. After Nixon, LBJ's effort to redistribute services to the poor was abandoned. The Great Society's strategy of targeting federal services on poor communities was replaced by a policy of "incipient universalism" that made middle-class citizens and communities eligible to receive federally funded services. In other words, as real spending for service programs either declined or leveled off, less money was spread across a wider set of individuals and communities. Thus, even though the main means-tested policies expanded to cover more people, a substantial portion of the very service programs that were calculated to move people out of poverty became less available to the inner-city poor.

The main reason federal resources were shifted to the middle class after 1974 is that federal services were increasingly distributed through general purpose and block grants-in-aid, which had few federal restrictions on eligibility or allocation. Broad-based grants accounted for 21 percent of all federal grants to state and local governments in 1980, up from 10 percent in 1972, and they were an even more important part of grants-in-aid for Great Society services.[8] During the eight years between the end of Nixon's first term and Ronald Reagan's election, social welfare outlays distributed through broad-based grants trebled in real dollars, while those for categorical programs declined by 35 percent. Three-fifths of all dollars spent on Great Society services flowed through broad-based grants in 1980, compared to just one-fifth in 1972. Important categorical programs were unaffected. For example, the allocation of resources in Title I of ESEA, Johnson's large compensatory education program, was more narrowly targeted by 1972 than at its inception in 1965.[9] Nevertheless, Lyndon Johnson's strategy of targeting resources on the poor by redistributing services went right out the window.

The advent of broad-based grants-in-aid led to a horizontal spread in the distribution of federal resources. For example, Thomas Anton concluded that the Department of Housing and Urban Development "appears to have made a determination to 'reach out' to provide program services to

8. Edward M. Gramlich, "Reforming U.S. Federal Fiscal Arrangements," in *American Domestic Priorities*, eds. John M. Quigley and Daniel L. Rubinfeld (Berkeley, Calif., 1985), p. 55.

9. Robert Plotnick and Felicity Skidmore, *Progress against Poverty* (New York, 1975), p. 216.

counties outside of its traditional urban constituency."[10] The number of counties receiving HUD's Section 8 housing program expanded from 269 to 2,070. Similarly, the Comprehensive Employment and Training Act initially shifted resources away from central cities, or from cities to counties, although the effects were diluted somewhat by a hold-harmless provision Congress inserted into the legislation to protect big cities. Even with funding increases as unemployment was rising, big cities experienced a decline in Title I or training funds. Suburban jurisdictions were the beneficiaries of this shift; one study found a relative decline in the share for core cities compared to suburban counties.[11]

The result, Richard Nathan observed, was that "thousands of local governments that never before received them," were now eligible for and received federal grants. The share of federal funds for cities with fewer than 100,000 residents increased from 20.3 percent in 1968 to 30.3 percent in 1976; in large cities of 500,000 people or more, the share declined from 62.2 to 44.4 percent. Small counties outside of metropolitan areas made stunning gains; federal funding in these counties increased by 74 percent over three years, compared to 22 percent in large counties outside metropolitans areas and 45 percent in large counties within such areas. Many of these new recipients were located in emerging Republican strongholds in the South and West—which should be no surprise.[12]

Despite these shifts, total federal funding remained more or less constant in counties with declining populations, precisely those urban centers in which poverty was concentrated.[13] But more of this money was funneled to cities in the form of broad-based grants. If big cities did not entirely lose out with the shift of resources to the suburbs, a lot of the money they did receive went to people who were not disadvantaged and were often middle class. A notable illustration of this phenomenon was Title XX, a program created in

10. Thomas J. Anton, Jerry P. Cawley, and Kevin L. Kramer, *Moving Money: An Empirical Analysis of Federal Expenditure Patterns* (Cambridge, Mass., 1980), p. 63.

11. William Mirengoff and Lester Rindler, *CETA: Manpower Programs under Local Control* (Washington, D.C., 1978), pp. 33–37. The share of CETA's employment training funds, which contained all of the Johnson-era categorical manpower programs, for fifty-six matched cities declined from 24 percent of the fiscal year 1974 (pre-CETA) allotment to 22 percent in fiscal year 1976 and then to 19 percent in fiscal year 1977. These amounts are adjusted for the hold-harmless formula.

12. Richard P. Nathan, "The Outlook for Federal Grants to Cities," in *The Fiscal Outlook for Cities*, ed. Roy Bahl (Syracuse, N.Y., 1978), pp. 76, 80; Anton, Cawley, and Kramer, *Moving Money*, p. 65, table 3.5.

13. Anton, Cawley, and Kramer, *Moving Money*, p. 69.

1974 to replace federal grants for social services to assist the poor. Federal bureaucrats intentionally shifted Title XX toward middle-class beneficiaries in order to inoculate it against political opposition. They set the income threshold for eligibility at 115 percent of state median income, although 50 percent of beneficiaries were supposed to be poor or means-tested. At its inception, 32 percent of Title XX recipients were non-means-tested; by 1977 the program served 3.5 million people, of whom 45 percent were non-means-tested. This shift was of enormous benefit to both the elderly and the large number of women who entered the labor market in the early 1970s. States had wide leeway to decide how to spend the money. About one-fifth of the outlays went for day care, and almost half of these funds went to "income eligible" clients—middle- and working-class women.[14] Yet funding for Title XX was capped at $2.5 billion annually, which meant that limited resources were spread over of a large number of beneficiaries, diluting the amount available to assist the poor.

Incipient universalism crept into some other federally run programs, notably the agencies on aging and community mental health centers. But it was in the big block grants—CETA and the CDBG program—that the sharpest reversal in targeting services on poor families took place. Employment training and Model Cities were among the most beneficial programs created by Great Society liberals to help the urban poor because they were among those most directly targeted at the inner-city poor. The two programs that replaced them, CETA and CDBG, shifted resources away from the poor to working- and middle-class constituencies. CDBG became less targeted on need between 1975 and 1978. In Boston, Cleveland, and St. Louis, for example, only one-third of CDBG benefits went to low- and moderate-income neighborhoods, or communities in which the average income was 80 percent or less of the city's median income. Local politicians had incentives to allocate CDBG funds as widely as possible.[15] They did the same with CETA funds.

Congress defined CETA's eligibility requirements broadly, which left all the important decisions to local program administrators. The job training title made about 27 million workers, or 25 percent of the work force, eligible for benefits. This capacious safety net caught many workers who were not poor: 42 percent were employed, and 53 percent had incomes above the

14. Neil Gilbert, *Capitalism and the Welfare State* (New Haven, Conn., 1983), pp. 54, 61.

15. James Fossett, "The Politics of Dependence," in Lawrence D. Brown, James W. Fossett, and Kenneth T. Palmer, *The Changing Politics of Federal Grants* (Washington, D.C., 1984), pp. 148–51; Anton, Cawley, and Kramer, *Moving Money,* p. 74, table 3.15.

legislatively defined threshold for eligibility.[16] Local officials used this latitude to put the most disadvantaged people in the training programs and reserve public service employment primarily for mostly middle-class men. After the 1974–75 recession, when funding shifted from job training to public sector employment, the distribution of benefits shifted away from low-income individuals. As Donald Baumer and Carl E. Van Horn cautiously put it, "the more direct and costly benefits have been distributed to a relatively more advantaged group of people, namely, those who are more competitive in the labor market because of their educational backgrounds, age, or work histories."[17] Furthermore, even though the job training component of CETA served poor people, it served fewer than did LBJ's categorical employment training programs. The proportion of trainees who were economically disadvantaged declined from 87 percent in the Great Society to 78 percent under CETA. This decline stemmed from the geographical dispersion of CETA resources and the inclination of local politicians to use CETA jobs as patronage and to substitute federal for local funding.[18]

Incipient universalism was partially reversed during the Carter administration. Requirements for targeting funds on low-income and very low-income population groups were reinstated, and there was a shift away from middle-class clienteles in both CETA and CDBG. But this occurred just at the moment that CETA funding took a nose dive, dropping by 45 percent between fiscal years 1978 and 1981. These two changes put the Democrats in a real bind. Their actions undermined political support for programs like CETA: "Many mayors and county executives," Baumer and Van Horn report, "felt that excluding the newly unemployed and serving only the poor put CETA in the same category as public welfare."[19] Yet diminishing funding left insufficient resources to make any real difference in the lives of most of the inner-city poor.

16. Williams Barnes, "Target Groups," in CETA: An Analysis of the Issues, Background Papers Prepared for the National Commission for Manpower Policy, Special Report No. 23 (Washington, D.C., 1978), pp. 75–76.

17. Donald C. Baumer and Carl E. Van Horn, The Politics of Unemployment (Washington, D.C., 1985), pp. 64, 78; Mirengoff and Rindler, CETA: Manpower Programs Under Local Control, p. 44. Funding for job training dropped from 42 percent to 23 percent during the first two years of the program.

18. Donald C. Baumer, Carl E. Van Horn, and Mary Marvel, "Explaining Benefit Distribution in CETA Programs," Journal of Human Resources 14 (1979): 181. The extent of substitution in CETA is a controversial issue. One should recall that some Nixon officials fully anticipated substitution and wanted to encourage it.

19. Baumer and Van Horn, Politics of Unemployment, pp. 149, 151.

Race and Gender under Conduit Colonialism

Transfers were effectively substituted for services, just as Nixon and Moynihan wanted, but the trade-off proved to be disastrous for the African American poor. For a sizable portion of poor African Americans, access to jobs or to education and other services that would provide avenues out of poverty was traded for relief. The thinning of services and other public investments made any escape from urban poverty terribly difficult. To see why, we must not focus just on the poor. Rather, we must ask whether different groups of men and women prospered or perished under the post-1960s social policies.[20]

Prior to the 1960s, the relationship of African Americans to the welfare state was defined by a pattern of inclusion and exclusion. After the civil rights revolution, African Americans were no longer excluded from social programs by virtue of discrimination. Nevertheless, and here is the nub of the matter, the structural relationship of poor African American families to the welfare state did not change after the 1960s. The welfare state for non-elderly citizens remained racially stratified, and, paradoxically, even though the number of poor black families on AFDC declined, the program remained the mainstay for black families trapped in poverty.

Despite an influx of white women onto the AFDC rolls, the transfer system sharply differentiated between blacks and whites, and between men and women. In fact, the persistence of the color line is most apparent among women, who were in many respects the main beneficiaries of the new transfer system. With rising numbers of single-parent families headed by women, poverty was feminized; that is, women made up a larger share of the poor after the Great Society than before. The incidence of poverty among female-headed families had always been very high, and the number of such families rose markedly from the 1960s. The proportion of female-headed families who received AFDC more than doubled between 1960 and 1977, rising from 19 to 46 percent. Poor women were not the only beneficiaries of federal transfers, however, either at the time or before; middle-class women benefited as well. Nationally, by 1975, 79 percent of female-headed families received a transfer payment, compared to 48 percent of all families. There was no difference in the proportion of white and black female-headed families receiving a transfer.[21] This statistic conceals very real differences in the

20. While I believe the evidence for differences in benefits presented is quite strong, a more systematic analysis is required. That analysis is beyond the scope of this study.

21. Eighty percent of white female-headed families received a public or private transfer payment, compared to 77 percent of black female-headed families. U.S. Bureau of the

relationship of white and black women to the post–civil rights welfare state. Although gender plays a central role in modern welfare states, all women are not treated the same way. Black women fare very differently than white women. Given the rigidity of ghetto walls, corporate disinvestment in central cities, and rising unemployment during the 1970s, the changes in the distribution of public social transfers and services sustained and reinforced the racial hierarchies within the welfare state and left African American women at a serious disadvantage compared to other groups.

It was in the South, not the North, where African Americans made the largest gains as a result of the War on Poverty. In the rural South, patterns of discrimination in the distribution of federal aid were reversed when newly enfranchised blacks turned out on election day. Elizabeth Sanders has documented a rapid expansion of social welfare benefits between 1962 and 1972 in southern black-majority rural counties, which she attributes to the mobilization of black voters.[22] Although the proportion of black families on the national AFDC caseload remained more or less unchanged between 1961 and 1977, blacks increased from 57 percent to 71 percent of the caseload in the eleven former confederate states and from 35 to 50 percent in border states.[23]

The gains made by blacks in the South were atypical of the rest of the country. Elsewhere the welfare explosion of the 1960s was of principal benefit to poor white women who, though eligible, had been deterred from applying for assistance. Blacks were clearly among the major beneficiaries of the growth of means-tested transfers, but the average monthly caseload for white families increased by 80 percent compared to just 2 percent for black families.[24] The proportion of white female-headed families that received

Census, *Money Income of Households, Families and Persons in the United States: 1980,* Current Population Reports, ser. P-60, no. 132 (Washington, D.C., 1982), pp. 120–22, table 37.

22. Elizabeth Sanders, "Electorate Expansion and Public Policy: A Decade of Political Change in the South" (Ph.D. diss., Cornell University, 1978), pp. 58, 89–91, 123–24.

23. Author's calculations from U.S. Department of Health, Education, and Welfare, *Characteristics of Families Receiving Aid to Families with Dependent Children,* November–December 1961 (Washington, D.C., 1963), table 3; *1977 Recipient Characteristics Study,* pt. 1, *Demographic and Program Characteristics* (Washington, D.C., 1980), table 8.

24. Barbara Boland, "Participation in the Aid to Families with Dependent Children Program (AFDC)," in *Studies in Public Welfare,* Subcommittee on Fiscal Policy, Joint Economic Committee, Congress of the United States, Paper no. 12, pt. 1 (Washington, D.C., 1973), p. 153, table 3. Also see Eugene Durman, "Have the Poor Been Regulated? Toward a Multivariate Understanding of Welfare Growth," *Social Service Review* 47 (1973): 344–45.

AFDC tripled between 1961 and 1977, rising from 11 to 34 percent. Indeed, the ratio of black to white female-headed families on the rolls declined from three-to-one in 1961 to two-to-one by 1977.[25] In many northern states the proportion of AFDC recipients who were black declined. In the heartland states of Illinois, Michigan, Ohio, Indiana, and Wisconsin, for instance, the proportion of blacks dropped from 59 to 47 percent, and in New England states, by 7 percent. Nationally, the proportion of black female-headed families receiving public assistance declined after 1975. In other words, although it is correct to say that African American households were among the main beneficiaries of means-tested policies and that discriminatory exclusion was no longer a significant problem, it is wrong to assume that the expansion of AFDC was mostly due to increases in black participation. It would be more accurate to say that women of all races benefited.

What is so striking about the post–civil rights transfer system is that the racial bifurcation between social insurance and means-tested policies that originated in the New Deal persisted, albeit in an attenuated form. White and black women have fared differently because white women usually have multiple sources of income regardless of their marital status. (See table 15.) Of white women, 59 percent received social security income, compared to 40.2 percent of black women. But only 13.2 percent of white women received any income from public assistance (including SSI and AFDC), while among black women the proportion was 47.6 percent. The proportion of blacks in noncash means-tested programs was even greater: 55.2 percent, compared to 16.4 percent for whites. These differences recall the heavy concentration of black families on federal relief rolls in the 1930s. And they are due to more than the relative poverty of black female-headed households compared to white female-headed households. (See table 16.)

Comparing black and white women by marital status and source of income reveals that, with the exception of never-married women, there are only slight or no differences in the proportion of black and white women who receive earnings. Yet black women find themselves relying upon welfare more than white women. Although, for example, 59 percent of black and white widows receive earnings, white widows are more likely to receive veterans payments, social security, and unemployment compensation, but much less likely to receive welfare. Sixty-two percent of white widows receive social

---

25. U.S. Bureau of the Census, *Statistical Abstract of the United States, 1961* (Washington, D.C., 1962), p. 43, table 41; idem, *Statistical Abstract of the United States, 1977* (Washington, D.C., 1978), p. 46, table 60.

Table 15. Receipt of cash and in-kind transfers by race and sex, 1980

	Both Sexes			Male			Female		
	Total	White	Black	Total	White	Black	Total	White	Black
Covered by employee benefit plan[a]									
Pensions	44.9%	45.5%	40.8%	51.0%	52.2%	42.9%	37.5%	37.5%	38.9%
Health	62.0	62.5	58.0	70.6	71.7	61.5	51.6	50.5	54.5
Cash transfers[b]									
All transfers	34.4%	34.0%	39.1%	32.9%	32.9%	34.0%	35.8%	35.0%	43.3%
Social Security	51.9	53.9	41.0	46.9	47.8	42.2	56.0	59.0	40.2
Public Assistance	13.3	9.7	36.5	7.4	5.7	19.2	18.2	13.2	47.6
AFDC/General	7.9	5.5	23.5	3.7	2.7	8.9	11.5	7.8	32.9
Private pensions	18.5	20.1	8.4	25.6	27.3	13.7	12.5	13.8	5.0
Means-tested transfers[c]									
Total	22.4%	17.3%	56.1%	20.4%	15.7%	51.8%	24.3%	18.7%	59.8%
Cash	10.0	7.1	28.3	8.7	6.2	25.4	11.1	8.0	30.9
Noncash	21.7	16.4	55.2	19.6	14.9	50.7	23.6	17.9	59.1
Food stamps	9.3	6.3	28.0	8.0	5.5	24.2	10.5	7.1	31.2
Transfers for poor families[d]									
Cash welfare	30.9%			20.4%	20.4%	38.2%		46.0%	68.0%
Noncash welfare	58.2			47.1	47.1	42.1		33.4	28.8

Sources: U.S. Bureau of the Census, *Characteristics of Households and Persons Receiving Selected Noncash Benefits: 1980*, Consumer Income, ser. P-60, no. 131, tables 14, 17; *Money Income of Households, Families and Persons in the United States: 1980*, Consumer Income, ser. P-60, no. 132, table 53; *Economic Characteristics of Households in the United States: Fourth Quarter, 1983*, Household Economic Studies, ser. P-70–83–4, table 2; Sheldon Danziger, "Budget Cuts as Welfare Reform," *American Economic Review* 76 (1983), table 1.

[a]Civilian wage and salary workers, 15 years or older, 1980.

[b]Persons 15 years or older, 1980.

[c]Excludes persons in farm households and group quarters.

[d]Nonelderly families only.

Table 16. Source of income for women by marital status and race, 1973 (percentage receiving income)

Source of income	Heads of households		Separated		Widowed		Divorced		Never married	
	White	Black	White	Black	White	Black	White	Black	White	Black
Earnings	72.9%	64.4%	63.2%	64.1%	59.1%	59.0%	80.4%	73.6%	78.9%	59.9%
Unemployment compensation	5.1	3.9	5.6	5.4	4.3	1.6	5.6	2.8	3.9	2.2
Veterans and workers compensation	6.7	3.4	1.3	0.8	18.8	10.7	4.9	2.2	0.9	1.1
Social Security	23.2	18.8	16.2	14.7	61.8	46.3	14.4	18.3	30.4	8.7
AFDC	15.8	47.9	28.4	52.0	5.2	48.0	19.3	32.2	6.4	51.1
Child support and alimony	24.8	10.9	24.6	13.4	8.7	0	39.0	18.7	2.5	6.0

Source: Frank Mott, The Socioeconomic Status of Households Headed by Women, R&D Monograph No. 72, U.S. Department of Labor (Washington, D.C., 1974), table 22.

security but only 5.2 percent receive AFDC; among African American widows, 46 percent receive social security, while 48 percent receive AFDC. More
astonishing are the differences among never-married women. Thirty percent
of white never-married women received a social security payment, most likely
for disability, compared to 8.7 percent of black never-married women. For
AFDC, on the other hand, the pattern is just the reverse. Only 6.4 percent
of white never-married women received AFDC, compared to 51.1 percent
of black never-married women. White women experience the welfare state
in very different ways than black women, despite the similarity in the two
groups' labor-force participation rates and earnings. White female-headed
households are, as Frank Mott concluded, "more likely than black households to have greater access to *every single* income source except welfare."[26]

Because black single mothers disproportionately must turn to AFDC rather
than other social policies, their income and well-being lagged behind that of
all other groups. Compared to single mothers who received survivor's benefits under social security, veterans, and recipients of benefits from the black
lung program, women receiving AFDC were at a disadvantage. By 1980 the
total number of women and children receiving survivors' benefits totaled
10.5 million, almost equal to the AFDC caseload of 10.7 million persons,
yet payments for survivor's benefits were substantially higher than AFDC
payments and rose more rapidly after the Great Society.[27] In real terms the
value of survivor's benefits rose from about one-and-half times the AFDC
value of AFDC benefits in 1967 (the low point) to a peak of three times the
AFDC value in 1981 (see figure 9). While AFDC mothers were taking a hefty
pay cut, women and children receiving survivor's benefits surged ahead of
the inflationary tide of the late 1970s.[28]

Transfer payments have had a greater effect in reducing poverty for whites
than for nonwhites, an outcome attributable to the greater access of whites
to non-means-tested transfers and to the higher benefits they received compared to recipients of means-tested policies. Sheldon Danziger found that
transfers reduced poverty rates by about 41 percent in 1980 (measuring the

26. Frank L. Mott, "The Socioeconomic Status of Households Headed by Women,"
R&D Monograph No. 72 (Washington, D.C., 1979), p. 54; my emphasis.

27. While the rise in the AFDC caseload has been the subject of never-ending controversy, the equally stunning growth of the OASI survivor's caseload, which rose from 3.4
million in 1960 to 8.3 million in 1980, has hardly been noticed.

28. Use of a measure of the combined AFDC/food stamps benefit package would not
change this conclusion much because states were substituting food stamps for AFDC; see
page 328.

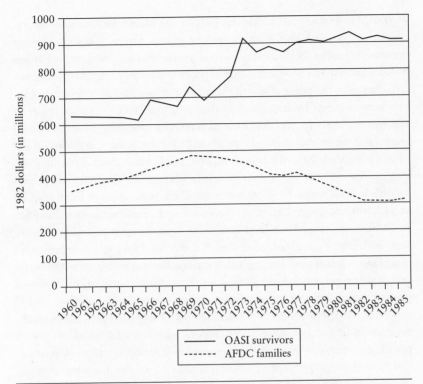

Figure 9. Average benefits to female-headed families by program 1960–1985. *Source: Social Security Bulletin, Annual Statistical Supplement, 1988* (Washington, D.C., 1988), tables 3.C4, 9.G1.

difference between pre- and post-transfer poverty rates). For nonelderly white male household heads, the percentage reduction was 30.6 percent; for black males, 21.4 percent; for white females, 22.4 percent; and for black females, just 13.7 percent. Over half of all black female household heads were left in poverty *after* receipt of transfers, almost twice the proportion of white female household heads. The transfer system betrays a gender bias: all female heads of household are more likely to receive means-tested assistance than male heads of household. But the proportion of white women and black men lifted out of poverty is about the same; that is, nonwelfare cash transfers have about the same effect for these two groups.[29]

Cash transfers were not only more effective in moving white families out of poverty, they were also more effective in raising their incomes. William

29. Sheldon Danziger, "Budget Cuts as Welfare Reform," *American Economic Review* 73 (1983): 66–67.

A. Darity Jr. and Samuel L. Meyers Jr. have calculated the combined effects of all transfers on families within specific income ranges. They asked what percent of families "with incomes within a given range . . . remain unchanged by [cash] transfers."[30] As a measure of the income-producing effects of transfers, they take the point at which the income of two-thirds or fewer of families is *unchanged* by transfers. At that point, only one-third or fewer of families are likely to find that their income rises as a result of transfer payments. For white male-headed families in 1976, this point is not reached until one exceeds a $25,000 annual income level. Among other families this income threshold is much lower. For black male and white female householders it is identical: $15,000 annually. Black women reach the threshold at $12,500 and single Latina mothers do worst of all, with the income for two-thirds unchanged at a level of $7,500. Transfers stop working to move families up the income ladder at a much lower level for black and Latina female family-heads than for any other group. The advantage of white males reflects their greater access to social insurance and other non-means-tested payments and their higher benefits, mostly because of their job histories.[31]

The irony of this is that cash transfers matter more to black single mothers than to almost any other group. Federal means-tested transfers have an enormous impact on their well-being, raising the incomes of black mothers and their children by 52 percent, compared to 31 percent for white mothers and children and just 11 percent for black male-headed families. Still, these transfer payments merely reshuffle black mothers along the poverty line; rather than being raised out of poverty, they are made less poor, an important but nevertheless insufficient outcome. As Darity and Myers put it, "while better off from transfers in the narrow sense that their incomes are higher, [they] are not much better off in the sense that they have moved considerably from their starting positions."[32]

30. William A. Darity Jr. and Samuel L. Myers Jr., "Transfer Programs and the Economic Well-Being of Minorities" (Mimeo, 1987), p. 34. Darity and Myers do not distinguish between the elderly and nonelderly, but Danziger's data show that this would not make a difference.

31. Ibid., pp. 35–38, table 9.

32. Ibid., p. 42. Darity and Myers do not include in-kind transfers as part of their analysis, and one might argue that the absence of food stamps biases the results. Black female-headed families are far more likely to receive food stamps and other noncash benefits, and thus the antipoverty and income effects of transfers would be greater than revealed by a study of cash transfers alone. There are inordinate technical difficulties to making this calculation, mainly because the Current Population Survey, March Supplement, does not include data on in-kind transfers. Aside from this problem, I am skeptical that it would make

The Great Society service programs might have offered a way out of poverty for many poor African American women, but changes in the distribution of federal services left them at the mercy of conduit colonialism. The job training programs utterly failed them. Dispersion of CETA funds to rural and suburban jurisdictions meant that fewer African Americans were served overall compared to the categorical programs that preceded CETA. The proportion of blacks enrolled in job training programs dropped from 46 to 40 percent between 1974 and 1978 and the proportion benefiting from public employment fell from 40 to 28 percent during the same period. But if blacks did less well than they had done under more targeted and centrally controlled categorical programs, they were overrepresented in CETA in relation to eligibility criteria. Women, by comparison, were by and large underserved in relation to need.

Eligibility decisions put fewer whites and fewer men in job training than in the more desirable, publicly funded jobs. One measure of this bias is the difference between eligibility and participation rates, which indicates whether a group is being served in relation to need. The gap between the number of women eligible and the number served by the training programs was negative 7 percent; there were, in other words, 7 percent fewer participating than were eligible. For the three public employment titles, the deficit for women was an average of 21 percent. Blacks made up just 17 percent of those eligible for training but 33 percent of the participants, or positive 16 percent. The net advantage for blacks in the public employment programs was much lower, just 5 percent.[33]

Not only did African Americans and other nonwhite groups get less than they did under a more targeted system of categorical grants, but programmatic boundaries continued to be demarcated by race, class, and gender. Blacks were almost 20 percent of those unemployed; they accounted for only 13.5 percent of those individuals receiving unemployment compensation and were disproportionate beneficiaries of CETA's training and public employment programs. When blacks and women were assisted they were banished to the Title I job training programs, which operated much as the 1960s programs had and functioned more as surrogate income-maintenance programs than as pathways to remunerative employment. During the first four years of the program, training for private sector jobs was de-emphasized in

much difference because states were substituting food stamps and Medicaid for AFDC payments throughout the 1970s, and the value of both food stamps and AFDC declined.

33. Barnes, "Target Groups," p. 79, table 4. It is next to impossible to get published breakdowns by race and gender for CETA.

favor of temporary, part-time employment. The structure of CETA programs was based on a distinction between poor families and the short-term unemployed, and discretionary decisions by program administrators perpetuated this distinction. Even within the training programs, racial and gender bias was at work. Sharon Harlan and Edward Hackett found that "black men and women were less likely than white women to be in on-the-job training and more likely to be in classroom programs," and classroom training was much less likely to lead to a permanent, unsubsidized job.[34] Blacks may have got more than their "share" of CETA slots, but they found themselves in a cul-de-sac.

It was AFDC mothers, however, who were mainly on the losing end of eligibility decisions. Title VI-B, a counter-cyclical job program that had the strictest eligibility requirements of any component of CETA, was reserved for women receiving AFDC, of whom 60 percent were eligible, and for the long-term unemployed. But AFDC mothers were a mere 12 percent of the participants in VI-B. The evidence indicates that a group in great need was deliberately denied access to a program that could have made a difference to their lives.[35] Nor did the Work Incentive Program (WIN), a work training program created specifically for AFDC recipients in 1967, help much. Federal regulations gave priority to unemployed fathers rather than single mothers. When questioned about this, a Nixon official told Congress that the policy was justified "because [men] have been in the employment market, and they do not have the problems that women are confronted with, without sufficient day care centers."[36] And in fact, the participation rate for men in WIN was double the proportion eligible. In 1978, for instance, about 9 percent of those eligible were unemployed fathers, but this group made up 16 percent of the beneficiaries.

Ironically, these distributive consequences were more severe in the most distressed and fiscally hard-pressed cities. Summarizing the results of a series of case studies of how federal money was spent in big cities, James Fossett

---

34. Sharon Harlan and Edward J. Hackett, "Federal Job Training Programs and Employment Outcomes: Effects by Sex and Race of Participants," Center for Research on Women, Wellesley College, Working Paper No. 129 (1984), pp. 6, 10–11. The racial disparity between on-the-job training and classroom training did not diminish when controlled for education, indicating that race has a separate effect.

35. Barnes, "Target Groups," p. 79, table 4.

36. The quote is from John Veneman, undersecretary of HEW, during hearings on the Family Assistance Plan in 1971. Cited in Sylvia A. Law, "Women, Work, Welfare, and the Preservation of Patriarchy," *University of Pennsylvania Law Review* 131 (1983): 1267.

wrote, "the share of CDBG and PSE [Public Service Employment] expenditures that benefited lower-income groups in the more prosperous cities was almost one and one-half times larger than in the poorer ones." In other words, it was precisely in those cities with sprawling ghettos, white flight, and disinvestment that incipient universalism did the most to subvert whatever was left of Lyndon Johnson's War on Poverty. Cleveland and Detroit stand out as two of the most egregious and interesting cases. Both cities were rigidly demarcated from white suburbs and their populations were at least two-fifths African American, but in each there was a clear middle-class tilt in the distribution of funds. Only one-third of public employment monies went to low- and moderate-income people, compared to an average of 63 percent in all poor cities and 96 percent in prosperous cities. Each city clearly distinguished between the clientele of training programs and the beneficiaries of public employment. In Detroit 92 percent of the funds for training went to low- and moderate-income people compared to only 25 percent of public employment dollars. Cleveland was not even this generous. Contrary to the law, the city used training funds to support public employment positions. The Brookings study estimated that 56 percent of the CETA benefits in Cleveland went to middle- and upper-income groups. Although blacks were major beneficiaries of CETA in Cleveland, only a small percentage entered unsubsidized employment. Of the operation of the public employment titles, Richard Tompkins concluded, "the most disadvantaged workers in the city have been under represented in the program and had the least promising outcomes."[37]

In addition to the entrenchment of racially segmented social policies, the distributive effects of the post-Nixon policy system put the inner-city poor in an excruciating bind. Although the welfare rights movement had been successful in establishing legal rights for the poor, federal social policy beginning with the 1967 amendments to the Social Security Act sought to condition cash transfers on work. Despite the disadvantages they faced in public employment and job training programs, many AFDC mothers mixed work and welfare throughout the 1970s. The labor-force participation rate for welfare mothers rose by 28 percent in the six years after Congress established explicit work incentives in 1967. In the early 1970s, it was estimated that 40 percent or more of women on welfare also worked, mostly in low-wage, dead-end jobs. National welfare policy in the 1970s was a de facto labor-market policy for

37. Richard Tompkins et al., *Case Studies of the Impact of Federal Aid on Major Cities: City of Cleveland* (Washington, D.C., 1981), pp. 42, 59, 61.

poor women, but it had less effect after 1974, when unemployment acceler-ated and disinvestment left inner-city mothers stranded.[38]

The failure to extend CETA jobs to this group except in the most minimal way created a bitter legacy. Work would be held up as the basis for success-ful welfare reform, a policy consistent with public preferences, but policy-makers failed to provide the requisite jobs. Bennett Harrison estimated that it would have taken 5.25 million jobs to accommodate the women who mixed work and welfare.[39] CETA never provided more than a fraction of the nec-essary jobs, and aggregate employment policies did not fill the gap. Although the process was less brutal and less visible than in the 1930s, once again white America had substituted relief for jobs. But, unlike the 1930s or even the 1950s, the political climate turned against social welfare programs, calling into question transfers for the poor and, ultimately, the welfare state itself.

The Post–Civil Rights Racial Divide over Social Policy

Post–civil rights social policy deepened racial divisions within the welfare state while doing little to remedy the underlying problem of African Amer-ican poverty. As the economy soured over the 1970s, resurgent Republicans manipulated white backlash against the Great Society and defined the moral rhetoric of a new policy regime. The Republican presidential victory in 1980 turned the enduring values of American political culture—self-reliance, hard work, and individual discipline—against the welfare state by invoking racial imagery deeply embedded in the history of federal social policy since the 1930s. By designating the inner-city poor as unworthy and dangerous, Ronald Reagan linked race and gender unmistakably to the failures of fed-eral social policy.[40]

---

38. Michael K. Brown and Steven P. Erie, "Women, Blacks, and Reagan's Assault on the Great Society" (paper presented to the American Political Science Association, Den-ver, Co., 1982), pp. 8, 11. The estimate of labor force participation rates is taken from Martin Rein and Lee Rainwater, "Patterns of Welfare Use," Working Paper No. 47, Joint Center for Urban Studies of MIT and Harvard University (Cambridge, Mass., November 1977), pp. 19–27.

39. Bennett Harrison, "Work and Welfare," in *Unemployment and Inflation,* ed. Michael J. Piore (White Plains, N.Y., 1979), p. 227.

40. See J. David Greenstone, "The Decline and Revival of the American Welfare State: Moral Criteria and Instrumental Reasoning in Critical Elections," in *Remaking the Wel-fare State: Retrenchment and Social Policy in America and Europe,* ed. Michael K. Brown (Philadelphia, Penn., 1988), pp. 165–82.

Republican success is often attributed by observers to a divisive racial consciousness promoted by black power ideology and civil rights militants. Moynihan believed black militants had a vested interest in fanning the flames of racial discord since they benefited from employment in social services and affirmative action. Jim Sleeper discerned similar motives at work. "While the language of the latter-day civil rights movement has remained that of legal rights," he stated, the black leaders have been more interested in distributing benefits according to race. "Such thinking [dodges] the reality of social class divisions, which are arguably more fundamental than racial divisions in perpetuating social injustice."[41] In this view, the racially coded rhetoric first used by George Wallce and then by many Republican politicians is a product of black militants, not of white racists. The problem with Sleeper's argument is that it evades the realities of the history of race and social policy in America, as well as entrenched racial privilege.

Race remained central to political conflict over social policy after the civil rights revolution because a form of Myrdal's vicious circle is sustained within the welfare state. Myrdal thought white racism was sustained by a vicious circle in which racial discrimination led to the economic degradation of African Americans, which in turn justified further discrimination. New Dealers had assumed that racially neutral social policies would raise the economic status of African Americans and diminish white racism. Myrdal's vicious circle was inverted, though, because federal social policies from the 1930s were implemented in racially discriminatory labor markets and used to bolster segregation in both North and South, which consigned African Americans to stigmatized means-tested policies. New Deal social policy ameliorated the economic plight of African Americans, but rather than diminishing white racism, it had the opposite effect and reinforced racial prejudices. A similar inversion occurred after the 1960s because of whites' insistence on maintaining the ghetto and the distributive legacy of the Nixon administration. Public transfers may have made life bearable for many, but the continued impoverishment and degradation of the black poor reinforced whites' antipathy to federal social policy and ascribed to all African Americans the invidious stereotypes of the black poor.

Conflict over federal social policy reflects a paradox: white racism created the racial hierarchies in the welfare state, which served, when retrenchment supplanted expansion, to justify white opposition to federal social policy. In this conflict, contrary to Sleeper and others, it is white Americans who keep

41. Jim Sleeper, *The Closest of Strangers* (New York, 1990), pp. 159–60, 163.

race alive as an issue by pursuing racially motivated opposition to new departures in social policy. African Americans acted in the 1970s, as they had since the 1940s, on a racially motivated interest in comprehensive, inclusive, and redistributive social policies.

Political support for specific social policies and for the basic obligation of the federal government to guarantee income or work rapidly deteriorated over the 1970s. Just when the welfare rights movement succeeded in articulating the idea of a right to income support, the public turned against welfare and governmental efforts to provide a guaranteed income for all citizens. Much of the public rejection of welfare and of any governmental obligation to assist the working poor was the expression of white hostility toward ADC and public housing that had begun to congeal during the welfare purges of the late 1950s. Most citizens were strongly divided along racial lines over many social policies, not just AFDC; only universalistic policies for the elderly were widely accepted. After examining public opinions across a range of social policies, James Kluegel and Eliot Smith concluded that, "race is the most frequently influential variable, with nonwhites significantly favoring all forms of redistribution toward the poor and away from the wealthy."[42] Blacks emerge from Kluegel and Smith's analysis as more likely to express "class consciousness" than do working-class whites.

This racial divide is apparent among both political leaders and voters. Black political leaders were obviously committed to improving the lives of all African Americans and asserting a black presence in American political and social life. But while most of them were influenced by the resurgence of black nationalism, they nevertheless advocated broad, universalistic social policies that would benefit all citizens. A survey of state and local politicians undertaken in the mid-1970s revealed that 76 percent of black elected officials believed that it is the responsibility of government to guarantee housing and income for all citizens, compared to just 30 percent of white elected officials. Leaders of civil rights organizations never missed an opportunity to point out the collective benefits of federal social policies and argue for a broader welfare state, much as an earlier generation had done in the 1940s. When he testified before the Senate Finance Committee on Nixon's Family Assistance Plan, Whitney Young Jr. argued strenuously for universal child care and employment training programs. Young's testimony was echoed by

42. James R. Kluegel and Eliot R. Smith, *Beliefs about Inequality* (New York, 1986), p. 169.

other civil rights leaders, and, importantly, by the Congressional Black Caucus (CBC).[43]

The handful of black legislators who founded the CBC initially saw themselves as the representatives of a national African American community and committed themselves to undertake "national case work" for the many blacks who lacked an African American representative or were represented by "white racist reactionary congressmen." CBC provided a mechanism of representation for thirty million blacks; "it allowed us," as one member put it, "to become congressmen at large."[44] Yet the CBC consistently advocated policies that would address "both the economic and political problems common to the nation and the black community."[45] For instance, they attached a proposal for a "universal voter registration act" to a demand to extend the Voting Rights Act. It was Augustus Hawkins, an African American congressman from South Central Los Angeles, who joined with Hubert Humphrey to sponsor the last attempt to create a national full employment policy. The budgets that the Congressional Black Caucus developed during the decade reveal an agenda and priorities that were anything but parochial.

Similarly, African American voters were substantially more likely than whites to believe that we spend too little on welfare and that the government has an obligation to guarantee an income for the working poor, to help people get medical care, and to guarantee jobs—beliefs that have not changed much over the last twenty years. Most African Americans actually have more in common with European attitudes toward the welfare state than with those of most white Americans. Surveys undertaken in the late 1970s showed four-fifths of Europeans believed that governments should guarantee a job for everyone who wants one; similarly about four-fifths of black Americans, agreed, compared with only one-third of all Americans.[46] African Americans

43. James E. Conyers and Walter L. Wallace, *Black Elected Officials* (New York, 1976), p. 31; Dona Cooper Hamilton and Charles Hamilton, *The Dual Agenda: Race and Social Welfare Policies of Civil Rights Organizations* (New York, 1997), pp. 185, 199–200, 202.

44. Augustus Adair, "Black Legislative Influence in Federal Policy Decisions: The Congressional Black Caucus, 1971–1975" (Ph.D. diss., Johns Hopkins University, 1976), pp. 29–30, 38.

45. *Congressional Record*, 94th Cong., 1st sess., vol. 121, pt. 5, p. 5413.

46. Kluegel and Smith, *Beliefs about Inequality*, pp. 170–74, figure 6.3; Tom W. Smith, "The Welfare State in Cross-National Perspective," *Public Opinion Quarterly* 51 (1987): 416. Michael C. Dawson reports differences between blacks and whites (based on the 1988 National Black Election Survey) every bit as large as those reported by James R. Kluegel and Eliot R. Smith. See *Behind the Mule: Race and Class in African-American Politics* (Princeton, N.J., 1994), p. 183.

were also more decisively in favor of explicit redistribution of wealth and government regulation of industry than were whites. The growth of the black middle class did not diminish African Americans' support for a comprehensive welfare state. Unlike whites, whose attitudes varied considerably depending on social class, blacks' attitudes were not significantly influenced by their socio-economic status. In fact, high-status blacks were more favorable toward redistributive policies than were low-status whites. Nor was the racial divide diminished by gender; white women's attitudes toward social provision were more similar to those of white men than they were to African Americans.[47]

Republicans and affluent voters display the most antagonism to the welfare state, but white Democrats are closer in their views on social policies and redistribution to Republicans (who are almost entirely white) than to black Democrats. For instance, 84 percent of black Democrats accept the proposition that the government has an obligation to assure the working poor a minimum income, compared to 54 percent of white Democrats and 36 percent of Republicans. And 61 percent of black Democrats consider poverty and jobs a very important issue, compared to just 35 percent of white Democrats and 27 percent of Republicans.[48]

In general, white attitudes toward federal social policy, especially those of white Democrats, relfect a mixture of fervent belief in America's individualist ethos and a consciousness of themselves as a group of beleaguered whites. White Americans consider success the result of hard work and individual self-reliance and reject policies they think benefit only blacks. The most alienated and hostile whites display a racial consciousness similar to what they suppose blacks adhere to, though few admit to it. Donald Warren called this group of whites Middle American Radicals and discovered that they were far more likely than other whites to identify themselves as whites who were excluded from power and influence as a consequence of the civil rights movement and black political mobilization. Warren's study showed that they felt "closer" to other whites than did low-income whites, highly educated whites, or other (though less radical) middle-class whites.[49] Among this group, white consciousness melded with middle-class individualism to fuel opposition to social policies for the poor.

The legacy of slavery and Jim Crow and the continuing experience of

47. One should not conclude from this that gender differences did not become important in the 1980s, yet a full treatment of this question is beyond the scope of this study.
48. Kluegel and Smith, *Beliefs about Inequality,* pp. 261–63, tables 9.8, 9.10.
49. Warren, *Radical Center,* pp. 96–98.

racial discrimination has given rise to a group consciousness that predis-poses African Americans, at least on questions of economic and social policy, to act more like European social democrats than practically any other group in America. In part this is a result of self-interest: the economic livelihood of many middle-class and poor blacks is tied to the public sector, whether through jobs or transfers. Yet self-interest alone is not a sufficient explana-tion. By the late 1970s and 1980s the black middle class was far less tied to public expenditures than it was at the outset of the Great Society, so some shift in attitudes might have been expected. This did not occur, and the rea-son, Michael C. Dawson suggests, is the strength of the perception of a linked fate, which "acts as a constraint on class divisions." Dawson argues that "regardless of economic status, the stronger the perceived link, the more likely one is to support policies of economic redistribution."[50] My analysis suggests that one crucial element of that linked fate is a stake in a welfare state that would rectify both racial injustice and economic inequalities and remove racial stigmatization from social policies.

There is no simple separation between race and class for African Ameri-cans. Since the New Deal, African Americans have understood that nothing less than both civil rights and viable social policies were required. This con-clusion was the outcome of the debate over race and class in the 1930s and the African American experience with the New Deal. Although the success of the civil rights movement changed the terms of this problem, it did not remove it. The main reason for this is that the fate of middle-class blacks is inseparable from that of poor blacks. "Middle-class blacks suffer from lower-class black life and circumstances," Raymond S. Franklin suggests. "They suffer because whites find it unreasonable in a quasi-segregated soci-ety, where resources and social amenities are distributed unequally, to make distinctions along class lines when it applies to African-Americans."[51] It is impossible for middle-class blacks to escape the black lower class (both lit-erally and figuratively, given the persistence of residential segregation); they therefore have an incentive to ameliorate the condition of the black lower class, an incentive that is more direct and concrete than it is ideological or humanitarian.

Whites' rejection of the Great Society derived, in part, from a profound sense of exclusion, which was tied to economic self-interest. Many middle-

50. Dawson, *Behind the Mule*, pp. 193–94.
51. Raymond S. Franklin, *Shadows of Race and Class* (Minneapolis, Minn., 1991), p. 112; also see pp. 121–23.

income whites believed they paid for Great Society programs but failed to benefit from them. There is no doubt some truth in this idea, and it was one of the motivating forces behind the tax revolts of the 1970s. But if the tax revolts were economic in origin and reflected unique circumstances, opposition to taxes was definitely tied to the racial bifurcation of federal social policy. Warren's Middle American Radicals, the most racially conscious group of white middle-class Americans, were twice as likely as other middle-class citizens to believe they should organize and protest taxes. Support for the California tax revolt was shaped more by racial attitudes than by partisan identification or ideology. White voters, regardless of party, opposed measures they thought benefited blacks and Hispanics. David O. Sears and Jack Citrin reported that among California voters "services whose clienteles are most widely thought to be racial minorities tend to be favored least. Welfare, public housing, food stamps, and unemployment compensation are the obvious examples."[52]

Economic self-interest alone is insufficient, however, to account for the racial polarization over Great Society social policies. For some whites, expressing disdain and hostility toward welfare was a way of asserting or at least reaffirming white superiority. Southern predilections can be understood in no other way. AFDC and food stamps expanded in the South, and African Americans were the main beneficiaries; southern whites literally hated it. A revealing anecdote drawn from FBI files during the height of the civil rights movement is indicative of southern views and the continuities between the welfare purges of the 1950s and the deepening disaffection with federal social policy in the 1970s. When three civil rights workers disappeared during the summer of 1964, the FBI launched an intensive search, fearing they had been murdered. While they dragged a river in Mississippi in search of the bodies, a local white farmer told them: "Hey, why don't you hold a welfare check over the water. That'll get that nigger to the surface."[53] Such odious racism was well-formed prior to the Great Society, and the linkage of blacks to welfare was used to rationalize opposition to Lyndon Johnson's social policies.

52. David O. Sears and Jack Citrin, *Tax Revolt: Something for Nothing in California* (Cambridge, Mass., 1985), pp. 47–49, 167–72; Warren, *Radical Center,* pp. 106–7; Clarence Y. H. Lo, *Small Property versus Big Government* (Berkeley, 1990), pp. 146, 162–65.

53. Quoted in Carter, *Politics of Rage,* p. 223; Sanders, "Electorate Expansion and Public Policy," p. 94. Sanders provides ample documentation of the racial split over AFDC and other Great Society policies in the South after the civil rights movement.

Some whites linked middle-class bootstrapping with racially stratified social policies, a phenomenon that antedates the Great Society. Warren provides striking evidence of this. Observing that the anger of Middle American Radicals cannot be assuaged by the mere augmentation of economic resources, he says:

> Efforts must be made to allow for the kinds of status differentiations which avoid having persons with identical homes living next to each other, or in the same neighborhood, when one of those individuals is paying half the rent of the other. Middle American Radicals are not against blacks having good housing, but they are concerned that in terms of some of the external trappings of status there was no basis for identifying those who had gone the conventional route and those who were being subsidized.[54]

White middle-class individualism, thus, is defined in opposition to blacks, who are seen as an excluded but ominous group who do not share white middle-class values. Warren argues there must be some recognition of how people arrived in the middle class, and "to wipe away . . . symbols of achievement and security is to undermine significantly the self-interest and psychic well-being of a major portion of the American middle class."[55] But viewed in light of the arguments in this book, one might say that such attitudes have allowed many white Americans to sublimate white advantage in the welfare state to black "dependence" and individual failure. By embracing a work ethos in opposition to what is seen as a racially based welfare state, many middle-class whites have been able to assert their superiority and deny blacks their individuality.

The Racial (De)construction of the Welfare State

After Nixon, public investment in the inner city for job training, public employment, neighborhood development, and other services diminished, leaving the inner-city poor on the receiving end of conduit colonialism. This is the 1970s version of what I have referred to in this book as the inversion of Myrdal's vicious circle. In the hands of resurgent conservatives, who were

54. Warren, *Radical Center,* p. 173.

55. Ibid., p. 174. Donald R. Kinder and Lynn M. Sanders provide some recent survey evidence for my argument. They note that "the [1960s] riots and inner-city life generally were interpreted by many whites as repudiations of individualism, sacred American commitments to hard work, discipline, and self-sacrifice." Hostility to African Americans is, today, "expressed in the language of American individualism" (*Divided by Color: Racial Politics and Democratic Ideals* [Chicago, 1996], pp. 105–106, 113–14, 118).

all too willing to invoke racial arguments, this inversion permitted the construction of a racial narrative that ascribed the failures of the Great Society to the emergence of an underclass nurtured by the federal government. In the 1980s, Ronald Reagan would follow Nixon's script; his budget changes intensified the distributive effects of federal social policy I have analyzed in this chapter. When combined with the exploitation of racial divisions within the electorate, the Republicans laid the foundations for an assault on the welfare state and ushered in the collapse of New Deal liberalism.

During Reagan's first term of office, funding for Great Society services was sharply reduced and what was left was folded into block grants. But Reagan rejected Nixon's substitution of transfers for services and sought to return federal welfare policy to its pre-1960 incarnation by repealing welfare benefits for the working poor and tightening up eligibility requirements. For all of the Reagan administration's preaching of the virtues of hard work, its social policies stripped away the work incentives and services that might have made a difference to poor women and men.

Budget outlays for Great Society services declined at an average annual rate of 6.4 percent in real dollars between 1979 and 1985 (see figure 8). This money was spread even more thinly. Title I of ESEA was cut by an average of 17 percent relative to fiscal year 1981 funding, and the targeting of funds on low-income children was reduced, effectively undoing one of the few remaining Johnson-era targeted programs. Title XX met the same fate. It was consolidated with other social service programs, funding was cut by one-fifth, and requirements for state matching funds and to restrict eligibility to the poor were repealed. The public service employment program was repealed, and CETA was replaced with a job training program that operated largely in the private sector and without the cash payments to trainees that had been federal policy since 1962. Funding was reduced by 35 percent, a "substantial decline in real funding for programs for the disadvantaged," noted the Congressional Budget Office.[56] Big cities, increasingly the location of the poor, suffered most from the cuts. Federal aid as a proportion of city expenditures dropped from an average of 22 percent in 1980 to just 6 percent in 1989 in cities with 300,000 or more residents.[57]

56. Congressional Budget Office, "Major Legislative Changes in Human Resources Programs since January 1981" (Staff Memorandum, Washington, D.C., August 1983), pp. 55–56, 61–62, 66.

57. Demetrios Caraley, "Washington Abandons the Cities," *Political Science Quarterly* 107 (1992): 11. According to Caraley, grants to cities declined by 46 percent in real dollars over the 1980s (p. 9).

Reagan repudiated the provision of public cash to any but the most destitute and rejected the notion of mixing work and welfare or the idea that income support should be conditioned on work. Work incentives were regarded as the equivalent of "dependency" incentives, and the administration proceeded to repeal the "thirty dollars and one-third rule," a 1967 policy, which had allowed AFDC recipients to keep more of their earnings. The Republicans also successfully limited eligibility to families with earnings below 150 percent of state need standards (which are typically lower than the official poverty line). This action created work disincentives by adding a large "notch" to AFDC and food stamps: individuals lose more than they gain if they earn too much, so they limit work (or lie about income obtained through work) in order to stay below the ceiling. The AFDC caseload was reduced by 447,000 women and children, or about 4 percent.[58]

The logic of Reagan's policies flew in the face of public opinion. Just as the public soured on welfare, a 1977 Roper poll found that 80 percent of those surveyed thought that "able-bodied" people should be removed from the welfare rolls and put to work and that public service jobs should be provided if there were insufficient private jobs. Three-fifths of Americans were in favor of guaranteed jobs at the end of the 1970s, and the racial divide was smaller on this issue than it was for cash transfers. Based on this kind of data, it was commonly argued that the public was not opposed to helping the poor or even opposed to the welfare state. The public in the wake of the 1960s had come to believe that the government should "help the poor but get rid of 'welfare.'"[59]

Hostility toward welfare abated in the wake of the Reagan budget cuts, but the perverse logic behind federal social policy after 1981 went unnoticed as the ground was dug out from beneath the urban poor, and poor black women and their children were demonized as a new and threatening underclass.

58. Robert M. Hutchins, "The Effects of the Omnibus Budget Reconciliation Act of 1981 on AFDC Recipients," *Research in Labor Economics*, vol. 8 (Greenwich, Conn., 1986), pp. 353–54, 365; Tom Joe and Cheryl Rogers, *By the Few, For the Few* (Lexington, Mass., 1985), pp. 34–37. Rather than substantially increasing work disincentives, Reagan's policies induced poor women to leave the welfare rolls. Between 55 to 75 percent of poor women mixing work and welfare prior to OBRA were off the rolls after 1981, but there was no substantial increase in the number of nonworking recipients (Hutchins, p. 373).

59. Seymour Martin Lipset and Earl Raab, "The Message of Proposition 13," *Commentary* (September 1978): 45.

PART V

THE PAST AND FUTURE
OF AMERICAN SOCIAL POLICY

CHAPTER ELEVEN

The Welfare State and Democracy in America

You must start with three facts: Most poor people are not on welfare. Most people on welfare are white, female and young. Two-thirds of the poor are women and children. A black mask has been put on the face of poverty. We must 'whiten' the face of poverty to change the dynamics of the debate.

— JESSE JACKSON

A despot who should subject the Americans and their former slaves to the same yoke, might perhaps succeed in commingling their races; but as long as the American democracy remains at the head of affairs, no one will undertake so difficult a task; and it may be foreseen that the freer the white population of the United States becomes, the more isolated will it remain.

— ALEXIS DE TOCQUEVILLE

Just before the 1994 congressional elections, the California Republican party mailed a glossy brochure entitled "The Welfare Mess" to many California voters. On the cover was a picture of food stamp coupons and hundred-dollar bills lying beneath a snub-nosed pistol, a marijuana cigarette, a bent spoon used to prepare heroin, and a syringe. Crime, drugs, welfare, and (implicitly) an "underclass" nourished by poor but irresponsible black women were sordidly related. The text inside linked welfare to social ills from teen pregnancy to declining SAT scores and warned voters, "If You Don't Vote, THEY WIN."

The saliency and power of this imagery were repeatedly demonstrated in Republican electoral victories throughout the 1980s but especially in 1994. Public opinion just prior to the election turned sharply negative toward both assisting the poor and racial equality.[1] Voter discontent with the federal safety net followed the collapse of President Clinton's attempt to create a national health insurance policy and culminated in the repudiation of forty years of Democratic rule in the House of Representatives in 1994. Just two

---

1. Times-Mirror Center for the People and the Press, *The People, the Press and Politics: The New Political Landscape* (Washington, D.C., 1994), pp. 29–32.

years later President Clinton and Congress agreed to repeal the AFDC entitlement and replace it with state-run block grants.

All welfare states face opposition today; none can escape the palpable hostility to tax burdens and fears that the large social insurance and transfer programs must be trimmed to maintain economic growth in a highly competitive global economy. Yet no other country has gone so far as America and repealed its basic cash entitlement for poor women and children. The comprehensive protection of European welfare states inspires solidarity or at least unified opposition to governmental proposals for austerity. Rather than accept minor reductions in social benefits sought by the government, the French shut Paris down for three weeks. Germans have been similarly intransigent when asked to accept retrenchment. But Americans, when faced with cuts in social provision, "don't mind throwing people overboard," one policy expert sardonically observed; "they just don't want to hear the splash."[2]

The United States is shredding its already weak safety net for working-age citizens at a time of widening income inequality, stagnant wages, economic insecurity among the middle class, and persistent, enervating poverty in big cities and rural communities. Class inequality, though, is overlaid by increasing racial inequality. The breach between the political and social rights of African Americans remains, and if anything has widened as a result of the economic turbulence of the last twenty years. For most residents of inner-city neighborhoods, life is isolated, precarious, and without hope. The proportion of blacks living in poverty remains unchanged since the mid-1960s—about one in three blacks remain below the poverty line compared to one in ten whites—but the absolute number of poor blacks in 1995 was about the same as it was in 1959 (10 million) while the number of whites in poverty has declined (by 4 million). Income disparities between the races remain wide. Thirty percent of black families had incomes below $15,000 (in 1995 dollars) in 1995 compared to 11.6 percent of white families. These data do not begin to convey the sense of hopelessness and futility that affects many young African American men and women who believe, with considerable justification, that they have been consigned to a nether world.[3]

2. "To French, Solidarity Outweighs Balanced Budget," *New York Times*, December 20, 1995, p. A1. The quote is from Robert Evans, a Canadian health economist, on a National Public Radio Broadcast, "Americans Ration Health Care." Evans was referring to the impact of the closure of county hospitals in northern California in the late 1980s.

3. *Statistical Abstract of the United States, 1997* (Washington, D.C., 1997), pp. 469, 476, tables 723, 728. One of the best studies of the relevant data and social implications is Troy Duster, "Postindustrialism and Youth Unemployment: African Americans as Har-

Nor has the black middle class escaped. The income and occupational gains brought by the Great Society have slowed dramatically or even been reversed. For instance, the earnings of full-time black workers dropped or remained constant relative to white workers over the last fifteen years at all levels of education. Remarkably, the greatest change in blacks' incomes relative to whites' was experienced by black male college graduates whose median income dropped from 85 percent to 72 percent of whites' median income. Both white males and females migrated to better-paying jobs over the 1980s, but black and Latino workers made at best marginal gains, moving from unskilled to semiskilled work. Moreover, blacks have been concentrated, according to Martin Carnoy, in jobs in which wages were more likely to stagnate or decline as a consequence of deindustrialization.[4]

Economic change and retrenchment exacerbates racial inequality at the same time that America's racially stratified welfare state fuels political discontent with patterns of social provision. In this book I have argued that the failure to construct a more integrated welfare state led to a racially stratified pattern of social provision in America. Both the failure of universalism and the contemporary racial divisions over social welfare call to mind Alexis de Tocqueville's prediction that racial equality is unattainable in America. Can the discrepancy between the political rights and social rights of African Americans be overcome? This question has renewed urgency in an era of persistent job insecurity, declining standards of living for many, and social conflict. As repeal of the federal entitlement for poor mothers and their children makes clear, this question cannot be separated from the issue of gender equality. Neither can it be understood without comprehending the antagonism between race and class at the core of America's welfare state.

Today many individuals would read race out of any discussion of social policy and poverty. Most conservatives believe (along with many white liberals) that the persistence of black poverty stems from a lack of motivation, not from an absence of jobs or from white privileges that deny or limit educational and economic opportunities. Many liberals, on the other hand, believe that the Democratic party cannot hope to reestablish itself as a vehicle for progressive social policies so long as it embraces the racial agenda of the 1960s; it will only become a majority party once again to the extent that it

bingers," in *Poverty, Inequality, and the Future of Public Policy,* ed. Katherine McFate, Roger Lawson, and William Julius Wilson (New York, 1995), pp. 461–86.

4. Martin Carnoy, *Faded Dreams: The Politics and Economics of Race in America* (New York, 1994), pp. 81–82, 89, 98–99, 102–4.

cultivates middle-class loyalties and sheds race-specific policies.[5] Neither of these views offers a way to break the knot of racial and class inequality. That requires understanding how the past has shaped our present opportunities. The history of race and social class in the political development of America's welfare state set forth in this book provides a critical perspective on these arguments and a basis for assessing our contemporary predicament.

Race, Money, and Universalism

The failure to construct a comprehensive, integrated welfare state that might have overridden the realities of America's color line—the legacy of both Jim Crow and discrimination in labor and housing markets—is best understood as the outcome of the choices of key policymakers, white southerners, trade unionists, and African Americans. These choices were shaped by conflicts over money and race.

In the two formative periods of welfare state building, Franklin Delano Roosevelt and Lyndon Baines Johnson failed to capitalize on their political leverage and ended up planting the seeds of racially stratified social policies, though neither intended to do so. FDR placed his faith in economic renewal, yet his social policies mocked the universalism of his rhetoric. He accepted contributory social insurance governed by stringent work-related eligibility requirements that excluded many workers; he vitiated the right to paid employment with a temporary work program that was so fiscally circumscribed that the distinction between work and relief was greatly diminished by the late 1930s and the program served only a fraction of those in need; and he turned over control of public assistance to states in order to limit the federal financial burden, but in the process stimulated passage of state sales taxes. FDR's welfare state was a means-tested, regressively financed affair that not only exacerbated the racial competition for jobs during the depression but also laid the foundations for a racially stratified welfare state.

LBJ set out to rectify black exclusion and to mitigate the social and economic consequences of migration. He responded to the racial and economic legacies of federal social policy by building a redistributive, rather than comprehensive, welfare state. Kennedy and Johnson, and their advisers, rejected proposals for public jobs programs and cash transfers, including universal-

5. See Michael Lind, *The Next American Nation: The New Nationalism and the Fourth American Revolution* (New York, 1995); and Thomas Byrne Edsall and Mary Edsall, *Chain Reaction: The Impact of Race, Rights, and Taxes on American Politics* (New York, 1992).

istic family allowances. Johnson's plan to build a redistributive state depended on a budget strategy that left him politically vulnerable and without alternatives once he launched the Vietnam War. Moreover, Johnson's effort to target money to ghetto communities was only modestly successful, as Congress was inclined to distribute the money across constituencies.

Money mattered to the choices of these two politically savvy presidents. Both framed their decisions so as to reconcile competing demands for social rights and capital accumulation. As he considered his choices in summer and fall of 1934, FDR confronted rising demands from senior citizens, workers, and the unemployed, on the one hand, and fearful, anxious investors, on the other. The policy settlement of 1935 and FDR's subsequent budget policies were driven by the necessity of managing these conflicting pressures. The budget strategy used by Kennedy and Johnson to launch their redistributive state was framed by the economic and political assumptions of the 1964 tax cut, which limited spending. Johnson persisted with this fiscally conservative strategy after his election, rejecting advice for additional spending programs in order to reassure investors that he was not about to give the store away.

Neither Roosevelt nor Johnson was oblivious to the need to craft policy in light of the institutional realities of federalism and separation of powers, and both men took these factors into account. Yet the evidence adduced in this study demonstrates the significance of money to their deliberations and choices, and, more broadly, the relevance of fiscal capacity to the development of welfare states. Any account of social policies which ignores the limits to state autonomy—the structural constraints of capitalism—is insufficient. Though the importance of investor and taxpayer resistance varies with the circumstances, no policymaker, especially none intent on adding new social policies, can escape the necessity of balancing the claims of entrepreneurs and taxpayers against the beneficiaries of new policies.

Money was also decisive to choices made by opponents of the welfare state. The liberals of both the 1940s and the 1970s tried to go beyond the New Deal and Great Society policy revolutions and enact broader, more comprehensive social policies that would rectify Roosevelt's and Johnson's failures. In each case they failed, though the outcome left a residue of social policies that incrementally added to the welfare state while shifting the distribution of benefits to middle-class citizens. The conservative coalition and the Nixon administration aimed to contain social spending and future tax increases by confining federal social policy to means-tested policies or, in the 1970s, block grants. The key here is that neither the southern Democrats nor Nixon were averse to using social policies to further their political aims.

In the 1940s, southern Democrats had most of the political leverage, joining with Republicans to defeat Roosevelt's and Truman's ambitious policies, but allowing northern Democrats to woo them with policies crafted to benefit the South. Expansion of public assistance and new spending programs were turned to southern aims, but only so long as northern liberals acquiesced in the use of federal funds to build a segregated welfare state. Nixon set out to remake the Great Society by trading services for transfers and carving out policies of benefit to middle-class constituencies. Block grants were the ideal political tool for Nixon's ambitions; they put a lid on spending but permitted its distribution to potential Republican constituencies.

The failure to build on the universal social insurance programs of the New Deal is usually ascribed to race-specific policies of the 1960s and the misguided adventures of black nationalists, who were blind to the wisdom of Bayard Rustin's call for an alliance with white workers. My analysis calls this interpretation sharply into question. Those who ascribe the political failures of the Great Society to African Americans also oversimplify the motivations of black political elites to acquire some control over federal social policies in the 1960s. The Community Action program, for example, was important to many blacks not just because of its political potential but because it was a source of leverage to erase the color line in federal social policy.

Nor can one argue that Rustin's effort failed because of the institutional impediments to the formation of broad political coalitions within the American political system. White workers were simply unwilling to sign on to universalistic social policies by the 1960s. This was partly due to their short-term economic interests. Unions negotiated private social policies when business executives made union security an issue in the 1940s. Although unions stimulated the growth of private pensions and successfully equalized the distribution of private health policies, they also lost interest in a more comprehensive welfare state after 1950. In addition, white workers acted on what they perceived to be their short-term interests in maintaining racial control over labor and housing markets and in preserving the color line. White flight from the Great Society is a far more cogent explanation for the persistence of racially stratified social policies and the failure to create a biracial political coalition than black nationalism, race-specific policies, or fragmented political institutions.

Ironically, African Americans, notably including black nationalists, have been the staunchest defenders of a federally controlled, universalistic welfare state from the 1930s to the present day. Martin Luther King Jr. regarded the Great Society as a failure, but for substantially different reasons than today's critics. The Great Society was unequal to the task of significantly diminishing the numbers of white and black poor, he thought; it failed on its own terms. Many whites have failed to understand Martin Luther King's insight that class and racial inequality are fundamentally linked and cannot be severed. Without this understanding, it is difficult to account for structural advantages and disadvantages that derive from differential access to the welfare state between blacks and whites, and men and women, or to see the possibilities for change.

The Divergent Fates of African Americans and White Americans

The racial narrative of the American welfare state has rendered invisible for most white Americans, the practices that have perpetuated ghettos and sustained white control of labor markets, obscuring the relationship between our history of racism and the development of collective instruments of social provision since the 1930s. This history belies the conventional wisdom about African American poverty. Far from being the moral hazard that many conservatives believe the welfare state to be, federal social policy has offset some of the perils of a racist society. There is no doubt that African American economic progress has depended on the welfare state. Limited though they were, New Deal relief policies rescued many African American families from despair and economic degradation. Without them, blacks would have been much worse off. Similarly, public housing and ADC served to stave off economic deprivation when African Americans encountered northern discrimination and stagnant employment during the 1940s and 1950s. It was the Great Society, however, that had the most dramatic effects on African American well-being. These were not limited to passage of civil rights laws, but encompassed public employment and many new service and transfer programs that were of inestimable value to black families.

Yet the political development of public social provision has also united racially stratified social policies with solicitude for the white middle class. This combination has had different consequences for the material well-being and economic opportunities of whites and blacks. Work is the main path to adequate social protection in America. The racial stratification of social policies is anchored by the denial of work to blacks and by occupational and wage discrimination against them. Although African Americans were disadvantaged by the statutory exclusion of agricultural and domestic workers from social insurance in 1935, it is mainly labor-market discrimination that has led to different benefits in social insurance programs and the substitution of relief, or means-tested benefits, for jobs. This process worked differently before and after the civil rights legislation of the 1960s.

The New Deal's racial liberalism assumed that broad social policies and economic reform would undermine the basis of white racism by equalizing the economic condition of blacks and whites. This vision was always something of a delusion, since New Dealers failed to confront the realities of southern apartheid and the labor-market discrimination that displaced African Americans and eroded the marginal economic gains they made during the 1920s. New Deal social policies acted to reinforce rather than mitigate labor-market discrimination, as displaced African Americans were relegated to general relief and then work relief while whites left to take private sector jobs. This pattern of social provision reappeared after World War II, when job discrimination and continued migration of both rural blacks and whites to cities intensified labor-market competition and coincided with structural unemployment as corporations shed manufacturing jobs. Blacks made striking economic gains as they moved from low-wage work in agriculture to jobs in manufacturing, yet their cumulative labor-market disadvantages reproduced depression-era conditions in which relief was substituted for work, particularly in northern industrial states. Both AFDC and public housing had become programs that predominantly served African American families in both the North and the South, and by the end of the 1950s racial distinctions had, in some ways, become as important as income thresholds in defining beneficiaries.

Passage and enforcement of the 1964 Civil Rights Act diminished labor-market discrimination and thus one basis for racially stratified social policies. But the Great Society failed to dismantle the ghetto, the other axis of America's system of racial stratification, and in this context Lyndon Johnson's social policies reproduced the color line in federal social policy. Kennedy and Johnson both chose to retarget federal services on impoverished black communities in response to the civil rights movement's demand for jobs. The Johnson administration pumped needed resources into impoverished communities—a process that was intensified as the Vietnam War drained off resources and the cities exploded—but federal employment and training policies, like the relief policies of the 1930s, cycled black workers between low-wage jobs and cash transfers or between low-wage jobs and training slots. Little was done to alter the structure of ghetto labor markets; indeed federal social policy served to reinforce the racial bifurcation of urban labor markets.

When the policy revisions of the Nixon administration diminished Johnson's service programs or replaced them with block grants, cash and in-kind transfers became the core federal social policy for the black poor, which left them trapped in economically declining ghettos with few avenues out. The poor were entitled to cash and in-kind transfers that diminished in value over the 1970s, while the massive outlays in job programs of the 1970s more or less by-passed them. White Americans chose to preserve the ghetto and paid for it with meager but racially stigmatized means-tested transfers.

Black disadvantage is only part of the story. The other side is white advantage. White control of labor markets gave them privileged access, progressively, to WPA jobs, to work-related public social insurance entitlements, and to private social policies extracted by unions from corporations. But white Americans have obtained more than protection against unemployment, illness, and old age from the American welfare state; the postwar expansion of the American welfare state has undergirded and sustained middle-class prosperity. Private health policies were tilted toward middle-class citizens, as were the tax breaks that underpinned them; veterans' readjustment benefits facilitated interclass mobility for many white men; discriminatory federal housing policies aided the white middle class in its flight to the suburbs. White southerners used their privileged access to the welfare state in the 1950s to offset pervasive poverty and lay the foundation for a new southern middle class that would find its political home in the Republican party after 1965. In the 1970s, block grants were of inestimable benefit to many middle- and lower-middle class families, and small, mostly suburban communities found themselves on the receiving end of a federal entitlement, revenue sharing.

The group of whites who have arguably and deservedly benefited most from the policy revolution of the 1960s were white women. The growth of AFDC in the 1960s, stimulated by the civil rights movement and the political activism unleashed by the War on Poverty, staved off economic degradation for many white women who found themselves beset by "husband failure"—abandonment, separation, or divorce—rather than market failure. And it was working white women who benefited from the incipient universalism of Title XX social service block grants.

Although women are disproportionately beneficiaries of the welfare state, either as providers or recipients, the history of social policy since the 1930s revises any notion that America's dual welfare state is based solely on a distinction between a social insurance channel for white, male workers and a public assistance channel constructed for women. Progressive Era social policy drew sharp distinctions based on gender. Social insurance was based on the assumption that incomes of male breadwinners should be protected; Mothers' Pensions, the first public assistance program of any consequence, reflected the assumptions of maternalism, the idea of a separate sphere for women.[6] Although Mothers' Pensions were retained as a separate categorical program, the gender basis of the dual welfare state was modified after 1939. Amendments to the Social Security Act that year extended the patriarchal logic of social insurance by adding survivors' benefits and drawing a distinction between different kinds of mothers—those whose benefits were legitimized by marriage and those whose benefits were not.

Yet it is not gender alone that defines AFDC; after 1939 AFDC was understood as a program for African Americans. The welfare purges of the 1950s were by and large racially motivated, fusing race and sex in explosive but pernicious ways. When white women moved onto the rolls in large numbers after 1965, they were folded into a program already encrusted by racial stereotypes. After the 1930s, in other words, race overlapped programmatic boundaries in a way that gender did not.

White and black women have had different relationships to the welfare state, even though both have been burdened by the implicit patriarchal assumptions of social policy—the male breadwinner model and the absence of any remuneration for household labor—and by labor-market discrimination. Both also have been disadvantaged by the operation of many post-1930s social policies. Until recently veterans programs excluded all women, except as survivors, and the War on Poverty singled out young men as the main recipients of federal intervention. Women have been most disadvantaged by the choices local governments made in selecting those who would participate in CETA. All women have had a stake in social policies that promised to give them economic independence and mitigate gender inequality, but the experiences of black and white women have been and continue to be profoundly different.

The cash transfer system protects white women against husband failure in addition to helping never-married mothers.[7] White women rely less on

6. Barbara Nelson, "The Origins of the Two-Channel Welfare State: Workmen's Compensation and Mother's Aid," in *Women, the State, and Welfare,* ed. Linda Gordon (Madison, Wisc., 1990), pp. 123–51; Linda Gordon, "Social Insurance and Public Assistance: The Influence of Gender in Welfare Thought in the United States, 1890–1935," *American Historical Review* 97 (1992): 19–54.

7. Mary Jo Bane, "Household Composition and Poverty," in *Fighting Poverty: What Works and What Doesn't,* ed. Sheldon H. Danziger and Daniel H. Weinberg (Cambridge, Mass., 1986), pp. 209–31.

AFDC than black women, and they have greater access to social insurance (OASI) and veterans programs, whether through marriage or through independent, work-related entitlements. For most black women the only alternative to AFDC is work, but not the kind of work that would typically support a family. This problem is compounded by the effects of the racial apartheid endemic to America's cities, an apartheid which influences the distribution of resources, sustains racially segmented policies, and intensifies the disadvantages of poverty.[8] Cash transfers, as we have seen, do more to raise white women out of poverty than they do for black or Latina women.

Both race and gender matter to the distribution of social protection, and it is the intersection of the two that has given the contemporary welfare debate its incendiary qualities. That debate reflects both the legacy of Progressive Era reformers (who used Mothers' Pensions as a tool to assimilate poor ethnic women to white middle-class norms) and the history of race and social policy since the 1930s. Daniel Patrick Moynihan has done more than any other major figure in the history of recent social welfare policy to fuse these two legacies. There is little that is truly original in the famous Moynihan report; not only did he rely on E. Franklin Frazier's depiction of black families, but he merely repeated what was the conventional wisdom within the social welfare establishment at the time. Yet the report transformed the debate over racial equality, shifting it from a question of access to jobs and unemployment to a matter of "illegitimacy" and the social consequences of female-headed families.

Moynihan's motives were always more benign and naive than his many critics have acknowledged, but his report recalled the racist imagery applied to ADC in the 1950s and reinvoked a history of coercive policies dedicated to "reforming" the character of poor women. Moynihan has erroneously ascribed the 1960s rise in the AFDC caseload to the breakdown of the black family rather than to the broadening of eligibility criteria, Supreme Court decisions that struck down residence requirements, and work incentives added by Congress in 1967. In doing so, he concocted a specious theory that now ties poverty to the behavioral choices of the poor. Moynihan assumed that falling unemployment rates and a rising AFDC caseload meant that the connection between unemployment and welfare had been broken, leaving illegitimacy as the main culprit behind the growth of the program. This conclusion willfully ignored the fact that far fewer women received AFDC

8. Douglas Massey and Nancy Denton, *American Apartheid: Segregation and the Making of the Underclass* (Cambridge, Mass., 1993), pp. 118–42.

benefits before the 1960s than were entitled to them. The precipitous rise in the caseloads had more to do with changes in the law and administrative decisions and a temporary decline in the stigma attached to AFDC than with changes in women's marital and reproductive behavior.[9]

Unlike most conservatives, Moynihan has always been an advocate of universalistic family allowances, which he assumed would have more political support among the public than programs created specifically for African Americans. At the same time, he remains one of the most forceful proponents of a behavioral theory of poverty that implicates the failure of women, particularly black women, to make responsible choices. This position is clearly articulated in some of his recent essays. Recalling the findings of *One-Third of a Nation,* a 1963 report on the wide differences in the physical and educational capacities of black and white men drafted into the Army, Moynihan allows that he was originally mistaken in thinking that poverty caused these differences. "What I had not adequately grasped," he wrote, "was the degree to which these unequal distributions of property were in turn dependent upon a still more powerful agent—the behavior of individuals and communities." From here it was but a short step to concluding that "behavioral differences" between groups, mainly differences in family structure, are the principal cause of poverty, rather than unemployment or the inequalities generated by capitalism or racial discrimination. In this indirect sense, Moynihan's interpretation paved the way for the draconian behavioral modification policies that are a staple of so-called welfare reform.[10]

Today many politicians blandly write off poverty as the product of a "welfare culture" and ignore gender inequality and the racism that perpetuates ghettos. They take refuge in the Moynihan Report, which has become the main weapon in a campaign that has destroyed the federal public assistance entitlements Senator Moynihan defends. The claim that welfare has led to the demise of the black family is open to serious question. Evidence that transfer payments have led to the break-up of two-parent black families is unpersuasive.[11] If welfare is detrimental to individual motivation and

9. Daniel Patrick Moynihan, *Family and Nation* (Cambridge, Mass., 1986), pp. 22–23. See also Moynihan's *The Politics of a Guaranteed Income* (New York, 1973), pp. 82–85.

10. Daniel Patrick Moynihan, "Toward a Post-Industrial Social Policy," *The Public Interest* 96 (Summer 1989), pp. 20–21, 23, 25.

11. See William A. Darity Jr. and Samuel L. Myers Jr., "Does Welfare Dependency Cause Female Headship? The Case of the Black Family," *Journal of Marriage and the Family* 46 (1984): 765–79.

leads to "dependence," as conservatives and many liberals believe, the explanation lies not with the generosity of the welfare state but with an un-willingness to provide alternatives to relief, such as work or even the accou-terments of economic opportunity—education, job training, health insurance, and adequate day care. Complaints that the Great Society wasted precious resources evades the truth. Johnson's social programs were underfunded, and even when money was successfully targeted on poor communities, the pro-grams could not overcome white control of labor markets. Resources that might have made a difference in ghetto communities were deflected during the 1970s.

In their quest to construct a politically powerful critique of the welfare state, many conservatives have merely embroidered upon the deleterious stereotypes that emerged during the 1930s with the coercive substitution of relief for work for African Americans and that were fostered during and af-ter World War II when black sharecroppers migrated northward. Many of the comments of more recent conservatives recall Newton Baker's fears in the middle of the depression that the high proportion of African Americans on relief in Cleveland could easily lead to social chaos. There seems to be a straight line running from Baker's worry to contemporary ruminations about a "welfare culture" and the "underclass." And the easy equation of black degradation with welfare is all too reminiscent of southern hostilities toward relief and transfers that flourished before and after the civil rights revolu-tion. There is hardly any difference between Jimmy Davis's vitriolic assault on black women on AFDC during the 1960 Louisiana gubernatorial cam-paign and the inflammatory brochure mailed to California voters by the state Republican committee in 1994.

African Americans have always understood the perverse logic of means-tested policies in a racist society and have demanded jobs rather than relief. Fears that the concentration of blacks on relief rolls during the 1930s would reinforce racial prejudice led the National Urban League to initiate a vigor-ous lobbying effort for a permanent public employment policy. African Amer-ican trade unionists and civil rights leaders of the 1940s lobbied fiercely for full-employment policies and universalistic social insurance. Roy Wilkins was fully aware of the threat that racial stigmatization of AFDC posed to the civil rights movement, just as Jesse Jackson today understands that por-traying poverty as a black affair feeds white prejudices and erodes support for any reasonable assault on poverty. Nevertheless, most black leaders—from John Davis of the National Negro Congress to Martin Luther King Jr.—and most black groups—from the National Welfare Rights Organization to the Congressional Black Caucus—have also defended guaranteed incomes for all citizens. African Americans, by and large, recognize the necessity of these policies in a society where the color line is still a reality.

Gunnar Myrdal assumed that the cycle of black degradation and white prejudice would be overturned with black economic progress. But the ironic result of the relationship between race and social policy since the depression has been an inversion of Myrdal's vicious circle: the alleviation of black suffering has reinforced pernicious racial stereotypes. Many white Americans have come to see blacks as both the authors and the defenders of policies they regard as odious. This assumption not only masks their responsibility for the construction of ghettos and the moral failure that allows them to persist, it also sustains whites' illusions about their own independence and obscures the advantages they receive from federal social policies by seeing blacks' ties to the welfare state as being based on "dependence" and individual "failure." All this of course has merely provided the true enemies of the welfare state with ample opportunities to manipulate racial hostilities for their cause. A crucial question is whether this historical link between race and social policy can be overcome.

Race, Poverty, and American Social Policy

Whether African Americans will continue to be "victims of democracy," to use Malcolm X's stinging phrase, depends on the willingness of Americans, especially white Americans, to grapple seriously with the deeply rooted problems of race, poverty, and despair. Breaking the link between race and social policy requires convincing white Americans to tax themselves for programs that, as Richard Titmuss put it, would "channel proportionately more resources [to poor people of color] without inducing shame or stigma."[12] The only sure way to do this according to some writers is either through universalistic social policies or through a "color-blind" politics. Although the former appeals to the class interests of whites while the latter presumes that only policies morally justified by nonracial appeals will succeed, either approach presumably would overcome the limitations of "race-specific" policies while permitting the redistribution of resources to inner-city communi-

---

12. Richard M. Titmuss, *The Philosophy of Welfare*, ed. Brian Abel-Smith and Kay Titmuss (London, 1987), p. 129.

ties.[13] Both arguments are based on dubious assumptions and evade the legacies of race and class for the American welfare state.

Large, completely universalistic transfer programs such as social security may mitigate overt racial distinctions, but such programs would have to be very large and very expensive to have any appreciable effect on ghetto poverty. Even if the Democrats were to regain congressional majorities (itself problematic), investors' fears of rising federal deficits and inflation along with widespread opposition to taxation would preclude adoption of comprehensive programs. Money still matters, and if anything the fiscal imperatives that have governed construction of the American welfare state are more powerful today than ever before. Any policymaker attempting either to expand social rights or to remedy poverty must face up to the *possibility* of retaliation by the market: the withdrawal of economic resources. In a globally integrated economy where capital moves in and out of countries with ease, new social policies are subject to a constant threat that any increase in spending or taxes may provoke a corresponding drop in investment and massive layoffs. And these threats have consequences. For example, in the 1994 legislative struggle over President Clinton's health care plan, just the threat of disinvestment—the claim that jobs would be lost if the government mandated an employer contribution for health insurance—proved influential in turning public opinion against the plan.

Is there a solution short of creating new universalistic programs? Is some form of "targeting" inevitable? William Julius Wilson argues that political conflict over social policy in America is not simply a matter of the divisive effects of means testing; it is less important whether social policies are targeted or universalistic than that any policy be "clearly race neutral."[14] The problem, Paul M. Sniderman and Edward G. Carmines suggest, is to convince those whites who are not opposed to federal social policies as a matter of principle but who oppose race-specific policies or any form of racial targeting, rather than to convince conservatives, who dislike expanding the social welfare responsibilities of the federal government. Public opinion data indicate that any policy that smacks of racial targeting erodes public

13. Theda Skocpol, *Social Policy in the United States* (Princeton, N.J., 1995), pp. 250–74; William Julius Wilson, *When Work Disappears: The World of the New Urban Poor* (New York, 1996), pp. 235–38; Paul M. Sniderman and Edward G. Carmines, *Reaching beyond Race* (Cambridge, Mass., 1997).

14. William Julius Wilson, "Another Look at *The Truly Disadvantaged*," *Political Science Quarterly* 106 (1991–92): 656.

support. For example, 70 percent of white Americans indicated in one survey that they would favor special tax breaks for businesses in poor neighborhoods, but only 43 percent would favor tax breaks in the ghetto. Like Wilson, Sniderman and Carmines think that race-neutral or color-blind policies would persuade many whites to support new or expanded social policies.[15]

This argument begs the question of what constitutes a "race-neutral" policy in a racially stratified society. Nonexclusive, race-neutral policies in America have a way of being particularized along racial lines. AFDC is the classic instance. But the difficulty is not limited to a means-tested cash transfer program which most people dislike anyway. Historically, one of the most legitimate social policies has been public education; but it has also been, and continues to be, one of the most racially stratified. "Separate but equal" obviously did not mean racially neutral, despite *Plessy v. Ferguson;* but neither does the contemporary acceptance of de facto school segregation as a consequence of voluntary housing preferences. It is hard to see what would constitute a race-neutral policy for public schools in a society with deep and enduring residential segregation. Whatever their feelings about education, white suburbanites have been reluctant to raise their taxes to rectify the deterioration of inner-city schools.[16]

New social policies might be nonexclusive, but they are unlikely to remove race from social policy. Proposals for neo-WPA programs illustrate the problem. Mickey Kaus believes that work relief would be both more acceptable to the American public and more effective in remedying urban poverty simply because it responds to the ideology of the work ethic.[17] But would a new public employment program continue to be viewed as part of a race-neutral safety net, especially as it became clear that the need for it would continue long into the future and that a disproportionate number of the beneficiaries were racial minorities? If the experience of the New Deal, or even the public employment programs of the 1970s, are any guide, Kaus's new WPA would inevitably be seen as relief for poor blacks. It is worth recalling that one social program eliminated outright in 1981 was public service employment,

15. Jill Quadagno, *The Color of Welfare* (New York, 1994), pp. 172–73; Sniderman and Carmines, *Reaching beyond Race,* pp. 105–9, 115–18, 153–54.

16. In *Pasadena City Board of Education v. Spangler,* 427 U.S. 424 (1976), the Supreme Court overturned a desegregation plan on grounds that remedies constructed to overcome voluntary housing preferences were unacceptable. For a disturbing portrayal of the racial stratification in public education, see Jonathan Kozol, *Savage Inequalities* (New York, 1991). I am indebted to Francis Fox Piven for suggesting the example of education.

17. Mickey Kaus, *The End of Equality* (New York, 1992), pp. 125–29.

a program in which blacks were disproportionate beneficiaries.[18] Any new programs to remedy inner-city poverty, moreover, will compete with other needs—for example, retraining of workers displaced by global economic competition—and likely reproduce the New Deal pattern of racially biased allocation of public resources combined with the stigmatization of whatever assistance is provided for the poor.

Those who seek salvation in comprehensive social policies or color-blind remedies cannot avoid confronting the question of race or the question of gender inequality. They cannot ignore, as Bayard Rustin did, the implications of white control of labor markets, an issue that remains salient today. Black political elites at that time did not assume that comprehensive public works or jobs programs would necessarily benefit blacks; in fact, they assumed that African Americans would be short-changed. This is the reason universalism was always coupled with strong civil rights policies. There is no reason to assume labor-market discrimination will not be a continuing problem, especially now that affirmative action policies are under attack. Even William Julius Wilson admits that "opportunity-enhancing programs that include race-based criteria" should be combined with race-neutral policies.[19]

The problem is similar to that faced by Lyndon Johnson in the 1960s: how to target limited resources to poor communities seen to be undeserving of any assistance. Johnson could not overcome the link between "race and dependence," even though his policies were designed by and large as race-neutral policies that "would permit, and should permit, the concentration of these programs in areas in which the beneficiaries would be predominantly Negro."[20] To break this link will require something more than policy engineering. Paul Sniderman and Thomas Piazza suggest that if the question of race is just as conflictual as it has always been, it is more amenable to solution precisely because questions of racial equality have now become part of a racial politics. White Americans, they argue, are open to persuasion; they may hold injurious stereotypes that preclude new policies to assist the urban poor, but they can be persuaded to change their minds.[21] Perhaps, though,

18. Donald C. Baumer and Carl E. Van Horn, *The Politics of Unemployment* (Washington, D.C., 1985), pp. 115–16, 159–165.

19. Wilson, *When Work Disappears,* p. 205.

20. Attorney General Nicholas Katzenbach to Califano, December 13, 1965, attached to "Civil Rights Program for 1966," p. 9, Harry McPherson Papers, box 21, folder "Civil Rights," LBJL.

21. Paul Sniderman and Thomas Piazza, *The Scar of Race* (Cambridge, Mass., 1993), pp. 166–178.

contemporary politicians have been more willing to inflame racial passions for electoral advantage than to educate citizens.

The tie between race and social policy in America cannot be removed by ignoring it, despite the ideology of a color-blind society. Nor can we put all our faith in incremental policy changes that might marginally improve people's lives, while at the same time ignoring the racial legacy of our social policies. Nor will black and white workers comprehend a common fate by sublimating race to class. African Americans and Latinos should not be asked to give up their claims for racial equality for the fantasy of reinvigorated class coalition. Whereas many whites tend to think that racial equality must be sacrificed to overcome class divisions, African Americans have always understood the necessity of reconciling the two. The legacy of Ralph Bunche and W. E. B. Du Bois, the antipodes of the black debate over the New Deal, remain the starting point for any consideration of ways to overcome divisions of race and class. The only question is whether those white citizens, men and women, who would benefit from a more durable and broader welfare state are willing to confront the realities of race and the history of American social policy.

Index

Abbott, Grace, 91
Ackely, Gardner, 240, 247, 258–59
African Americans: family, 93–94,
  210–11, 368; and Great Society, 239,
  267, 324–25; migration and welfare
  policies, 88–89, 166, 195, 210; and
  New Deal relief, 77–81, 84–87; poverty,
  358; and social security, 2, 14, 61–62,
  82; unemployment, 69–70, 192–93,
  206, 215–17; and unions, 16, 67–68,
  164, 271, 278–79, 282–84; veterans,
  9, 189–91; and welfare state, 26, 165,
  346–49, 363–64; women, 90–91, 93,
  189, 190–91, 334–40, 366. See also
  Racial discrimination
Agnew, Spiro, 309
Aid to Families with Dependent Children
  (AFDC): attacks on, 167–69, 357; and
  CETA, 342; in Chicago, 187, 195;
  development of, 90–91, 125, 174–75,
  213, 254–55, 327–28, 353; growth of
  caseloads, 93, 171–76, 255, 331; and
  race, 185–86, 311–12, 331–35, 346; in
  South, 126, 175–76, 194, 198–99, 334.
  See also Racial stigmatization of social
  policy
Albert, Carl, 214
Alexander, Will, 64
Altmeyer, Arthur, 56, 58, 104, 112–13
American Federation of Labor (AFL),
  136, 141–42
American Federation of Labor & Con-
  gress of Industrial Organizations
  (AFL-CIO), 26, 161–63, 282
American Medical Association, 137
Antidiscrimination amendments, 111–12,
  132–33, 207, 213, 216
Arnold, Thurman, 122
Auto Workers (UAW), 140, 146–47, 150,
  283–84. See also Reuther, Walter

Baker, Newton D., 77, 369
Baltimore Commission on Governmental
  Efficiency and Economy, 171
Bethune, Mary McLeod, 66
Bilbo, Theodore, 107, 134, 197
Biracial political coalitions: and African
  Americans, 66–67, 76, 164; in Great
  Society, 265–66, 278–80, 362. See also
  Rustin, Bayard
Block grants-in-aid, 298, 305, 343; devel-
  opment of, 317–20; middle-class bene-
  fits of, 329–332
Boone, Richard, 276
Brademas, John, 315
British Trades Union Council, 137
Brown, J. Douglas, 57–58
Budgets: and deficit spending, 52, 54–55,
  228–29, 238, 241, 315–17; outlays and
  GNP, 238, 240, 247–48, 260, 319; and
  presidential decisions, 60, 121–23, 234,
  237, 242–46, 301–3, 318–19, 321,
  328–29, 352. See also Business confi-
  dence; Retargeting of federal programs
Bunche, Ralph J., 63, 66–67, 95, 374
Bureau of Apprenticeship and Training
  (BAT), 220
Burns, Arthur, 303, 309–12
Burns, Eveline, 137
Busby, Horace, 238–39
Business Advisory Council (BAC), 208,
  242, 247
Business confidence: effects on policy
  making, 6, 18–20, 24, 317, 361; and
  Great Society, 224, 237–38, 246–47;
  and New Deal, 38–39, 51, 60–61, 69
Businessmen: on collective bargaining,
  148–49, 154–56; on Great Society,
  246–47; on New Deal, 34–36, 40, 51
Byrd, Harry, 45–46, 107–8, 134, 228–29
Byrnes, James, 107